The British Problem, c. 1534–1707

PROBLEMS IN FOCUS SERIES

Each volume in the 'Problems in Focus' series is designed to make available important new work on key historical problems and periods. Each volume is devoted to a central topic or theme, and the most important aspects of this are dealt with by specially commissioned essays from scholars in the relevant field. The editorial Introduction reviews the problems of the period as a whole, and each essay provides an assessment of the particular aspect, pointing out the areas of development and controversy, and indicating where conclusions can be drawn or where further work is necessary. An annotated bibliography serves as a guide for further reading.

The British Problem, c. 1534–1707

State Formation in the Atlantic Archipelago

EDITED BY

Brendan Bradshaw and John Morrill

St. Martin's Press
New York

THE BRITISH PROBLEM, c. 1534–1707
Preface and editorial matter © 1996 by Brendan Bradshaw and John
Morrill; Chapter 1 © 1996 by John Morrill; Chapter 2 © 1996 by Brendan
Bradshaw; Chapter 3 © 1996 by Hiram Morgan; Chapter 4 © 1996 by
Ciaran Brady; Chapter 5 © 1996 by Peter Roberts; Chapter 6 © 1996 by
Jenny Wormald; Chapter 7 © 1996 by J. G. A. Pocock; Chapter 8 © 1994,
1996 by University of Chicago Press; Chapter 9 © 1996 by Mark Goldie;
Chapter 10 © 1996 by Jim Smyth

St. Martin's Press, Scholarly and Reference Division,
175 Fifth Avenue, New York, N.Y. 10010

First published in the United States of America in 1996

Printed in Malaysia

ISBN 0–312–16042–9

Library of Congress Cataloging-in-Publication Data applied for

Contents

Preface

In 1988 we jointly created an option for students taking Part II of the Historical Tripos at the University of Cambridge and called it 'The British Problem, c. 1534–1707'. The problem was how to conceptualise the relationship between the Kingdoms of England and Scotland and their relationship with the Kingdom of Ireland and the Principality of Wales; to trace the development of a multiplex composite or triple monarchy with the accession of the Scottish House of Stewart to the thrones of England and Ireland in 1603; and to examine the reactions of the various peoples of the islands of Britain and Ireland to the growth of the English state. It was and is a study of state formation and the emergence of new nationalisms.

We begin our course with the 1530s because of the extraordinary succession of formal changes that were clustered together in the first decade after Henry VIII's schism from Rome: the expansion of royal authority throughout England – the effecting of a new ubiquity of royal writs and the forging of a new and omnicompetent instrument of royal policy, the parliamentary statute; the development of a new doctrine of imperial monarchy; the destruction of the regional magnates who for decades controlled the Tudor borderlands of Ireland, the Welsh March and the Anglo-Scottish borders; the creation of the Kingdom of Ireland with its ambiguous relationship to the Crown of England in 1541; the incorporation of the Principality of Wales into the Kingdom of England between 1536 and 1543; and the crushing defeats inflicted on the Scots in the 1540s, accompanied by demands for dynastic union and the reassertion of English feudal claims to suzerainty over Scotland. The course ends in 1707 with the formal union of the Kingdoms of England and Scotland and the creation of a Parliament for the whole of Britain. In Irish or Anglo-Irish relations 1707 is

not a key date. Nevertheless, it follows closely the treaty of
Limerick of 1691 and the enactment of the penal laws by the
Irish Parliament, which together marked the completion of the
process of political and constitutional transformation inaugurated by the Tudor Revolution of the 1530s, a process that
resulted also in the radical transformation of landowning and
a radical transfer of social, political and cultural power.

Together – and ably assisted by David Smith, Jim Smyth and
John McCafferty – we have taught this course to some 150
Cambridge students over the past seven years. And the more
we have taught it, the more convinced we have become that
the relations of the peoples of these islands need to be seen
in terms of their interactions. It is not the only way in which
they need to be seen; but it is *an* essential way of making sense
of their history. John Pocock, the great pioneer of 'British
History', provides the motto for this volume: 'British history
denotes the historiography of no single nation but of a problematic and uncompleted experiment in the creation and interaction of several nations' (or, as he also put it, British history
must show how the component parts of these islands 'interacted so as to modify the conditions of one another's existence'). As the years went by, we found that many other scholars
had also responded to Pocock's invitation and challenge, or to
their own inner convictions. Many others recognised the importance of the debate but were unconvinced by the claims
being made for the new approach. To some it risked degeneration into English historiographical imperialism or simply into
a celebration of the growth of the English state.

We found ourselves increasingly involved in debates and discussions with fellow-scholars about the merits and hazards of
the enterprise, not least with Steven Ellis who pioneered a similar
course at University College, Galway, and who has been a regular
'guest' lecturer in the Cambridge course. And more and more
conferences have been held to debate the issues. We felt it
was time to explore the themes in a form that would lay out
the issues before as wide an audience as possible. We therefore approached Macmillan with a view to putting together a
collection in their enterprising **Problems in Focus** series, which
we knew from experience managed to get onto the reading
lists and into the classrooms that other collections of essays
cannot reach. And to our delight, Macmillan, in the person of

their then History Editor Vanessa Graham, agreed to publish a collection with the same title as the Cambridge course: *The British Problem, c. 1534–1707.*

To facilitate the preparation of the volume, we decided to get the authors together for a weekend colloquium. This was held in Cambridge in early July 1993, with generous funding assistance from the Faculty of History Trevelyan Fund and additional assistance from the Master and Fellows of Queens' College who hosted the occasion. We are deeply grateful to both bodies.

We invited John Pocock to attend and to give a keynote address to inaugurate the discussion; and that paper was so brimful of ideas and suggestions that we co-opted it to the volume in place of an article on 'The War(s) of the Three Kingdoms and the Unification of Britain' which one of the editors had intended to write. However, this left the 1650s untreated, and it was with great pleasure that we heard about and read Derek Hirst's distinguished essay on 'The English Republic and the Meaning of Britain', due to be published in the *Journal of Modern History* (1994). We are delighted to be able to republish it here and are grateful to Professor Hirst and to the *Journal* for permission to do so. The other eight essays were written especially for this volume.

Between them we hope that these essays cover most of the major issues comprehended by the title of this book. The authors do not share a common view on what the British Problem was, only that historically there *was* one (and that historiographically there *is* one). We hope this volume will enable readers to achieve a fresh perspective on the historical process by which the political and constitutional relationships between the communities of the two islands were transformed in the early modern period and through which they gained a new sense of their own identities as national communities.

BRENDAN BRADSHAW
JOHN MORRILL

Acknowledgements

Derek Hirst's 'The English Republic and the Meaning of Britain' was first published in *The Journal of Modern History*, 66:3 (1994) pp. 451–86, and is reproduced by kind permission of the University of Chicago Press.

1. The British Problem, *c.* 1534–1707*

JOHN MORRILL

I

This book does not set out to supplant the histories of England, Ireland, Scotland and Wales with a new British history. The history of Ireland or Scotland within Britain is not the same thing as the history of Cornwall within England or of Fife within Scotland. There are innumerable historical problems which are best seen and best accommodated within the traditional 'national' frameworks.

What this book does claim, however, is that some of the most stubborn and insoluble problems in the history of each kingdom require a British dimension in order to be fully understood.[1] For this is a story about a process of state formation if not the formation of a single state; and – in John Pocock's words – there is a 'British history [that] denotes the historiography of no single nation but of a problematic and uncompleted experiment in the creation and interaction of several nations.'[2] For Pocock, this vitally affects the history and the historiography of each nation in different ways.

Let me begin with some claims which represent my own conviction after several years of teaching and reflection: they are highly contentious and the purpose of this book is not to demonstrate them but to test them. My starting point (as I have suggested elsewhere)[3] is that historians of England need to accept that the expansion of the English state is part of a much larger issue – the formation of a British federated and composite state. However, this is not a problem for the historians of the northern and western kingdoms and principalities. Coping with, and devising strategies to deal with, the reality of the superior might of the English is part of the warp and woof of Irish, Scottish and Welsh historiography. But there remains a tendency in those historiographies to play down the effects on the Irish,

1

Scottish, Welsh and English peoples of the dialectical processes involved, to understate the degree to which each native culture did not so much heroically resist acculturation and integration as interact one with another so as to experience profound change and adaptation. Englishness is self-evidently the product of the complex interactions of peoples and cultures (Britons, Romans, Saxons, Norsemen, Normans). Scottishness, Irishness, Welshness too are the product of complex interactions of peoples, one of them the English.[4]

This book seeks to tell the story of three kingdoms in search of a defined relationship one to another, of four or more peoples in the process of refashioning themselves in the light of much heightened contact and friction. It is a story of how men and women both developed a new or transformed sense of themselves as Irish, Scots, Welsh, English, and came to recognise themselves as subjects of a British king, while also developing – in some but not all cases – new and varied senses of themselves as Britons.

II

In 1500 only about two-thirds of the inhabitants of the British Isles could speak variants on the English language;[5] the varieties of English within England itself and across the archipelago made it difficult for regions to communicate and identify one with another (a good reason for elite and church Latin and Law French). The monarch's writ did not run in some parts of England, in much of Wales, in most of Ireland; and the writ of the independent monarch of Scotland barely ran beyond the Highland line where a majority of the population lived.[6] The same can be said of the legal systems that were rooted in amalgams of Roman, Saxon and feudal codes and practices and which prevailed in most of the south and east lowlands of Britain, but not in most of Ireland or in Celtic Britain.[7]

By 1700 all this had changed. Although the proportion of those speaking Celtic tongues had not shrunk substantially, the proportion who spoke *only* Celtic tongues had shrunk, and the elite and the more prosperous farmers, artisans and traders throughout the archipelago were anglophone. A best guess would be that the total proportion of English speakers had risen from 65 per cent to 85 per cent; and there had been a radical stan- dardisation of the English spoken and written, most impor- tantly because all 'English' Bibles were printed in London and Oxbridge in southern English.[8]

More importantly, by 1700 a single ruler was recognised by almost all the inhabitants of the archipelago. Even that minor- ity who refused to recognise William III as their king recog- nised the exiled James II as ruler of the whole archipelago – i.e. all Jacobites believed in a pan-archipelagic monarchy. There were many and various disagreements about how the compo- nent parts of the British composite monarchy should relate one to another, but very few sought to dis-integrate them. There were no independence movements of the kind that in the early modern period saw the secession of the United Provinces or Portugal from Habsburg rule. The Scots who in the years 1703–7 threatened to break the regal union unless they could get a union of the kingdoms that met their grievances were engaged on a high-risk bluff that worked.[9] In 1707, there had emerged a truly British state comprising the whole of England, Scot- land and Wales with one imperial and omnicompetent Parlia- ment, one central executive, an open and increasingly integrated economy, one language of law and government, and parallel if not identical social structures, systems of inheritance, and of property holding and justice.

Ireland was as it was to be for all the nine centuries to 1922, semi-detached. It now had its own Parliament controlled by English and Scottish settlers and its own executive manned by those same English settlers but usually headed by an English- man. Both Parliament and Council were subject to review and direction from Whitehall and Westminster. Ireland also had its own structure of lawcourts, which were subject to judicial review by the Judges in Westminster Hall and by the English Privy Council. Ireland was English (if not Old English) in theory and in practice a subordinate kingdom. It could be argued that while Wales and Scotland were being institutionally and constitutionally Briticised, Ireland was being institutionally and constitutionally Anglicised.

III

The nine authors whose work is gathered in this volume have very different points of departure, very different convictions about the nature and extent of the interactions between the various peoples that make up what some would call 'the British Isles', others the 'Atlantic archipelago', others 'these islands'.

There are modern sensitivities about the use of the term 'British Isles', with its prejudgement of the historical relationship between 'mainland Britain' and Ireland. It is used in this book simply because it was in regular use amongst the cartographers and geographers (especially in the Latin form *insulae Britannicae*) by the later sixteenth century, and maps of 'Britain' began routinely to show Ireland alongside the island of Britain and as part of the whole.[10]

Yet it is a treacherous term. For then, as now, the word 'British' was *only* made to comprehend Ireland in that loose, strictly geographical sense. No commentator tried to extend the term descriptively, let alone prescriptively, to include the political claims of the Houses of Tudor or Stuart; and certainly not to describe the juridical or cultural integrity of the inhabitants of the two islands. The sixteenth and even the seventeenth centuries saw English historians refurbishing and re-presenting the myth which had its most forthright expression in the work of Geoffrey of Monmouth in the twelfth century. This related how Britain had been first settled by refugees from the Trojan War under King Brutus. This British kingdom had subsequently been divided between his three sons, the eldest inheriting England and the younger ones Scotland and Wales.[11] Some Scottish historians – without invoking Brutus – argued for a shared origin and common destiny of the peoples of Britain;[12] but no alternative or adaptive myth was created by the English or Irish (or Scots for that matter) with a view to incorporating Ireland into the story.[13]

The alternative way of claiming English suzerainty over Scotland was by feudal right: the recital of the large number (by the 1540s almost thirty instances were listed and published) of occasions of which the king of Scotland had sworn fealty to kings of England.[14] This claim was advanced for essentially dynastic reasons in the sixteenth century, to legitimate the rights of the English Crown to manage the affairs of the kingdom of

Scotland during the minority caused by the death of James V and the infancy of Mary, including the disposal of the Queen in marriage. In Ireland the situation was complicated by the fact that English claims to the whole of Ireland resided principally in papal grant and confirmations which the Tudors were unlikely to remember after the schism from Rome; and *present* and *future* conquest did not require a historical origins-myth. As an adjunct to that, there is the question of the status of the Church of Ireland and its autonomy from the Church of England. In the early seventeenth century, continental European scholars became interested in the ancient patriarchies of the Church. Their concern was to build up the independence of the Churches against the pretentions of the papacy, but their interest in the British patriarchy, which claimed to give the archbishops of Canterbury jurisdiction over the whole of the British Isles, could have been very readily appropriated as part of a claim to imperial kingship, with the archbishop as a patriarch answerable to an imperial supreme governor. Yet even Charles I and William Laud hesitated to appropriate the title.[15] The British Isles existed as a geographical term; but there was no term for, and no *concept* of, a single polity, entity, state incorporating the islands of Britain and Ireland.

IV

The British Isles contained a number of peoples; and over the early modern period, those peoples' sense of themselves changed significantly.[16]

We can say that in 1500 there was very clearly an English sense of Englishness and a Welsh sense of Welshness; and while there was a Scottish sense of Scottishness, it was essentially a Lowland sense of Lowland Scottishness. The Irish sense of Irishness must be left on one side for the moment.

Rees Davies has argued powerfully that we should talk about the peoples, in Latin *gentes*, of Britain and Ireland not the nations. A *gens* is a people with a sense of its own historical identity and integrity, a people descended from a single founding Father or progenitor. Those who moved away from the *patria*, mingled with another people, as in the case of the English in Ireland in the later Middle Ages, were said to degenerate – lose their identity.[17]

The English were the first to develop their name and identity, separating out their 'English' from their 'British' (= Celtic) origins, and clearing the confusion between their 'Angle' and 'Saxon' identity. By the thirteenth century, all the insular inhabitants of the territories acknowledging the Plantagenet kings were content to be seen as 'English' and to call the realm the kingdom of England. By 1300, forms of the same word covered the territory of England, the language, and the inhabitants who spoke the language. The English had a strong sense of regnal identity, of being subjects of a king to whom they owed loyalty and from whom they derived justice and protection; and a strong sense of the boundaries of an English kingdom.[18] Nothing that was to happen in the sixteenth century would weaken this English sense of Englishness. The realm of England, as against the personal loyalty owed to the King of England, was everywhere made more evident – the ubiquity of the royal writ, the destruction of the liberties and franchises, the fusion of Church and state, the heightened visibility of a national Parliament creating new local structures and devising new devolved strategies that still looked towards an integrated economic, social and legal culture all point towards it.[19] The English seem to have treated Wales as part of England and their readiness to appoint bilingual Welshmen to high office in church and state without seeing them as different from the inhabitants of any other region suggests a diminishing contempt for – because a diminishing awareness of? – the distinctiveness of the Welsh. The *Welsh* dimension of the English civil war was seen by both sides as a single theatre of *the* war. For the English, the Welsh were as English as the Cornish were.[20]

The situation in Scotland was more complex. There, fluid boundaries and the delayed appearance of regnal solidarities allowed chronic conceptual instability to prevail – the five or more 'peoples' of north Britain inhabiting '*Scotia*' or '*Alba*'. One of the few certainties was that the *Scoti* inhabited the lands north of the Clyde and the Forth and that they were the 'people' both of the Highlands and of Ireland (commonly known as *Scuitt*).[21] Only gradually did 'Scottish' triumph as the name of the people (singular) who occupied Scotland, but even then the sustaining myth of a single people, bound together under a single king and with ancient territorial boundaries, appears first in a Lowland account crystallised out at the time of the declaration of Arbroath of 1320 and in the subsequent writings of John Fordun, Andrew Wyntoun and Walter Bower.[22] Passionately anti-English, this still saw the Gaelic-speaking inhabitants north of the Forth as the semi-civilised and only partially assimilated descendants of Irish invaders and settlers. The Lowland Scots viewed the Gaels much as the English Palesmen viewed the Irish.[23] All this represents the triumph of the Anglo-Norman settlement of Scotland in the twelfth century, when feudalism and the characteristic legal, social and military institutions of the Anglo-Norman *imperium* were imported into Scotland and came to dominate the Scottish Lowlands. Both England and Scotland for centuries consisted of an Anglo-Norman core with a bare and fluctuating control over the mountainous wholly Gaelic-speaking borderlands to the North and West, and the Norse speaking fastnesses beyond those borderlands.[24]

The Celtic-speaking people of Wales came over the centuries before 1000 to call themselves *Cymry* (which literally means 'people of this region') instead of the older term *Brytanaiad*.[25] Welshness was very territorially located – it was the country between the sea and Offa's dyke (extended by the rivers Wye and Dee); but within that it was defined as the bloodstock of those who spoke the Welsh language, lived by the customs of the Welsh, resisted the language, law and arms of the English: 'a basic fault line between two peoples – natives and settlers, vanquished and victors – now ran across the face of Wales...'[26] Welshness was bleakly defined by the shared experience of resisting the English.

But at least in Wales forms of the same word covered the territory of Wales, the language, and the inhabitants who spoke the language (*Cymry, Cymru*).[27] In Ireland things were more fragmented still. The categories of 'Irish' and 'English in Ireland' used by the English and by the English in Ireland were clearer in concept than in application, given the de*gen*eration of so many of the heirs of the Norman settlers. Furthermore, as the early modern period wore on the Catholicism of a majority of the English in Ireland came to distance them from a sense of both Englishness and Britishness. The native population had a series of overlapping identities: that of the tribe, clan or sept; that of the region; that of the people of Ireland (*fir Erenn*); and that of the *Gaedhil*, an identity which united the Celtic peoples of Scotland and Ireland. These distinct and overlapping identities ebbed and flowed in relation to one another over time and between regions. For many, the primary identity would always have been with the sept or clan, linked to a strong regional identity (men of Ulster etc.). Beyond that a strong case can and has been made for the primacy of both of the larger entities. On the one hand the notion of the men of Ireland – *fír Erenn* – had deep cultural resonance in the mythological and literary landscape of the bardic poets. Nor is this confined to the poetry. It is thus possible to point to the Remonstrance of 1317 as an Irish Declaration of Arbroath,[28] and one can find the concept of high kingship long surviving the erosion and evaporation of the term *rí* as the primary descriptor of Gaelic lordship.[29]

But by the later Middle Ages, it has been suggested that the fundamental languages of community within the political culture of the Gaelic revival of the fourteenth and fifteenth centuries were those of lordship (*tighearnas*) and of the great fault line that separated the *Gaedhil* from the *Gaill*: tribal loyalty on the one hand and ethnic identity against the Norman – the Norman in Ireland, Scotland or England. As Steven Ellis – and in a more hesitant way others – have been stressing recently, it may be that we have assumed too readily that the use within Ireland of the *Gaedhil/Gaill* distinction betokens a sense of Ireland as a national territory, the *patria* of the *Gaedhil*.[30] Even though it should be stressed that for many *fír Erenn*, the West of Scotland was a former colony of Ireland, and Ireland the true home of the Gaelic diaspora, the fact remains that ethnic identities within Gaeldom were more complex than elsewhere within the archipelago.

No claim in this introduction is more contentious than this one, and I make it very hesitantly. But there is a possibility that the growth of Irish identity was a product of the period we are studying in this book.[31] In such a view, the processes at work in the ninth to eleventh centuries by which English high kingship and English boundaries emerged out of the Heptarchy, and by which over a longer period Scottish high kingship emerged from the ethnic and political complexities of the earlier period, were also at work in Ireland; but they were stayed by the Norman irruption and the introduction of notions of feudal lordship and landownership. By the time changing military imperatives, the economic recession and cultural renaissance

generated the Gaelic revival, there may have been less a sense
of an identity rooted in island-identity and Irish (as against
Gaelic) high kingship than of one that stressed a *Gaedhil*-soli-
darity that straddled the Irish Sea. As Steven Ellis has put it,
'the evidence concerning power and senses of identity in the
Gaelic world as a whole rather suggests the possibility of . . .
the emergence of a consolidated Gaelic polity in the far north
west. In the late middle ages, the Irishry of Scotland may be
seen as an extension of the Irishry of Ireland, rather like the
relationship of the English Pale in Ireland to the English mainland.'[32] The implications for a very different outcome to the
British problem are obvious.

V

In all this the oscillating importance of 'Britishness' is very
much a sub-plot. The Romans had a strong sense of 'Britannia' and of the British and it was the British who were colonised and inculturated by the Saxons wherever they settled.
By the ninth century, the ealdorman Aethelwald said that 'Britain
is now called England thereby assuming the name of the victors.' And as we have seen, the surviving Britons in Wales came
to abandon their sense of themselves as inhabiting *Brytanaiad*
in favour of *Cymru*. Geoffrey of Monmouth – with momentous
consequences – kept the term alive in the twelfth century, but
in a story which ends in the defeat and utter dejection of the
Britons.[33]

None the less it was on the basis of Geoffrey of Monmouth's
prophetic hope that the Tudors grounded their cultural imperialism; and that James VI and I tried to refound his *imperium* as
Great Britain and redesignate England as South Britain and
Scotland as North Britain. On this basis, on the basis of regnal
union and incorporation, English, Scots and Welsh were invited to consider themselves Britons, and in fact many Scots
and Welsh did recognise and acknowledge that they were Britons as well as Scotsmen and Welshmen. The Welsh were descended from English settlers, their families had intermarried
with the English, they traded with the English, they spoke the
English language, they spent time at the English court, and so
on. Anglicisation was a phenomenon within the principality

throughout the later Middle Ages preparing the way for the Tudor political incorporation. Even the Welsh-speaking people of Wales recognised themselves as the descendants of the original settlers of Britain; and there is no strong evidence that between the sixteenth and the twentieth centuries they wished to be politically detached from the British state or from a dynasty that so assiduously proclaimed in Welsh and English its Welsh/British origin. The Welsh accepted – often welcomed – incorporation into the English state;[34] Welsh-speakers contributed many men to the King's army in the 1640s and few to the Parliamentarian army; they embraced English law and English religion and to a lesser extent the English language or aspects of English farming practice.[35]

Even more complicated is the fact that while Ireland was never part of 'Britain' or even 'Great Britain', and although the English of Ireland almost always referred to themselves as just that – the English of Ireland or the *Anglo-Hibernici* – the Scots in Ireland frequently referred to themselves as 'the Britons in Ireland'.

Which brings us to the recognition that the one group who most resolutely and consistently refused to regard themselves as Britons were the English in England. If they use it at all it is without any sense that it is other than a synonym for English.

VI

All this bears out John Pocok's dictum that British history is a tale of how the component parts of these islands 'interacted so as to modify the conditions of one another's existence'[36] and also his claim that 'British history denotes the historiography of no single nation but of a problematic and uncompleted experiment in the creation and interaction of several nations.'[37]

But it also suggests that he is right to stress that it was the story of 'the increasing dominance of England as a political and cultural entity'.[38] In that sense British state formation is very much of a piece with French or Spanish state formation. In the course of the fifteenth century, the English had been driven from their territories and *heritages*[39] in western and southern France, the independent duchy of Brittany had been absorbed by dynastic chance and the independent duchy of

Burgundy by conquest, and the House of Valois was settling down like a contented boa-constrictor to create a constitutional mulch out of these various prey. Dynastic chance brought the amalgamated Crowns of Aragon into union with the Crown of Castile, and further dynastic chance backed by *force majeure* was for several decades to incorporate Portugal into this composite monarchy.[40] Even more complex circumstances were to lead during the early modern period into the emergence of the Habsburg monarchy in Austria and the Balkans, and of composite states as in Prussia and throughout Scandinavia. This was the age of multiple or composite monarchy, with monarchs everywhere torn between two options. The first was to create common social, political, legal and cultural institutions throughout their dominions. The second was to maximise their power in accordance with the particular and particularist arrangements in their various dominions. Over the early modern period the kings of 'France' and 'Spain' balanced these two largely contradictory approaches in different proportions – the Valois/ Bourbons favouring more of the former, the Habsburgs (especially the Austrian Habsburgs) more of the latter. British monarchs adopted the first policy within Britain and (eventually)[41] the latter within the archipelago as a whole.[42]

Looked at from this perspective, various features of the British experience throughout the early modern period seem fairly familiar: the attempt to create an imperial court, a homogenised aristocracy, central, imperial bodies for the management of imperial defence, a de-emphasis on centralised representative institutions and the systematic corruption of peripheral representative institutions to turn them into tools for the implementation of metropolitan political and fiscal imperatives.[43] Equally the destabilising effects of composite rulership – the persistence of unrest and rebellion in peripheral regions threatening the stability of pacified and effectively governed metropolitan regions – can be seen in the British experience (as in the 1590s, 1640s and 1690s where crises in England were very much consequent upon the collapse of royal authority in Ireland and (after 1603) in Scotland).

But the British experience also had some uncharacteristic features. First, the internal colonisation of Ireland between 1547 and 1700, especially in the 1650s, was only approached in extent and severity (and even there not matched) by the ruthless supplanting of the Bohemian elite in the wake of the Battle of the White Mountain.[44] The title to more than half of the total land of Ireland (and perhaps two-thirds of the cultivable land of Ireland) passed into the hands of those who lived in Britain or who came over from Britain. Secondly, three-quarters of the population of Ireland and a substantial though unknown proportion of the Scottish Gaels remained stubbornly and resolutely Catholic while the overwhelming majority of the monoglot English-speakers, along with most Welsh and many bilingual Scots, became Protestant. Unlike their contemporaries in Spain, and (in a more destabilising way) their contemporaries in seventeenth-century France, Austria or Prussia, British monarchs were forced to confront the religious pluralism of their peoples. And this was in the age of the confessional state – *cuius regio, eius religio* in the famous formula associated with the Treaty of Augsburg of 1555. The relationship between these two distinctivenesses – the extraordinary violence meted out by the English to the Irish and the almost complete failure of the Protestant Reformation amongst the Gaelic peoples of Ireland and its substantial failure amongst the Old English communities of Ireland – is one of the themes explored in the chapters that follow.

Within the British Problem there is, then, a specific problem – why the Irish were not assimilated to the British state in the same way that the Welsh and Scots were assimilated. And the chapters that follow – especially that of Brendan Bradshaw (Chapter 2) – suggest some reasons for this. A further reason, one not fully explored below, perhaps needs airing here: the thesis first advanced by David Quinn and developed by many other scholars – most notably by Nicholas Canny – namely that we need to see the history of English relations in the period not as part of the Renaissance-European phenomenon of composite monarchy but as part of the transatlantic phenomenon of English colonisation.

This is an interpretation with much to commend it. Many of the early investors (intellectual and financial) in Irish Plantation were the same men who invested in Virginia or the Caribbean colonies. There was a violent literature of colonial expropriation in which the de-humanisation of the native population of Ireland can be strictly likened to the de-humanisation of the native population of the Americas. The economic policies of successive English governments treated Ireland in the same way as they treated American colonies; and the systems of government – English governors, colonial assemblies subject to metropolitan oversight and over-rule – came more and more to resemble one another.[45]

And yet – as Hiram Morgan has pointed out in influential reviews of the most intelligent and thorough statement of the 'colonialist' case[46] – there are a series of respects in which this misleads:

> it is based on position papers and political tracts which express the opinions and objectives of certain interest groups . . . [and] ignores the meat and drink of politics – warfare, marriage alliances, faction fighting, litigation . . . and the constant manoeuvring at Court. There is nothing colonial about any of these activities: they are all recognizably European and all Irishmen of whatever ethnic background participated in them to a greater or lesser extent.

Gaelic Irish, unlike native Americans, were incorporated as full subjects of the Crown; Gaelic chiefs, unlike native American chiefs, were given feudal titles; Gaelic chiefs like O'Rourke and Maguire who rebelled were – unlike native American chiefs – brought to England for trial and public execution. Despite the gripes of some, official government policy in London and Dublin remained the assimilation and civilisation of the Gaels. The worst things that were said by the English in Ireland about Irish Gaels were said by James VI about the Scottish Gaels, but he persisted in the belief that their savagery was nothing that protestantism, patriarchalism and primogeniture could not put right.[47] When pressure from England for assimilation of the hinterlands of the *imperium* of the Crown caused desperate and bitter rebellion and where rampant planter self-interest went unchecked, the English were well capable of pursuing vengeful and vindictive policies, as can be seen in the Cromwellian proposals for confining the Irish Catholic population within Connacht and Country Clare or in the later Highland Clearances.

There is also no doubt that the wars in Ireland – in the thirteenth century as much as in the sixteenth and seventeenth centuries, and on the Irish as on the English and English/Scottish settler side – were bloodier, more brutal, more vicious than those in Britain. Whatever passed as the Geneva conventions of the early modern period were generally observed in England during the civil war, for example; but not in Ireland. There was little taking of prisoners and little honouring of surrender terms. The worst excesses of the first civil war – Rupert's storming of Leicester and Bolton – resulted in a loss of civilian life which was but a tithe of that exacted by Cromwell as policy at Drogheda and Wexford. But the different behaviour of the English in Britain and in Ireland does not make the latter a colonial pattern of (mis)behaviour, but a specific English-in-Ireland pattern of (mis)behaviour.[48] Finally, it is all too easily overlooked that whereas the native populations of so many of the colonies were either devastated by disease or dispossessed and driven away from European areas of settlement, the natives of Ireland failed to dwindle to politically insignificant numbers.

The conclusion, however, remains clear. Whether we attempt to view the British Problem as an example of the development of 'composite monarchies' or as an aspect of the colonial expansion of the Atlantic-seaboard powers, Ireland is a special case. It just will not fit into any of the established patterns.

VII

Many historians will argue, of course, that there is no such thing as 'British history' before 1603 and no such thing as a British history that incorporates Ireland at any stage. Or at any rate, they would argue that the primary units of study should be English, Irish, Scottish and Welsh history, and the secondary history the account of how those histories collided and intersected during this (or any other) period. British history, it is said, is only a *real* history in the sense that European history is a real history. Indeed, British history can be seen as no more than an aspect of a loose European history. Given the way the history of England, or of the British Isles, has generally been taught at school and university rigorously segregated from the history of continental Europe, it is suggested that the way forward is the integration of the history of the archipelago into a European context.[49]

I will argue against the adequacy of such an account in due course; but there are many things in favour of it. Much of the story of the sixteenth-century interactions of England, Ireland and Scotland only makes sense in a dynastic context or in a European geopolitical (or rather georeligious) context. This case is powerfully made by Hiram Morgan in Chapter 3 of this book. Thus, English policy towards Scotland can be seen as dynastic, in the application of feudal claims of suzerainty to the problems of managing the three Scottish royal minorities that occupied well over half of the period from the battle of Flodden in 1513 to the Union of the Crowns in 1603, and in binding the royal Houses of Tudor and Stuart together and keeping the House of Valois out of Scotland. It can also be seen as determined by the need to ensure that Scotland was on the same side of the widening confessional divide. Similarly the increasingly obsessive concern of the English with Ireland can be seen as a growing fear that Catholic Ireland would be a staging post for their superpower Catholic enemies intent on undermining Protestant monarchy in England.

Such a view needs to embrace the fact that the early modern centuries unquestionably represent an epoch between the central drive of medieval king and aristocracies – the building of an Anglo-Norman English/Continental Empire straddling the English Channel – and the central drive of the eighteenth and nineteenth centuries – the building of an English (though actually very much a *British*) colonial Empire in the Americas, Africa and Asia. In this epoch – a period spanning the period from 1453 to 1707 – the central drive of English kings was to expand not south and east but north and west, first by incorporating the borderlands of Wales and the Scottish Marches, and then by restoring a viable Pale in Ireland, and finally by absorbing and pacifying the Celtic regions.

In the sixteenth century, the dynastic chances that flowed from James IV of Scotland's marriage to the elder daughter of Henry VII of England gave each royal house a vital interest in the internal affairs of the other. The international and national security crises engendered by the Reformation merely quickened and intensified the processes of interaction between the peoples of the British Isles which were already in train for reasons that were sufficient unto themselves. Thus the seventeenth century can properly be termed the age of triple monarchy and the crisis of the mid-seventeenth century the war(s) of the three kingdoms. Surely where all but the tiniest number recognised a common ruler, where every inhabitant recognised a duty of obedience to the same monarch, and where policies that affected all inhabitants were conceived or confirmed in London, a single history was happening?

It may of course be objected that if we set out to study the history of cuckoos, should we concentrate on the history of the nests in which they leave their young? If, once in its history, a nest has to endure the presence of a cuckoo chick, does that make it a unit in the history of cuckoodom? Is Portugal to be studied principally as an aspect of Iberian history because for sixty years between 1580 and 1640 it shared its monarch with Spain and struggled free of the attempts of Spanish rulers to incorporate it into the Spanish *monarchia* and royal ambitions for an aggrandisement of Spanish power? Even if Scotland has been conjoined to England for almost three hundred years (or Wales for five hundred years) after being independent of English rule for thousands of years, does that make Scottish history from the time of the union an aspect of British history in much the same way as Cornish history is an aspect of English history? Even more, is Irish history part of British history because of the effective claim of sovereign power by the English Crown which dates back to 1169 (and was sustained uninterruptedly for longer than in the case of Scotland and Wales)? Or because about half the inhabitants of Ireland affirmed an English or British identity for 400 years after 1169? Or because of the spasmodically-effected participation in sovereign power of the English Parliament, a claim sustained over the whole of Ireland for more than 400 years (but not up to the present), and sustained over only part of Ireland up to the present? One answer to this is, of course, no – because the great majority of the Gaelic population of Ireland have always disowned a British identity (while taking a long time to establish an 'Irish' identity). After all, most Scots and Welsh have had a greater and longer sense of their identities as peoples; and have been well able to recognise themselves as 'British' while still in varying degrees despising the English.

Yet this raises very large issues indeed. It is surely a variant of Whiggery to take as the unit of study only the modern unit of territorial sovereignty; to say that because Ireland is no longer part of the British state system, it should not be studied as such at the time when it was part of that state system; or to assert that because many Scots wish to see a *future* Scotland independent of England they must deny not only the attempted Anglicisation of Scotland, but also its Briticisation. The paradox of British history is that while a British *state* was created throughout the archipelago, a British *people* (later a British *nation*) was only created in Britain and in one corner of Ireland. Whatever many Scots and Welsh might wish for their future, they cannot escape a past in which their ancestors in the period in and after that covered by this book were Scots *and* Britons or Welsh *and* Britons.

The problem takes us back to the opening section of this introduction, and lies in the half-submerged elision of the history of the peoples and of the states they find themselves in. Yet, as Hugh Seton Watson has shown, it is rare and not common for a nation to be co-terminous with a state, and it is not necessarily a source of stability when it is so; states can exist without a nation, or with several nations among their inhabitants. Most states have had national minorities within them.[50] The unit of study can be the history of a 'people' (= nation); but that must not be made to masquerade as the history of the 'polity' (= state), or to absolve historians from the responsibility of working out the messy relations of different peoples within a single, if diffuse, state.

This matters for another reason. If we can see the limitations of the response of a little-Englander, or little-Scotlander kind to the claims for a 'British' history, then we must also confront the response of those who would claim that the greatest cultural influences on *each* of England, Scotland and Ireland in this period were *not* the interfaces with other parts of the Atlantic archipelago but those with continental Europe – with the continental Reformation and the continental Renaissances. For example, it can be claimed that it was French not English influence which shaped the Scottish Reformation,[51] that it was the continental counter-reformation not a resurgent Celtic Catholicism which shaped Irish Catholic religious identity,[52] that the legal and political cultures of all three kingdom were stimulated more by the inpouring of fifteenth-century Italian, sixteenth-century French and seventeenth-century Dutch ideas rather than by the interplay of indigenous ones. The answer to all this is that such considerations represent a *further* layer of explanation not an alternative layer, let alone an excuse for

ignoring the *British* layer of explanation. Ideas know no boundaries and carry no passports, and the arrival of printing unquestionably changed the extent to which bodies of thought
penetrated beyond courts and universities. But that does not
change the ineluctable fact that most of the Scots, the Welsh
and the Irish had constant inter-personal, intellectual, cultural
and material exchanges with one another and with the English which cannot but have had a primary effect on the way
each developed as a people. Indeed, the differing ways in which
each was exposed to separate bodies of continental ideas would
contribute to how each reacted to the others; continental influences were variables within the breaking and remaking of
identities within a British crucible. And – with the exception
of Scotland in the 1550s – the real, hard institutional framework within which changes occurred was a British one not a
continental one.

It is still possible to write British history in a triumphalist
Anglo-centric way:[53] to see British history as the story of the
expansion of the English state, and the reason for studying it
as the solution to ineluctable problems of English historiography.[54] At times it seems that this is something Conrad Russell
is guilty of, and Keith Brown has been quick to point out the
hazards of an approach that can use Tudor and Stuart political imperialism as a subject designed to achieve a late twenti-
eth-century English historiographical imperialism.[55] It need not
be like that. This book seeks to show some of the ways in which
an *holistic* or *organic* account can bear dividends. Holistic does
not mean wholestic; and organic does not mean wholesome,
peaceloving, balanced and integrated. For the story which
emerges here is one of new identities forged by conflict and
the meeting of incompatibilities; of communities imagined and
lived out by some, and simultaneously rejected, disowned by
others who then created their own imagined alternatives. It is
a story in which all communities are transformed into something new and specifically conditioned by the processes of interaction. It suggests that the peoples of Britain are in a real
sense new peoples, not refined, stripped back to elements of
their old identities, but remade as a result of their interaction.
What defined the English and the Scots was to be precisely
what limited their recognition of their Britishness; what defined each community in Ireland was precisely the extent to

which it acknowledged or denied its relationship to England, Scotland and indeed Britain. John Pocock's aphorism bears one more repetition: 'British history denotes the historiography of no single nation but of a problematic and uncompleted experiment in the creation and interaction of several nations.'[56]

VIII

This fuller, more *holistic* history of the British Isles is, then, the story of an incomplete and ultimately (from the perspective of the 1990s) reversible experiment in state formation, and of a series of interactions of peoples within an expanding polity, interactions which dramatically reshaped those people's sense of themselves and their relations with one another.

Within such a framework, the years from around 1534 to 1707 are of fundamental importance.[57] In no other period did such extensive growth of the state and the fisc take place. No other period witnessed such movement of peoples within the archipelago. In no other period was there such violence visited by the peoples on one another, either in the name of the Crowns or in the names of the liberties of the peoples; in no other period was there such profound ideological conflict, as the Reformation process worked its way through and was integrated into a series of refashioned ethnic identities. And yet, even within this period, there is an ebb and flow. The periods when the affairs of the three kingdoms were most intertwined, when the constitutional, political, religious and cultural histories of each are so entangled that it simply does not make sense to treat them apart (as has been too often done in the past), include 1534–47, 1559–72, 1592–1609, 1637–60 and the whole of the Restoration period. This introduction will conclude by looking at each in turn. My aim in doing so is to provide a narrative framework to support the chapters that follow this introduction and not to provide an overall narrative.

IX

There are throughout British history a few defining moments when changes take place which produce a fundamental new climate or environment. They represent a kind of constitutional rite of passage, as a political system passes from one stage to another. The Revolution settlements of 1688/90 were one such defining moment; the Great Reform Bill of 1832 was another; the election of the Labour Government of 1945 a third. They liberated a torrent of reform in other areas and by and large, although conservative voices lamented the changes, these voices sought more to limit their consequences than to reverse them.

It can be said that the passage of the Act in Restraint of Appeals (1533) and of the Act of Supremacy (1534) were just such a defining moment or constitutional rite of passage. In the remaining fourteen years of Henry VIII's reign, the face of English government was transformed. Much of the wealth of the Church was appropriated and the independent social power of churchmen was destroyed. The many 'liberties and franchises' (grants of rights and jurisdiction created – the technical term is *alienated*, which means irrevocably surrendered – by Henry or by his predecessors) were abolished and a new ubiquity and universality of royal writs and government officials was established. The authority of his Great Council in Parliament as the instrument for reshaping and extending the king's imperial authority was greatly enhanced, with the establishment of what has been rightly termed 'the sovereignty of statute,'[58] so that this awesome instrument could be used even to determine the order of succession to the throne after the king's death (a power no other western European prince could claim). By the same token there began the programme of legislative action which was to create a greater degree of state responsibility for regulating economic activity and social welfare than was found anywhere else in Europe. Henry VIII and his ministers transformed the way in which England was governed.[59]

Yet this was only part of a wider programme of transformation. Intimately if elusively the ecclesiastical schism as applied to the peripheral dominions was to have profound effects on the lives of all those who lived in the principality of Wales, the lordship of Ireland or the independent kingdom of Scotland.

It began with the near-simultaneous destruction of the powerful regional magnates to whom Henry had devolved responsibility for managing the borderlands of his dominion. Between 1531 and 1534 Rhys ap Gruffydd in the Welsh Marches, Lord Dacre in the Northern March and the Earl of Kildare in the English Pale in Ireland were all arraigned on treason charges; and two were executed, one sidelined.[60] In the aftermath of these cynical and deliberate acts the regional councils in all three regions were remodelled and bureaucratised and then more effectively incorporated into the realm of England.[61] Brendan Bradshaw and Peter Roberts explain in Chapters 2 and 5, below, just how the English and Celtic landowners of the principality of Wales were offered the opportunity to benefit from the more beneficent aspects of Tudor rule. Within a few years an even more dramatic offer was made to the Irish within and beyond the Pale. The erection of the Crown and Kingdom of Ireland in 1541 was an attempt to abolish the distinction between the medieval 'Englishry'[62] (that shrinking area controlled by Anglo-Norman lords within which prevailed the social and legal institutions of the Anglo-Norman state) and the 'Irishry', and to grant to all inhabitants the rights of freeborn Englishmen. This policy was to be accomplished by the strategy of Lord Deputy St Leger, known as surrender and regrant, by which the Gaelic lords recognised Henry's kingship in return for feudal charters confirming title to and common-law possession of the land they occupied together with (for the greatest of the lords) peerages conferred by their king. These social changes were to be underpinned (exactly as in Wales) by the shiring of Gaelic Ireland and the penetration of common-law process and adjudication at local as well as national levels. Why, and to what extent, this policy foundered in Ireland when it was so successful in Wales is explored below by Brendan Bradshaw and Ciaran Brady in Chapters 2 and 4.

Henry VIII made no attempt to proclaim himself King of Scotland, even after the death of the son-less James V. He was not in the least interested in 'uniting' Britain. But as his adoption of new and distinctive ways of extending royal power throughout England, Ireland and Wales reached its crescendo, he did develop interventionist policies towards the Northern kingdom. If he did not claim immediate sovereignty over Scotland, he did claim suzerainty: that is, he did claim that Scotland had been for centuries a feudal dependency of England.[63] Rather than waste time reheating the rather dog-eared mythological account of Brutus's claim to the whole

island of Britain,[64] he looked back to the twelfth-century Norman migration to Scotland and the numerous subsequent oaths
of fealty sworn by Scottish kings to the kings of England. This
was pure opportunism: the need to legitimate his interventions
in Scotland during a minority. As feudal lord, he could claim
the right to supervise the arrangements for government during the minority and – even more important – to control the
marriage of the heir to the throne. What made this so urgent
was that the heir was a woman. In effect, whoever married Mary
would bring Scotland into the ambit of his own family. Henry
wanted both to acquire Scotland by a dynastic marriage between Mary and the Prince Edward, and perhaps even more to
prevent her falling into the clutches of the royal house of
France.[65]

So Henry (and Cromwell) largely ignored Scotland throughout the 1530s, his only concern being with the possibility of a
Franco-Scottish (Catholic) pact. His relations with Scotland were
essentially an aspect of his foreign policy.[66] Once his fears were
realised and he was faced by a war on two fronts in 1542 as
the Scots sought to take advantage of his war with France to
invade England, he took up a policy at once aggressively dynastic (represented by the Treaty of Greenwich) and militarily
punitive (represented by the Rough Wooing). Such policies
drove those Scots nobles who survived the carnage of the Battles
of Solway Moss and Pinkie into the arms of France. Henry had
over-reached himself. Mary, Queen of Scots, was transported
to France for education and marriage. At the time of Henry's
death, the prospect of his adding Scotland to his family's *imperium*
had faded, to be replaced by the prospect of Scotland becoming the kind of appendage to France that the Netherlands had
become to a monarchy based in Spain.

X

The events of the twenty-four months following the death of
Mary Tudor represent one of the greatest crises in British history. They were months dominated by rites of passage – the
marriage of Mary of Scotland to the Dauphin of France, the
death not only of Mary Tudor, but of Henry II of France, Mary
of Guise (widow of James V and Regent of Scotland), and of

Francis II, husband of Mary of Scotland. Each of these was of crucial significance to the outcome of British history. But the greatest of all was the rite of passage which did *not* take place: Francis II died before he could father the son who in French and papal eyes would have been heir to the Crowns of France, Scotland and England. Instead of almost half a century of dynastic shadow boxing which was to result in the peaceful accession of the Scottish James VI to the throne of England, an early and bloody war of the English succession would surely have followed.

All this is grist to Hiram Morgan's mill (below, Chapter 3), where he argues that in the sixteenth century the British problem was essentially part of a wider pan-European geopolitical struggle. And yet what was at stake was the future constitutional and confessional relationship of the component parts of Britain. The marriage of Francis and Mary and the contracts by which Mary handed over the government of Scotland to her husband did indeed threaten the independence of Scotland. Already the Regent had been shifting from a low-key, non-coercive religious and civil policy to one that was more assertive, grounded on French styles of government, a more severe policy towards Protestants, and an increasing reliance on French 'advisers' and French troops.[67] This coincided with the return of Scottish ministers with their English friends from continental exile in Germany and the Rhineland. Somehow, a heady mix of new religion and patriotic defensiveness produced the startling gathering of the Lords of the Congregation as well as the unsuspectedly large numbers of protestant lairds at the Scottish Parliament of 1560 and the rushing through of legislation abolishing papal authority and the practice of the Mass. Protestantism was a glue that stuck together the improbable alliance of anti-French interests which challenged the authority of an ailing Regent and then of the grieving 18-year-old widow despatched from France to secure her inheritance.[68]

It was a European-wide crisis but the outcome was essentially British in form and content. The Spanish looked on aghast, willing to engage themselves if either France of England appeared likely to incorporate Scotland. The French were prevented by civil war from reinforcing their garrisons in Scotland. Both superpowers watched as the English invaded just long enough to secure an agreement that *all* foreign troops – English and French – should be withdrawn. It was a manoeuvre that led to a Scotland dominated by anglophile, Protestant nobles and a powerful group of ministers who had strong links with leading dissident clergy in England. It created a series of paradoxes that provided the dialectics of Anglo-Scottish relations for the next 150 years.[69]

Meanwhile, an edgy English government sought to secure its authority over Ireland. The more secular aspects of this struggle are outlined to Ciaran Brady below (Chapter 5). However, the religious aspects might need some mention here. The English Church Settlement of 1559–63 was truly hybrid. What emerged was a church thoroughly Protestant in its doctrine, traditionalist in its government and discipline except that the Queen subsumed the jurisdiction that had hitherto lain with the Pope, and a liturgy and worship that, in Conrad Russell's splendid phrase, 'looked Catholic and sounded Protestant'.[70] it was also a church in thrall to the laity, subordinated to the Crown and to the Crown-in-Parliament. This was a pattern the Crown attempted to repeat in Ireland. Only slightly modified versions of the English Acts of Supremacy and Uniformity were pushed through the Irish Parliament of 1560. But the situation in Ireland was inherently different. Brendan Bradshaw describes, below, the very different political and cultural context of the Irish Reformation that attended the extension of the Reformation to Ireland, finding here the explanation for its rejection by the colonial community (Chapter 2). We need here only to remind ourselves that the enforcement of the Henrician schism was less stained in blood and plunder in Ireland than in England and that the violent oscillation of the Edwardine protestantisation and Marian restoration in England passed Ireland by. As a result there was no church-property-glutted indigenous elite and convinced Protestant caucus, nourished by the martyred blood of their friends and neighbours, to launch Protestant Ireland. The Irish Act of Uniformity provided for the services of the *English* Prayer Book to be provided in the English tongue (in areas settled by the English) and in Latin (in Irish areas) but not in Gaelic. Indeed, the Latin Prayer Book used contained rather more reminders of the old religion than were contained in the 1559 Book of Common Prayer.[71] No attempt was made in 1560 to subordinate the Church of Ireland to the Church of England, and subsequent evolutions in the Church of England – even the 39 Articles – were not paralleled in Elizabethan Ireland. The Churches of Scotland and Ireland were, in their different ways, ribs out of the side to the Church of England; and the Church of Ireland was to have a very complex relationship with the Church of England (and indeed with the Church of Scotland) in the following centuries.[72]

Related but divergent branches of the same Reformation blueprint were introduced into each kingdom, but the consequential failure of that reformation to incorporate so many of the inhabitants of one (but only one) of the kingdoms provoked bloody resistance and conquest. This was, after all, the age of the confessional state. In the 1560s, religious pluralism was no more conceivable in a composite monarchy than in a single monarchy.

XI

Anglo-Scottish relations in the years 1560–1603 were dominated by dynastic tensions, as both the English and the Scots pondered what would happen after the death of an ageing and childless Elizabeth. Mary Queen of Scots, driven from her kingdom into the imprisoning embrace of her English cousin, toyed with conspiracies to overthrow her and was finally executed in 1587 – albeit fifteen years after most Englishmen thought she should have been.[73] If Elizabeth had predeceased her its seems certain that there would have been a succession war in England, with proponents of legitimacy and religious conservatism backing Mary against whatever Protestant claimant(s) came forward. It would have been an internal war that both Habsburg and Valois would have itched to join. In the event, the deferred execution of Mary and the impeccable Protestantism of the son led to a progressive decline in tension and the eventually uneventful accession of James VI and I.

Elizabeth's childlessness cast a long and disturbing shadow, but there is a sense in which her reign witnessed a long standoff in Anglo-Scottish relations. It was Elizabeth's refusal to become drawn into Scotland's Wars of Religion – 1567 (or earlier) to 1583 (or later) – that defines Anglo-Scottish relations. Despite the attempts of her counsellors to make her consider a British policy based on mutual interest and a common religion rather than suzerainty, they only once and briefly managed to persuade her to send military aid to the Protestant Regents of James VI.[74] Otherwise she stubbornly closed her ears to pleas from north of the border to encourage a 'conformity of kirks' or other forms of closer co-operation between the kingdoms.[75] Her gaze was fixed on Scotland but it was a mute stare. Indeed, as I have suggested elsewhere, there was much more Scottish interest in interfering in the internal affairs of the English church than vice versa.[76] James VI and all his nobility waited in largely paralysed hope to see what would happen when the ageing Queen died, but they committed little to paper and entrusted little to one another that has left traces in the archives. Indeed Jenny Wormald suggests below, in Chapter 6, that perhaps the more James thought about the English succession and yearned for it, the less clear he became quite what to do with it.

If Elizabeth refused to get drawn actively into the affairs of Scotland, she was dragged reluctantly and savagely into the affairs of Ireland. Hiram Morgan (Chapter 3) and Ciaran Brady (Chapter 4) explore the nature and consequences of the perhaps mis-called 'Elizabethan conquest' of Ireland.[77] If Anglo-Scottish tensions tapered off as the sands of time ran out for Elizabeth, the violence in Ireland climaxed with the greatest of all early modern rebellions and with the landing of Spanish troops on Tudor soil. Hiram Morgan has fruitfully explored the events of the Nine Years War – 'Tyrone's Rebellion' as he prefers to call it,[78] and especially the significance of O'Neill's letter to the Pope in 1600 informing him that he was fighting '*pro Romana et libertate patriae*' (for the Roman faith and the liberty of the fatherland).[79] It was, he argues, a doomed attempt by one still temperamentally committed to the values and traditions of Gaeldom, to appeal to the interests of the Old English, and to a set of proposals which 'would have made Ireland a kingdom in fact, not just in name'.[80] Catholicism would have been fully re-established. All posts in the Irish administration would have been filled by Irishmen (under an English-born viceroy). And an Irish Parliament unfettered by Poynings' Law would have made law for the Irish people. Morgan fruitfully explores the rhetoric of O'Neil as a mirror-image of the patriotic language of the Dutch rebels against Philip II.[81] However, there is a vital difference. O'Neill did not disown Tudor sovereignty, only English domination of Irish affairs. Central to his programme was the appointment of a viceroy who would sit on the English Privy Council. Perhaps the most fruitful of all ways of looking at this climacteric is one suggested by John Pocock in Chapter 7 with reference to the Scots in the 1640s, when he draws on the ancient Roman distinction between a *bellum civile* and a *bellum sociale*, a war *inter cives*, between citizens of the same polity, and *inter socios*, between members of polities associated in a system comprising a multiplicity of states – the violent demand of a peripheral region for a redefinition of its relationship with, but not separation from, a metropolitan centre.[82] The Queen called O'Neill and his allies rebels. He preferred the term Confederates. His slogan – *pro Romana et libertate patriae* – neatly prefigures that of the Confederation of Kilkenny in 1642 – *pro fide, pro rege, pro patria*. And the Confederates were clearly fighting a *bellum sociale*, not a war of independence.[83]

XII

James VI and I failed substantially in his attempts to extend the union of crowns into a union of kingdoms, attempts which Jenny Wormald suggests in Chapter 7 may have been less fully developed than has been suggested hitherto. Yet all three kingdoms changed considerably as a result of the creation of a composite monarchy. There was now a recognised and authorised Scottish presence both in Ulster and in Munster. Migration and intermarriage across and amongst the elites produced an English presence in Ireland that was much closer to the centre of the court and government. There was a strong Scottish presence within the royal Household and on the royal Council at Whitehall. James had brought Scottish ideas about equity and conscience to bear so as to halt the advance of the claims of the English common lawyers to a monopoly of jurisdiction and judicial arbitration within England. And Protestant sensibilities formed in the Scottish context – especially a commitment to a learned preaching clergy – had brought a distinctive new royal headship to the Church of England. Of course the effects were dramatic outside England. In Scotland, the effect of the union had been principally felt in the Church, where

James had borrowed and *adapted* English ideas to suit prevailing Scottish conditions. The introduction of the royal supremacy and of the Court of High Commission capped the fundamental development – the reconstruction of a distinctive form of episcopacy. Scottish bishops were not autonomous rulers of dioceses, but chairmen of diocesan boards of governors ('constant moderators' of synods and presbyteries).[84] However, they were also the conduits through which the king could now transmit his royal orders to the Kirk and by whom he could be briefed on what was happening. It meant that royal supremacy had meaning. In addition the reconstruction of episcopacy provided the mechanism by which James could strengthen his control of Scottish Parliaments. Indeed in both Scotland and Ireland, increasing subordination of representative assemblies and alliance with new nobilities – Planter nobles in Ireland, planter Lords of the Erection (lawyer-administrators newly endowed with former church lands) in Scotland – point to trends common to the emergent 'new absolutisms' of continental Europe, and it is a striking fact that a substantial majority on the Council of each of his kingdoms at the time of his death comprised men elevated to the peerage by James himself.

This is the base from which Charles I set out. He had far less interest than his father in promoting the union of his kingdoms. His preoccupation was to increase royal authority in each kingdom by whatever means came to hand. This naked authoritarianism eroded his authority in each of his kingdoms and it brought him to grief in each kingdom in turn. How best to understand the *British* dimension of the mid-century crisis is a contentious issue, however; as inevitably is the nature of the series of interlocking wars that ensued – encapsulated by John Pocock's unease, below (Chapter 7), about whether to refer to the *war* or *wars* of the three kingdoms.

For Conrad Russell, a crisis of *British* monarchies caused the *English* civil war. England was a diesel-engineered state and spontaneous combustion within it was impossible. The nobility of England had been disarmed and rendered impotent, so that only a Scottish 'invasion'[85] could create the pressure required to allow them to negotiate the political concessions that handed them control of the levers of power; and only the Irish slaughter of Protestants could legitimate their supervision of military preparations and thus the raising of troops when Charles failed to make the concessions many of them still thought necessary for their long-term security and for the further development of English Protestantism.[86]

It may be that Russell underestimates the ability (as against the will) of the English to mobilise for war by themselves. After all, the Scots removed and disbanded their troops in the last months of 1641 and the English managed to regiment perhaps 60,000 men with modern weapons by the autumn of 1642 and probably 150,000 by the summer of 1643. Work in progress suggests that the number of men with military training and experience was far greater than hitherto suspected and the stockpiles of arms and knowledge of foreign suppliers more than sufficient to create fully professionalised armies with extraordinary rapidity.[87] It was the lack of will not the absence of a capacity to fight that delayed civil war in *England* until events elsewhere in the archipelago produced new and different circumstances.[88]

This matters for two reasons. First, that effort of will was, to an extent that varied from person to person, conditioned by what was happening outside England and within the British Isles. Secondly, elsewhere in the British Isles the will to resist the king's authority, and to change the ways in which authority was exercised, was, to an extent that varied from person to person, also conditioned by what was happening in England. Conrad Russell has brilliantly demonstrated the first; but we must not forget the second. The collapse of royal authority in Scotland and Ireland is not an exogenous factor. It is part of a single process of a political system imploding.

Charles I's authoritarianism in each of his kingdoms took a distinctive form appropriate to the prevailing circumstances in each. But in each case, the aim was the same: to repair the wealth, jurisdiction and dignity of the established Church, to promote a particular style of evangelism; and to use extra-parliamentary means to secure a balanced budget that would permit the king to carry out what he perceived as his God-given duties without the necessity of bargaining with self-interested elites. In each case the result was widely perceived as an attempt to undermine the Protestant identity of the Church and the security of the subject in his property.

I have written at length elsewhere about the attempts of Charles and Laud to reform the Churches of England, Ireland

and Scotland. They had sought not a fusion of the churches
or a narrow uniformity, but three independent churches with
common goals and specialised local resources.[89] Here let me
comment on the perceived attack on property rights. In each
case the reclamation of (mis)appropriated church lands was a
target. In each, however, it was only part of a wider review
Charles instituted into the titles of landowners to the property
they believed that they held by secure title. In Ireland, this
was presaged by the appropriately sinister-sounding 'commission
for defective titles'; by the high-profile attack on the ill-gotten
gains of recent planters such as Richard Boyle, 1st Earl of Cork;
and by an unconcealed ambition for a massive new round of
Plantations, especially one to be made at the expense of the
Gaelic Irish in the West.[90] In Scotland, it was predicated upon
the Act of Revocation, the royal (not parliamentary) demand
that all grants of land by the Crown since the accession of the
Stuarts be surrendered, prior to a regrant on terms more
favourable to the king.[91]

However modest the Crown's plans in reality, the theoretical
basis was corrosive of all trust – as the Lord Chancellor of
Scotland himself put it in private, it put in jeopardy every title
to land rooted in a grant since the reign of Fergus (the Scottish
equivalent of King Arthur). In England, commissions into the
title to lands reclaimed from the sea, anxieties about the Court
of Chancery (not a common law court) creating for itself an
effective jurisdiction over title to land, combined with rumours
of inquiries into titles to former monastic lands, all created a
major panic by 1640. It is not coincidental that by far the greater
number of those whose landed fortunes rested upon former
church lands were Parliamentarian in 1642.[92] That these relatively
minor incursions created so much panic can be explained in
part by the simultaneous application of 'fiscal feudalism' to
create a stronger fiscal base for the Crown independently of
Parliament, but also by the recognition of the greater invasion
of property rights in the outlying kingdoms. This is a point
stressed years ago by Terence Ranger as a context for the English
attack on Strafford's invasion of property rights in Ireland.[93] It
is a suggestion that has, perhaps, been rather overlooked in
more recent discussions.

It is difficult to think of two more lethal ways in which a
seventeenth-century king could undermine the loyalty of his

subjects than by appearing to subvert true religion and to take away the security of property rights. The result was a rapid erosion of trust in each kingdom, a progressive disintegration of obedience and a slide into rebellion. Rebellion started last in England because it was the most pacified state with the most sophisticated mechanisms of legitimised and non-violent dissent; because the degree of provocation was least there; and because Charles's incomprehension at the effects of his policies was less extreme there. Because rebellion broke out last there, it broke out in ways that were conditioned by the events in the prior rebellions in Scotland and Ireland. Let us take two simple examples. First, it is now clear that there was a large measure of co-ordination between leading Covenanters and leading critics of royal policy in England throughout the years 1639 and 1640, and this co-ordination helped to shape the demands of the Long Parliament in 1641.[94] As a further corollary, the fact that the king knew that they had conspired with rebels elsewhere in Britain created a fear for their own safety amongst the English politicians that made the prospects of a settlement in England all the bleaker.[95] Secondly, the fact of the Irish rebellion, and the exaggerated accounts of all-too-real massacres, stoked the fires of English anti-popery and patterned English responses to the unfolding crisis of 1642.[96]

But to say that the English Great Rebellion would not have broken out as it did but for the prior rebellions in Scotland and Ireland is not to say that it *could* not have broken out at all without them.

This point is perhaps made all the clearer by the circumstances of the Irish Rebellion of 1641. As Ciaran Brady makes clear in Chapter 4, Wentworth's rule had been predicated on 'a redefinition of the nature of Charles's Irish kingship and with it a reshaping of kingship in the Stuart realms as a whole'.[97] This led him to humiliate and to challenge the most cherished vested interests of every important group in Ireland, and by 1640 he was – to sequester Christopher Hill's description of the Cromwellian regime in England[98] – sitting on bayonets, governing by fear and by force. Although rebellion was not inevitable, it was predictable. But it took the form it did because of the actions of the Long Parliament in interfering in the internal affairs of the Irish kingdom, which thereby made it clear that MPs would develop policies of direct rule from

Westminster if not Whitehall and (egged on by the Covenanters) that they would intensify the proscriptions on the Catholic community. The Rebellion of 1641 therefore took on a
pro-Charles and anti-Parliament hue that was not predictable.
The British dimension is necessary for an understanding of
the *hows* of rebellion rather than the *whys* of rebellion.

Thereafter there was what can be called both a war of the
three kingdoms and the wars of the three kingdoms. I have
explored the sense in which it was both elsewhere.[99] John Pocock
offers his own analysis of the problem in Chapter 7, below.
Some people saw it as one conflict in several theatres, others
as three interlocking conflicts; and the wars in England, Ireland
and Scotland can be seen as different kinds of war. I have a
feeling there is a lot more to be said on these issues.

In the 1650s, of course, the Cromwellians attempted a very
robust solution to the British Problem. English armies completed a military conquest of Ireland and of the Lowlands and
Western Highlands (but not the Northern Highlands) of Scotland.[100] The Instrument of Government of December 1653
presumed that Scotland and Ireland had been incorporated
into an enhanced English state, creating a single, sovereign
Parliament for one Commonwealth comprising the three former
kingdoms, and locating executive authority in a single Council
of State in Whitehall with branch offices in Edinburgh and
Dublin, with no greater freedom of action than the Council of
the North or the Council of the Marches had enjoyed in the
century before 1641. The English spelt out their intention of
making English law effective throughout the archipelago.

XIII

Henry VIII's constitutional and institutional revolution may have
created a 'unitary realm' of England; Cromwell's reforms did
not create a 'unitary' Commonwealth of Britain. Derek Hirst
explores in Chapter 8 the ambivalences and hesitancies in this
state-building exercise.

There is a central and defining paradox about the 'unions'
of the 1650s. The English intended the Irish settlement to rest
on conquest, ethnic cleansing, and the 'extirpation of the catholic
religion'.[101] They intended the Scottish settlement to rest on

the shadow of consent, a redistribution of social and political power within the indiginous population and not from them, and on the export of English concern for the liberty of all tender (Protestant) consciences.[102] The two settlements were to contrast the blackness of the souls of the wicked Irish Catholics and the reformable souls of misled Scottish Protestants. Yet in the event the two settlements came more and more to resemble one another.

First, internal dynamics proved a leveller. Although the English attempted no mass confiscation of Scottish lands,[103] the factions of the Kirk had effectively done that already for many of the nobility by the Act of Classes.[104] Meanwhile the attempt to expropriate all the Catholic landowners and tenant farmers of Leinster, Munster and Ulster 'according to their respective demerits'[105] ran up against administrative and legal difficulties (not least the need to establish the degree of guilt of each individual) and against the lobbying of the English Adventures[106] who could not find English tenants to work their Irish estates and who wanted the existing tenants to remain (suitably coerced and hedged around by demobilised English soldiers on their own holdings) rather than being herded together into Connacht. Secondly, as the canker of want dulled the highmindedness of Protectoral counsels, the need to make the Irish and Scottish operations pay for themselves rather than act as a sieve in the Exchequer caused a modification of policy in both areas. Catholics were readmitted to the economic if not the political life of Ireland; the English takeover of major aspects of Scottish local government and the judiciary had to be backpedalled. More and more responsibility was handed back to trusty Scots (and the English were never very good at working out who those were likely to be). For all Cromwell's anti-Catholic venom during his conquest, the lot of Ireland's Catholics in practice in the later 1650s was little different from that of Scotland's Protestants.

This is not to deny but that the long-term experience of the afforced 'unions' of the 1650s was more lasting in Ireland. The social engineering in Scotland produced no long-term effects, although in the fifty years after the Restoration the Scottish nobility were less visible in London than in the preceding or succeeding periods – they too were making good their losses from the mid-century crises.[107] Since no English had moved permanently to Scotland, there was no colonial or post-colonial problem. In Ireland, however, the change was to be lasting. The land settlement of the Interregnum was no more than tinkered with at the Restoration: more than a third of the land surface of Ireland moved from Irish Catholic to English Protestant ownership, and as a result the proportion of land held by those of recent English origin and who were effectively monoglot, anglophone and Protestant rose to almost 80 per cent. The proportion of the population that was Protestant, however, was closer to one-fifth than four-fifths; and that one-fifth must be called the Protestant communities of Ireland in the plural because of the three-way antipathies amongst them as to the nature of their Protestant identity: Church of Ireland, Presbyterian, dissenter (Baptist, Quaker, Congregationalist),[108] which in turn betokened their kingdom of origin and their time of arrival, each of which remained an essential part of their colonial identity. So although in the Restoration there is a clear sense of a greater homogeneity within the Catholic population – the New Irish or *Nua Gaedhil* – it is rash to speak too readily of the Protestant Anglo-Irish Ascendancy. These are issues explored below by Jim Smyth in Chapter 10.

XIV

The archipelagic dimension of later Stuart history arose less from the degree of interaction between the component nations and kingdoms than from the unnatural degree of isolation of each from the others. After the early Stuart push for some form of integrative union, and after the ruthless process of incorporation witnessed in the 1650s, the startling thing about the Restoration settlement from the British perspective is the dis-integration of the polity.

Charles II entrusted the government of Scotland entirely to Scotsmen – for much of the reign the formidable Duke of Lauderdale – and the government of Ireland principally to members of the Protestant communities of Ireland, most notably to the Old English Protestant Duke of Ormond. Foreign policy continued to be made for all kingdoms by English ministers and was ratified as and when necessary by an English Privy Council with a number of Irish and Scottish Lords sitting on it. Under the renewed Navigation Acts, Irish and Scottish merchants were more rigorously excluded from English colonial markets than they were before the wars, and discriminatory tariffs were raised against the import of goods from Ireland and Scotland that would compete with English goods (e.g. Irish linens and Irish hides for the leather industry). Yet in the thirty years after 1660 there were few in any of the kingdoms who called for a change in the constitutional relationship between them.[109]

The Scottish nobility needed time to lick their wounds, recover their fortunes and fleece their tenants, over whom they had resumed a stranglehold. They were content to make a strong collective bond with the restored monarchy in the creation of a fairly autocratic state. Never hitherto had the Council's legal power to use torture against dissidents been so widely deployed. Scotland was restless and there were major rebellions in the later 1660s, 1670s and mid-1680s, each of which was put down brutally. There were always more English troops stationed in Scotland than in England, and the Scottish Parliament gave the Crown sweeping powers to raise troops to deal with disorder. That disorder stemmed largely from the survival of many hardline Covenanters, made all the more incorrigible by persecution.[110]

If the Restoration in England was backdated to 1641, in Scotland it was backdated to 1633 (the year of Charles I's coronation). This meant that Charles II was freed from the constraining bonds of the Scottish reform process of 1638–41, but the Scots were freed from the radical royal religious innovations of 1633–7. However, this restored bishops, as James VI had left them in Scotland. Together with the ban on the use of the liturgies and other documents of the Westminster Assembly, this was too much for many of the clergy. Almost one-third resigned and set up in opposition to the state Church. Although periodically the authorities in Edinburgh tried to ease the terms of membership of the Church so as to lure moderates back in, the spasms of persecution were more intense and vindictive than in England. Thus in 1670 when the English Parliament enacted that repeated offenders in holding illegal conventicles were to be deported, the Scottish Parliament approved the 'clanking act', which included the death sentence for anyone preaching at a conventicle, and in 1677 Scottish landowners were made legally responsible for the religious conformity of their tenants. These extreme measures were the product of Covenanter militancy, and they only served to reinforce it. The climax was the ambush and murder of Archbishop James Sharp as he neared St Andrews in 1679. The brutal suppression of the Cameronian rebellion in the south-west of Scotland, known as the 'killing times', saw a reign of terror unparalleled on mainland Britain in the seventeenth century, and preceded by a year or two the equally brutal French army suppression of the Huguenot towns in France following Louis XIV's Revocation of the Edict of Nantes. The killing times, presided over by the Duke of York, the king's brother and heir to the throne, provoked no great backlash in England.[111]

The Scottish Parliament dominated by these complaisant nobles, and rendered safe by the fact that the single-chamber assembly simply voted yea or nay to proposals put forward by a steering committee effectively chosen by the king or his representative, assisted rather than hindered the growth of royal pretension: in 1681 (as the English Commons sought to pass another Exclusion Bill), the Scottish Parliament declared the inviolability of divine, hereditary right.[112]

The brutalisation of the tenants by the lords, and the noble contempt for the Covenanters for the latter's oppression of them in the 1650s led to the bitter irony that in 1685 when the Earl of Argyll rose up against the accession of the Catholic King James VII, neither his tenants nor his peers rose with him.

The Restoration settlement in Ireland consolidated the political power of the Protestant communities and left the Catholic communities marginalised. Its history is dominated by the 1st Duke of Ormond. He had been unflinchingly loyal to Charles I, however often that king went behind his back, and he spent much of the Interregnum at the exiled court. He had two long spells as viceroy, the first from 1662 to 1669, the second from 1679 to 1685. Ormond held senior office in the English royal Household, and was better able than many of his predecessors to get a number of his closest friends and clients into key positions around the King, watching out for his interests while he was in Ireland.[113]

The Protestant head of the Catholic Butler clan who had been a major family in southern Ireland since the Norman settlements there in the twelfth century – Ormond did not so much straddle and balance the various factions as find himself being denounced by all. Charles sought to square several circles created by the land settlement of the Interregnum, and when the dust settled almost every interest was outraged. The Cromwellian settlers had to surrender less than the one-third originally envisaged, but they resented every acre reclaimed. The Catholics thought the proposed settlement far too harsh and its administration corrupt and falling insultingly short of what was promised.[114]

The other predominant issue was the religious settlement. Viceroys attempted to reach accommodations with the Catholic hierarchy to allow *de facto* toleration if the hierarchy could deliver a guarantee of the political loyalty of their flocks, and much time was wasted trying to draw up binding oaths of loyalty acceptable to the viceroy and his Council, to the Catholic majority, and to Rome. The inevitable result was a bitter division within the Catholic leadership that was useless to the state. But Catholics fared better than those Presbyterians and Congregationalists whom the bishops ruthlessly drove out of the Church of Ireland – Bishop Jeremy Taylor evicted thirty-six Scots from livings in his diocese in a single day. And once outside the Church, Protestant dissenters were more likely than their Catholic neighbours to feel the weight of the law against illegal conventicles.[115]

In a sense, the Restoration was a breathing space in Irish history. After a century of aggression, and despite calls for further plantation, the English rested with what they had, and did not seek to take more. Indeed they discouraged those who had settled in Ireland from taking more. But they also had no interest in a closer constitutional or economic relationship with Ireland. Not quite a security threat, not quite a commercial opportunity, the English lost interest in Ireland. Denied what they saw as their just rights to restitution, denied a political voice and denied the religious freedom they thought both Charles II and his father had promised them, the Irish Catholic community felt even greater alienation from the Anglo-Irish state. And the English in Ireland tended to drift from being just that, men and women whose families, property and vistas straddled the Irish Sea, into a colonial settler community, increasingly frustrated and angered by the kid gloves that viceroys were required to wear when they dealt with the conquered natives of Ireland. Restoration Ireland was not a happy place.[116]

In 1689 James VII and II was overthrown. There is scope for a full study of the kind Conrad Russell and others have attempted for 1637–42 of the 'billiard-ball' effect of the way events in each kingdom affected events in the others. Certainly the English were anxiously aware that James's policies in Scotland and (especially) Ireland showed a naked authoritarianism he was half-concealing in England. He stopped short of meeting Irish Catholic demands for a reversal of the Commonwealth land transfers, but in every other respect he handed power in Ireland over to a Catholic Lord Deputy, Catholic lords, the Catholic bishops and a Catholic army. The effects of James's actions in Scotland and Ireland on his downfall in England have yet to be fully calculated.

In this case, it is probably appropriate to use such anglocentric language. For in 1688, unlike 1642, England led and Scotland and Ireland followed (though, in truth, it was the Netherlands which led England). James was deemed to have deserted the kingdom and thereby forfeited the throne (the Scots forthrightly but subsequently deposed him as a tyrant and the Protestants in Ireland just did what the English told them). The full implications of Ireland's dependent status were made clear. No constitutional instrument transferred the title to the Irish Crown from James to William. He was deemed to have deserted his Irish kingdom by deserting his English throne. Only the most myopic of historian ostriches can call the Glorious Revolution bloodless. William had to wade through seas of blood to secure his Scottish and Irish thrones, and the resultant political compromises in Scotland and resultant religious and ethnic pogroms instituted in Ireland shaped and stained the British politics of the next twenty-five years. As Mark Goldie shows in Chapter 9, the insecurities of the war years, and the further constitutional divergence of England and Scotland, created the context out of which another compromise produced in 1707 the Union of the kingdoms of England and Scotland into the British state, with one Parliament, one economic system but two legal systems and two national churches. Once again Ireland was left in an anomalous situation. It is appropriate that this introduction, like the book as a whole, and like the history it describes, should end in ambiguity and a sense of incompleteness. These are the early days of a historiographical quest for an explanation of a story without an end . . .

2. The Tudor Reformation and Revolution in Wales and Ireland: the Origins of the British Problem

BRENDAN BRADSHAW

I

The outcome of the Tudor Reformation and Revolution in Wales and Ireland provides a contrast fraught with significance for the political evolution of the two islands that comprise the Atlantic Archipelago.

In the case of the Reformation in Wales, historians are agreed – the protests of puritan evangelists concerning the persistence of superstitious observances notwithstanding – that by the end of the reign of Elizabeth the religion 'by law established' had secured the loyalty of the Welsh community and concomitantly Roman Catholicism had been discredited by association with subversion and the threat of foreign invasion.[1] The outcome in Ireland by the same time was more complex but no less clearcut. On the one hand the last of a series of rebellions conducted in the name of the Catholic faith – the so-called Nine Years War, 1594–1603 – had been defeated, giving the English monarch as Supreme Governor control of the formal structures of the Church throughout the island. Yet the aftermath of the rebellion was to show – the protest of Counter-Reformation missionaries concerning the persistence of superstitious observances notwithstanding – that the struggle for 'hearts and minds' had been resolved in favour of the proscribed religion of Roman Catholicism.[2] The contrast here delineated, set in the context of the European conflict between the Reformation and the Counter-Reformation, brings to light an ominous anomaly. The result throughout Europe was to produce a reconfiguration of the political map in line with the confessional formula, 'one king, one faith, one law', enunciated – in the form *cujius regio, eius religio* – in the treaty of Augsburg in 1555 as a means of ending the Wars of Religion in the territories of the Holy Roman Emperor.

In the light of the confessional norm, then, the outcome of the extension of the English Reformation to Wales is found to be unexceptional (although, as we shall see, this is not to render it unproblematical, much less to dispense with the need to explain it by reference to a unique set of historically contingent circumstances). Nevertheless, viewed in the light of the same norm, the outcome in Ireland is seen to be ominously exceptional: a kingdom in which the vast majority of the subjects persisted in refusing to conform to the religion of the monarch 'as by law established.'[3]

Furthermore the political corollary of the ecclesiastical Reformation, the Tudor Revolution in Government – as it has come to be called following Sir Geoffrey Elton – provides a very similar contrast.[4]

In Wales all the indications are that the implementation of the programme launched by the Cromwellian regime in the 1530s proved unproblematical from the beginning. Here, to take a lead from M. E. James, the history of rebellion provides a significant indicator. As James has shown, the spate of rebellions in England from the Pilgrimage of Grace, 1536–7, to the Northern Rebellion, 1569, attests the resentment elicited by the assault which the Revolution entailed on the quasi-autonomy of the outlying regions. Yet Wales remained tranquil: not a splutter of rebellion is recorded there throughout the period or at any time thereafter down to the death of Elizabeth.[5] Indeed, by her reign, the Welsh literati took to eulogising the new dispensation. The antiquarian David Powell exemplifies the common refrain in his *Historie of Cambria* (1584), which celebrates the way in which Henry VIII had been 'willing to make a plenary Reformation of what his father had easily begun'. Thus also, his contemporary and fellow antiquarian, George Owen, vented the theme in more patriotic form in proclaiming that the Henrician reforms showed the king's 'affection to be more towards that country [Wales] than to any other part of the [English] realme'. To the Welsh elite of this generation, therefore, as Peter Roberts has explained, the Tudor Revolution in Government appeared as a benevolence.[6]

The response from Ireland indicates a very different perception. In that regard, to return to the lead of M. E. James, the history of rebellion in sixteenth-century England and Ireland provides an illuminating comparison. For by that measure the intensity of resentment registered against the encroachment of Tudor reform in the quasi-autonomous regions in England pales by comparison with the resentment it elicited in Ireland. Thus the Fitzgerald rebellion of 1534–5, and its sequel, the Geraldine League of 1539–40, represent the most extensive and the most sustained manifestation of violent protest offered to the Cromwellian programme of the 1530s anywhere in the Tudor dominions: the Pilgrimage of Grace was a decidedly tame affair by comparison. Thereafter, whereas rebellion withered away in England, it took on a new menace in Ireland where it increasingly assumed the aspect of a nationwide struggle, culminating in a Nine Years War which did indeed engulf the whole island. And while religion provided the ideological catalyst for these later rebellions there is no doubt that, as the Tudor Revolution pressed inexorably forward, resentment at its practical implications provided the precipitant in the localities.[7]

Paralleling all of this and of no less significance, disaffection found constitutional expression. One manifestation was widespread resistance, frequently exploding into riot as noted above, against payment of cess, the tax imposed to sustain the army – the coercive instrument of the Revolution. More critically in constitutional terms, resistance manifested itself also in parliamentary opposition. In that regard comparison with the English experience once more is illuminating. Here – to follow a lead of Sir Geoffrey Elton – from the Irish Reformation Parliament of 1536–7 onwards, with the exception once again of the tractable last parliament of the reign of Henry VIII, 1541–3, parliament in Ireland functioned as a 'point of conflict' between Crown and community, not, as in England, as a 'point of contact'. Increasingly effective filibustering on the part of the dissenting majority, and increasingly ruthless intimidation and carpet-bagging on the part of government over half a century, reached due consummation in the addled parliament of Lord Deputy Perrott, 1585–6, which brought the legislative process to a virtual standstill. A twenty-seven-year 'tyranny' followed – only for the gladiatorial struggle to be resumed all over again in the Irish parliaments of the Early Stuarts.[8]

Finally, the contrasting response to the Revolution is manifested in the way in which humanist-inspired patriotic rhetoric came to be deployed in different ways in the two territories. In Wales, as already noted, the 'plenary Reformation' introduced by Henry VIII was eulogised as a signal expression of the special affection of the Tudors towards their '[native] country'. In Ireland, however, such rhetoric was appropriated by opponents of the Crown's policy who claimed to act from the 'natural affection' they bore their 'native country'. By the reign of Mary these had begun to style themselves a 'commonwealth party' and, as such, defenders of the kingdom against the self-interested agents of the Revolution, the New English.[9]

Extending the focus as before to set the contrast delineated above in the context of the reconfigured political map of Europe, the Irish response is found once more to resist the thrust of a major dynamic of early modern European state formation. This was the assimilation of peripheral territories by their cores under the impulse provided by Europe's consolidating Renaissance monarchies striving to transmute their disparate feudal patrimonies into centralised unitary realms by arrogating to themselves the absolute sovereignty vested in the Roman Emperor in the Civil Code of Justinian in accordance with the maxim of humanist jurisprudence, *rex est imperator in regno suo*.[10] In that light, then, the submission of the Welsh to the Tudor Revolution – designed on precisely such lines – is seen to set Wales on a path of development in tune with trends throughout Europe generally. In contrast the increasing intransigence elicited by the Revolution in Ireland sets in apart once more as an ominous anomaly.

Turning now to the British Problem, the significance of these contrasts for the political evolution of the Atlantic Archipelago becomes abundantly evident from the vantage-point of hindsight. As history was to show, the process of confessionalisation and assimilation set in motion by the Tudor Reformation and Revolution marked the first phase of a tortuous evolution through which the Archipelago's regional polities were resolved into a United Kingdom, governed unitarily by a Protestant British monarchy based in the English capital, London. And as history was also to show in the case of the Welsh and Irish peripheral dominions, the evolutionary process continued as it began. The integration of Wales within the unitary system proved to be unproblematical. Resistance was rare and politically insubstantial: latter-day attempts to generate a national movement for secession have consistantly failed to mobilise a substantial popular constituency. Not so with Ireland. It consistently proved itself a reluctant participant in the evolutionary process. It remained stubbornly Catholic. It was the last of the regional polities to be incorporated fully within the Union – by a combination of bribery and bullying in 1801.[11] And it was the only one to insist on secession – more or less successfully – after little more than a century filled with increasingly violent agitation towards that end, in 1922. The legacy of the 'unfinished business' of Ulster – as the partition expedient then adopted seems from an Irish perspective – has remained to bedevil the politics of the Archipelago to the end of the twentieth century. In short, in the light of hindsight Ireland emerges as the unassimilable element within the unitary British state that evolved from the Archipelago's regional polities in the early modern period: as such it has constituted a chronic source of instability within the unitary system. It seems not too much to claim first that Ireland constitutes *the* historic British Problem, and secondly, that the roots of the problem are to be traced to the anomalous outcome of the extension of the Tudor Reformation and Revolution to the island in the sixteenth century.

The object of the present study is to seek to explain the origins of the British Problem in these terms. The specific question to be addressed therefore is why Ireland emerged as an anomaly in the first place. The answer will be sought by continuing to explore the implications of the contrast that brought the question to light, in the expectation that it will also be found to contain germs of a solution. The comparative perspective will indeed prove to yield rich interpretative insights in what follows, not least to begin with, by exposing the superficiality of the received wisdom concerning the Irish outcome and by directing attention to a more fruitful line of enquiry.

Conventionally the challenge posed by the impasse that resulted from the extension of the Tudor Reformation and Revolution to Ireland has been missed or too easily dismissed by invoking the island's location as medieval Europe's *Ultima Thule*. This has been wielded as a kind of Archimedean key to explain, on the one hand, the resistance offered by the inhabitants and, on the other, the inability of the Crown to overcome it. Thus, ingrained conservatism, a traditionalist culture and immunity from innovative intellectual currents operating elsewhere, all stemming from the island's remote borderland location, are brought forward to account for local resistance construed, plausibly enough it would seem, as the negative response of a backward society to the forces of modernisation represented by the Reformation and Revolution. Likewise the remoteness of Ireland as a peripheral dominion of the English Crown is held to have rendered the law a blunt instrument of enforcement.[12]

The inadequacy of such an explanation comes to light by reference to the Welsh comparison. Wales provides the example of a region where similar geocultural and political structures prevailed and yet where the outcome of the Tudor project was altogether different. As to the first, Wales comprised, with Ireland and Scotland, medieval Europe's westerly borderland, the frontier region demarcating the feudal societies of Northern Europe from the Celtic communities who, as the surviving remnants of the prehistoric settlers of the Archipelago, maintained a tenacious toehold along the fringe of the Atlantic littoral. As to the second, Wales and Ireland shared similar forms of political organisation in consequence of a phase of conquest and incomplete colonisation conducted by Anglo-Norman adventurers owing allegiance to the English king in the course of the high middle ages. The result was the annexation of both territories as appendages of the Crown of England, and a bipartite system of government which allowed native Celtic forms to operate among the indigenous inhabitants in the westerly uplands and English feudal forms among the colonists who occupied the easterly lowlands.[13]

Against that background, the contrasting outcome of the Tudor Reformation and Revolution in Wales and Ireland presents an insoluble paradox for the received wisdom. The crux is that if the region's remote Celtic borderland status holds the key to the Irish impasse the same situation must have resulted in Wales, where in fact the outcome was altogether different. The most that such considerations can plausibly explain, it seems clear, are differences in the degree of the success achieved, as for instance, between the level of popular religious conformity secured in Wales and in the home counties. However, they do not suffice to explain the substantive differences that set Ireland apart as an anomaly.

Ironically, however, the more fruitful line of enquiry indicated by the Welsh contrast entails approaching the paradox
from the inverse direction. That is to say that, since the Tudor
project of reform proved capable of surmounting the obstacles placed in its way in Wales by the region's remote Celtic
borderland status, it must also have been capable of surmounting
them in Ireland, other circumstances being equal. Presented
in those terms, then, the paradox seems amenable to resolution by means of a two-stage analytical exercise. First, the means
must be identified by which the Tudor Reformation and Revolution were enabled to overcome the obstacles placed in their
way in Wales by the region's Celtic borderland status. Secondly,
having done so, the findings must be brought to bear for the
purpose of a comparative analysis designed to identify the
specific differences that account for the failure to overcome
the same obstacles in Ireland. That is the task to which the
remainder of this chapter is devoted. Here indeed, it will tran-
spire, lies the Archimedean key to the Irish paradox.

II

In the light of the circumstances that attended the introduction of the Tudor Reformation and Revolution to Wales the
successful outcome seems scarcely less paradoxical than the Irish
failure. The puzzle relates, first, to the success of the religion
'by law established' in eliciting confessional allegiance from
the Welsh in the absence of those religious dynamisms 'from
below' which were exploited to secure ideological commitment
to the ecclesiastical revolution 'from above' in England. Immu-
nised like Ireland by its remote location and by its conservative
and traditionalist cultural environment, Wales remained largely
unaffected, so far as the records show, by the late medieval
traditions of anti-clericalism and of populist Lollard heresy that
provided ideological grist for the erastion royal ecclesiastical
supremacy in England. Nor, for the same reason, could the
state-sponsored religion in Wales derive ideological sustenance
from the corrosive critique of the medieval Church mounted
by English humanists from the early decades of the century.
Finally, again corresponding with the Irish analogy, the radical
currents of Protestant heresy that began to infiltrate England

from the early 1520s, failed to penetrate Wales to any appreci-
able extent before the inauguration of the Tudor ecclesiastical
revolution there in the mid-1530s.[14] The puzzle then is how to
account for the confessional allegiance secured by the religion
'by law established' in this remote peripheral dominion in the
absence of the intellectual preconditions that disposed so many
to such commitment in England. The puzzle, it should be noted,
to point up its paradoxical aspect, is not simply that such a
highly conservative and traditionalist society yielded unresisting
obedience, however superficial, to the novel and apparently
heterodox regime of belief and observances established by law
as the religion of the reformed church of England. It is more
that the chauvinistic Welsh came to identify themselves with
the religion of the reformed church of *England,* as such –
therefore with a novel and apparently heterodox regime of belief
and observance rendered doubly repugnant, it might be
expected, as intruded 'from the centre' by the heartily resented
Saxon conqueror.

   The acquiescence of the Welsh in the Tudor Revolution in
Government seems to present *prima facie* an even more
perplexing paradox. The purport of the Revolution in Wales,
it will be recalled – conforming to a process of state formation
now in train throughout Europe generally under the inspiration
of the ideology of imperial monarchy – was to comprehend
this peripheral dominion within the frame of an integral
sovereign realm, governed unitarily from the English centre.[15]
The radical implications in constitutional terms may be gleaned
by reference to the sonorous preamble of the so-called Act of
Union of 1536 where the constitutional conception that informed
the project is set forth and ideologically vindicated. Here it
was decreed first that the status of Wales as a separate polity
constituted an intolerable affront to the sovereignty now
discovered to inhere in the Crown of England in virtue of its
imperial status, accordingly that Wales was to be incorporated
'as it rightfully is and ever hath been . . . [as] a very member
and joint of the English realm', secondly, as a necessary concomitant, that those distinctive features that constituted the
badge of Welsh political and cultural identity – laws and customs,
forms of government, language – were to be eliminated.[16] This
then was the radical conception. It was given juridical effect,
in accordance with the classic strategy of the 'architect of the

revolution', Thomas Cromwell, by means of three massive statutes dating, in addition to the Act of 1536, from 1534 and 1543 respectively. Finally, the substantive provisions of the statutes found administrative expression in the form of a programme of reform designed to apply the conception in practice.

The radical implication of the Revolution for Wales ultimately therefore may be observed by reference to the consequences of applying the device – again in accordance with the classic Cromwellian reform strategy – on which the reform programme pivoted. The ploy was to extend the English shire system comprehensively throughout the territory.[17] By this means, first and fundamentally, the medieval frontier between the kingdom and the outlying dominion was abolished and Wales was integrated within a unitary jurisdictional frame with the English kingdom. Secondly, as a necessary corollary of this process of jurisdictional assimilation, a process of juridical assimilation was also implemented. Welsh law and its judicial institutions gave way to English practice, to the common law, its courts and judicial procedures, supplemented by the system of equitable justice exercised under the Crown's prerogative.

Finally, jurisdictional and legal assimilation provided the means of setting a process of cultural assimilation in train by privileging English as the language of public intercourse. Its use was decreed for the conduct of local government and for all legal transactions; in the former case Welsh was proscribed on pain of forfeiture of office.[18] The paradox presented by the outcome of the Revolution in Wales therefore, is that the execution of such a radical design, encompassing the annexation of Wales 'as a very member and joint of the English realm', not only failed to elicit the slightest whimper of protest from the Welsh but, as noted as the outset, came to be eulogised by their literati as a benevolence.

These then are the elements of the paradox that require explanation in accounting for the successful outcome in Wales of the Tudor Reformation and Revolution. In addressing the problem, the interpretative strategy adopted here assumes as a starting point that, in view of the region's remote borderland location, the success is not to be accounted for in terms of the sheer effectiveness of government from the centre: *pace* the administrative genius of Thomas Cromwell and the Draconian proclivities of Bishop Rowland Lee, the central administration's local representative. The effect is to return the quest for a solution to the local context. More specifically the effect is to raise the obvious but neglected question of the internal dynamics of the Welsh episodes, of the operation of forces within the territory that provided a local momentum for the revolutionary initiative from the centre. The analytical task imposed by this line of enquiry then is to seek to identify a range of countervailing circumstances locally that would serve to explain how the initiative from the centre, despite its radical design, was enabled to overcome the obstacles placed in its way in Wales by the region's remote Celtic borderland location. The result of this enquiry will be to belie the paradox. It will emerge that, appearances to the contrary notwithstanding, the Tudor revolution in Church and state in Wales was favoured by its moment.

Embarking now on the analysis, the conundrum posed by the revolution in the Church requires little enough discussion. That is because the explanation for this first element of the paradox is contained in the explanation for the second. What favoured the inauguration of the ecclesiastical revolution in Wales, analysis shows, was not subversive religious currents infiltrating – feebly at most – from England or the continental mainland in the prelude. What favoured it rather, odd though it may seem, was precisely its magisterial provenance, its inauguration as the corollary of the Tudor Revolution in Government. The point is that the programme of the Revolution, examined in the local context, presents a highly enticing prospect in that it is found to address needs and sensibilities by which the local socio-political elite were keenly exercised. The 'spin-off' for the revolution in the Church therefore was that its inauguration in conjunction with a revolution in the state which the Welsh socio-political elite had very palpable reason to regard as beneficent, disposed the latter to accept the apologia offered for the state-sponsored Reformation at face value. They accordingly responded to it not as a heterodox innovation imposed by the Saxon conqueror but as the restoration of the usurped authority of their lawful monarch and the liberation of the Church throughout his dominion from papal greed and extortion. Pursuing this line of enquiry, then, the explanation of the paradox presented by the success of the Tudor Reformation and Revolution in Wales comes to hinge

on the explanation of Welsh acquiescence in the project of
the Union. To unravel that puzzle requires a rather more in-
depth analysis of the local context than was necessary in the
present instance. Here *la longue durée* transpires to hold the
solution to this puzzle. The explanation emerges, in the form
of a conjuncture of historically contingent developments such
as to dispose the Welsh elite to perceive the prospect of incorporation in altogether different terms from those adumbrated
in the imperialistic preamble of the Act of Union.

Proceeding therefore to reconstruct the historical context
that conditioned the local perception of the Union, the feature
that first claims attention as the *sine qua non* is a gradual shift
in the local power structure. The crucial factor in that development was a process of attrition to which the Welsh magnate
kindreds were subjected throughout the fifteenth century: a
process precipitated by the collapse of the Glyndŵr Rebellion
early in the century with its sequel of demoralisation and royal
retribution, and accentuated in subsequent decades by the
depletion of the great lineages through natural wastage, es-
cheat and attainder. Meanwhile the impact of the decline on
the local power structure was consolidated by its corollary. This
was the accumulation by the Crown, through reversion, of a
cluster of rich Welsh magnate patrimonies – most spectacularly
the Duchy of Lancaster – to the extent that by the end of the
century the monarch had become, in the words of Glanmor
Williams, 'incomparably the most powerful landowner in Wales'.[19]

The consummation of these reciprocal processes then, so
auspicious as an augury for the moment of the Revolution,
was twofold. First they procured the early withering away in
Wales of the late medieval system of power-brokerage known
to historians as bastard feudalism, the survival of which on
the peripheries elsewhere proved such a bane to the consolidation of monarchical power embarked on by the Tudors. In
Wales, on the contrary, the effect of magnate decline, again
to cite Glanmor Williams, was to render a magnate conspiracy
against the intrusion by the Crown on local liberties a virtual
impossibility.[20] The second effect, following upon the first –
and an even more auspicious augury for the onset of the Revolution in the event – was to thrust the Welsh gentry to the
fore as the residuary legatees of the leadership role in the
localities.[21] It is the needs, aspirations and sensibilities of this

emergent gentry that must be explored therefore as the crucial determinant of the perception brought to bear in Wales
on the project of incorporation. In moulding these two, further features of the medieval Odyssey of Wales come to attention as crucial determinants of the fateful conjuncture.

The origins of the first is to be traced, ironically, to the be-
grudging constitution granted to Wales by Edward I in the
aftermath of his conquest in the late thirteenth century. This
decreed a bipartite system of law and government. In the
Principality, occupied by the indigenous inhabitants, an amal-
gam of native custom and the Draconian English criminal law
– the worst of both worlds – was imposed under the code of
the statute of Rhuddlan (1284). In the colonised lowlands, the
so-called 'laws of the March' applied: a body of uncodified
custom, largely feudal in provenance, and variously defined
through the exercise of the regalian powers invested in the
lords of the Marches.[22] One way or the other the pertinent
consideration for present purposes is that the subsequent
evolution of the two communities demographically, economically
and socially was such as to render the constitutional constraints
which these arrangements imposed particularly burdensome to
the emergent gentry in the circumstances of the sixteenth
century. One drawback was the limited opportunities which they
afforded for participation in government service and its
perquisites by comparison with the possibilities that were offered
in England through the shire system as it had developed there
and through representation in parliament.

Probably an even more palpable source of dissatisfaction
related to the vital matter of land tenure. Increasingly through
the late medieval period the operation of demographic and
economic forces in Wales facilitated the accumulation and
consolidation of private land holdings. The trouble was that
the Welsh custom of collective ownership and partible inheritance rendered such enterprises legally vulnerable. The remedy lay in access to the common law of England, according to
which individual tenure and inheritance by primogeniture were
generally held sacrosanct. However, under existing arrangements
access was difficult, requiring the grant of a special 'charter of
privilege' by royal patent.[23]

It can well be understood how the Welsh elite in the 1530s,
chafing under these constitutional disabilities, were disposed

to perceive incorporation in quite different terms from those
elaborated in the preamble of the Act of Union. What they
saw was not the suppression of the community's distinctive 'rights,
usages, laws and customs'. Rather they saw the extension to
the Welsh of the 'privileges and liberties' for long enjoyed by
English subjects: government by consent through representation in parliament; increased opportunies for the accumulation of status and profit through participation in local
administration under the English shire system; above all open
access to English common law as a means of securing vulnerable
property titles.[24] Propitiously also, as it happened, that convenient construction of what incorporation entailed was facilitated
by a development that transformed Welsh perceptions of the
English monarchy itself in the half-century preceding the onset
of the Revolution.

This second convergent development was the turn in the
dynastic struggles around the throne miscalled the Wars of the
Roses, that resulted in the accession of Henry Tudor following
upon the Battle of Bosworth in 1485. As the bardic eulogies
that marked the event attest, what impressed the Welsh about
Henry VII's lineage was not his descent from the illegitimate
stock of John of Gaunt but his tenuous claim to a 'British descent'
through the line of a single Welsh grandparent, Owain Tudor.
Accordingly, their jubilation at the installation of the Tudor
dynasty centred not, as in England, on the intertwining of the
white rose of York with the red of Lancaster, but on the revival
of the ancient British monarchy, and, thereby, on expectation
of liberation from Saxon thraldom. With customary shrewdness
Henry VII cultivated this helpful conceit at little cost to himself:
by displaying the British ensign – the Red Dragon of Cadwaladr
– on the royal arms and on his coinage; by naming his heir
after the legendary chivalric British hero Arthur; and, at the
practical level, by a characteristic strategy of 'kicks and ha'pence',
balancing an intimidatory policy of bonds and recognisances
towards unruly marcher lords and their stewards with a display
of royal liberality – at a handsome profit by way of fines – in
grants of charters of privilege.[25] Modest though these gestures
were, they sufficed to sustain a mood of euphoric expectation
in Wales through the opening decades of the reign of Henry
VII's more neglectful son. The relevance of all of this to the
question in hand is, therefore, that the accession of the Tudors

served to engender an ideological climate in Wales, centred on the conceit of a revived British monarchy, which facilitated a perception of incorporation, in view of the benefits it bestowed, not as the annexation of the nation as a 'very member and joint of the English realm', but as its liberation by the long hoped-for British deliverer.[26]

Seen in local historical perspective, then, the sanguine response elicited by the radical programme of reform in Church and state implemented in Wales in the name of the Tudor Reformation and Revolution becomes comprehensible. Set in the context of the needs, aspirations and sensibilities bequeathed by history to the emerging gentry now assuming the leadership role in Welsh society, the alteration in religion and the dissolution of the medieval polity prescribed by the programme appeared neither as apostasy in the one case nor as tyranny in the other. Rather, the gentry, combining self-interest and patriotism, were disposed to perceive the programme as the culmination of a process directed to the reinauguration of the ancient British kingdom and the liberation of the Welsh, as the lineal descendants of the ancient Britons, from papal and Saxon oppression.

In that light, in turn, the explanation emerges for the success of the radical initiative in surmounting the obstacles placed in its way in Wales by the region's remote Celtic borderland status. The explanation has to do with a further implication of the strategy devised to effect incorporation. No doubt in persisting with the scheme to extend the English shire system to Wales holus bolus in the teeth of Bishop Lee's dismayed opposition, Thomas Cromwell had in mind the reform strategy that dictated the extension of the shire system to the outlying areas in England: administratively, the establishment of a unitary frame of government pivoting on the administrative centre of the imperial regime in London; politically the realignment of local power structures to the advantage of the Crown by constituting the 'county community' a countervailing force to the overweening influence traditionally exercised by powerful lords in their localities.[27] However, the strategy had a further dimension, of crucial significance for the outcome of the Revolution. This was to devolve the administration of Crown government in the localities on the gentry elite from whose ranks the offices of the shires and the panels of the commission of the peace were recruited. Here ultimately lies the key to the paradoxical outcome of the Tudor Reformation and Revolution in the Welsh Celtic borderland.

In the first place this explains how a vigorous campaign on behalf of the revolutionary programme of reform was mounted in Wales at all, given the problem of supervision posed to Crown government by the remoteness of the region and the traditionalist and chauvinistic dispositions of the local community. The momentum that sustained the initiative from the centre was supplied by the local elite, who, as its beneficiaries, were willing to implement the programme. Secondly, however, the same consideration explains the limitations of the achievement. These bring into focus the self-subverting aspect of the Cromwellian strategy. The effect of placing the administration of the Welsh shires in the hands of the local elite was, of course, not only to constitute them the agents of Crown government in the region but its arbiters also. It was, to cite Glanmor Williams finally, to grant the Welsh home rule, at least in the sixteenth-century sense of the term.[28] Thus it was that the Welsh elite were enabled to apply the Tudor Reformation and Revolution to Wales in accordance with their own conservative and patriotic predilections. The outcome – to encompass four and a half centuries of history in one pithy sentence – was to secure the successful assimilation of the Welsh polity within the evolving United British Kingdom while ensuring the survival of a sense of a distinct cultural identity among the inhabitants of the territory in defiance of the imperialistic design of the Union.[29]

III

Returning in that light to the British Problem it remains to be considered what insights the foregoing analysis has to offer concerning the contrasting outcome to the process of assimilation set in train simultaneously in the English Crown's other Celtic borderland dominion. More particularly it remains to be considered – returning by the same token to the Irish paradox – what insights the analysis may provide into the origins of the problem: into the circumstances that account for the violent concatenation precipitated by the inauguration of the Tudor Reformation and Revolution in Ireland in the mid 1530s. In that regard the value of the analysis lies in providing the means of conducting the comparative exercise proposed at the outset as the Archimedean key to the Irish paradox. The proposal, it will be recalled, is to bring to bear the circumstances that account for the success of the Tudor project in Wales in analysing the context that conditioned the response to the project in Ireland with a view to identifying the specific differences that would account for the Irish failure. That is the task to which this final section of the chapter is devoted. Sure enough the result will be to identify a range of variables as between the circumstances that conditioned the inauguration of the Tudor programme in Wales and in Ireland such as to endow the prospect of 'reform from the centre' with connotations in the latter case altogether different from the euphoric expectations which, as has been seen, the prospect generated in the case of the former.

Embarking on the comparative exercise, then, the initial effect nevertheless is to heighten the paradox. For it transpires that the project devised for the reform of the Irish polity in the 1530s fell far short of the radical scheme for the incorporation of Wales as a 'very joint and member' of the English kingdom. True, a policy of conquest was urged at the time by hawkish reformers within the Irish Council as the only feasible strategy whereby royal sovereignty could be asserted in the territories occupied by the 'disobedient Irishry', and the 'land of dis-obedience' could have been comprehended within the frame of effective royal government. However, as once before during the regime of Thomas Wolsey, the king and his principal min-ister baulked at the cost. Their cheaper alternative was to con-centrate instead on consolidating the colonial territory, the 'land of obedience', as a bastion of monarchical power and govern-ment, thus providing a base from which in the short term the Crown might be enabled to exercise indirect control more ef-fectively over the 'disobedient Irishry' and from which in the fullness of time its direct jurisdiction might be extended through-out the island.[30] As it applied to the Irish dominion, there-fore, the Revolution in Government was designed within the frame of existing constitutional arrangements. The island main-tained its status as a Lordship appended to the English Crown, bestowed upon it in complicated circumstances in the aftermath of the twelfth-century Anglo-Norman conquest. Furthermore,

the bipartite arrangement under which the Lordship was governed, as formalised in the statute of Kilkenny in 1366, was
preserved intact. The import of that statute had been that the
monarchy, bowing to political reality by accepting the fact of
the 'uncompleted conquest', confined the conduct of Crown
government as such to the area occupied by the colonial community in the east and south, contriving to exert external control as best it might beyond the frontier in the territories
occupied by the Gaelic septs and those Anglo-Norman kindreds
on the periphery of the colony which had 'gone native'.[31] Devised, then, within the frame of existing constitutional and
political arrangements, the project for the reform of the polity
launched in Ireland in the mid-1530s was, in the strict sense
of the term, conservative in conception. It was directed towards
reformation rather than revolution.

Thus the interpretative challenge presented by the Irish paradox can be seen to hinge on the problem of why the comparatively moderate initiative through which the Tudor Revolution
in Government was inaugurated there in the 1530s should have
precipitated a phase of chronic instability as outlined earlier.[32]
That is the specific question that provides the agenda for the
analysis that follows. The upshot will be to bring to light a
series of historically contingent developments in Ireland that
converged in such a way as to dispose the elite of the colony
to bring an altogether different range of concerns, aspirations
and sensibilities to bear on the prospect of the reform of the
polity from those that disposed the Welsh elite to respond so
sanguinely to the prospect of the Union.

In Wales it will be recalled, the effect of a process of attrition
that set in in the aftermath of the Glyndŵr Rebellion was to
undermine the power structure and the culture of bastard
feudalism, thereby ensconcing the gentry as the residual legatees
of the leadership role in the localities.[33] The concomitant process
in late medieval Ireland provides a striking contrast. There the
effect of trends that gained increasing momentum in the aftermath of a no less disastrous native rebellion a century earlier
– the Bruce adventure in the second decade of the fourteenth
century – was to entrench a power structure and a political
culture in both the native and the colonial territories of the
island that brought the dynastic lords a degree of dominance
in their localities unparalleled elsewhere in the Tudor dominions.

To delineate the process that led to that ironic sequel would entail traversing the entire course of late medieval Irish political history. It must suffice here instead simply to draw attention to its dynamics. One stemmed from, on the one hand, the disappearance of the institution which hitherto provided a national frame – however flimsy – for native politics, the Gaelic high-kingship, and on the other hand, the increasing disengagement of English monarchs from their Irish Lordship – while they were otherwise occupied with the recovery of their continental inheritance and later with the dynastic struggle of the 'Wars of the Roses'.[34] The effect was the reversion of politics and government to a predominently local frame throughout the late medieval period. Further, the effect, to point up its particular relevance to the present enquiry, was to enfeeble royal government within the Lordship and thereby to enable resident dynasts with the requisite resources and capacities to turn the ensuing crisis of law and order within the Lordship to their political advantage by supplying the need locally on their own terms, namely by consolidating and extending those networks of patronage and protection, reciprocated by dutiful allegiance – the bonds of 'good lordship' – on which the bastard feudal system was structured.[35]

A second moulding force had the effect of compounding and reinforcing the first. This is the phenomenon which anthropologists describe as acculturation: the process through which an individual or group assimilates a different culture in consequence of close and continuous contact with it. In the specific instance of late medieval Ireland, then, the element to be considered is the process lamented in contemporary documents as 'degeneracy' or, as recent historiographical coinage has it, 'Gaelicisation': the process through which the colonial community came to adopt a whole range of native cultural modes, from language, dress and literature to features of native political, legal and military organisation.[36]

The pertinent consideration here is the latter aspect in so far as the features adopted served to advance the power and the effectiveness of the colonial dynasts as local governors. First, the feature known as buyings (ceannaíocht), a form of political clientship, enabled the greater magnates to circumvent the pyrammidic structure of feudal political relationships and to extend their networks of protection and patronage and of

reciprocal allegiance across the frontier between the feudalised
colony and the Gaelic or Gaelicised 'land of disobedience'.
Secondly, there was *kincogish*, collective, kin responsibility, invoked as a rough and ready means of maintaining law and
order in areas lacking the necessary infrastructure for the effective
operation of the common law system. Thirdly and most importantly, 'coyne and livery' was a means by which the colonial
lords were enabled to recruit and maintain private armies on
a scale comparable to those of the native dynasts.[37] The effect,
then, of the convergence of these elements was to precipitate
an evolutionary process through which the colonial dynasts, in
the manner of their Gaelic counterparts, were transmuted from
feudal vassals to local warlords and as such proceeded to entrench
themselves as regional satraps.

By the late fifteenth century the bastard infeudalisation of
the colony had advanced to the stage where the earls of Desmond
on its south-western perimeter had withdrawn from all formal
contact with royal government. Meanwhile, at the other extreme
(in more senses that one), the earls of Kildare on the outskirts
of the Pale – Dublin and the four shires in its hinterland where
alone royal government operated directly and regularly – had
rendered themselves so indispensable to the maintenance of
the Crown's tenuous hold on the Lordship as to have succeeded
in engrossing the machinery of the central administration more
or less as a hereditary fiefdom.[38]

The first significant variable to emerge from a comparative
analysis relates to the composition of the local power structure
in Wales and Ireland in the immediate prelude to the phase
of reform in Church and state inaugurated by the Tudor Revolution of the 1530s. Whereas in the former the historical process
conspired to remove the 'overmighty subject' as the dominant
feature of the political landscape and to bring the gentry to
the fore as local leaders, the trend of developments in Ireland
was in the inverse direction: towards ensconcing dynastic magnates as local warlords and regional satraps, elevating them to
a degree of power and status unparalleled elsewhere in the
Tudor dominions. Therefore, following this lead, the enquiry
henceforth will focus on the variables between the historically
contingent developments that conditioned the response of these
differently composed elites to the Crown's reforming initiatives.

In Wales, it will be recalled, the Tudor Revolution in Church and state was favoured by its moment. Reviewing the auguries that attended the extension of the reform to the irish Lordship it becomes clear that historical forces there conspired to provide no such favourable moment. On the contrary, the effect first of all was to pre-empt the possibility that the extension of the Revolution to Ireland could hold out the prospect of the kind of cornucopia that so palpably disposed the Welsh towards the Union. This was because Ireland, having been conferred upon Prince John by his father, Henry II, as a feudal patrimony, then acquired the status of a Lordship appended to the English Crown on John's unanticipated succession to the throne of England.[39] These were the circumstances through which the Lordship came to boast in like manner to the English Kingdom an 'ancient constitution', and came to be governed accordingly as a self-subsistent polity by means of a set of political instruments which duplicated those of the kingdom.[40] So far as the moment of the Revolution is concerned, then, the opportunity was pre-empted whereby it might have promised those legal and political amenities as well as the opportunities for administrative office which the prospect of incorporation held out to the aspiring Welsh gentry.

Secondly, the moment of the Revolution was still less fortunate in the ideological climate it encountered. In contrast to the receptive atmosphere generated in Wales by the accession to the throne of England of what was locally regarded as a native dynasty, the ideological legacy bestowed by history on the colonial community in Ireland was such as to dispose the elite to look upon the prospect of reform from the centre at best with reservations and at worst with downright hostility. True, the community's historical experience as the defenders of a receding colonial enclave served to instil in the elite a keen awareness of their ethnic origins and, as a corollary, served to mould an ideological posture of loyalism through which they defined themselves, over against the 'disobedient Irishry', as 'English by blood' and, as such, the King of England's faithful and obedient subjects. At the same time however, their experience as the self-perceived victims of centuries of metropolitan political bullying, economic fleecing, cultural *hauteur* and, in time of need, indifference and dereliction, served to instil a countervailing anti-metropolitan sensibility and with it the consciousness of a distinct colonial identity predicated upon

Ireland as the community's historic *patria*. Here then is found the emotional spring of a burgeoning ideology of separatism through which the colonists affirmed their distinct identity, over against the 'English by birth', as 'Irish born', 'of the land of Ireland', '*populus Hiberniae*' and as such the historical legatees of a self-subsistent Lordship, appended to the same Crown as the English kingdom but separate from the latter; the legatees furthermore, in virtue of the same circumstance, of an 'ancient constitution' through which they claimed the 'liberties and privileges' of subjects equally with the inhabitants of the kingdom.[41]

The force of this patriotically driven separatist ideology as it operated to corrode colonial loyalism will shortly appear. Immediately, however, one incidental casualty of major significance must be emphasised. The effect of the emergence of a colonial patriotism predicated upon Ireland as the community's *patria*, their native land, was to pre-empt the development of a British consciousness also, the burgeoning of which in Wales so effectively camouflaged the imperialist designs of the Union from the chauvinistic elite of the territory.

However, the ominousness of the thrust of the political evolution of the colony for the prospects of the Revolution emerges fully only in the light of the impact upon the colonial elite of a turn of events in later fifteenth-century English politics which, as in the Welsh case, though to very different effect, served to mould their expectations of 'reform from the centre'. This was the revival of monarchical government that got under way with the readeption of Edward IV and gained increasing momentum in the reign of Henry VII, being further augmented under Wolsey's administration in the period immediately preluding the revolutionary moment.

The first significant consideration here is that, as the revival impinged on the colonial elite, it took the form mainly of a succession of reformist missions from London at least one every decade from the 1460s – sent thither to restore the effectiveness of monarchical government in the Lordship.[42] The second noteworthy point is the tension observable between the priorities of the reformative commissions and the problem of government that exercised the elite of the colony most palpably. The reforms invariably got under way with a purge of the Dublin administration involving the removal of the local Fitzgerald magnate

as Lord Deputy in favour of the head of the commission, and
the intrusion of a bevy of English officials to the jeopardy of
Kildare's clients ensconced in the plum offices of the
administration. Invariably, as a corollary, the missions entailed
an assault upon bastard feudalism in the localities – thus jeop-
ardising the structure on which the political hegemony of the
magnates rested – by the deployment of bonds and recognisances
ad terrorem in accordance with the strategy adopted to such
telling effect in England.[43] As an ancillary task only, the efforts
of the commission were directed to what, so far as the colonial
community were concerned, constituted the Crown's most urgent
problem of government, the need to curb the debilitating
encroachments of the 'disobedient Irishry' on the colony.

The outcome was that the series of reforming initiatives inaugurated by the 'new monarchy' in the Lordship from the
1460s onwards, as they impinged on the mundane concerns of
the colonial elite, deeply jaundiced the elite's perception of
the monarchical revival – by contrast with the Welsh elite's
experience of the accession of the Tudors. Against that
background a third feature calls for more detailed consideration in that it brings to attention the special relevance of the
revival of monarchical government to the reception of the Tudor
Revolution in the Lordship: the effect of the reforming missions
launched for the purpose in providing a catalyst that transformed the compound of inherited ideological solvents operating as a corrosive force upon colonial loyalism into an ideology
of opposition to 'reform from the centre'.

The feature requiring examination in that regard is the resistance predictably encountered by the reformative commissions
as the colonial elite rallied to protect their interests. The catalytic
function of the resistance derived from the impact of the
experience on the political consciousness of the colonists. First
their hostility to the encroachments of the reformative
commissions served to rekindle smouldering resentment at the
long history of perceived metropolitan overbearance and
exploitation, and to project it upon the monarchy's reforming
initiatives, these being taken to constitute the latest additions
to the grievous catalogue. Concomitantly the effect of the
resistance was to re-energise the associated ideology of separatism that operated from of old to corrode colonial loyalism,
directing it also now against the reforming initiatives of the

monarchy. Thirdly, the resistance acted reciprocally to suffuse the colonial elite's immediate, materially motivated hostility to the reforming initiatives with this inheritance of ideologically informed sensibilities. Finally, the outcome of the fusion was to appropriate the colonists' inherited separatist sensibilities as an explosive ingredient of an ideology of opposition to 'reform from the centre'. Specifically, the effect so far as the Tudor Revolution was concerned – the project of reform in which the monarchical revival culminated – was to dispose the elite of the colony to view the prospect of the reform of the polity first, in material terms, not, as in Wales, as promising a cornucopia of patronage and of legal and civil amenities but as an assault upon those long cherished; and further, in its constitutional implications, not, as in Wales, as the harbinger of a long hoped for liberation but as an untoward encroachment upon the Lordship's no less cherished 'ancient constitution'.

Set in that context the catalytic function served by rebellion as a mode of resistance to the reforming initiatives of the reviving monarchy deserves special consideration. Its function in that regard stemmed from the impact upon the political consciousness of the colonists of materially motivated resistance in re-energising the sensibilities associated with the conditional bond of the bastard-feudal code of honour. In analysing the outcome of the interaction thus engendered the crucial consideration is that, set within the frame of the honour code, the encroachments on the colonists' material interests entailed by the monarch's reforming initiatives assumed the aspect of a flagrant breach of the 'good lordship' enjoined upon the English king in respect of the colonial elite's much vaunted 'service' as the historical custodians of the Crown's Irish patrimony. The reciprocal effect of the interaction of materially motivated hostility and inherited, ideologically informed sensibilities in this instance therefore was twofold: to suffuse the colonists' resentment at the encroachments upon their material interests with a sense of moral outrage, and in doing so to mould a perception of the monarchy's reforming initiatives as the latest additions to the chronicle of grievous injustices to which the traditional custodians of the Crown's Irish patrimony had been subjected by an overbearing and exploitative metropolitan government. In that light finally the precise catalytic function of rebellion as a mode of resistance to the reforming initiatives of the reviving monarchy emerges. The effect of the fusion thus engendered, in sum, was to appropriate the conditional bond of the code of honour for the colonial elite's burgeoning ideology of opposition to 'reform from the centre' as a norm of political conduct that served to elevate defiance in arms to the level not merely of a chivalric obligation of honour, but of a patriotic duty imposed by the call of defend once more the 'liberties and privileges' justly due to the traditional custodians of the Lordship of Ireland in the age-old struggle against metropolitan overbearance and exploitation.

To complete this survey of the baleful auguries that attended the extension of the Tudor project of reform to the Irish Lordship in the 1530s it remains to consider a historically contingent development at the centre which operated reciprocally with local resistance to augment the explosive potential of the monarchical revival. The source of this development is found in the opportune convergence, in the course of the late fifteenth century, between the political aspirations of the reviving monarchy and the concept of monarchical power and authority that emerged from the reception of so-called 'court' humanism in England. More particularly the source lies in the achievement of a coterie of royalist legists and rhetoricians in appropriating the exalted concepts and values associated with princely rule by court humanists in High Renaissance Italy for the purpose of inflating the status and accordingly the pretension of England's reviving feudal monarchy. The ideological transmutation thereby precipitated manifested itself in the form of a developing imperial consciousness on the part of the monarchy, a development that found expression, *inter alia*, in the increasing resort of the first two Tudors to imperial iconographical and rhetorical motifs as royal insignia.[44] The implications of this burgeoning imperial ideology for the monarchical revival have to do with the implications in turn for the suzerainty traditionally exercised by the Crown of the imperial status now claimed for it by appeal to the axiom of humanist jurisprudence, *rex est imperator in regno suo*.[45]

Addressing the question in those terms a lead is provided by recent research that draws attention to the gradual awakening of Henry VIII, under the tutelage of erastian-minded common lawyers and political commentators, to the radical implications of his imperial status for the competing jurisdictional claims of Church and state within his dominions. The upshot ultimately was the revolutionary solution of the king's matrimonial crisis by the assertion of a royal ecclesiastical supremacy and accordingly the repudiation of papal authority as a 'foreign usurpation'. The point that needs emphasis here is that the king's perception of the suzerainty exercised by the Crown in relation to secular *loci* of power within this dominions underwent a similar process of radicalisation in the prelude to the so-called Tudor Revolution in Government, the secular corollary of the ecclesiastical Reformation.

The inflation of the regime's jurisdictional aspirations is well demonstrated by the history of the monarchical revival as promoted under that conniving absolutist and energetic centraliser, Henry VIII's first chief minister, Cardinal Wolsey. The novel perception of royal suzerainty that found expression in Wolsey's determined if chequered attempts at jurisdictional consolidation can be glimpsed in two moments of high-visibility. One is provided by the famous debate at Baynard's Castle in 1515 concerning the respective jurisdictions of the civil and the ecclesiastical courts, which the king himself concluded by claiming, apropos of his royal prerogative, that 'kings of England in times past have never had any superior but God alone. Wherefore know you well that we shall maintain the right of our Crown and of our temporal jurisdiction as well in this point as in all others.'[46] The second is provided by the less well known but perhaps even more revealing claim made by the king six years later in the course of correspondence with the Earl of Surrey, then engaged in yet another ultimately ineffectual mission for the reform of the irish polity. The claim, in so many words, was that '[we] of our absolute power be above the laws'.[47] In these two incidents, then, Henry VIII points unambiguously to the nexus between the perception of royal suzerainty now being brought to bear upon the monarchical revival and his mounting imperial pretensions. In a word, the nexus is provided by the attribute of sovereignty (*imperium*) which, according to the civil code of Justinian, inhered in the emperor as law-giver, representing as such the attribute from which the law derived its sanction, in so far as it elevated the ruler above all other *loci* of power and authority within his dominions.[48]

These two incidents reveal the king in active pursuit of that imperial sovereignty which was first formally claimed for the Crown only in the 1530s – in the ringing preamble of the seminal

Act 'in restraint of Appeals' of 1533. At the same time the inconclusive outcome of both episodes in practical terms demonstrates that the means to the end continued to elude the monarch. It was in no small measure the achievement of Thomas Cromwell as 'architect of the Revolution' in the 1530s to provide them. Apropos of which – to turn the coin – it now becomes possible to grasp the ominousness of the ideological transmutation at the centre that fuelled the Revolution in injecting yet another explosive tension into the climate that attended its inauguration in the Irish Lordship. The situation was that, on the one hand, the success of the resistance hitherto offered to the reviving monarchy's reforming initiatives emboldened the Geraldine cohort that dominated politics and government in the Lordship to persist in conducting their relationship with the Crown within the frame of the conditional bond of the code of honour. On the other hand, the criterion of imperial sovereignty to which Henry VIII had now recourse was altogether incompatible with the notion of political obligation as in any way conditional. The effect of Henry VIII's burgeoning imperial pretensions was to render the obstructionism of the colonists increasingly insufferable.

Against that background it is possible to draw to a necessarily peremptory conclusion. Set in the context of the *hereditas damnosa* delineated above, the resistance elicited from the Irish Celtic borderland to the assimilative process set in train by the Tudor Reformation and Revolution loses its paradoxical aspect. Indeed, as is now clear, the effect of the monarchical revival, compounding the medieval Irish Problem, was to set relations between the regime at the centre and the socio-political elite on the periphery on a course which rendered it well nigh inevitable that the comparatively moderate project for the reform of the Lordship inaugurated there in the 1530s would explode upon the local ruling elite with the impact of an irresistible force upon an immoveable object.

It needs only to be added by way of gloss that the concern of the present analysis has been to trace the historical *origins* of the British Problem. As such it constitutes a necessary but not a sufficient explanation of why the resistance elicited by the first tentative initiative towards assimilation should have hardened rather than moderated over time, first developing the character of a struggle for national autonomy under the

British Crown and then that of a movement directed towards breaking the British connection altogether. The rest of the explanation is to be found largely in the sequel to the original cataclysm: in the catastrophic history of Ireland down to the Treaty of Limerick, 1691, in consequence of the unique strategy eventually adopted by the Tudors to secure the assimilation of their intransigent peripheral dominion, conquest and colonisation; a solution which in the event served only to transform the English Crown's medieval Irish Problem into the British Problem that continues to bedevil the Atlantic Archipelago.[49]

3. British Policies before the British State

HIRAM MORGAN

Was there a British policy in the sixteenth century? This chapter argues that a growing awareness of a British problem on the part of English Statesmen did not axiomatically lead to a more coherent policy for the British Isles. In fact the growing disparity between policies towards Ireland (conquest and colonisation) and Scotland (alliance and union) suggests that the overall aim was by no means integrationist – towards the establishment of a unitary British state. Rather, what was coherent was the underlying purpose of English policy – to keep foreign powers out of the British periphery. In which case management of the ongoing situation might either be formal (by expensive direct rule) or informal (by a cheaper system of proxies) but the same result was aimed at. This was developed as a result of security needs, when policy-makers had to steer stormy waters after Henry VIII cut loose from Rome, and must be seen in the larger context of western European foreign policy. Since the underlying assumptions were strategic, it is fair to say that England was not alone in having a British policy. France and Spain developed British policies as they vied with each other for hegemony – when one was in alliance with England the other endeavoured to keep the English preoccupied in Scotland or Ireland. The Scots had a British policy, which involved intrigue in Ireland, but it was mainly the official expression of the dynastic ambitions of James V, Mary and James VI. The Papacy had a policy to recover its position in the British Isles, which was largely dependent on the good offices of other Catholic powers. Nevertheless, the most influential and consistent British strategy emanated from Whitehall and its examination requires an introduction to the English official mind which produced it.[1]

The Post-Reformation Tudor administrative elite had a distinctive outlook. English officials were educated at Oxford or

Cambridge or one of the Inns of Court and may have undertaken some foreign travel. Many were from the gentry, a group
that benefited from the dissolution of the monasteries or were
in the process of joining them as a result of successful careers
in Crown service. Most of these were Protestants anxious to
maintain the supremacy of their religion at home; some of
them were committed to its triumph abroad. This English elite
had a particular view of the history of the British Isles. The
historians whom they patronised reiterated the myths concocted
by Geoffrey of Monmouth and Giraldus Cambrensis in the Middle
Ages so as to claim superiority over Scotland and Ireland on
spurious historical grounds.[2]

Policy aims were highly conservative – to maintain and strength-
en control and only to extend it at the least possible cost. The
main strategic goals of English policy were to prevent foreign
interference in Scotland and Ireland – the so-called postern
gates of England – and to ensure that the near continent was
not dominated by a hostile foreign power. These traditional
goals became attenuated when England adopted Protestantism
and was left diplomatically isolated. Henry VIII's establishment
of a national church to facilitate his divorce from Catherine of
Aragon destroyed the lynchpin of English foreign policy which,
since the treaty of Medina Del Campo in 1499, had provided a
powerful ally against France and good relations with the Low
Countries. In the period of heightened insecurity which ensued,
new approaches to old strategic problems had to be tried. It is
intriguing, though perhaps entirely unrelated, that the English
state showed more interest in cartography – in maps of England
itself and of its neighbours – than the other European states
of the period.[3] Strategy became the stuff of political maxims,
which could be varied to match the particular problems at hand.
'Who so would England win / at Scotland he must begin'[4] could
serve a turn but 'He who would England win / Must with Ireland
begin'[5] was equally serviceable. With high levels of continental
involvement in Scotland and Ireland, it is obvious that British policy
so-called was in many respects the exercise of foreign policy in
England's own backyard. Arguably the priority in its Irish dependency
had as much to do with defence as with administrative centralisation or internal colonialism. At one point during the crisis of the
1590s the Queen complained to her Irish government that its in-
adequacies were 'as things too common in foreign service'![6]

On the the other hand, ministerial servants of the Crown were representatives of the political nation and were often more interested in the problems of the near abroad than monarchs, whose main concern was princely reputation on the international scene. In pursuing their novel British policies, ministers were able to create jobs and in turn patronise a host of minor officials. Indeed the rule of minors and female monarchs during this period of English history gave administrators unprecedented freedom of action to pursue their ambitions as regards both policy and patronage. In these circumstances it was the state's weak resource base which limited the prospects of schemes that were too grandiose in conception or motivated by an excess of religious zeal. Likewise the pursuit of long-term policies was frequently stymied by the vagaries of court politics, which depended on the changing likes and dislikes of the monarch. This was a period when government was not yet rigidly departmentalised. Secretaries of State in particular dealt with all aspects of government. Such ministers received correspondence from officials in Ireland, JPs in the shires, soldiers and spies abroad, as well as having to deal personally with the monarch, courtiers, petitioners and ambassadors. Their own correspondence reflects this multiplicity of concerns which they were having to juggle and prioritise. In consequence of this holistic approach it was easy to see linkages, or imagine conspiracies when, in dealing with the problems of Ireland or Scotland it was necessary at the same time to consider looming continental dangers. Thus did Ireland and Scotland naturally form part of a wider strategic picture. In this way it can be argued that the policies of the beleaguered English state towards other areas of the British Isles, even at their most aggressive, were in many respects reactive to threats or perceived threats to English interests. A major problem for English ministers was that intelligence received from officials and soldiers on the ground was often exaggerated. These 'men on the spot' shared the same official mind as their patrons in Whitehall but, underpaid and slackly controlled, they created troubles and threats where none had hitherto existed in pursuit of their own immediate aggrandisement.

Using the Tudor official mind as a paradigm in the way set out above necessarily invites an analysis of developing British policy which is as much about process as causation.

1. THE BREAK WITH ROME

At the end of the Middle Ages the kings of England exercised little or no control in the Gaelic and Gaelicised parts of Ireland and none at all in the kingdom of Scotland. They had little inclination to go beyond occasional haphazard interventions in these peripheries because their reputations were made in the wider European theatre. In the borderlands of the Tudor state itself (the North of England, Wales, the English Pale in Ireland and the Calais Pale in France) a somewhat more formal control was operated through the delegation of authority to locally-based aristocrats who, as cheap proxies for the king, were allowed to pursue their own interests whilst in his service. This system of concentric circles suited Henry VIII until his divorce and break with Rome highlighted a frightening lack of peripheral control amidst growing diplomatic isolation. The new departure, engineered, like so much else, by Thomas Cromwell, was aimed at the bureaucratic overhaul of the Tudor borderlands by direct rule. Thus far the aim was more the creation of a unitary Tudor state than of a unitary British one.

Henry VIII preferred glamorous continental warfare to the task of consolidating the British Isles. Before the Battle of Flodden when the Scots invaded England in 1513, he had declared himself with characteristic bluster 'the very owner' of Scotland, but he made no attempt to prosecute the claim after such a crushing victory. He preferred peace with Scotland, if necessary by maintaining a pro-English faction there. The logical match in terms of the future unification of the British Isles would have been the marriage of James V and Princess Mary who until 1533 was Henry VIII's only heir. However, when it was mooted in the early 1520s it was plain that Mary, who was already on offer to the Dauphin and the Emperor, was a mere pawn in short-term diplomacy.[7] Nor would Henry recognise James's place in the English succession – he described the request of his sister Margaret, the dowager Queen of Scotland, and her erstwhile husband, the Earl of Arran, that James be made Prince of Wales and be given lands in England as 'haughty and covetous'.[8] On the contrary Henry wanted his own male heir, which put him to the trouble of establishing his own national church to dissolve his marriage to Catherine of Aragon.

If Scotland was a nuisance, Ireland was a responsibility suffering benign neglect. In 1520–2 European peace permitted Henry VIII to experiment with a new government of Ireland under the Earl of Surrey. Grandiose aims soon disappeared under the costs of direct rule with little local support. Surrey advised an army of 6,000 men for a rapid conquest and 2,500 men for a slower one; Henry VIII proposed instead to integrate the Gaelic and Gaelicised Irish within the frame of Crown government by conciliating them. But even this pious hope evaporated as Henry was threatened by war on the continent, where 'greatly dependeth his honour and estimation'. The government of Ireland was eventually returned to the Earl of Kildare, who by a mixture of marriage diplomacy and main force was able to keep the Gaelic interior quiet. Such was English disinterest that the aberrant Earl of Desmond was able during the 1520s to intrigue first with France and then with Spain without unduly worrying the authorities.[9]

On the frontiers and in the borderlands, where the king's writ did run, government had been undertaken successfully and cheaply in the late Middle Ages by aristocratic delegation. The 1520s saw a period of experiment – the Councils of the North and the Marches of Wales were restored and there was much chopping and changing of personnel in these areas and in Ireland but there was no irrevocable change. When problems occurred in the borderlands in the early 1530s, the heightened tensions of the Reformation crisis made central government more apt to mistake the intentions of 'overmighty' subjects on the periphery. In Wales Rhys ap Gruffydd was executed in December 1531 on the grounds of conspiracy with James V of Scotland, which is pretty unlikely since he had already refused the blandishments of Chapuys, the Imperial ambassador. In the North, Lord Dacre, the warden of the West Marches, was arrested and put on trial for treason.[10] In Ireland, Kildare's defiance of Henry VIII in an attempt to hold onto the reins of power, with which the dynasty had been so frequently entrusted, came at the very point when Cromwell was pushing the Reformation-enabling legislation through parliament. When the authorities in London over-reacted by imprisoning the Earl of Kildare, his son Silken Thomas, Lord Offaly, staged a full-scale rebellion in the Pale, declaring his allegiance to the Pope and requesting the support of Charles V. Such overtures meant that the rebellion had to be crushed and in its aftermath it was impossible to go back to a system of aristocratic delegation.

Cromwell devised a more bureaucratic solution with the appointment of an English Lord Deputy backed by a garrison to defend the Pale. In the North of England the Pilgrimage of Grace (with which the Kildare rebels were in contact) was directly related to the Reformation and so the Council of the North was similarly remodelled to provide closer supervision.[11] The English authorities were particularly fearful of the interference of the Scottish king in this conservative region and as a result they continually urged him to follow suit by breaking with Rome, but such a move held no material benefit as the Scottish Church was already heavily taxed.[12] The difficulties in Ireland and the North prompted reforms in Wales, where lawlessness and fractionalised jurisdiction also made it a weak link. The legislation of 1536 granted the Welsh the same laws and liberties as the English, abolished the marcher lordships in favour of shires, which were henceforth to send MPs to Westminster, and established the framework of an English system of justice. Any Catholic or imperial hopes for Wales were therewith dashed: indeed the so-called Act of Union was a great success. The Welsh were already proud that they had supplied the ruling dynasty; now their gentry class accepted the established Church, participated in economic development and even encouraged a Welsh cultural revival.[13]

Also in 1536 the government of Calais was overhauled and was given the right to send MPs to parliament. There is no doubt that Cromwell was pursuing similar reforms in the borderlands – for instance the investigating commission sent to Ireland in 1537 had a similar brief to that of the one sent to Calais in 1535.[14] These Cromwellian reforms, designed to abolish anomalies, to make outlying regions pay their share and to make the periphery more accountable and responsive to the needs and dictates of the centre, are rightly described as an attempt to create a unitary state, but they should equally be seen as a bureaucratic response to the increased security fears attendant on the break with Rome.[15] These new constitutional structures were the political equivalents of the castles Henry VIII built on the south coast!

2. ASSIMILATION AND AGGRESSION

Shoring up the frontiers of the Tudor realm did nothing to relieve Henry VIII of his international pariah status. Indeed the reforms in the Irish Pale affected the delicate balance beyond, and facilitated the Catholic dynastic intrigues of James V of Scotland. Gaelic Ireland and Stewart Scotland were now potential springboards for France and major strategic headaches to Protestant England. The first response was a cheap assimilationist approach. Pushed by St Leger, Henry VIII assumed the Kingship of Ireland and adopted a policy of integrating the Gaelic lordships by a process of enfeudalisation, so-called 'surrender and regrant'. In Scotland assimilation was to be achieved by a dynastic union secured through a shotgun marriage in the wake of King James's early death. When these policies of assimilation faltered, military conquest became the order of the day. In the absence of an adult king seeking peer group recognition on the continent, Lord Protector Somerset was able to pursue an expensive policy to establish English control in the British periphery. The invasion of Scotland was at first a military success but Somerset eventually lost what had effectively become a two-front war with France. In Ireland, on the other hand, a more limited military operation beyond the borders of the Pale showed all the signs of becoming a process of piecemeal conquest. Far from securing formal control in Ireland and Scotland, Somerset merely forced disgruntled Irish lords and the Scottish governing elite into the hands of France, further beleaguering the isolated Protestant kingdom of England.

The real security crisis for England came at the end of the 1530s. The Franco-Imperial truce brokered at Nice in 1538 brought constant fear throughout 1539 of an invasion of England. Symptomatic of England's diplomatic isolation were Comwell's overtures to German Protestant princes and the king's disastrous six-month marriage to Anne of Cleves. However, the main threat came from Scotland via Ireland. Cromwell's new measures may have been sufficient for the Pale but the militaristic approach of Lord Deputy Gray caused havoc in Gaelic parts of Ireland where the Kildares had formerly imposed a degree of stability. Manus O'Donnell gained possession of the Kildare heir, Gerald Fitzgerald, by marrying his aunt and guardian and then established the Geraldine League together with Conn O'Neill.

The main aim of this Gaelic combination was the re-instatement of the house of Kildare but it also recognised the Pope's supremacy in ecclesiastical matters and was willing to make James V King of Ireland. The Scottish king sent the league military assistance and was ready to come himself to Ireland until it was decisively beaten at Bellahoe in 1539.[16] These events proved to the English the strategic unreliability of Gaelic Ireland as well as the weakness of their claim to sovereignty, which in international terms rested on the grant of the Lordship of Ireland by Pope Adrian in 1155. The consequence was a fundamental shift in English policy under Lord Deputy St Leger.

In 1541 the Irish parliament passed 'An act for the kingly title' to make Henry VIII King of Ireland; at first Henry balked at the potential costs and responsibilities of such an honour but eventually he accepted. Linked to the Kingship Act was a policy to incorporate the Gaelic lords into the revamped polity, a variant on the idea originally mooted by Henry himself in his exchange with Surrey in the early twenties. The incorporating mechanism is now known as surrender and regrant, because it entailed Gaelic lords surrendering their lands and having them regranted as feudatories of the Crown. In doing so they accepted primogeniture as the method of inheritance instead of tanistry and relinquished the use of their surnames as titles in anticipation of receiving a noble title. There were settlements along these lines with Clanrickard Burke, O'Brien and Fitzpatrick but the greatest success in this regard was the submission of Conn O'Neill and his creation as Earl of Tyrone, which took place amid great publicity in London in September 1542. However, this key settlement contained the seeds of its own failure because Conn O'Neill had been allowed to prefer an adopted son, Matthew, as heir over his eldest son, Shane. Furthermore the whole policy was necessarily gradualist, requiring time and money, but the former expired with Henry VIII and the latter afforded by the dissolution of the Irish monasteries was squandered by his ministers.[17]

In Scotland the untimely death of James V following the defeat of his army by the English at Solway Moss in 1542 allowed for a different approach to British integration. The Scots were forced into the Treaty of Greenwich (1543), by which they accepted the betrothal of Prince Edward to their child queen, Mary. The successes in Ireland and Scotland allowed Henry to return

to the altogether more glorious pursuit of bashing the French
in combination with his old ally Charles V. Boulogne was
captured in 1544 with the aid of Irish kerne provided by the
Gaelic lords and as a result the Pale of Calais was extended
southwards. This was the solitary English gain and they were
soon left to face the French alone when the Emperor sued for
a separate peace the same year. In retaliation the French were
rumoured to be planning an invasion of Ireland to set up Gerald
Fitzgerald who was now a fugitive in France, and as a result
the Dublin government made defensive preparations. Not surprisingly, however, the naval force collected at Nantes was
directed instead to Scotland, which was higher on France's list
of priorities.[18] It was obvious that there could be no going back
to pre-Reformation policies for Henry VIII because the strategic
realities were changed utterly. England had to keep up the
'Rough Wooing' of Scotland, which had in the meantime
repudiated the marriage treaty. In 1544 Edward Seymour raided
the Lowlands and sacked Edinburgh. In a move similar to that
practised by James V in Ireland, relations were opened up with
Donald Dubh MacDonald, claimant to the Lordship of the Isles,
through the agency of the Earl of Lennox. In return for an
annual subsidy of 2,000 crowns and the use of bases in Ireland,
the islanders agreed to serve Henry VIII against the regent of
Scotland. But the expedition to the West of Scotland failed
and Donald Dubh died in Drogheda.[19]

Henry had preferred a conservative and cheap British policy
which allowed him maximum opportunity to flex his muscles
on the continent, but in the last years of his reign he had
been forced into a more radical policy. The main activist for
an aggressive British strategy, Edward Seymour, became Lord
Protector of the new king and Duke of Somerset. Using a French
expedition to evict the assassins of Cardinal Beaton from St
Andrew's castle as a convenient pretext, Somerset launched a
full-scale invasion of Scotland to force it into a dynastic union
with England. The English army did not fall back after the
crushing victory of Pinkie, as in the past, but instead established
garrisons in southern Scotland. From bases defended by *trace
italienne* fortifications, English armies were able to wreak devastation on the Lowlands and to establish a zone of occupation
known as the Pale. They gave pensions to Scottish Protestants
who were willing to collaborate and extended protection through

bonds of assurance to 950 others, most of whom submitted
out of fear. The invasion was acompanied by a barrage of propaganda which, in addition to traditional claims of English suzerainty, emphasised a manifest destiny which was both British
and Protestant. The Scots were urged in Somerset's *Epistle* 'to
take the indifferent old name of Britons again' and 'to make
of one isle, one realm in love, amity, concord, peace and charity'.[20] However, blandishment, bribery, Britishness or brute force
could not win over the Scots. As Adam Otterburn, the Scots
ambassador to England, told Sir Ralph Sadler during the crisis:

> If your lad were a lass and our lass a lad, would you be so
> earnest in the matter? Our nation, being a stout nation, will
> never agree to have an Englishman to be king of Scotland.
> And though the whole nobility of the realm would consent
> to it, yet our common people and the stones in the streets
> would rise and rebel against it.[21]

In fact Somerset's invasion merely created a far worse strategic
threat than had existed before by pushing Scotland into the
hands of France. The arrival of French armies, which built
fortresses of their own, forced the English onto the defensive,
and eventually the beginning of a two-front war, with French
attacks on Boulogne, compelled an English withdrawal from
Scotland.[22]

There were similarities with contemporary English policy in
Ireland but the results were quite different. The consequence
of English direct rule in Ireland after 1534 was not only a non-
native governor but an embryonic standing army. This made
resort to a military solution to the problems of Gaelic Ireland
beyond the Pale more likely. The militaristic approach by Lord
Deputy Leonard Gray in the late 1530s was a forewarning. The
change came towards the end of Henry VIII's reign and then
gained force when Bellingham was sent to Ireland by the
Somerset regime. A revolt by the O'Mores and O'Connors was
suppressed in the Midlands and then fortifications, elaborate
by Irish standards but less sophisticated than those in Scotland,
were built at Daingean and Ballyadams to house garrisons. This
led in turn to the confiscation of Leix and Offaly and the
beginnings of plantation.[23] As a result the O'Connors sent George
Paris, whose family had been displaced in the earlier Kildare

rebellion, as an agent to the French Court. The French were interested – D'Oysel, their supremo in Scotland, considered the Pope's ability to transfer the sovereignty of Ireland and suggested an invasion of the North by the Earl of Arygll and a simultaneous expedition to southern Ireland to bring home Gerald Fitzgerald. A French fact-finding mission was sent from Scotland. It assessed the military capacity of the Irish but received no commitments from O'Neill and O'Donnell, who were not directly affected by the developments in the Midlands. This was the extent of French interest in Ireland because the English sued for peace after their reconquest of Boulogne. When Paris returned to the French Court together with Cormac O'Connor in 1551, their requests were politely ignored.[24] Lord Deputies Bellingham and Croft had built forts on the southern Irish coasts to counter this possible threat but Northumberland's peace with France staved it off.[25]

This was a critical phase in British policy. The official mind of an isolated, committed Protestant regime was working overtime unrestrained by the different ambitions of an adult monarch. Scotland had a civil society which was cohesive enough to withstand English invasion and one which was deemed stable enough to be worth receiving French aid. In Ireland the establishment of garrisons beyond the Pale began a process of piecemeal conquest. The process antagonised the Gaelic lords, forced them to seek foreign intervention and created strategic threats where none had hitherto existed. Irish society was not cohesive enough to resist conquest and was usually considered too unstable to merit foreign assistance. Furthermore the local English commanders responsible for this moving frontier often exaggerated the rumours of foreign intervention, thereby drawing the support of Dublin or London into the interior to suppress troubles which their very presence had provoked.

3. THE FRENCH THREAT

Between the mid-1550s and the late 1560s England was in alliance with Spain, either by marriage between Mary Tudor and Philip II or thereafter as a matter of convenience to prevent French and Guisan domination of the British Isles. After the fall of Calais, Ulster seemed exposed as a strategic weakspot because of its close proximity to Scotland, which was ruled by a French regent, Mary of Guise. However, it was the escalating military and colonial activity in Ireland that created this weakness, forcing the native Irish into making contacts with foreign rulers, which overtures English commanders in turn exaggerated to further their own aggrandisement. William Cecil pursued a policy by which he hoped to rid Scotland of French influence and Ulster of Scottish influence. The basic idea was that the Earl of Argyll, influential in the new Protestant elite in Scotland, would sort out the Ulster problem for the English. Cecil's radical British policy was tempered by the conservative penny-pinching of Queen Elizabeth. In the mid-1560s the French threat loomed large again with Mary Queen of Scots, the Catholic candidate for the English throne, riding high in Scotland and Shane O'Neill following suit in Ulster. However, the assassination of Shane in 1567 and the flight of the Scottish queen into England in 1568 seemed to abate these northern threats. Whether such threats were more imagined than real hardly matters because they had had real consequences for the development of British policy.

In Mary Tudor's reign the conquest of Ireland gained momentum. In 1556 the plantation of Leix-Offaly was reorganised and there were more expeditions against the MacDonnell settlement in Antrim, which were considered to be a vanguard of a Franco-Scottish invasion. The English were now returned to their natural alliance with Spain, but Calais, England's last continental possession, was lost to the French and Mary was forced to refortify Berwick in case it was similarly lost in the half-hearted war against the Scots. The main reason was not the Spanish marriage but England's military weakness resulting from the expensive wars of Henry VIII and Edward VI in France and Scotland and the related debasement of the currency. The national hand-wringing over the loss of Calais was more about honour and symbolism than reality. The disaster stopped any foolish notions of re-establishing a land-based continental empire and put more emphasis on the need for a strong navy. It would be interesting to know how many civil and military personnel displaced from Calais eventually found employment on the northern borders with Scotland or in Ireland. However, England's interest in the near continent was by no means reduced – intervention was still required there to protect her interests when necessary. On the other hand it did prevent any inadvertent involvement, because Calais would almost certainly have become a magnet for French and Netherlandish Protestants during the civil wars which soon after enveloped those countries.

If the fall of Calais did give birth to a new, insular British policy, William Cecil, Queen Elizabeth's chief adviser, is the man we might expect to supply it. He had been a rising star of the Somerset regime, had fought at Pinkie and had helped produce Unionist propaganda during the Rough Wooing. Jane Dawson shows Cecil's lifelong interest in the new cartographic science, which involved collecting maps and even commissioning ones of Ireland. Whereas Elizabeth preferred short-term European policies, Cecil wanted to create a British Isles which was both united and Protestant. In this regard it is also claimed that Cecil favoured a stronger navy – he referred to it as 'the wall of England – and the establishment of a native arms industry. At the start of the reign the main strategic priority was to succour the Lords of the Congregation in Scotland, especially after the arrival of French reinforcements to suppress the Protestant coup d'état. The Queen was reluctant to intervene but Cecil got his way after threatening to resign from office. In the Treaty of Berwick, concluded with the new Scottish regime, the Scots were on this occasion treated as equals to be rendered temporary military assistance rather than to be invaded and occupied, as in the 1540s. As a result the French withdrew.

The Treaty of Berwick had also introduced a new element – Ireland. The Scots, in particular the Earl of Argyll, were to provide repayment by solving the Irish question or at least the most pressing part of it. Argyll would use his military forces to defeat Shane O'Neill with the assistance of Calvagh O'Donnell and James MacDonnell. The latter had entered into a bond with Argyll to resist a French invasion in the hope of getting his lands in Ireland confirmed. By this *linkage*[26] Cecil hoped to kill two birds with one stone. That the Scots favoured the linkage, or purported to do so, is revealed in their proposed marriage of Arran and Elizabeth in 1560/1:

France and Spain have of late so increased their estates that they are nothing like what they were and yet England remains always one, without the accession of any new force. For avoiding the peril thereof, united strength, by joining the two kingdoms, having Ireland knit thereto, is worthy consideration. By this means Ireland might be reformed and brought to perfection of obedience and the Queen would be the strongest Princess in Christendom upon the seas and establish a certain monarchy by itself in the ocean, divided from the rest of the world.[27]

Cecil could not have put it better himself but the linkage never worked. In Ireland Sussex was forced to make peace with Shane, and Elizabeth, much to Cecil's annoyance, favoured the expedition to support the French Huguenots whereby she hoped to swop Le Havre for Calais. Cecil's British strategy received its death blow when Mary married Darnley, and Elizabeth stood aloof, refusing to back the Scots Protestant nobles. Moray, when he rebelled, was left to stew in his own juice and Argyll was abandoned to such extent that he became unco-operative and downright hostile.[28]

Ireland became heavily militarised under Sussex and Sidney and the army captains they brought over with them. Under female monarchs, the western realm was a perfect terrain in which to dissipate the energies of the military men but they created more problems than they solved. The French threat to Ireland which loomed during most of Mary's reign was suddenly heightened by the fall of Calais. The Dublin government, on receiving the 'dolorous news' about Calais, was worried by rumours of a Scottish–French invasion in the North and fears that the Irish would assist them.[29] In the Autumn of 1558 Lord Lieutenant Sussex took preventive action with an expedition against the Scottish islanders and their kinsmen in Ulster.[30] Yet there is little doubt that English governors in Ireland exaggerated this strategic threat. Despite the Treaties of Cateau-Cambresis and Edinburgh, in late 1560 Sussex was still harping on a possible French takeover in Ireland – 'the matter, if it be attempted by a foreign power and aided by civil faction, so easy to be compassed and the resisting thereof so difficult'.[31]

The problem was that the English had bred a civil faction of their own by their mismanagement of Shane O'Neill. After Sussex failed to defeat him, Sidney took up the task in 1565. The interesting thing about Sidney's appointment with a programme similar to that of his predecessor is that it comes hard on the Darnley marriage in Scotland, which by combining the two

Catholic claims to the English throne turned up the pressure on Elizabeth. This point has been missed by historians. Of course Sidney's subsequent moves against Shane merely forced the latter into the hands of the Queen of Scots – O'Neill made overtures to Mary through the agency of Argyll who had now switched sides, offered the Crown of Ireland to Charles IX of France, and professed himself a defender of the Catholic faith.[32] In April 1566 Sidney remarked on Shane's connection with the Scots and the potential loss of Ireland rivalling the disaster of Calais, and in December came an unsubstantiated report from Carrickfergus that if Mary was not recognised as heir apparent in England Argyll would invade Ireland to help Shane O'Neill.[33] Nevertheless Sidney managed to succeed where Sussex had failed – he had Shane assassinated by proxy.[33]

4. THE SPANISH THREAT

The French threat did not vanish entirely. It merely became compounded in a wider Catholic threat in which the Pope took the lead by absolving subjects from their allegiance to a heretical English queen. The growing fear was that Spain's attempts to reconquer its Netherlandish possessions would ultimately lead to an English clash with the leading Catholic power. The danger was isolation, war and absorption. The strategic spotlight now fell on the southern Irish province of Munster, facing as it did the westward projection of the Iberian peninsula. English interference in this province precipitated the flight of James Fitzmaurice Fitzgerald to the continent and his return via Spain with an indulgence from the Pope and the remnant of a larger Papal army in 1579. The new Desmond war was thus engendered by the over-reaction of uncontrolled English commanders in Munster to a militarily insignificant expedition. This occurred at a critical juncture in English policy. William Cecil, now ennobled as Lord Burghley, was playing a conservative role and advocating that the queen marry the Catholic Prince of Anjou to underwrite an Anglo-French alliance against Spain. He was opposed by Walsingham. This radical Protestant was trying to cover all the angles including Burghley's old policy of supporting the Protestant regime in Scotland and keeping the lid on Ulster. The Anjou crisis led to the temporary collapse of Walsingham's

British policy. He resuscitated it afterwards but the outbreak
of war with Spain meant that the reform of Ireland could no
longer be justified as a priority.

Just as the Franco-Scottish threat was diminishing, relations
with Spain worsened. As early as 1567 Sidney had informed
the queen how easily Philip of Spain might dispossess her of
Munster and Connacht and reminded her of the need for greater
security on the south coast of Ireland.[35] Sidney wanted to establish
provincial presidencies to bring law and order into these outlying
provinces. When Edward Fitton, a client of Cecil's, was appointed
to the presidency of Munster, he sparked off a magnate revolt.[36]
When Warham St Leger, Sidney's candidate for the Munster
job, was rejected, he petitioned instead as part of a consortium
to launch a private colonisation of the Irish parts of Munster.
This consortium echoed Sidney's fears about the threat of Spain,
wanted to break the local connection with Spanish merchants
and asserted that Munster's resources would be better developed
by Englishmen. The colonial scheme and simultaneous land-
grabbing by Sir Peter Carew, together with Sidney's attempts
to demilitarise the South, brought a widespread revolt led by
James Fitzmaurice. 'A parliament' of the Munster Irish dispatched
the Catholic archbishop of Cashel to Spain to request that Philip
appoint a Habsburg prince as King of Ireland on the grounds
that Elizabeth was trying to impose heresy on the country. Philip
was unresponsive but the proclamation of Pius V's excommuni-
cation of Elizabeth saw the beginning of a decade of aggressive Papal policy. After repression by Gilbert and Perrot,
Fitzmaurice submitted in 1573 and went into exile in 1575. As
if their earlier petitions had been self-fulfilling prophecies, the
would-be colonists were now demanding extensive confiscations
but were ignored.[37]

In Ulster the local lords also united to oppose colonisation.
After the death of Shane O'Neill, Sidney put forward extensive
plans for the reform of Ulster but they were too expensive and
became less urgent after the fall of the Scottish queen. The result
was the private colonial ventures of Sir Thomas Smith and the
Earl of Essex to take over the lands of the Clandeboye O'Neills
and the MacDonnells. 'The Enterprise of Ulster' (1571–5) proved
beyond the means of the individuals involved, received little support
from the Dublin government who feared it would 'bring the
Irish into a knot to rebel' at a time when it was under orders

to cut costs and discharge troops, and ended in massacres by the frustrated colonists at Belfast and Rathlin.[38] The Ulster interlude drew the attention of a Spanish agent and the interest of the French ambassador but luckily there was no real strategic threat to England at this time for the Irish to call upon.[39]

In the 1570s William Cecil became less radical. In the late sixties he had poured cold water on Sidney's grandiose colonisation scheme in Ulster, though he later invested in Smith's private scheme and supported that of Essex. In 1573 he supported the expeditionary force to scotch the last remnants of Mary Stewart's party holed-up in Edinburgh Castle. With Scotland now less of a threat, Burghley, as Lord Treasurer from 1572, and possibly too busy lining his own pockets, was keenly aware of the costs of a forward policy. He became a conservative, following the same tack as the queen. The radical role was now played by Sir Francis Walsingham as Secretary of State from December 1573, and Keeper of the Privy Seal from April 1576. He wanted to safeguard England, unite the British Isles and defend the Gospel. To do this, he patronised soldiers and sailors, sought to advance England's interests in Scotland and Ireland, to support Protestants on the continent, and to contest Spanish hegemony world-wide. Walsingham wanted the English Crown to regularise its relationship with the Protestant regime in Scotland with a treaty of amity, to spend more money on its supporters there and if necessary to intervene on their behalf. In Ireland he wanted Ulster reformed, he wanted to break the link with Scotland, and favoured presidencies to establish law and order in the outlying provinces. Basically he shared Sidney's assumptions about the reform of Ireland and the Irish though he disapproved of his more adventurist tendencies. Using his pivotal position of secretary, Walsingham was able to build up clients in English embassies abroad and in the central and provincial government in Ireland.

As a result of the Anjou marriage negotiations, Walsingham's careful plans came completely unstuck. Until recently historians viewed the Anjou business from its inception as a means of delaying the war with Spain, a mere tactic. However, new research by Mitchell Leimon suggests that the conservatives led by Sussex and Burghley propounded it seriously, believing that the threat to England was urgent and required immediate action. The basic goal was the maintenance of the balance of power, which would reduce England's isolation, staunch the Spanish threat, prevent French predominance in northern Europe and save England from a war it could not win. The marriage negotiations distracted government from Ireland and Scotland, and wrecked Walsingham's British policies and his influence over developments, especially during his banishment from court between October 1579 and February 1580. England failed to take preventive action in Ireland even though there was forewarning of Fitzmaurice's Papal-backed landing at Smerwick. Walsingham had supported Desmond's attempt at reform, as had Sidney before his departure in 1578. Now Walsingham had no control over his main military client, Sir Nicholas Malby, who pursuing his own interests forced the unfortunate Desmond into rebellion. The queen was furious with Malby because of the vast strategic quagmire and money-pit which had been opened up but the New English, who put all the blame on Desmond, saw it as a golden opportunity for large-scale confiscation and colonisation. In Scotland Elizabeth and Burghley refused to help the carefully nurtured Morton regime. In August 1579 the Privy Council, distracted by the marriage proposal, ignored Morton's agent and the following month Esmé Stewart, sieur d'Aubigny, arrived and won the young king's confidence. Ambassador Bowes insisted that England could secure her position in Scotland for £2,000 but nothing was done. Morton was arrested on 31 December 1580 – an English army was raised and disbanded – Morton was executed on 2 June 1581. Esmé Stewart was now in power as the Duke of Lennox; French and Guisan influence seemed to be restored in Scotland, and Ulster again seemed a weak link because Turlough Luineach O'Neill was in cahoots with Argyll. The English had spent too little too late trying to back up Morton; now they were forced to spend a great deal more reinforcing their first line of defence at Berwick.[40]

In the years following the collapse of the Anjou marriage negotiations, Walsingham rebuilt his position and achieved some of his basic policy goals. He was influential in the appointment of Perrot as Lord Deputy of Ireland in 1584. Alleging a Franco-Scottish invasion threat, Perrot intervened in Ulster, attempting to evict the MacDonnells from Antrim and simultaneously to demilitarise the province in a 'composition' whereby the local lords agreed to exchange their Scottish mercenaries for English troops. In 1585 Walsingham secured English intervention in the Netherlands. This meant the end of Perrot's grandiose schemes; as the Secretary of State told him in February 1586, it was now 'impossible to draw Her Majesty into any further charge, having many necessary occasions to use the money elsewhere'.[41] Likewise many of the composition troops were recruited by Sir William Stanley to fight in the Netherlands.[42] Walsingham also secured the treaty of amity with Scotland after Lennox's successor regime under the Earl of Arran had been destabilised. In a treaty of mutual assistance against foreign invasion the English bought Scottish friendship with a pension of £4,000 for James VI and the Scots agreed to restrain their military activity in Ireland. Linked to this were the orders sent to Perrot to wrap up the dispute with the MacDonnells. As a result Sorley Boye MacDonnell submitted to the Lord Deputy in return for legal status and confirmation of lands. By these agreements England ensured her postern gates were shut as she prepared for an epic struggle with Spain.[43] In 1587 Walsingham secured his final objective – the destruction of Mary Stewart, something he had determined even before he entered political office, when his agents set up the increasingly desperate ex-queen in what is known as the Babington plot.[44]

5. CONQUEST AND CONVERGENCE

The English victory over the Armada was only the beginning of a long struggle against Spain in which Ireland proved one of the most decisive theatres. The diversion of funds to engage the Spaniards on the continent and the high seas beggared the queen's service in Ireland. The death of Walsingham and the disgrace of Perrot turned Irish servitors, many of them cronies of Burghley, into freebooters who pressed hard on the Irish lords. These lords were forced to look for a Spanish alliance and the intensity of the warfare on this occasion brought their appeal more tangible (though equally fateful) results than did previous Irish overtures for foreign backing. The English authorities also knew that O'Neill and the Irish confederates would have access to Scottish mercenaries. Ironically it was only when Spanish intervention became a reality that James VI, fearing for the security of his future inheritance, moved to close down the trade in mercenaries. The Nine Years War in Ireland, both in its causes and its course, was a case of the tail wagging the dog. This final phase of the Tudor conquest of Ireland cost close on £2,000,000 – more than the subsidies and soldiers sent to the Dutch and Henry IV, and eight times the cost of any previous Irish war.[45] Apart from the old formula of linkage, there was no self-conscious British strategy for a war which by March 1603 gave unimpeded sovereignty of the archipelago to a single monarch.

The defeat of the Armada of 1588 far from alleviating the Spanish threat to England merely highlighted its potency. In the war which dragged on until 1604, England's weakest point was undoubtedly Ireland. During invasion scares in 1589–90 and 1595–6 contignency plans were laid to rush reinforcements to Ireland.[46] The fact that Stanley's regiment, which had deserted to Spain at the siege of Deventer, was mostly Irish and still intact increased fears that Ireland would be a specific enemy target.[47] The Irish crisis, as it developed, might have been less severe had the active Sir John Perrot been allowed to return to its government but after the death of Walsingham in 1590 he was brought into disgrace by Burghley and his corrupt client Sir William Fitzwilliam.[48] The conflict which broke out in Ireland in 1593 was not caused by big, programmatic-style government but by reform on the cheap by an inactive, avaricious government in Dublin and by various local commanders, put into front-line positions by earlier policies, who now acted in their own self-interest.

In the West, Sir Richard Bingham, his kinsmen and clients were overrunning North Connacht step by step. Their pretext was intrigue by the local population with shipwrecked Spaniards from the Armada and the strategic threat posed to advances already made. Having reached the limits of Connacht, Bingham began complaining about interference from Western Ulster and demanding the right of hot pursuit there.[49] Then came Fitzwilliam's settlement of Monaghan with its double-dealing and backhanders, which extinguished the Lordship of the MacMahons and partitioned their territory, leaving no room for compromise between the Ulster lords and the state. The main beneficiaries were Sir Henry Bagenal, local commander at Newry and prospective Lord President of Ulster, and his fellow army captains. As a result Hugh O'Neill and Hugh O'Donnell opened lines of communication with Spain. Offers of Spanish support did not arrive until 1596. By then a Gaelic confederacy had fought the English to a standstill and a compromise was on the table which effectively called off the conquest of Ireland. However, the Gaelic lords refused to trust the English and listened instead to Spanish agents, whose promises exceeded the scope of their commission.[50]

In January 1596 Geoffrey Fenton, the secretary of the Irish Council, had discounted Spanish overtures to the Irish.

> They have no reason to be confident in the support of Spain, considering how vain and fallible the Spanish promises have been heretofore, both to them and others in this realm and it may be thought that the uttermost that Spain will do at this time, is to bear up the quarrel with money, whereby a war may be kept on foot, to the end to divert Her Majesty from the aid of the Low Countries or Brittany, or to hold her engaged in Ireland, that she may have the less means to trouble the Spaniard in some parts of his own territories.[51]

This was a fair assessment but the Cadiz raid in the summer of 1596 affronted Spanish pride. Another armada, one hundred ships strong, was hastily assembled – Ireland was targeted but the fleet was wrecked by storms off the coast of Brittany on 28 October. The Irish victory at the Yellow Ford in 1598 enabled the extension of the war to Munster, where the displaced and discontented overthrew colonists planted on confiscated Desmond estates, leaving the southern province wide open.[52] In 1599 and 1600 Philip III sent arms shipments to O'Neill and in 1601 a Spanish expeditionary force finally landed at Kinsale. This was the last Spanish fling against Queen Elizabeth, and on the eve of the battle, with the English army wedged between the Spaniards and their Irish allies, it looked like a strategic masterstroke to win the war. However, the Irish attack miscarried and became a rout; the Spaniards made a deal with Lord Deputy Mountjoy and withdrew in a welter of recriminations with their defeated allies.[53]

When O'Neill forswore allegiance of foreign potentates in his submission to Mountjoy at Mellifont, he had, unbeknownst to himself, a new sovereign in the person of James VI and I. During the war in Ireland James had kept his options open with the various parties, who themselves had an eye to the future.

From 1587 he had James Hamilton and James Fullerton, masquerading as schoolmasters, as his agents in the Pale, the former even becoming a fellow at the new Trinity College.[54] James remained in contact with O'Neill and the English intercepted a letter to the Scottish king in which O'Neill acknowledged James's 'accustomed goodwill and princely affection towards me'.[55] Scotland itself was strategically important for the participants in the Irish war. O'Neill purchased gunpowder in Glasgow and hired auxiliaries from the Highlands and Islands. In 1595 an English naval squadron managed to intercept a fleet of galleys filled with mercenaries at the mouth of Belfast Lough but this was exceptional.[56] Robert Cecil had plans, not dissimilar to those of his father, that the English should recruit Scottish Redshanks themselves. Yet even after the disaster of the Yellow Ford, the English authorities shied away from this expedient fearing that the cure might be worse than the disease. Instead subsidies were paid to the clan chiefs to keep their soldiers in the islands.[57] English pressure also induced James to issue proclamations against Scots mercenaries going to Ireland and against Scots merchants selling munitions to the Irish confederates. Generally James was glad to offload the underemployed clansmen; it was only after the Spanish landing at Kinsale that he began to co-operate seriously, offering to raise a force himself for the Queen's service and issuing a proclamation describing Tyrone's rebellion as a danger 'as well to the liberty of the true religion as of the crowns and estate of this whole Isle of Britain, whereof Ireland is a proper dependence'.[58]

CONCLUSION

During the sixteenth century England did develop a British policy of sorts. It was conceptualised within a wider western European framework in which the security needs of England were paramount. Thomas Cromwell tried to shore up the defences of the Pales of Calais and Ireland and to re-energise the administrations of outlying regions generally. As England's strategic position worsened in the mid-century, the search for British policies intensified. These were often pre-emptive of, or reactive to, the British policies of other powers. Similarities in Somerset's Scottish and Irish policies can be detected and it is plain that the Cecils and Walsingham saw a linkage of issues relating to the problem of Ulster. This was representative of a budding official mind characterised by a use of maps and by having a distinctly Protestant edge. However, none of the British policies they pursued were successful. The more conservative policies of Henry VIII, Elizabeth and William Cecil (in his metamorphosis as Lord Burghley) usually held sway. Even Walsingham had to give up his Irish policy in 1585 to make possible intervention on the continent – money was always the key factor. The object was to reform, not conquer, Ireland. It was not so much grandiose reform policies which provoked the conquest as the flotsam and jetsam left behind when they proved too expensive. These 'men on the spot' exaggerated foreign strategic threats and their aggrandisement created threats where none had hitherto existed. England was drawn into expensive Irish wars. The last one, against O'Neill, which brought the Tudor regime close to disaster, was only won by debasing the Irish currency.

After the failed attempt to force Scotland into a British union in the 1540s, England employed a mixture of direct intervention, destabilisation, cajolery and bribery in an attempt to keep its northern neighbour in line. Walsingham thought modest and timely payments to key individuals could keep Scotland sweet – 'Money', he said, 'can do anything with that nation'.[59] Elizabeth and Lord Burghley were more contemptuous of the Scots, wanted to keep them at arms length and believed with some truth that the Scots king and his nobles would act in their own interests however much they were given. At the close of the period English ministers finally achieved the active co-operation of the Scottish monarch in Ireland but only when his dynastic interests were threatened.

England's policies towards the other parts of the British Isles were likewise self-interested. In fact they are best described as Anglo-British because they were all determined from an Anglocentric viewpoint and predicated upon English interests. Elizabeth's striking out of the clause for mutual naturalisation in the 1585 treaty of amity with Scotland is surely indicative of English hostility to equitable British policies even in their mildest form![60]

4. England's Defence and Ireland's Reform: The Dilemma of the Irish Viceroys, 1541–1641

CIARAN BRADY

I

The Irish viceroyalty in the sixteenth and early seventeenth centuries was the single most powerful office in English regional administration. And it was also the most dangerous. Formally the proxy of the monarch, the viceroy (styled lord lieutenant, lord deputy or lord justice, according to the holder's social and political prestige), was the head of the largest civil and military establishment outside central government. Commander-in-chief of the largest standing army in the British realms, he enjoyed the leadership of usually (after 1580) more than 3,000 troops and frequently a good deal more; and he had the right of appointment to scores of commissions in the infantry and cavalry as well as to the several constableships of castles and wards in the island. In terms of civil administration his powers were almost as great. Though he was required to consult with and take advice from the Irish Council, the discretionary nature of such an obligation was made clear by frequent admissions from the Crown that he might choose a select group with whom he should consult, and by royal admonitions to the councillors that they show proper respect to their governor. Independently, the viceroy could issue leases and grants, give pardons, and deliver judgments, make treaties and proclaim rebels, all under his own seal. And in certain respects, most notably in his use of the prerogative powers of purveyance and military service, his practical authority was even greater than that of his monarch.[1]

Yet for all its extraordinary powers the Irish chief governorship remained of all high offices in the Tudor and Stuart regimes the least secure. In the century under discussion no less than four of the viceroys were charged, found guilty and condemned to die for high treason.[2] Many more ended their careers in disgrace.[3] Several died in office amidst their labours; some collapsed under the strain.[4] Many suffered serious financial loss; only a handful left office with any share of those prime desiderata of early modern public service: glory and profit.

Simple explanations of such unhappy careers have been readily forthcoming when the cases have been reviewed individually. That one viceroy was over-ambitious and another incompetent has always been easy enough to argue. But such essentially qualitative judgements have never been measurable: what is the upper level of ambition, the lower level of incompetence? And as an explanation of viceregal failure in general they carry little conviction. Yet the one common factor linking the ruin of so many viceregal careers simply raises rather than resolves a problem. All of the governors who failed were brought down by troubles that originated primarily not in Ireland, but in England – in palace coups, or campaigns of courtly intrigue and slander, by sudden political reversals or by profound constitutional conflicts – where the actual character of their conduct in Ireland was either of secondary importance, or of no importance at all. There existed, therefore, a paradox inherent in the English viceroyalty in Ireland that made the office which had been granted the greatest degree of independent authority and autonomy available within the Tudor and Stuart administrative systems so vulnerable to alterations and upheavals far removed from its primary concerns.[5]

II

The paradoxical vulnerability in the powerful Irish viceroyalty was a reflection of the anomalous and indeterminate status which the Irish polity had acquired within the Tudor and Stuart realms. Unlike either Scotland or Wales, Ireland enjoyed no direct link to the English monarchy through dynastic ties, and the history of its gradual assimilation under a common sovereignty over the previous centuries had been very different. Unlike Scotland, Ireland had largely been conquered for the English Crown by

English and Welsh colonists, who had dispossessed or subdued leading Gaelic families in most parts of the country (Ulster remaining throughout a partial exception) and in doing so had seriously distorted political and constitutional developments within the surviving Gaelic lordships, permanently inhibiting the emergence of a centralised dynastic state. English law and its supporting administrative and judicial institutions had been widely introduced by the middle of the thirteenth century. The royal writ, it is true, was never current throughout the whole island and over the later Middle Ages its authority declined significantly. Yet its prevalence was such that whenever the aim of establishing legal and constitutional uniformity over the island was considered, it was uncritically assumed by advocates both of conciliation and of coercion that it was the framework of English law, rather than the particularist and unsystematised principles of the Gaelic law tracts, that provided the only possible means of securing this objective. Any further constitutional development in Ireland was to be primarily a matter of English revival rather than of adaptation, compromise and consensus. Thus while Scotland, despite many feuds, invasions and periods of anarchy, continued to retain its potential for independent political and consitutional development, the evolution of Ireland from the twelfth century on was determined by an English conquest which had wholly succeeded in its work of destruction while abandoning the obligation of cultural reconstruction which was then made necessary.[6]

For the same reason, Ireland at the beginning of the Tudor period could not be made comparable to Wales. And though many English commentators in the sixteenth century were wont to apply the experience of England's success in assimilating Wales, they were bound to recognise that for Ireland there had been no Edward II to complete the war and no Henry VII to consolidate the peace. Thus the contrasts with Wales persisted. The English Crown held little land directly in Ireland, and no dynastic links at all. The descendants of the first conquerors had grown further away rather than nearer in their allegiance to the Crown; and while there is evidence that leading Gaelic families had adopted some of the feudal customs and practices of the would-be conquerors, the rate of actual anglicisation among them had been negligible. The fundamental differences between the two regions were recognised formally between 1536 and 1541 when Wales was assimilated under the English Crown by an act of Union and Ireland was recognised as a separate kingdom in its own right.[7]

This new definition of Ireland's status as a sovereign entity seriously oversimplified matters and was at best aspirational. The Act for the kingly title itself qualified Ireland's independence by the acceptance that the Irish kingdom was forever 'united and knit to the Imperial Crown of the realm of England': equality granted on the condition of permanent inseparability. This constitutional anomaly was reflected in a number of practical means by which Irish autonomy was modified: by the persistence of Poynings' Law, which required the permission of the English Privy Council for the summoning of the Irish parliament, and its ratification of all proposed pieces of legislation; by the rights of appelate jurisdiction claimed by the English courts; by the appointment of an English-born viceroy and by the frequently declared royal preference that the chief administrative and legal officers of the realm and the bulk of the military establishment should be English. Though it may seem surprising, it is clear that the continuance of such practical restrictions was not perceived by English administrators themselves to contradict the spirit of the Kingship Act. But underlying such an apparent contradiction was the usually unspoken assumption that Ireland was a kingdom in an inchoate sense only, a polity that was in the process of becoming a kingdom but which required successive stages of political, administrative and cultural reform before it would realise its potential. Its unfinished constitutional status thus committed Ireland's viceroys to a reformist and constructivist mode of government that was unique within English administration.[8]

Such a formal location of Ireland in the framework of Tudor and Stuart rule should not, however, obscure the importance of the changes which had occurred within the Irish polity itself during its medieval experience of alternating conflict, coexistence and neglect. Though the war of conquest had severely retarded political development within the Gaelic lordships, fostering militarism, retarding social and economic change and concentrating power in the hands of small dynastic elites, it is clear that over time tensions within the lordships began to appear as groups from within the ruling families and their vassals asserted a greater economic and political freedom from their military protectors and began to challenge the value of protection and patronage upon which government within the lordships rested. The outcome of such challenges was far from predictable. In some cases the total dissolution of the chieftaincy seemed threatened. But in many more, the direction of these tendencies was far from certain, and their one clear consequence was a general and often sudden de-stabilisation of regional and provincial peace. The complexity of early sixteenth-century Irish politics strongly accentuated the interventionist ambitions of English government, providing at once an opportunity to encourage developments within the lordships which would hasten the process of peaceful anglicisation and a potential problem for England's international security. But the opportunity soon appeared to be more intricate and more difficult to exploit than had at first seemed likely, while the challenge proved to be severe and urgent.[9]

In the early sixteenth century, the internal instability of the Irish lordships, their expansionism and most seriously their tendency to seek mercenary aid from abroad – from Spain and France potentially, and from Scotland regularly – presented a continuing worry to England's defences. And in the crisis years of the 1530s such anxieties grew immeasurably more serious as the Henrician regime became isolated in Europe, a prey to rumours of foreign intrigue and invasion and fearful of rebellion in the least governable extremities of the realm.[10]

Initial attempts to cope with this imminent security crisis were modest and based upon remarkably optimistic assumptions. The dependence of the Irish lords on their great private armies made necessary by the chronic instability of the island's politics was proving so expensive and so dangerous that many observers both in Dublin and at Court believed that with proper persuasion a majority of the island's powers could be made amenable to reform. If the great lords could be convinced that their real power – already under threat through the costs and risks of the system under which they worked – would be better preserved by the revival and extension of English law, then their collaboration in a policy of anglicisation could eventually be enlisted. Such a policy required, of course, some delicate diplomacy; but in the anxious years of the early 1530s the immediate challenge presented by the threat to England's security overrode the desirability of such a gradual procedure. Pressed to agree to reform and sensing the Crown's panic, the Anglo-Irish Fitzgeralds of Kildare, the most powerful individual dynasty

within the island's politics, which had enjoyed almost uninterrupted tenure of the viceregal office for over fifty years, bolted,
forcing the Crown to confront a challenge it had sought to
evade. Their defeat in 1536 alleviated King Henry's immediate
security fears, but left the country bereft of the most important
potential indigenous support for reform.[11]

Thus from its very beginnings the revived English government
in Ireland was torn between two distinct imperatives, which,
though based on the same assessment of political conditions
in Ireland and of the problem they presented to England, tended
in actual practice to be sharply in competition with each other:
a conservative urge to defend territory, secure borders and
suppress dissent; and a progressive requirement to cultivate in
Ireland the constitutional and political stability which would
offer the most permanent guarantee of its future loyalty.

III

It was these opposing but inescapable forces which, regardless
of all questions of personal ambition and practical ability,
provided the fundamental terms of reference of the English
viceroyalty in Ireland in the sixteenth and early seventeenth
centuries, defining the limits of all that was considered desirable
and all that was regarded as necessary. Every governor, knowingly
or not, operated within these conditions, and the viceroys' success
or failure was a measure of their ability to retain control of
their office against these competing drives.

At the outset, it can be said, there was little that was exceptional
in the manner in which the Tudor viceroys attempted to survive
under these conditions. All of them sought, naturally enough,
to satisfy both requirements simultaneously, and at first the
post-1536 governors, Lord Leonard Grey and Sir Anthony St
Leger, sought to do so by the fairly obvious strategy of fashioning
alliances for themselves from among the existing factional
interests in the island. The grounds for such an approach were
simple enough. On considerations of short-term exigency alone,
a willingness to minimise conflict and forgive past injuries allowed
at least a temporary alleviation from security anxieties for a
governor required to survive with the modest military force
allowed to him by the English treasury. But in terms of grand

strategy it was clear that the major internal upheavals which followed upon the destruction of the Kildare Fitzgeralds had created an opportunity for providing an alternative focus of political allegiance. This was something which the English viceroy, by a judicious use of patronage, shrewd arbitration and manipulation of rivalries, might exploit in the interests of the Crown. Commitments to immediate security and long-term reform could thus be honoured by allowing personal loyalties and political alliances to precede legal reform and cultural change.

There were serious risks entailed in such a political balancing act. It made enemies for the viceroy among disappointed rivals of the Fitzgeralds in Ireland and left him open to suspicions of favouritism at Court; and when Grey unwittingly fell victim to the palace coup that destroyed Thomas Cromwell in 1540, it was these two forces that combined to ruin him.[12] By enframing his own extensive diplomatic activities within the grand constitutional declaration of the 1541 Act, St Leger made himself far more secure. Yet despite his superior skills as a politician and undoubted breadth of vision, the continuing assumption that diplomatic alliances could provide the foundation for legal and cultural reform was practically viable only so long as the problem of external security did not once more become acute. And when it did, his consensus-seeking government lacked the material capacity and the political credibility to re-define itself as an effective policing agency. Thus at mid-century, when the government at Whitehall once again became convinced (largely without justification) that an invasion of Ireland was imminent, and every report of Irish unruliness became a further confirmation of this threat, the tolerance of St Leger's regime was seen to be insupportable.[13]

Yet, as the brief mid-Tudor administrations of Sir Edward Bellingham and Sir James Croft were to show, such a rapid transformation proved to be impossible. The high cost of policing – the funding of an enlarged garrison, the expense of building and re-fortifying forts, the necessity of uncovering and suppressing dissent – placed a huge strain on the government's financial and administrative resources; while the good will of the native lords, which had been carefully cultivated over the previous decade, steadily evaporated. The perceived need to meet an immediate security crisis threatened in fact to create the conditions in which such an emergency would be permanent.[14]

It was the desire to escape from this trap, where the needs of security and the demands of reform actually cancelled each other out, that gave rise to the most important policy innovation in Tudor viceregal government in Ireland. This was a strategy that sought, like its predecessors, to meet the requirements of defence and reform simultaneously not by the sober drifts of gradual diplomatic conversion, but by means of a rapid and comprehensive programme of institutional construction.

Sometimes viewed, a little too simply, as primarily a means of preserving the viceroy from the charges of partiality, private interest and prodigality which were the stock in trade of slanders at Court, this programmatic approach to Irish government in fact had deeper roots. It is doubtless true that the viceroys who initiated and developed it – the Earl of Sussex (1556–65), Sir Henry Sidney (1566–71, 1575–8) and Sir John Perrot (1584–8) – saw such an advantage in stating their objectives, setting their timetable and agreeing their expenditure in advance. But rather more important than such uncertain tactical benefits was the promise which the construction of a government programme held out for resolving the fundamental dilemma of the viceroys in facing the dual requirements of defence and reform.[15]

It was the Earl of Sussex who provided the first account of the assumptions upon which this government by programme was based. In keeping with Grey and St Leger, Sussex recognised that England's security needs in Ireland could not be met in the long term by military force alone but only by persuading the indigenous powers to accept English law as the best way of defending their rights and settling their disputes. But against his predecessors, Sussex insisted that the methods of diplomacy and factional manipulation they had employed were the principal obstacle in the path of reform. Ireland's basic problem, he contended, was not its violent style of politics, which everyone accepted was self-destructive and ripe for change, but the factional alliances which continued to sustain it. These great factional structures, which had sucked the life out of conventional legal procedures everywhere in Ireland, should not be cultivated but must be opposed directly by the rapid construction of an alternative institutional framework which would supply an immediate source of redress at law to those who had suffered injustice at the hands of the great factional powers. In his plans Sussex envisaged the simultaneous introduction of varying levels of justice throughout the different regions of Ireland – the revival of assizes in the Pale and the surrounding Anglo-Irish earldoms of Ormond and Kildare, the introduction of provincial councils in Munster and Connacht, a special re-enforced council for administration in Ulster, the development at a lower level in Gaelic areas of special circuit courts, in which the equitable procedures of chancery would be blended with the precepts of Brehon law, and the establishment of an Irish Star Chamber – the Court of Castle Chamber – which would enable the council in Dublin to use all its authority to root out the secret intimidations of the great.[16]

Sussex would have liked three thousand; but in the end he was willing to accept a force half that size which, if adequately deployed, would be sufficient to meet these initial priorities while still providing an adequate bodyguard to protect the lawyers and to discourage intimidation of plaintiffs and juries in the first stages in this new programme of infrastructural reform. The demands which such an enlarged garrison would make upon the local communities of the island would not, Sussex realised, be negligible; and he attempted some administrative reforms which would minimise the burden. Yet he remained convinced that there existed sufficient support for this institutionalist assault upon factionalism amongst the many interests small and large which had been victims of its oppressions. And his confidence was bolstered by the assurance of the nominal leader of one of the great factions – the Earl of Ormond – that he himself was willing to have all existing disputes over land, feudal obligations and the like which had hitherto sustained his faction settled by recourse to English law. His problem then lay only in addressing the unreconstructed factionalism of the Geraldines, the remaining allies of the house of Kildare, and he believed that, left to themselves without any promise of favour such as they had enjoyed under Grey and St Leger, and opposed in the courts by their own tenants, vassals and clients, their influence in the country would gradually wither away.[17]

As it turned out Sussex overestimated the ability of the Earl of Ormond (who was in fact a genuine ally) to uphold his promises; and more seriously, he underestimated the ability of the Geraldines to launch a counter-attack of their own. With the political support of the rising favourite Lord Robert Dudley, who was for reasons quite unrelated to Ireland Sussex's principal political rival, the Geraldines orchestrated a highly publicised visit to Court by Shane O'Neill, the powerful Ulster lord whom Sussex had committed himself to destroying, in a manner designed to cause the deepest embarrassment to the governor. The visit did not succeed in reconciling Shane to English rule, but it so undermined Sussex's credibility as viceroy that even though O'Neill was once again in rebellion against the Crown, Sussex was never again able to muster enough support in Ireland to suppress him.[18]

But despite this setback, the framework Sussex laid down was followed by his two most active successors, Sidney and Perrot. They introduced, of course, refinements of their own. Sidney soon learned that the simple introduction into Ireland of provincial councils similar to those that were operating in Wales and the north of England was impossible: despite the efforts that were made to accommodate them on the councils, the great lords remained suspicious, viewing the new presidents through their own factional lenses; while the expected surge of plaintiffs seeking impartial justice did not materialise. He came to recognise also, following the failure of this rudimentary exercise in institutional transferral, that the programme of reform must be shifted one stage backward, that English government should not simply oppose, but directly attack the factional systems. By imposing its own superior form of military rule over the whole country, exacting tributes and supplies for its troops in the traditional manner, the government could demonstrate its ability to supersede any one faction in its own practices. But once this had been accomplished it would offer a general commutation (composition) of all exactions on the condition that similar commutations would be concluded by the lords over their vassals and tenants. The new fiscal arrangements between the lords and their vassals and between both groups and the Crown, would from henceforth be administered under English law by English-style provincial presidencies. In their early stages, however, these 'composition' presidencies would bear little resemblance to the English and Welsh models. They were in effect military agencies operating under martial law in the loosest sense. But following the initial composition agreements, the presidents, it was understood, would oversee the holding of general sessions, the (re)establishment of shire government, and the construction of regional councils.[19] Perrot in the main adopted Sidney's composition plan. He took a slightly different view of Ulster, where he believed that military rule would be required for longer, but in Connacht he quickly made clear the intrinsic connection between composition and the introduction of English law by the establishment of a major legal inquisition headed by the leading law officers in Dublin, which aimed to provide a comprehensive review of the actual political and social structure of the province.[20]

Thus, such strategic developments aside, the major Elizabethan viceroys from Sussex onwards shared the same basic approach to the government of Ireland. All attempted, that is, to satisfy the injunctions of security and reform by means of intensely active institutional programmes whose implementation would at once assert the immediate political power of the royal government while creating the conditions whereby such power would be accepted by all of the island's communities as permanently legitimate. In drafting their plans, all accepted, moreover, that the maintenance of their autonomy was of greater importance to the success of their administrations than any benefits which the cultivation of local interest might bring. And though they took steps to limit the risks of this self-imposed withdrawal, securing the support of influential figures both in Ireland and at Court for their particular plans, each accepted the costs that followed inevitably upon the abandonment of traditional political practices.

In the event these costs were to prove too high: and disappointed local interests moved to wreak revenge. The Geraldines worked to undermine Sussex by exploiting the factional tensions of the early Elizabethan Court. The Earl of Ormond moved similarly to protect the interests of his following against the hostility of Lord Deputy Sidney by capitalising upon his special place of influence with Elizabeth herself. Burdened by the increasingly onerous demands of the enlarged garrison, the gentry of the Pale appealed to their sovereign as freedom Englishmen in order to persuade the Queen to withdraw support from her governor. And when all else failed, desperate local parties like the Desmond Fitzgeralds and the Burkes of Clanrickard had recourse to rebellion.[21] Such action seriously endangered the credit which the advanced commitments given by the governors had purchased at Court; and more seriously, they made clear that, however much Ireland was officially regarded as an as yet unfinished kingdom whose development required the careful application of reform measures, it could not in practice be isolated from the immediate political, financial and defence concerns of the English state. This was the fundamental weakness which, for all its conceptual and strategic attractions, lay at the heart of the Elizabethan enterprise in Irish reform. And it was to become all too clear in the troubled viceroyalty of Sir John Perrot.

The modifications which Perrot had made to his predecessor's strategies proved on one level to be remarkably successful. His revised composition in Connacht was largely acceptable to the lords in Clanrickard and Thomond and the new settlement was concluded through an extensive series of agreements with little resistance. In Ulster too, Perrot made more progress than any previous governor, making peace with the Scots, negotiating a major division of Tyrone between the reigning lord, Turlough Luineach, and his rival Hugh O'Neill, whom he elevated to the earldom of Tyrone, and securing initial composition agreements in most of the lordships of the province. Like Sidney, Perrot encountered trouble with the Palesmen in his attempt to override their constitutional objections to the establishment of a composition tax and his determination to impose the Oath of Supremacy on all holders of public office. But thanks to the support of influential local councillors, he remained confident that he could contain the Pale's resistance.[22]

Unexpectedly, however, Perrot found himself faced with more serious opposition from a group which had hitherto been the most loyal support of the reform governors: the English-born councillors, office-holders and captains of the Dublin administration. The emergence of a distinctively English office-holding or 'servitor' group concerned with its own furtherance and protection against local interest had been a possibility since the expansion of the Dublin administration in the 1530s; but the development of such a 'New English' identity had been inhibited by a number of factors. Initially, the number of English officers who came to settle permanently in Ireland was small, and among them marriage into the old colonial community was common.[23] It was only under Elizabeth, when the size of the civil and military establishment grew substantially and an extensive new plantation was settled among the O'Mares and the O'Connors in the midlands, that new English servitors ar-

rived in sufficient numbers to constitute a recognisably different group. The change, moreover, was not simply quantitative.
As the reform governors after St Leger maintained their determination to be as free as possible from local factions, so they
came to depend more heavily on a small group of professionals
who had little personal connection in the country and no loyalty other than to the administration which had appointed them.
Further, as increasing numbers stayed on, exploiting the rewards
of land grants and government sinecures which came their way,
religious difference – the fact that most of them had in England fully subscribed to the Anglican settlement, which had
yet to be realistically enforced in Ireland – sharpened the sense
of distinctiveness of this new official class. In the early 1580s
these processes were rapidly accelerated when rebellions in
Munster and Leinster gave rise to a massive increase in the
size of the army, made vast tracts of land available for plantation, and brought the Anglo-Irish locals and the new English
servitors into open confrontation.[24]

It was in these circumstances that the reforming governor
and his administration came into conflict for the first time.
There were some particular reasons why the confrontation should
have occurred when it did. Perrot was by temperament iras-
cible and in his dealing with his councillors he displayed an
impatience bordering on belligerence.[25] But underlying such
conduct there were deeper forces at work. His disputes with
the Council were the result of his conviction that the Dublin
administration was corrupt and partial, and that within it there
existed many who for their own personal reasons were secret
enemies of reform.[26] In his national plans also, Perrot posed a
threat to the New English. An outspoken critic of the way in
which the plantation in Munster was being carried out, he demanded that planted areas should be made answerable to the
composition tax being imposed elsewhere, and proferred support to natives in the province who were prepared to acknowledge the tax.[27] But most seriously of all, the success of his
programme among the landholders of Connacht and Ulster
promised a resolution of all outstanding doubts over land title
in the province and with it an end to a major source of profit
for the servitor interest.

Behind the servitors' revolt, then, there lay more important
reasons than the fact that the man was impossible. The case

against Perrot was so absurd that it seems impossible to see how he should have been convicted. It has been speculated that Lord Chancellor Hatton, who had extensive interests in Munster, or the aging Burghley, who feared Perrot's potential, were anxious to destroy him.[28] But whatever the immediate motivation, the destruction of the most active and successful of the reforming viceroys in the interest of a servitor group signalled a major change in English attitudes towards the Irish Office and towards the government of Ireland in general. The significance of this alteration began first to become clear during the viceroyalty of Perrot's successor, Sir William Fitzwilliam.

Even by the time he took office, in 1588, Fitzwilliam was already the most experienced English administrator in Ireland. A holder of high office since the mid-1550s, he had deputised as lord justice for Sussex and Sidney and first acted as lord deputy between 1571 and 1575. It was perhaps his witness of the failure of so many viceroyalties that made Fitzwilliam such a sceptic of the reform programmes by the time of his second term in office. But the deputy had more personal reasons for adopting such an attitude. At the end of his service as vice-treasurer and treasurer at wars in the 1560s Fitzwilliam had been held responsible for a massive deficiency of £10,000 st. revealed by the audit of his ten-year account. Elizabeth grudgingly waived half of the debt; but from then on Fitzwilliam's attitude to office become frankly exploitative. The way in which he chose to operate was, however, clearly defined. Sharing with his fellow Elizabethans a distrust of local interest, he did not attempt to return to the ways of St Leger; but neither did he show any enthusiasm for innovative projects, such as the extension of plantations or the raising of a composition, in which the deputy might have hoped to have a share in the profit. For the risks which either of these alternatives had entailed were plain enough to see. Instead, he looked to the governor's primary obligation to service the security needs of the Crown, as a means of repairing his personal fortunes. Exploiting Whitehall's perennial fear of invasion and rebellion, Fitzwilliam persuaded the Crown to allow him to organise a semi-formal constabulary of small companies throughout the country and then, battening on his vast experience as paymaster of the army, he used his position as chief of these several mobile, short-lived operations to employ all the techniques of patronage and peculation in order to take his share in the dues exacted by the captains from both the Crown and its subjects.[29]

Fitzwilliam's security state was a fragile conception, based on the ambivalent proposition that while peace and order were being preserved under his supervision, imminent danger everywhere required that he keep his captains on a permanent (and lucrative) alert. It implicitly begged the question raised by the reformers that, if England's hold on Ireland was so vulnerable, new policies must be devised to strengthen it. It was on this basis that Fitzwilliam was displaced by Sidney in 1575, and he feared that he might suffer the same fate during his second appointment. More seriously, Fitzwilliam's disguised inaction left him unwilling and unable to cope with genuine crises which arose. His failure to assure the Geraldines' position in Munster almost precipitated rebellion there in the 1570s; and in the early 1590s his refusal to address the grave internal tensions provoked by Perrot's abortive composition scheme in Ulster actually did. Ulster discredited Fitzwilliam. Yet it is ironic that, despite the part he played in provoking the great conflagration of the Nine Years War, the style of viceregal management which Fitzwilliam initiated was to become the model of future governors for almost four decades to come.

IV

The crisis of the 1590s simplified the viceroys' task in a number of respects. Security was now not simply a major priority, but the only one. Relieved of any commitment to reform of any sort, the governor was reduced merely to the role of commander-in-chief, who could identify himself exclusively with his captains and soldiers, seeing (not always successfully) to the provision of their official allotments of food, munitions and pay, and seeking (often with far more success) alternative means of rewarding loyalty and good service by the distribution among his preferred captains of confiscated land, cattle, head-money and the general spoils of war.[30] As the size of the army grew (by 1602 it had reached almost 20,000) and arrears of pay mounted, the war governors, Sir William Russell, Sir Thomas Burgh and Lord Mountjoy, maintained the loyalty of selected captains by the means of 'concordatums' – warrants issued at the viceroy's discretion directing that pensions, expenses, leases on lands etc., be issued by the Irish exchequer to individual petitioners as a sign of special favour. Though such practices had been frequently condemned in the past, they came in the war years to be regarded as legitimate not only on grounds of necessity, but on the more significant claim that the wealth that was being expropriated in this way was that of rebels or their secret sympathisers, and was therefore fair game for loyal servitors who were risking their lives to preserve England's security.[31]

Such a frankly expropriative approach was defended in a large body of treatises, strategic proposals and personal memoirs produced by servitors in the war years – of which Spenser's *View of the present state of Ireland* is the best known example. In these writings the servitors asserted that the unofficial profits made during the war were not only the just desserts of good service, but provided an essential foundation for the future security of Ireland. The development of a system of small plantation garrisons throughout the island, in which trusted military men would settle themselves as landlords and as policemen was, they argued, the only way in which the long-term security aims of the Crown could be satisfied. The public needs of government were in effect identical with the private ambitions of its officers; and the kingdom of Ireland was to be integrated with the other territories of the English monarchy, not by the processes of diplomatic persuasion or institutional reform, as the Tudors had attempted, but by the simple means of allowing the new English servitors to establish their social and political dominance in the island by whatever means available.[32]

Confirmation of this change in the viceroy's role, first heralded under Fitzwilliam, took place in the first decade of the new century. Though he was the first governor ever to enjoy unopposed authority over the whole country, Lord Mountjoy showed no desire to seize the unique opportunity for political reform presented to him, and elected instead to become an absentee. From this vantage he made some gestures towards maintaining continuity with the pre-war era in his protection of the ex-rebel Tyrone and his support for the establishment of a commission intended to make safe the titles of native landholders. But such attitudes were qualified by his more immediate concern to favour and advance his old associates' claims to be confirmed in lands seized during the rebellion,

and whose plans for the further extension of garrison government into post-rebellion Ulster he fully endorsed.[33]

No such ambivalence affected the outlook of his chosen successor, Sir Arthur Chichester.[34] Though he had served in Ireland for some years, Chichester himself never canvassed for
the office and accepted appointment in 1605 only after considerable hesitation. His reluctance had little to do with mod-
esty, but arose instead from his very clear perception of England's
true interest in Ireland and how he should best serve it. From
the beginning of his Irish service in 1599 Chichester was a
soldier who shared with the writers of the 1590s the view that
Ireland was best governed by constant military policing. Pri-
vately Chichester would have preferred to have played his own
role in such a policy more directly, as Constable of Carrickfergus
or as the military President of Ulster (a post he continued to
seek even as viceroy). But once in office he set about advancing the soldiers' cause in every way he could. He appointed
senior soldiers to his Council, and saw to the appointment of
lesser military men to office in local and regional government.
He constantly pressed the English Treasury for the payment of
arrears, fought to have the pensions of selected captains maintained and subsidised by the abolition of payments to absentee pensioners, and argued for the establishment of a special
Irish pension fund which would enable him to supplement the
standing army whenever emergency arose.[35] More importantly,
he strove to increase the number of soldier–planters in the
island. His efforts to increase the permanent military presence
in Ulster provoked the flight of the Earls of Tyrone and
Tyrconnell from Ireland in 1607 and the rebellion of Sir Cahir
O'Doherty in 1608. But far from being discomfited by these
events, Chichester regarded them as an opportunity to advance
a full-scale garrisoning of the province with an extensive network of small military settlements controlling the remaining
native residents. These relatively modest plans were overtaken
by a more grandiose scheme of dispossession and plantation
preferred by King James.[36] But even then he succeeded in securing some 54,000 acres for his servitor group and acquired
for himself a substantial allotment around the O'Neill stronghold of Dungannon, becoming in the process the first English
viceroy ever to take a private share in government plantations.[37]

The governor, however, did not rest there. Disappointed that

the military men had not acquired an even greater stake in
Ulster, he set about devising a whole range of lesser schemes –
in Wexford, Longford, Leitrim and the midlands – where he
hoped soldiers could acquire a greater representation. Chichester's pursuit of ways of falsifying native titles in order to legitimate their dispossession was ruthless. But though he was without
scruple in advancing the material interests of the group with
which he himself identified, Chichester's strategy should not
be too simply defined as graft. The plantation schemes about
which he was particularly concerned were regarded by him as
strategically vital, being set in areas which were notoriously
difficult to govern or close to settled English regions.[38] And
though he accepted defeat in regard to Ulster, he continued
to complain about the failure of the non-servitor planters to
honour their military obligations, and he expended a good
deal of his own fortune to convert the Dungannon allotment
into a model for the whole plantation. In this frank identification of group interest and public service Chichester was simply
making concrete the fundamental change that had taken place
in viceregal attitudes since the fall of Lord Deputy Perrot: that
is, the realisation that the simultaneous pursuit of the dual
aims of political reform and strategic security in the hope that
one would eventually supply the needs of the other was hope-
less, and that England's greater needs in Ireland would only
be served when the social substance of the island had been
entirely transformed.[39]

It was for this reason that, despite the inevitable criticism
which his various initiatives generated at Court, Chichester, in
contrast to his Elizabethan predecessors, remained mostly immune from political intrigue. Having never sought office, or
made any undertakings in relation to policy, Chichester was
unusually free of the obligations that had fettered the reformers.
From the beginning the deputy signalled that he was ready to
respond to the direction and advice of the then all-powerful
minister, the Earl of Salisbury, who in the early years of James
I exercised more control over Irish affairs than any of the
Elizabethan secretaries. Under Salisbury, Chichester enjoyed a
unique position of dependence and trust that was sustained by
the fact that he was forever willing to include clients of the
minister within his party and that the minister himself understood that the governor never conceived that his party's interest

should ever conflict with that of the Crown.[40] It was because of this essentially impersonal link between governor and minister that Chichester was able to shift his allegiance easily to the Earl of Northampton who inherited the mantle of the king's great minister after Salisbury's death. Northampton was more demanding in his exercise of patronage than Salisbury; but again the willingness of the viceroy to comply in most cases and Northampton's acceptance, encouraged by the advice of Salisbury's Irish Secretary Sir Humphrey May, that both parties, whatever their particular interests, shared a common concern for the welfare of the Crown, allowed a rough and ready compromise to evolve.[41]

But beneath such good relations there remained two profoundly disruptive forces which were not to be so easily resolved. The first was the problem of government finance. The Irish wars of the late sixteenth century had well-nigh bankrupted the English treasury, forcing the Crown to resort to unprecedented parliamentary taxation and to become heavily indebted to both foreign and domestic creditors. The heavy debt, lingering army arrears and most seriously the continuing high cost of current expenditure on Ireland gave new life to two familiar policy imperatives at Whitehall that were in practice quite contradictory: first a determination to cut subventions from England to a minimum, and secondly an insistence that new sources of Irish revenue must be found to make the country self-sufficient.[42]

The combined effect of both of these imperatives on the viceroy's freedom of action was considerable. In administrative terms alone Whitehall's search for increased savings and profits led to the establishment of two major commissions of inquiry (in 1611 and 1613) with powers to make recommendations to the Crown over the head of the deputy.[43] In 1611 also, the Privy Council established a commission for Irish causes as a permanent sub-committee through which all Irish business was to pass before decisions were taken.[44] Such interventions circumscribed the governor's authority in principle; but while Chichester, often through the good offices of May, was generally successful in moderating the personal tensions that occasionally arose, the need to respond to the Crown's financial imperatives seriously affected the standing of the viceroyalty in general. Cost-cutting on salaries, pensions and discretionary

expenditures by means of concordatums severely threatened
the viceroy's means of patronage, and left him increasingly
unable to satisfy the expectations of dependants. The obligation to raise revenues was less directly restrictive – and during
his time Chichester increased domestic income from c. £16,000
p.a. to over £28,000 p.a.[45] But such gains were purchased at
some cost. The parliamentary subsidy which accounted for about
£4,000 p.a. had been extracted with difficulty from a troublesome parliament, it was only slowly and grudgingly being paid,
and it was due to expire in 1625.[46] Other means of increasing
revenues, through the more vigorous collection of rents, the
increase of customs rates, legal fees, and fines for breaches of
the Act of Uniformity, were even more controversial, and
threatened to give rise to serious trouble in the near future.
There remained, of course, one major alternative by which Crown
revenues might be raised: the acquisition of new lands by plantation and the exposure of defective titles. And Chichester had
his own advanced views in this regard. Yet from the outset the
ability of his administration to develop a coherent policy of
official plantation was restrained by the second of those fundamental forces shaping the character of the viceroyalty: the problem of Court patronage.[47]

In the early days of the reign James was content to leave the
management of Irish affairs largely in the hands of his minister and his viceroy. But where matters of direct royal patronage were concerned the king's will was irresistible. Thus, despite
the concern for retrenchment, lavish pensions were issued from
the Irish civil list on the royal authority, and membership of
the Irish peerage multiplied with the addition of wholly absentee creations without any consultation with the viceroy.[48] But
more serious conflict arose in regard to Ulster. Chichester, as
we have seen, had very particular strategic plans for the province and the alternative scheme of introducing large numbers
of migrant settlers in the area in the wake of extensive native
clearances was, he believed, impracticable and would inevitably
collapse. But such arguments counted for little with a king already
committed for reasons of patronage and indebtedness to the
grander scheme; and Chichester was overruled.[49]

It was the one serious reversal experienced by Chichester.
Yet the Ulster plantation revealed the continuing vulnerability
of the Irish viceroyalty in English politics even in its consider-

ably reduced post-reformist role. Without the protection of powerful ministers the governor could not expect to discharge even
his modest responsibility as England's policeman in Ireland
without interruption from Court; and the ministers themselves,
it was clear, could not continue to offer such protection in-
definitely. Such underlying faults in the viceroy's position became evident in the closing years of Chichester's rule.

By 1614, after almost a decade in office, a disgruntlement,
due largely to the diminishing opportunities for advancement
which were the inevitable consequences of the political and
financial restraint, began to emerge within the ranks of Chichester's own administration. There was nothing intrinsically
threatening about such complaints; but they became more serious
when they were related to a Court-centred campaign against
his second great patron, the Earl of Northampton.[50] The movement against Northampton was a disjointed affair, a coalition
of disappointed place-seekers and genuine promoters of financial reform, but its unity was sustained by a general hunt to
uncover corruption and neglect in government in which, with
the help of Chichester's critics, Ireland was selected as a prime
target. The coalition was temporarily outmanoeuvred in the
parliament of 1614, and the challenge to Chichester evaporated.
But in the wake of Northampton's death, the disgrace of the
Earl of Somerset, his followers' most important link with the
king, and the rise in the king's affections of the young George
Villiers, the anti-Howard group was in the ascendant; and the
government of Ireland was again under review.[51]

There is no reason to assume that Buckingham's rise precipitated Chichester's fall. For his recall, though sudden, was accompanied by no hint of disgrace. Rather it seems best to
conclude that once the fragile conditions at Court which had
sustained his long tenure of office had ceased to exist, Chichester was happy to withdraw to cultivate his estate at
Dungannon. But the ease of his passing and the absence of
any accompanying recriminations has tended to obscure the
degree to which the constraining forces of financial restraint
and factional Court politics were made even more oppressive
for the Irish Office by the circumstances of his departure.[52]

The extent to which its operating conditions had changed
became clear during the administration of Sir Oliver St John
(1616–22), the first of Buckingham's clients to assume the vice-

royalty.[53] A leader of complaint against Chichester in the past, he began with the credentials of a reformer, promising to curtail expenditure drastically and to increase revenues in every sector. Yet as Buckingham's man (and a relation by marriage) he was required, in a way Chichester had never experienced, to answer the increasingly voracious demands of the favourite on all of the potential resources of Irish wealth in order to sustain his proliferating patronage network. This was a dilemma from which St John never escaped; and though it has been argued that his commitment to reform was genuine, it was his obligations to his powerful patron which always came first. It could hardly have been otherwise. For in the years of St John's government Buckingham rapidly gained control over all of the channels through which Irish business was managed at Court, ending the commission for Irish causes, overriding Sir Humphrey May, the Irish Secretary who had lent such support and continuity for Chichester under Salisbury and Northampton, and ensuring that the most important matters should be processed directly in the Bedchamber where he himself was omnipotent.[54]

The ways in which Buckingham set about raiding Irish resources were several. He procured wardships, escheatments, export licences and some small monopolies for his supporters, and secured for himself a 50 per cent share in the general farm of the Irish customs, whose annual yield had been greatly enhanced by the revised rates established in 1613. But his greatest interest lay in the acquisition of Irish land. Routinely he favoured the petitions of clients in their quest for the purchase of concealed lands, and more covertly he intervened in the operation of the Ulster plantation, by securing, on the ostensible grounds of reform, a licence to collect fines from those settlers who had failed to fulfil conditions concerning the restrictions on the number of native tenants. And most importantly of all, he set about acquiring, usually by secret devices, an extensive Irish estate for himself in lands demarcated for plantation (on dubious legal grounds) in Leitrim.[55]

In all of these affairs St John was either actively collusive or powerless to intervene. When he raised some obstruction to Buckingham's scheme for the customs, he was effortlessly brushed aside; and his objections to the way in which the earlier Ulster planters and their tenants were to be treated under the terms of Buckingham's new licence were similarly disregarded. But the problem of improving Irish finances still remained, now made worse by the governor's patent inability to exert control over the very areas where progress was to have been made. Revenues showed little improvement, while, with the annual deficit approaching an average of £18,000 st, subvention from England remained high and the debt to the army continued to climb: by 1622 it stood at £75,000 st.[56]

The crisis materialised for St John, as it had for Chichester, with the summoning of an English Parliament in 1621 where once again a complex coalition of forces presented the problem of Ireland as the epitome of royal prodigality and incompetence.[57] Hostile parliamentary investigation was once again diverted by means of another commission of inquiry – the largest in terms of both personnel and scope yet established. And having once removed it from the control of his enemies in Westminster the favourite took elaborate measures to limit its operations and findings. In the meantime he secured St John's honourable recall (he was raised to the peerage as Viscount Grandison) and replacement by another client, Henry Cary, Viscount Falkland. By these means scandal was averted but not suppressed. Though the commission's reports generally avoided placing blame and pursued no trails to the favourite himself, they did reveal vast amounts of waste, neglect and dubious accounting practices, and so deepened the predicament of the viceroy, torn between the need to service the appetite of an all-powerful patron and an increasingly desperate financial situation.[58]

Inevitably the crisis recurred. Under mounting pressure from Lord Treasurer Middlesex, who wished to end all English subventions, but unable to address the abuses (so profitable to Buckingham) which the commission had uncovered, Lord Deputy Falkland looked desperately to two alternative ways of raising revenues. The first was a vigorous enforcement of the Crown's right of wardship through a new Court of Wards established on the commission's recommendation in 1622. The second was a stricter enforcement of the fines against recusancy. Though it was potentially a major source of income, the collection of fines for recusancy (authorised by statute since 1560) had, except for a brief period under Chichester, never been exploited, principally because the fine had been seen as a policing measure to threaten the fractious, rather than as a means of financial gain. But Falkland believed that systematic enforcement could net the exchequer as much as £20,000 a year before recusancy itself began to decline. The move against recusants, moreover, would carry the additional advantage of rallying servitor groups to the new viceroy's side, persuading them that, whatever his dubious Court connections, the governor was still, in the old Chichester way, favouring the Protestant 'New English' over their 'Old English' Catholic rivals.[59]

Such hopes, however, were dispelled when James, egged on by Buckingham, declared war on Spain in 1624. As this new emergency dawned, the deputy found himself suddenly circumvented by the Old English gentry whom he had so ably alienated, who offered to solve at once the Crown's security and fiscal problems by raising a trained militia and maintaining it at their own costs in return for certain legal and tenurial concessions.[60] Profoundly mistrusted by the Old English and committed also to the servitors whose support he had enlisted by his initial policies, Falkland found himself quite unable to carry out King Charles I's instruction to negotiate the terms on which a deal could be reached. Discussions in Dublin became deadlocked, and in June 1627 the viceroy was simply sidelined when Charles agreed to deal directly with Old English agents at Court.[61] Characteristically, Charles's own negotiations over 'the Graces' soon became bogged down in duplicity and mistrust. But the lengthy isolation of the viceroy from such matters of high policy completed his discredit. In the country at large the extortions of the army he had been ordered to deploy but was unable to pay alienated both natives and planters alike; while on the Irish Council opposing official factions openly bickered with one another without regard to his nominal authority. In August 1628 the assassination of Buckingham, who had done little in his final months to protect his client, merely hastened moves in Ireland to unseat him. Cynically, his enemies on the Council now exposed the particularly crude way in which Falkland had moved to suppress the rights of some native Irish families in order to confiscate their lands, and then, in a desperate hurry to conclude agreement with the Old English, Falkland finally humiliated himself by summoning a parliament without following the procedures of Poynings' Law. The parliament had to be abandoned. Falkland was regarded by the Old English as a shameless deceiver, and by his enemies in Dublin and at Court as a fool. He was recalled in disgrace in April 1629.[62]

V

Thus ended the third major effort to define the role of the
viceroy in the unformed Irish kingdom. Like the old diplomatic persuaders and the institutional reformers of the sixteenth
century, the guardians of the English servitor interest failed
also, because even their narrowly conceived view of their responsibilities in the country failed eventually to satisfy the Crown's
dual requirements of immediate security and long-term reform.
The full extent of the collapse was registered in the hiatus
which arose after Falkland's recall. No decision was made concerning a successor, and in the interim, as Falkland struggled
vainly to rehabilitate himself, the factionalism of the Irish Council
deepened under the encouragement of rival caretaker governors,
Sir Richard Boyle and Sir Adam Loftus. Yet the political vacuum that had thus arisen served to create an opportunity for
the initiation of the boldest and most short-lived experiment
in viceregal government: the administration of Sir Thomas
Wentworth.[63]

Though he had showed no prior interest in the Irish Office,
Wentworth, whose appointment was announced only in January
1632 and who arrived in Ireland some eighteen months later,
sought to implement the most complex viceregal strategy ever
attempted in Ireland – and also the simplest. It was complex
because Wentworth was to encompass several of the leading
features of all the preceding styles of government. It was simple
because all of these borrowings were to be reshaped and reduced
under one guiding principle: the imperative to serve the
immediate interests of his Prince without regard to any other
consideration.

Like his Tudor and unlike his Stuart predecessors, Wentworth's
avowed purpose was to impose a common unity over the island's
inhabitants in common obedience to the same sovereign. His
appointment was accompanied by a spate of officially inspired
publications – histories, antiquarian studies, memoirs of the
Elizabethan wars – all of which purported to show that the
divisions and conflicts of Ireland's past were accidental and
ephemeral, and that all of the island's inhabitants could now
celebrate the fact that, in the words of Sir James Ware, Wentworth's principal publicist, '*iam cuncti gens una sumus*'.[64]

More concretely, even before his arrival in Ireland, Wentworth made it clear that he would be no simple cipher of a New English Protestant interest, by opening negotiations directly on Catholic causes with the Old English Earl of Westmeath and by publicly rebuking Boyle and Loftus for their too vigorous enforcement of recusancy fines. Shortly after his arrival also, Wentworth announced his intention of summoning a parliament in which he would deal with the country's grievances not by means of special or private petitions, but by public debate.

But Wentworth's conception of unity had nothing of the transformative aspirations that had characterised the Tudor governors. He understood it simply as an external effect based upon a common obedience to the will of the sovereign in any matter.[65] And for Wentworth, unlike the Tudors but like his Stuart predecessors, the matter which he viewed as paramount was the extraction of a substantially increased revenue from Ireland. To this end he employed all the devices used by recent viceroys to milk Irish resources – defective titles, concealed lands, and increased fines in the Court of Wards. But he did so in a more ruthless manner than ever. Brutally disregarding the confirmation of tenurial security which had been implied in the sixteenth-century composition of Connacht and the indentures that had been drawn up on that basis, Wentworth found the bulk of the native residents to be without title, and seized half the province for plantation. Yet he did not simply direct his attention to the vulnerable native Irish. He planned a similar investigation of all titles in the Munster plantation and urged the confiscation of the Londonderry Company's holdings in the Ulster plantation. More generally, he employed the ecclesiastical courts and the prerogative Court of Castle Chamber to launch a widespread recovery of Church lands in a manner that particularly threatened the New English who had benefited most from the appropriation of ecclesiastical properties. And he restored to the Crown the customs revenues which had hitherto been let out to New English speculators. The result of all these efforts was substantial. During his time in office, Crown revenues doubled in Ireland to almost £80,000 p.a. By 1640, the Irish treasury was for the first time in annual surplus, and the huge debt was gradually being whittled away.[66]

Like the other Stuart governors, however, Wentworth also regarded the Irish Office as a means of advancing his own private fortune, and by the end of his service he had acquired a massive landed estate, several commercial monopolies and a share in re-appropriated customs farming. Wentworth was exceptional not simply in the extent of his avarice, but in his openness. All of his enterprises were fully reported to King Charles, along with their likely profitability (usually overstated) and an offer made to share any profits with the Crown should the king deem it appropriate. And in all of this the king remained complaisant, for Wentworth had acquired a status that no other Irish governor had ever attained. He was not only the Irish viceroy, he was also, in a peculiar way, a court favourite.[67]

Wentworth's personal relations with Charles were never close. He could on occasion be discomfited, as when the Earl of Clanrickard launched a brief counter-offensive against his conduct in Connacht. But if he was never a familiar of the king, he had no other favourite to contend with, and he enjoyed from the beginning the full confidence of the only other men on whom Charles most depended, Archbishop Laud and Lord Treasurer Weston. Their initial support and advice secured his position, and as his successes mounted Charles's confidence in his Irish minister became complete. At Court he overrode the recriminations of the Old English gentry, the servitors' cries of tyranny and corruption and the pathetic pleas of the victims of his various plantation schemes with an ease allowed to none of his predecessors.[68]

'The most novel feature of Wentworth's rule', it has been observed, 'was the integration of Anglo-irish governmental structures which it achieved'.[69] The achievement was in part a matter of convenience: a unique agreement between the king and his viceroy that the only priority in Ireland was making money for the Crown. But beneath such considerations lay Wentworth's understanding that the realisation of the notional Irish kingdom would occur not by internal reform nor by the wholesale displacement of the natives by imported English subjects – alternatives chosen by all of his predecessors – but only by a redefinition of the nature of Charles's Irish kingship and with it a reshaping of kingship in the Stuart realms as a whole.[70]

It was for this reason that, despite the immediate improbability and unfairness of their charges, the viceroy's accusers in 1641 were at heart right. For to Wentworth, Ireland was not merely to serve as a source of money and men to defend the

English Crown's interests when needed; it was to be a model for the conduct of royal government throughout the British realms. Thus his ruthless and impolitic suppression of support for the Scots in Ulster, and his extraordinary pleas to be allowed to send an Irish army to make war in Scotland, were not simply the overconfident impulses of a man flushed with success; but the ultimate expression of the assumptions on which he had governed Ireland from the outset.[71]

In the end, as we know, Wentworth was abandoned by Charles to his enemies in England and Ireland, for the king, in the last analysis, did not share the same confidence in the future which his minister had mapped out for him. Blinded, like Grey and Perrot before him, by a vision of what Ireland might yet be, Wentworth lost sight of what his own English monarch thought permissible in serving the Crown's immediate interests in Ireland, and perished. But like Grey's and Perrot's also, his individual tragedy was simply a limiting case – a monument to the fundamental dilemma of the viceroys in Ireland as a whole. Charged with the task of defending England's interest in a kingdom that they had yet to construct, the repeated failure of the stratagems they devised to transcend such opposing imperatives offers only testimony to the fact that the fluid and fissiparious states of Ireland could never be fitted into the complex conceptual structure of the multiple British monarchy.

APPENDIX

A list of the most important Vice Royalties, Ireland 1536–1641

Lord Leonard Grey (LD)	1536–1540
Sir Anthony St Leger (LD)	1540–1548
Sir Edward Bellingham (LD)	1548–1549
Sir Anthony St Leger (LD)	1550–1551
Sir James Croft (LD)	1551–1552
Sir Anthony St Leger (LD)	1553–1556
Thomas Radcliffe, Earl of Sussex (LL)	1556–1565
Sir Henry Sidney (LD)	1565–1571
Sir William Fitzwilliam (LD)	1571–1575
Sir Henry Sidney (LD)	1575–1578
Sir William Drury, Sir William Pelham (LJ)	1578–1580

Lord Arthur Grey, Baron of Wilton (LD)	1580–1582
Adam Loftus, Archbishop of Dublin;	
Sir Henry Wallop (LJ)	1582–1584
Sir John Perrot (LD)	1584–1588
Sir William Fitzwilliam (LD)	1588–1594
Sir William Russell (LD)	1594–1597
Sir Thomas Burgh (LD)	1597–1597
Sir Thomas Norris, Archbishop;	
Sir Robert Gardiner (LJ)	1597–1599
Robert Devereux, Earl of Essex (LL)	1599–1599
Charles Blount, Lord Mountjoy (LL)	1600–1604
Sir Arthur Chichester (LD)	1605–1615
Sir Oliver St John (LD)	1616–1622
Henry Cary, Lord Falkland (LD)	1622–1629
Adam Loftus, Richard Boyle (LJ)	1629–1632
Sir Thomas Wentworth, Earl of Strafford (LD)	1633–1641

5. The English Crown, the Principality of Wales and the Council in the Marches, 1534–1641[*]

PETER ROBERTS

I

Accounts of 'Tudor policy in Wales' have been beset in the past by unresolved problems of definition. What do we mean by 'policy' in the age of monarchs who ruled as well as reigned; and what, or when, was Wales?[1] What is incontestable is that there was no systematic approach to the government of the country as a whole on the part of English kings until the formation of the unitary state in the 1530s. Wales was the creation of the Henrician 'union' with England in the sense that it then achieved territorial integrity for the first time in history. Incorporation with the realm brought with it an unprecedented measure of administrative uniformity. Although the Welsh people were recognised in the Middle Ages as forming a distinct nation, they had never inhabited a single polity; the limited unity achieved by Hywel Dda in the tenth century had not been matched by any subsequent Welsh ruler, while the medieval kings of England had never exercised direct rule over the whole country.[2]

After the Edwardian conquest the 'land of Wales' belonging to the last independent prince had been annexed to the Crown as one of the king's dominions, but neither it nor any other area of Wales formed part of the realm of England. The conquered lands of Gwynedd had been shired by the Statute of Wales of 1284 and in them, as well as in the older shires of the west, English criminal law and a mixture of English and Welsh civil and land law had been administered. Since 1301 these five shires had formed the principality with which the

118

heir to the throne was usually invested at, or soon after, his creation as Prince of Wales. With the incorporation of Wales with the realm in the years 1536–43, the separate history of the principality seemed to be at an end. The 'Act of Union' of 1536 did not mention it except for a passing reference in the preamble, and yet the concept of a principality survived the process of transformation, to be reformulated in the territorial sense.

The country which Henry Tudor invaded and traversed in 1485 was still divided according to the pattern established in 1284. Between the shires of the principality and the realm the lordships of the March formed a barrier of quasi-independent jurisdictions. Within these lordships native law co-existed with marcher customs in communities of Welshries and Englishries, while in the shires English settlers were concentrated in the 'plantation boroughs', from which the Welsh, the native 'aliens', were initially excluded.[3] In the private lordships the king's writ did not routinely run and the problem of law enforcement in the Marches was complicated by the perpetuation of mutually exclusive jurisdictions. Criminals, particularly cattle thieves, could cross the boundaries to flee from their pursuers with impunity, and the special extradition treaties arranged between one lordship and another, and between the Marches and the English and Welsh shires, were rarely effective. Between the fourteenth and the early sixteen century Parliament, in response to petitions from the inhabitants of the English shires, enacted a series of laws against border raids by the Welsh, which were difficult to enforce in the lordships.

Lawlessness had been endemic in the Welsh lands of the Crown and in the Marches throughout the later Middle Ages, and the social conditions and customs which sustained it were comparable in some of their essentials to those obtaining in other frontier societies. There had been uprisings at intervals since the Conquest, the most serious of which was the Revolt of Owain Glyndŵr in 1400–10. A series of emergency measures passed in Parliament to contain the rebellion was retained on the statute book as a penal code which inhibited the Welsh from intermarriage with the English and from acquiring land in England or in the English boroughs in Wales. It was one of the few incursions of statute law into the country before the transformations of the 1530s. Under the terms of the Statute of Wales, the 'lands of Wales' remained subject to laws made by the king and his council. Only in cases of treason and rebellion, or of problems between lordships, was the king prepared to override marcher customs or to allow Parliament to legislate for any part of Wales.[4]

The conflict between York and Lancaster weakened royal authority in all the king's dominions, the lack of governance in the realm being matched by the failure of the marcher lords, including the king, to maintain control over their lordships. With the changes of ruling dynasties and as a result of the casualties of the Wars of the Roses, lordships fell to the Crown through confiscation and inheritance. Within these estates Yorkist and early Tudor kings exercised their seigneurial, rather than their sovereign, rights: royal writs were not current and justice had to be administered at a remove. In the absence of resident lords in both private and royal lordships, power was devolved upon stewards, while in the shires of the principality the Crown became increasingly dependent on the Welsh squirearchy acting as deputies, despite the prohibitions of the penal laws.

The special arrangements made by Edward IV to govern Wales arose out of the need to safeguard his own position and to administer the Crown possessions in both the principality and the Marches. In 1473 the king met the marcher lords at Shrewsbury and, in his capacity as Earl of March, entered into indentures with the other lords which reaffirmed their reciprocal obligations to administer justice. Between 1471 and 1476 the group of advisers attendant on the Prince of Wales, Edward of Westminster, acquired administrative and judicial commissions which extended into the principality, the lordships and the English border shires. Based mainly at Ludlow, the caput of the earldom of the March, this was the foundation of what was to become a permanent council in the Marches of Wales.

Regional conciliar government, in the North of England as well as in the Welsh borderland, was one of the most important features of Edward's rule to be resumed by the Tudors. The acquisition of many more lordships by Henry VII and Henry VIII eased some of the problems of law enforcement but did not, in the first half-century of Tudor rule, lead to radical reform or a re-ordering of jurisdictions. Henry Tudor's most striking contribution to the government of Wales was the systematic adoption of the 'indentures of the Marches', whereby lords and royal stewards alike were bound to observe the rule of law in their lordships. Henry also conferred charters of privileges, including English forms of land tenure, on the Welsh inhabitants of a group of lordships in the northern Marches and on those of the three shires of the ancient principality. By the early sixteenth century most of the Marches was in royal hands, the last great marcher lord, Edward Stafford, the 3rd Duke of Buckingham, was destroyed in 1521 for allegedly having compassed the king's death. Ten years later Rhys ap Gruffydd, scion of the house of Dinefwr in the southern principality, was also executed on a trumped-up charge of treason, based on allegations that he had entertained prophecies foretelling the eclipse of the Tudor dynasty.[5] The humbling of these two magnates removed the most powerful surviving aristocratic dynasties, while the reduction in the number of private lordships made the king the only marcher lord of any consequence.

There is no evidence that this situation was regarded as an anomaly before the 1530s. During Wolsey's ascendancy traditional expedients were resorted to, and administrative reform was restricted to an extension of conciliar control over the borderland. In 1525–7 the Princess Mary resided at Ludlow as the nominal head of a council which exercised greater administrative and judicial powers devolved from the centre, but after her withdrawal this body declined under the weak presidency of Bishop Veysey. Reform of the structure of the Marches, as distinct from the institution of conciliar government, was first formulated in a series of memoranda addressed by some of the 'king's commissioners in the Marches of Wales' to Henry VIII and his council in the early 1530s. Though the problem of disorder in Wales appears regularly in Thomas Cromwell's own memoranda for these years, he was not responsible for devising the solution that was eventually adopted. The first of these proposals to shire the Marches and to introduce English common law uniformly throughout Wales was advanced at least five years before the reforms were realised in the 'first Act of Union' of 1536. They were not taken up in 1531–4 partly because the king was preoccupied with his 'great matter', but also because the conditions for their implementation were not favourable.

Cromwell chose instead to introduce a more rigorous regime into the Marches with the appointment of the redoubtable Bishop

Rowland Lee as Lord President of a reconstituted Council. Lee's hand was strengthened in 1534 by a series of Acts of Parliament which made inroads into the privileged status of the lordships and abolished the more disruptive marcher customs. A hanging bishop, Lee vowed that the would 'make one thief hang another', and his strong-arm methods of terrorising offenders did succeed in curbing the worst lawlessness in the lordships if not in establishing the rule of law, and this process may have been regarded by Cromwell as a necessary prerequisite to the dismantling of the marcher system. If this was the case, he did not take Lee into his confidence, and when the new policy was announced in 1536 the Lord President denounced it as premature and ill considered. On the other hand, the changes may not have been preordained, and the reform proposals may not have been seriously entertained before 1536. As late as 1535 an item in Cromwell's memoranda hints at a possible return to the Lancastrian penal code against the Welsh.

A complete reversal of policy emerged in 1536, a decision to bring Welsh laws and institutions into line with English, not as an administrative convenience for its own sake, but because uniformity in the pattern of jurisdictions was now considered by the makers of policy to be desirable, if not indeed essential, for the successful enforcement of the statutes of the Reformation Parliament. Wales had to be brought within the parliamentary system if statute law were to apply there without exception or ambiguity.[6] The reform of the laws and government of Wales was not embarked upon until it was judged to accord with considerations of high policy. The presence in Cromwell's circle of a prominent Welshman such as the humanist and civil lawyer Sir John Price may have been a decisive influence in countering Lee's advice and persuading the king's secretary that the reforms were feasible. Price was one of the commissioners investigating the monasteries in England and was to be appointed Secretary of the Council in the Marches in 1540. The transformation of Wales was to coincide with the dissolution of the monasteries, and the newly enfranchised Welsh gentry, as justices of the peace and members of the Commons, were able to join their English counterparts in securing a share of the dissolved monastic lands, and with it a vested interest in the Henrician Reformation.[7]

II

The Tudor revolution of Welsh government was not imposed from above or outside upon an unreceptive people. Individuals and communities in north and central Wales are on record as having petitioned for the introduction of English law and land tenure in particular. But though petitions and memoranda sent to the king and council paved the way for legislative change, there is no trace of those discussion documents such as have survived for Ireland in this period: no 'discourses' invoking 'the common weal' to indicate that the reforms were conceived according to 'humanist principles'.[8] That the policy adopted in 1536 did represent a change of heart on the part of the regime in its attitude to Welsh government is manifest in the preamble to the Act 27 Henry VIII, c. 26, the so-called 'first Act of Union'. This castigates those 'rude and ignorant people' who 'have made distinction and diversity' between the king's subjects in his realm and those in the dominion and principality of Wales. These invidious distinctions, which have given rise to discord and sedition, have proceeded from the differences in laws, customs and languages, and so the king, 'of a singular zeal, love and favour that he beareth towards his subjects' in Wales, has with the advice, consent and agreement of Parliament, ordained that all persons born in Wales shall enjoy the same liberties and laws as his English subjects.

The premise of the enactment is a convenient piece of constitutional fiction: the 'dominion, principality and country of Wales' is declared to be, and ever has been, incorporated, united, annexed and subject to and under the 'imperial crown of this realm'. This was to misrecite the tenor of the Statute of Wales of 1284, in which Edward I had annexed the lands conquered from Llywelyn the Last, previously held by feudal right, to the Crown (though not the realm) of England. In effect, it reflected Henry VIII's imperial policy, the first practical application of the territorial implications of the concept of 'empire' which had been reformulated in the Act of Appeals of 1533, though it was no longer couched in terms of feudal suzerainty. The fiction consists in the assumption that the Edwardian incorporation had involved the whole of Wales, for this was to ignore the separate status and history of the marcher lordships. It was all the more remarkable because the majority of the Act's provisions dealt with the Marches, which are now converted into shireground, while the three shires of the northern principality are to serve as a model for the judicial arrangement to be introduced for the rest of the country.[9] Within this framework the Welsh were to enjoy the benefits of English law in every part of the country.

This masterstroke of statecraft (or of 'policy' in the contemporary sense) was rendered possible, as was acknowledged in the Act itself, because the king himself was the greatest marcher lord: the remaining lords were of no political account and their rights could be overriden. Thus were the feudal enclaves of the borderland, in theory at least, legislated out of existence by asserting the king's *imperium*, though the coup de grace was delivered in another Act of this session, the Act against franchises and for 'recontinuing liberties in the crown', which was of wider application but devised with the Marches in mind. Henceforward these areas were subject to direct royal administration, and no-one except the king would have the right to appoint justices or to issue pardons and original or judicial writs. A third Act empowered the Lord Chancellor to appoint commissions of the peace and of gaol delivery in the County Palatine of Chester and the existing Welsh shires, as a preliminary to the extension of the shire system into the Marches once the lordships had been dissolved.[10]

The Act 27 Henry VIII, c. 26, which historians call 'the first Act of Union', was entitled on the statute roll 'for laws and justice to be ministered in Wales in like form as it is in this realm'. The keynote was administrative uniformity and the abolition of Welsh laws and marcher customs in favour of the common law. The gentry were entrusted as sheriffs and justices of the peace with responsibilities in their own communities, the Welsh shires were made subject to parliamentary subsidy, and newly formed constituencies were to send their knights of the shire and burgesses to future Parliaments. Wales was to be brought into the parliamentary system at the same time as the County Palatine of Chester and Calais, and the administrative settlement formed part of a strategy conceived and co-ordinated in 1536 for the integration of the peripheral areas into the realm. Thomas Cromwell may not have been the only begetter or originator of the reforms, but he may be regarded as the architect of the legislative programme for the extension of the realm which gave them reality.

Having enunciated the general principles and listed in detail the administrative divisions, the Act set up commissions to supervise the transition of laws and the drawing of boundaries. It was expected that the transformation would take several years to effect. Two enabling clauses added in a schedule to the bill during its passage through Parliament authorised the king, for a period of five years, to erect courts of law and appoint justices, and also, if need be, within five years, to suspend, amend or repeal the Act in whole or in part. This last proviso in particular has been read by historians in the past as signifying a tentative approach: the legislators were entertaining second thoughts about proceeding with such a radical innovation, and had doubts about the wisdom of enfranchising the wild Welsh before they were ready for such mature treatment. A more convincing explanation is that the king was concerned that the settlement of Wales should proceed in step with the mainstream events of the Reformation, with his matrimonial plans and with his overriding desire for a son and heir who would be Prince of Wales. Thus Henry saw to it that he could complete the settlement at his own discretion in the light of the reports of the commissions of inquiry, and if necessary alter its character so as to take account of new developments at court, and especially in the royal Bedchamber. The birth of a prince was never far from the king's mind during these months: when the bill made its way through Parliament, he was preoccupied with putting away his second queen and marrying his third.

The timetable of the Act's implementation, and perhaps its ultimate aim, was implicit in its provisos. In a proclamation of February 1537 Henry used his suspensory powers to postpone the greater part of its provisions for a further year. The redrawing of the map of Wales involved in the 'shiring' of the Marches was not completed until 1540 and the system of new courts was not fully in operation until the following year. It was at this point that thought was given to a novel supervisory authority for the Welsh judicature. The 'effectes devised for Wales' considered over the winter of 1540–1 proposed the replacement of the Council in the Marches with a Welsh Court of Chancery, also to be based at Ludlow Castle. This was to be the seat of a new principality embracing the twelve shires of Wales to be created for Prince Edward, then five years of age. In the years between 1541 and 1543 these ambitious plans were abandoned and the other provisions whittled down, so that the final enactment, known to historians as the 'second Act of Union', merely confirms and consolidates the settlement as envisaged in 1536. Nevertheless, the king still retains, under this last Act, an extra-parliamentary right to make laws for Wales, much wider powers than those recognised in 1536 but similar to those retained in the Statute of Wales of 1284, when Edward I had appropriated the legislative authority which Llywelyn ap Gruffydd had exercised in his own lands. The Council in the Marches was continued in existence by the Act 34 & 35 Henry VIII, c. 26, which thus gave statutory recognition to a prerogative court. The Act itself had originally been drafted as a royal ordinance and its preamble claimed that this had been enacted in parliament at the suit of the king's subjects in Wales. This was the first Parliament to which the Welsh representatives were returned, and they would have had an opportunity to review the details of the bill, if not to influence the major decisions which it enshrined.[11]

Edward may have been considered too young, and the king perhaps too old, for the erection of an apanage for the heir apparent to be practical politics at this time. The plan may even have been frustrated by the complexities of faction politics at court in the last years of the reign. The prince's Seymour uncles, Edward and Thomas, may have been loath to repeat the political mistakes of the Wydevills in Edward IV's reign by allowing the prince's household to be removed to Ludlow, and so putting at risk their purchase on the 'reversionary interest' in the succession to the throne. There were rumours of the impending creation of Edward as Prince of Wales shortly before his father's death. Had he lived longer, Henry might well have exercised his extraordinary legislative discretion to erect a principality on the pattern proposed in 1540–1. In the event, the special relationship of Wales with the Crown was preserved even as uniformity of law and administration was established. Although at its repeal in James I's reign the discretion was adjudged to have been personal to Henry VIII, this is unlikely to have been the legislative intention in 1543. The Tudors' country of origin enjoyed a distinctive status on account not of dynastic sentiment but of hereditary principle. Henry may or may not have intended to use his extraordinary power to make laws for Wales without reference to Parliament, but concerned as he was with questions of inheritance and succession, he ensured that Parliament recognised this as an important prerogative of the 'imperial crown'.

David Powel, writing in 1584, assumed that, as a result of the Tudor 'union', the principality as a separate estate was irreversibly subsumed in the realm. The proposal to create an enlarged principality as an apanage for Edward late in Henry VIII's reign shows that the estate and dignity of a prince continued to be latent in the 'imperial crown', and suggests that this might have been revived had another male heir been born in the Tudor line. The 'union' of the two countries can thus be regarded as contingent on a dynastic accident. The projected Edwardian principality would seem to represent a departure from what is known about Thomas Cromwell's vision of a unitary state. It may have emerged unheralded in 1540–1 as one of the refinements of the settlement of Wales conceived by one of his successors among the king's advisers. Like the conversion of the lordship of Ireland into a kingdom in 1541–2, the creation of a principality along these lines would have been a radical retreat from Cromwell's policy of unification. On the other hand, as has been argued above, such an eventuality may have been foreseen when the legislation was first framed in 1536. Cromwell was nothing if not a pragmatist where his master's interests were concerned, and it may be that the depiction of him as an inflexible centraliser of government should be revised.[12]

III

The whole of Wales had been integrated into the realm, and yet there continued to be a certain ambivalence about the country's constitutional status. The twelve shires came to be described in state documents as 'the principality', even in the absence of a prince. Acts of Parliament and proclamations could still refer to 'the realm of England and the dominion (or principality) of Wales', and many of them rang the changes on the formula found in the Acts of 1536 and 1543: 'the country, dominion and principality', though no longer 'the king's dominion'. Not only the country's designation but its boundary continued to be imprecisely defined. The eastern borders of the marcher shires were determined somewhat arbitrarily through the reallotment of hundreds rather than by following geographical divisions or diocesan boundaries. Many Welsh communities were attached to the English border shires and kept their 'Welshry' until the nineteenth century, while Monmouthshire was treated as supernumerary to the 'twelve shires of Wales'. The country retained several distinctive features which qualified the impression of administrative uniformity. The Council in the Marches continued to exercise its jurisdiction over Wales and the border shires – an area now consisting of 18 shires until 1569 and 17 thereafter. While this arrangement maintained the character of provincial government by a prerogative court, it did not perforce respect the boundary between the two countries, and to that extent 'union' of a kind was achieved. However, the Welsh and English shires were not equal in all respects, for the provision for parliamentary representation recognised certain differences. As a concession to the relative poverty of a more sparsely populated country, only one knight was to be returned for each of the twelve shires, and (with two exceptions) one burgess to represent the 'contributory boroughs' which were to cast their votes in the shire town. Monmouthshire was treated as an English shire, with two knights of the shire and a burgess of parliament to be returned exclusively by the shire town of Monmouth. The county was also attached to the Oxford circuit of assize, thus permitting the formation of a symmetrical system of higher justice for Wales consisting of four three-shire circuits of great sessions.

With this enfranchisement came the obligation to pay the taxation voted in Parliament. After 1543 Wales was subject to the two last Henrician subsidies, but on Edward's accession, a 'mise' was levied on the whole country for the first time. This was the customary tribute paid on the entry into his inheritance of a lord or prince and, though it could be regarded as a continuing sign of 'dominion' status, it now earned for Wales a postponement of the 'relief' voted in Parliament in 1549. On every subsequent Tudor accession the payment of a mise led to a respite in the collection of the subsidy in Wales, and an exemption was written into the subsidy bills in every Parliament until 1571. Only in the Parliament of 1576 was a parity in the incidence of the subsidy achieved to cement the 'union' of the two countries.[13] The Crown did not resort to its exceptional right to issue ordinances for Wales, except in the form of instructions and commissions sent out as before to the Council in the Marches. On the other hand, Parliament was to amend or revise the Henrician legislation in particular details on several occasions throughout the period up to 1641. Most of these revisions were made by the government in public Acts, though the first of them, the Act of 1544 (35 Henry VIII, c. 11) making special provision for the prompt payment of the fees and wages of the Welsh members of the Commons, was evidently promoted by the interested parties. Certainly the Act of 1554–55, which protected the residual rights in marcher lordships of the ecclesiastical lords (the Bishops of Hereford and St Davids) and the heirs of temporal lords, was based on a petition submitted on their behalf to Philip and Mary. Some members succeeded in securing the passage of a private bill, as a boon for their constituents, either adjusting the original provision for the location of a county court, or arranging for the alternating of the county days between two towns. A number of Elizabethan Acts made good some deficiencies in the legal provisions of the settlement, but most of these were government bills, introduced mainly in the Lords. On occasion a reforming bill was passed which addressed a problem or a defect brought to the Privy Council's attention by officials in Wales, such as the appointment of a second justice in each court of great sessions (18 Elizabeth, c. 8: 1576).

Sir Geoffrey Elton concluded that the relative dearth of legislative initiatives taken by Welsh members in the Commons in the four decades after their first entry into Parliament 'must call in doubt whether an entity to be called Wales had much reality in the middle of the sixteenth century.' Far more private than public bills were promoted by them, and there is no trace of anything approximating to a 'Welsh party' in the Commons.[14] On the other hand, members from Wales played their part in the making of laws for the whole realm, though they did not always succeed in gaining special provisos for their own country. The most effective moves to effect both legal and religious reforms for the principality in Elizabethan Parliaments came from the Lords. The one partial exception to this rule, the Act of 1563 authorising the translation into Welsh of the Bible and the Book of Common Prayer, was to have the most momentous impact of all on Welsh religious culture. This origi-

nated as a Commons bill, sponsored (according to a contemporary source outside Parliament) by the burgess for Denbigh,
the antiquary Humphrey Lhuyd, and in the Lords by the Bishop
of St Davids, Richard Davies. The bishop was himself to contribute to the work of translation undertaken chiefly by the
Protestant humanist William Salesbury. By recognising Welsh
as an official language of worship in those parishes where English was not understood by the congregations, this Act was to
have a countervailing influence on the process of anglicisation
inherent in the operations of the 'language clause' of the Act
of 1536, which insisted on the exclusive use of English as the
language of the law.

The Elizabethan regime allowed the Scriptures to be trans-
lated into a second mother tongue within the realm as a means
to save the monoglot Welsh from irreligion and Catholic 'superstition'. William Cecil was later to record his approval of the
Act as a weapon in the Protestant armoury against the forces
of the Counter-Reformation. The Welsh New Testament and
Prayer Book were published in 1567, followed by the whole
Bible in 1588 in a new translation by William Morgan. The
translations were to have far-reaching consequences for the
survival of the language and the national identity, but the Act
itself bore the marks of a reluctant concession, motivated in
party by an impulse to encourage the Welsh to become bilingual.
Y Testament Newydd is dedicated to Queen Elizabeth, who is
acclaimed as surpassing the leading women of British history
in 'their singular learning and heroical vertues'. In his preface, Salesbury also paid tribute to the benefits for the Welsh
of Tudor rule, which had brought them release from bond-
age, first from oppression and inequality and now from spiritual desolation. The Scriptures in their own tongue were
represented as the latest gift of the Tudors to their fellow-countrymen.[15] However, the translations were of limited influence
until the publication of the portable edition of the Welsh Bible
in 1630 and the growth of literacy made them truly accessible
to laity as well as clergy. In the long term the triumph of Protestantism helped to preserve the language, while the impact
of the religious texts on the sense of national identity effected
a cultural transformation quite as significant as the changes
brought about by the 'union' in the legal personality of the
country.

George Owen, the historian of Pembrokeshire, also spoke for the Protestant gentry of Wales when in his unpublished writings towards the end of Elizabeth's reign he praised the 'sweet and wholesome laws' of Henry VIII, which had wrought 'a joyful Metamorphosis for Wales'. Even the language he uses to describe this Tudor revolution is revealing of the extent to which he believed the two countries had been united:

> No country in England so flourished in one hundred yeares as Wales has done, since the government of Henry VII to this tyme, in so much that if our fathers were now living they would think it some strange country inhabited with a foreign nation, so altered is the country and countrymen, the people changed in heart within and the land altered in hue without, from evil to good, and from badd to better.

Moreover, the Welsh had accepted the abolition of Welsh laws in favour of the common law of England 'quietly & without great grudging & some rebellion'. In his manuscript 'Dialogue of the Government of Wales', Owen did not hesitate to criticise features of the Henrician legislation which, fifty years on, required revision in the light of experience. One of the interlocutors proposes at the end of the 'Dialogue' that some of the reforms discussed should be brought to the attention of Parliament, so that the knights and burgesses for Wales 'were all made acquainted therwith & to join together to seek reformation'.[16] This did not happen: the tract, with its (admittedly mild) criticism of the system of justice, did not lend itself to publication, and there was to be no occasion on which the Welsh members took the initiative in concerted action in support of any parliamentary measure in the late sixteenth century. There were also calls in this reign for a resolution of the confusion in land tenure arising largely from contradictory clauses in the Acts of 1536 and 1543. In the event the only remedy obtained for these ambiguities resulted from litigation rather than legislation, with an Exchequer decree which related not to any statute but to the status of the charter of liberties granted by Henry VII to North Wales.[17]

The most persistent attempts to amend the 'union' legislation came not from Wales but from representatives of the English border shires. They were concerned to rescind the clause in

the Act of 1543 which confirmed the jurisdiction of the Council in the Marches over these shires. The city and County Palatine of Chester (with the connivance of their Chamberlain, the
Earl of Leicester) escaped from its orbit in 1569, and the shires
of Salop, Hereford, Worcester and Gloucester were to cite this
as a precedent in their later petitions for exemption. The borderers' representatives in Parliament allied with the common
lawyers of the Westminster Courts in a campaign to confine
the Council's authority to Wales. A bill of secession for the
border shires was introduced in the Lords early in 1598 but
failed to proceed beyond a second reading before the end of
the session. The campaign was to gather momentum, in and
out of Parliament, in the next reign.

IV

The marcher lords had been supplanted by the service aristoc-
racy of Tudor England and Wales even before the Henrician
'union'. The Earls of Worcester had lost the prominence in
Welsh government they had enjoyed in the last years of the
Marches with the rise to power of the Herberts, Earls of
Pembroke, the only Welsh family ennobled by Henry VIII. The
1st and 2nd Earls of Pembroke were entrusted by Mary and
Elizabeth with the lord presidency of the Council in the Marches,
but became increasingly less attached to their seat at Cardiff
Castle. They continued their patronage of Welsh bards and
men of letters, but as members of the Court aristocracy they
gravitated more towards Wilton House and their Wiltshire estates. For most of this period the Somersets of Raglan identified themselves with their country of adoption and were to a
degree cymricised. The bard Dafydd Benwyn hailed William,
the 3rd Earl of Worcester (1526–89), as a naturalised Welshman through his marriage with a Herbert, while Edward, the
4th Earl (1553–1628), was commended by the lexicographer
Thomas Wiliams of Trefriw for his readiness to speak and honour
the Welsh language, 'dearly loved Briton that he was'.[18]

There were no resident magnates in North Wales, where contacts with the royal Court after the 'union' retained a traditional pattern until early in Elizabeth's reign. Courtiers still
held the office of Chamberlain in the three shires of the old

principality, while the north-eastern shires remained within the orbit of the justice of Chester. Elizabeth conferred the lordship of Denbigh on Leicester in 1564, and also made him Chamberlain of Chester and Chief Ranger of the Forest of Snowdon. His sway over the country did not go unchallenged: his wishes in the nomination of candidates for election to Parliament were flouted, and Sir Richard Bulkeley of Beaumaris, one of the queen's gentlemen pensioners, persuaded her to overturn one of the earl's inquisitions into encroached Crown lands in Caernarfonshire. Leicester began to build a large church at Denbigh but he did not have a residence there; whatever plans he may have entertained for the barony were cut short by the premature death of his son and heir in 1584 and the distractions of the Netherlands campaign. He prepared himself for that command from an early date: in the lordship of Denbigh by inserting a clause into the renewed leases of his tenants requiring them to provide military service.[19] This was redolent of the feudal tenures of the former marcher lords, and it may well be that the account in the libel, 'Leicester's Commonwealth',[20] of his unpopularity in North Wales was not exaggerated.

At least the earl did not try to compel his tenantry to vote for his nominee in elections to Parliament, as one Elizabethan squire, John Edwards of Chirk, did in 1585.[21] This seems to have been a singular case, even on this estate, and Edwards's recusancy may have prevented him from exploiting the advantage to the full. Such tactics were to become common practice among landlords only in a much later age, and there is little sign that the political culture of the Welsh shires was very different from that in Elizabethan England. The greatest difference arose out of the less generous provision made for parliamentary representation in the Welsh constituencies in the legislation of 1536–44. Welsh gentlemen responded eagerly to the opportunities of serving in the House of Commons, particularly in the reign of Elizabeth. Thomas Bulkeley of Beaumaris declared in 1584: 'I am one that loves to see fashions and desires to know wonders; therefore, if I be elected, I will not refuse it.'[22] Bulkeley was a younger son and a lawyer with his way to make in a wider world, but for the heads of families and their heirs the knighthood of the shire betokened a recognition of their prominence in the community. Because there was only one county seat in the Welsh constituencies to satisfy the ambition of such men, contested elections were that much more frequent than in England. It was on these occasions that the rivalry of county families broke out into factional conflicts which disturbed the peace and, to an extent, belied the sense of 'county community' which was supposed to be fostered by the shire system and service on the commissions of the peace.[23]

The Cecils, like the Tudors, were of Welsh descent, and Burghley in particular exercised some influence in Wales on that account. He did not set up a network of dependants to counter-balance Leicester's clientage in the country, but he was cultivated by his family connections on the Welsh border, as was Blanche Parry, the queen's gentlewoman and his 'kinswoman', by hers. Many families from all parts of Wales had friends at Court (as indeed they had had, though at a lower level in the royal Household, for generations past) and these contacts were as important as any in forging the 'union' under Elizabeth. In Pembrokeshire the queen's putative half-brother, Sir John Perrot of Haroldston, acted as a counterweight to Devereux interests in the area, until a marriage alliance arranged at the end of the century brought a temporary truce. The 2nd Earl of Essex assumed Leicester's mantle in Wales as well as at Court. He built up the Devereux clientage from its base in Lamphey in the south-west by recruiting justices of the peace, sheriffs and deputy lieutenants in other counties into his service. A group of adventurers from the north-eastern shires were among those knighted by Essex in Ireland; his promotion of their interests in Wales led to clashes with the Lord President, Pembroke, which came near to paralysing royal authority in the country. Essex's exploitation of this, the most dangerous connection built up by any Elizabethan nobleman, threatened the stability of the regime and the bonds of loyalty that tied Wales to the Crown.

The waning of powerful courtier connections did not lead to peaceful conditions in the countryside: the election of 1601 in Denbighshire was bitterly fought between rival factions among the county gentry now released from the shadow of any territorial magnate.[24] If, as recent revisionists insist, England was still largely an aristocratic society by the end of the sixteenth century, this was much less true of Wales, where the gentry, newly enfranchised by the 'union' legislation, came into their own. There were remarkably few new landed families among them, few that is which derived their fortunes exclusively from the further opportunities thrown up in the wake of the Reformation and the 'union'. The Welsh concept of gentility, *bonedd*, laid more stress on length of pedigree than on broad acres – as needs must in such a relatively poor country – and most of the Tudor gentry claimed descent from *uchelwyr*, the medieval nobility of free men.[25] Until the outbreak of the Civil War, most of them also remained rooted in their communities, for all that they explored the avenues of advancement in England and especially in London. The anglicisation in speech and values which was eventually to alienate the gentry from their cultural heritage did not become general until the late seventeenth century, and was not complete even in the eighteenth.

V

While county factions in Wales did not revolve in the orbit of the Court to any significant extent until the 1590s, the conflicts among the councillors at Ludlow certainly did reflect tensions within the Privy Council from early in the reign. The longest-serving Elizabethan lords president, Sir Henry Sidney and the 2nd Earl of Pembroke, were allies of Leicester and his interests were guaranteed a sympathetic hearing at the court there. One potential conflict of interest lay in the question of the Council's authority within the County Palatine of Chester, where Leicester was Chamberlain and where the Chief Justice, Sir John Throckmorton, was *ex officio* a councillor at Ludlow and one of the earl's followers. The problem was resolved in 1569 with the recognition of the privileged status of the city and county of Chester.

Another source of friction between the councillors was the difference of approach to the mounting law suits with which the court had to cope. The litigiousness of the Welsh after the 'union' became proverbial. As more of them took advantage of the freer access to English legal process, their feuds increasingly took the form of contests at law – which can in a sense be regarded as a measure of the success of Tudor policy. Sidney took a lenient view: 'a happy place of government it is, for a better people to govern or better subjects to their sovereign

Europe holdeth not'. The civilian Dr David Lewis, the first Principal of Jesus College, Oxford, disapproved of Sidney's lenience and was remarkable for his dispassionate opinion of his fellow-countrymen. He deplored the lack of respect for the Council and in 1576 he warned Walsingham: 'My country is far out of order at this time as doth require severe remedy . . .'[26] For the Vice-President, Sir William Gerard, as for Lewis, the exemplary Lord President had been Rowland Lee, but while he argued for a return to the regime of peripatetic councillors, he believed that 'in Wales universally, are as civil people and obedient to law as are in England'. After 1570, when Sir James Croft of Croft Castle, Herefordshire, was reinstated in the queen's favour in the royal Household and the Privy Council, his presence at Ludlow ensured that other counsels, critical of Leicester as well as of Sidney and Pembroke, were given a hearing even if they did not prevail. Another independent voice raised in opposition to Sidney's tolerant attitude to Welsh litigants was that of John Whitgift, who sat on the Council as Bishop of Worcester and acted as Vice-President during Sidney's absence in Ireland.

The Council in the Marches, for all that its reach exceeded its grasp in controlling the flood of litigation, was equal to the task of ruling the country for the Tudors. When they were resident at Ludlow, both Sidney and Pembroke kept a vice-regal court which for a few years revived the tradition of patronage and hospitality associated with the princely Households of Arthur and Mary. The frequent absences of the President, however, undermined the Council's authority and exposed them to the damaging criticism of their adversaries. The last years of Pembroke's presidency were overshadowed by illness and the quarrel with Essex.[27] As Lord Lieutenant of all the Welsh counties, he found his deputies deficient and in 1591 he berated them for their factiousness:

> For how can your minds be united in public defence, when they are devided by private quarrels. . . . All men cannot be deputy lieutenants, some must govern, some must obey.

Early in 1590, in a letter to the deputies in Caernarfonshire, he spelled out the public duty expected of them with an appeal to their allegiance to the Crown and to the larger patriotism engendered in post-union Wales with the reception of Protestantism. The performance of their present service to the 'state' in its time of peril would be a measure of 'what hearts you bear to our dread soveraign under whom, and to our dear native countrey in which, we live'. Pembroke was forever justifying himself against criticism by parading his duty to queen and country, but the warning and appeal directed to his subordinates on this occasion did not go unheeded. There is some evidence that the deputies came to assume a more responsible attitude towards meeting the shire's contribution to defence. But the results failed to satisfy the Lord President or the Privy Council. Pembroke was impatient of the real difficulty experienced by the deputies in raising money within the shire, and in 1596 he scathingly reminded them of the illicit exactions still being imposed by some of the gentry on their communities:

You have ever bene forward in *comorthas* for your owne privat gains, wherefore I conceive you will be much more forward in this *comortha* for the public good of the whole state.

The Privy Council was far from satisfied with the quality of the levies raised in the Welsh counties for the Irish service, but the failure lay not so much in the chain of command as in the unrealistic assessment of the resources available.[28]

VI

The Welsh reconciled themselves to the succession of a Scottish king by recognising him as the true heir of British monarchy. Since James derived his title to the English Crown from his descent from Heny VII, the transfer of allegiance was relatively painless except for those Catholics who had committed themselves to the Spanish claimant. In 1604 James was treated to an unsolicited Welsh translation by Robert Holland of his *Basilikon Doron*, undertaken to enable 'the very remnant of the ancient Britons . . . to enjoy so great a benefit as to hear your Majesty so speak unto them as they might well understand'.[29] James for his part remained comparatively ignorant of Wales, and the language remained a mystery to him. When Robert Cecil lavished extravagant praise on another of the king's early publications, James modestly dismissed the work as written 'in very rude Scottish spelling', blaming the copyists for this, 'so as it is now good Britain language or rather Welsh'. Cecil himself shared none of his father's and elder brother's curiosity about their Welsh forebears. When a Welsh genealogist claimed to have traced his pedigree back to one of the native princes of Wales, Cecil dismissed it contemptuously: 'I desire none of these vain toys, nor to hear of such absurdities.'[30]

The king's Welsh servants accorded far more respect to these matters. Among the number of Welsh-speaking councillors whom James had confirmed in office on his accession were William, 3rd Earl of Pembroke, and the 'second secretary', Sir John Herbert, whose 'perfection in languages' qualified him for several diplomatic missions. Sir John Trevor also survived the transition to the new reign as a naval administrator enjoying the patronage of Howard of Effingham. Welsh commoners and churchmen were elevated to higher positions than they had occupied under Elizabeth in London as well as Ludlow. Under James, John Williams became, in 1621, Bishop of Lincoln and Lord Keeper of the Great Seal, his climb in the royal favour having been eased by an impressive court sermon and the patronage of Lord Chancellor Ellesmere, with his connections in the Welsh borders. James's principal favourites, unlike Elizabeth's, did not have important estates in Wales: Philip Herbert, Earl of Montgomery (1605), was of the second rank in his favour. Herbert was granted the lordship of Denbigh and the chamberlainship of North Wales, which were the traditional preserves of courtiers, and he retained Welshmen in his household as tutors and chaplains (his kinsman George Herbert, and Griffith Williams, later Bishop of Ossory, were among his protégés), but otherwise his contacts with Wales were tenous. On his brother's death in 1630, he succeeded as the 4th Earl of Pembroke, but though he was later rewarded with appointments in traditional Herbert territory, his links with Wales remained distant and formal. Over three generations the Herberts had become increasingly estranged from their country of origin; the alienation of the family estates there began in earnest after the Restoration.[31]

The relationship of Wales with the Crown in the reign of James I involved a reinterpretation of some of the basic elements of the Tudor settlement. This impinged on discussions of other constitutional issues of the reign, some of which were publicised in print or enmeshed with Court politics, but as far as Wales was concerned most of the activity took place in Parliament, or rather in the Commons. It focused on the authority of the Council in the Marches and the status of the principality in relation to the royal prerogative, particularly as this was defined in the Act of 1543 (34 and 35 Henry VIII, c. 26).

The Tudor settlement of Wales was cited as a precedent in the Jacobean tracts advocating a larger union of laws to complement the regal union between Scotland and England, as well as in the parliamentary debates on this, the king's pet project. It was in James's mind when he addressed Parliament on 30 March 1607: 'Do you not gain by the union of Wales? And is not Scotland greater than Wales?' Two Welsh members, Sir Richard Bulkeley and Sir Robert Mansell, were placed on the commission to discuss the issue of union with the Scots, but no-one was more vociferous on the subject than Sir William Maurice of Clenennau, who sat for Caernarfonshire. In the Commons debate in 1609 Maurice urged the king to rename his dominions 'Great Britain' and to assume the title of Emperor. It may have been Maurice who was responsible for suggesting the style of 'King of Great Britain' which James had adopted earlier in the reign. Maurice's sister certainly believed so, for she wrote to him in February 1604, during one of his visits to London, to recommend that he should request James to intervene in support of his interests in suits at law, because 'you are his God father and entitled his highnes "King of Great Britain"'. The bard Richard Owen dubbed Maurice in his turn 'penn plaid brytaniaid' (the chief of the British party). There was no such party in the Commons, and Maurice does not seem to have fired even his fellow countrymen there with his zeal for the Scottish union.[32]

VII

If the Welsh representatives, or a significant number of them, took a prominent part out of all proportion to their numbers in the exchanges and transactions over the question of a larger union with Scotland, they were only marginally involved in the debates on another cause touching the royal prerogative which came before Parliament in this reign and which, ostensibly at least, had a more direct bearing on their country's interests. This was the issue of the jurisdiction of the Council in the Marches in the English border shires.

Whereas very few Welsh judges found preferment in their own country, the numbers of Welsh squires appointed as lay members of the Council had increased considerably since 1590. It was not, however, the prominence of this Welsh element, but the entrenched power of the lawyers at Ludlow, that caused the border gentry to renew their attack on a court which was proving to be too intrusive in their affairs and which they represented as oppressive. In their campaign they made common cause with the lawyers of the Westminster Courts, who had professional reasons for objecting to the jurisdiction of a rival court. Welsh litigants may have had less cause to resent its authority as long as it maintained its reputation for dispensing impartial justice. The formidable Sir John Wynn of Gwydir was a councillor from the beginning of the reign, and yet he did not escape its discipline when he transgressed. In 1615 Wynn was summoned before his fellow councillors on several charges of intimidation of his less powerful neighbours, and imprisoned; a grudging submission and a heavy fine saved him from greater indignities.

Though James appointed more Welsh gentry as councillors at Ludlow, he continued the policy adopted by Elizabeth at the end of her reign of ensuring that the presidency was in the hands of a nobleman without local landed connections. Lord Zouch was confirmed in office in 1603, and he was to be succeeded by Lord Eure (1607), Lord Gerard (1619), and Lord Compton, Earl of Northampton (1617). The Jacobean Council thus ceased to form the virtually vice-regal court for Wales which had flourished in the time of Sidney and Pembroke, with their sentimental attachment to the country, and was functioning more than ever as a court of law. The presidencies of Pembroke (d. 1601) and Zouch were weakened by quarrels between these two proud noblemen and the lawyers over influence and precedence. After 1604 the councillors began to close ranks to defend the Council's jurisdiction against the external challenge to its authority.[33]

In the legal arguments deployed in and out of Parliament, the case for exempting the English shires from the Council's

jurisdiction came to depend on the meaning to be attached to
the word 'Marches' in the clause in the Act of 1543 confirming its continued existence, and whether this described the
former marcher lordships or the borderland in general.[34] Francis
Bacon argued before the judges in 1608, and in a report to
Robert Cecil, that the Council was an essential component of
the Henrician settlement. It was the mainstay of the 'commerce
and intercourse' between the English and the Welsh, which
subsisted so long as each had equal remedy against the other
in an accessible court of law. To grant the requested exemption would be to reduce the status of the Welsh, who would be
again 'cantonised'. It will dissolve the union betwixt England
and Wales, by breaking of their great traffic, their mutual alliances, and their equality of right.' Other defenders of the
prerogative court averred that to reduce its authority would
'make the Welshmen despised by the English, who are now by
their common government holden in terms of love'. It would
stir up the ancient enmity between the two peoples and revive
the old confusion (the argument here contained a distinct echo
of the preamble to the 'Act of Union' of 1536 with its ration-
ale for the legislative change); the Welsh might even rebel if
the English shires were excluded 'upon any concept of bond-
age' – that is, if the reason advanced for the exemption was
release from arbitrary authority. In the event of such a distur-
bance, the Lord President would be deprived of the means to
suppress it, which was to cast the borderers in the role once
played by the marcher lords.

    Alternatively, the defenders of the *status quo* reasoned, to
admit the claim of the borderers for exclusion would be to
encourage the Welsh to follow suit, and then the inhabitants
of the North of England might wish to be released from the
sway of the Council at York, 'especially now, when the happy
union of England and Scotland may happily admit more pre-
tences [claims] for the same than heretofore'. On the one hand,
the Tudor settlement of Wales was cited as a precedent for
the Anglo-Scottish union and for the removal of boundaries.
On the other, so James and the defenders of his regality argued, to dissolve or weaken the supervisory body which made
the first union a reality would be to set a precedent for other
unwelcome demands to remove divisions within the realm which
were perpetuated by regional government by prerogative courts.

In other words, these champions of the prerogative took the view that the case for unification could be taken too far, and that some historical distinctions should be maintained. There may have been some inconsistency of attitude here, as there was in the conduct of the 'gentlemen opposers' (as they were called in contemporary accounts) from the English border shires, who did not improve their case by flouting the king's will in the debates on the Scottish union. They were consistent only in voting 'agin the government', which suggests that there was an irreducible core of opposition to the Crown by the same group of members on more than one issue of constitutional principle in Jacobean Parliaments.

VIII

The Welsh members did not identify themselves with the cause against the court's jurisdiction in this reign. In the parliamentary session of 1610, when Sir Herbert Croft and his fellow critics from the English border shires introduced a bill in the Commons to repeal the clause of the 1543 Act recognising the Council 'in the Marches', the members from Wales were more concerned to revoke the clause in the same Act giving the king the right to legislate for Wales independently of Parliament. They petitioned the king for an act of grace to repeal this as part of the conditions in the negotiations for the 'great contract'. That bargain was not struck, but the bill of grace was reintroduced in each subsequent meeting of Parliament until it was finally passed in 1624. It was not unanimously supported by the Welsh members, despite the manoeuvrings of the knights of the border shires, who were politicking for support for their cause by focusing attention on common concerns in interpreting the statute of 1543. James was content to relinquish this legislative power, although he insisted that it was part of his inherited prerogative. When the Welsh petition for the repeal of what modern constitutional lawyers have called the 'Henry VIII clause' was repeated in subsequent Parliaments, the delay in obtaining a bill of grace from the king induced them to voice their apprehension of a future arbitrary government should the royal legislative right be exercised. James did not take this amiss, since it was not a shaft directed at him. What he would not accept was the judges' opinion expressed in 1608, and repeated by Sir Edwin Sandys and others in Parliament, that the discretion had been personal to Henry VIII. He refused to agree to the repeal of the other clause of the Henrician statute when the 'gentlemen opposers' were supported by Sir Edward Coke and other champions of the cause of the Westminster Courts against the rival jurisdiction of the Council in the Marches. James would not be moved by any disparagement of Henry VIII's government: 'the abuse of a king's predecessor be not a ground to deprive his successor of his lawful and rightly used privilege'. In his response to the petition in 1610, however, he acknowledged the 'Henry VIII clause' to be 'a mark of conquest'; he did not propose to alter any law by royal decree and he wished that England and Wales might be equal in this respect. His ostensible concern was that 'the country of Wales be not too justly grieved by dismembering from them their ancient neighbours', for this would lead to inequality of a different order.

James was also concerned that the attack on the Council should not impair the principality he proposed to bestow on his son and heir. Members of the prince's household had begun to draw the thirteen-year-old Henry's attention to the patronage attached to the dignity in June 1607, but the earliest discussion of the potential of the patrimony seems to be that contained in a manuscript tract presented to the king by George Owen of Henllys, Pembrokeshire, which is dated 1 March (St David's day) of that year. Owen argued that the principality had not been abolished when Wales was incorporated with the realm. Contrary to the impression given in David Powel's *The Historie of Cambria, now called Wales* (1584), Edward had borne the title of Prince of Wales though there had been no formal creation or investiture in Henry VIII's reign. The principality had been absorbed in the Crown not by legislation, but with the prince's succession as king in 1547. Thus the honour was dormant and could be revived again for the heir apparent. The 'gentlemen opposers' also referred to Powel's *Historie*, but as an authority in their case for the contention that at no time in the past had the principality extended beyond the Severn.[35]

In the event, the principality with which Henry and Charles were endowed in their turn was an honorific one. The ceremonies of creation and investiture in 1610 and 1616 were based on the arrangements made for the future Henry VIII in 1504; he had not, like his brother Arthur, been sent to Ludlow with a household and council in attendance. In the intervening century, the Crown lands in Wales had substantially declined in value (some had been made over to Court favourites), and the Stuart princes' endowments had to be supplemented with grants from other sources, including a contribution from Parliament and mises from their Welsh subjects. The letters patent for Henry's creation, dated 4 June 1610, conferred upon him the authority 'to preside over, direct and defend' his principality. Henry died in 1612 and, though something is known of his other ambitions, there is no record of his own perception of the dignity he had so actively sought. On Charles's investiture in 1616, Daniel Powel expressed *The Love of Wales to their Soveraigne Prince* and that of 'your proper Meridian of Ludlow'. But Charles was not sent to what had become the virtual capital of Wales to take possession of his patrimony. The campaign against the existing Council in the Marches had virtually collapsed: in 1617 Croft turned Catholic and departed the realm, while new instructions issued to the new Lord President, Lord Compton, restored to the Council its full judicial rights.

When the bill of grace repealing the 'Henry VIII clause' passed into law in 1624, the Welsh were reported to be content that a power which had never been invoked, and whose original purpose was imperfectly understood in the Commons debates, had been removed from the statute book. Thereafter, at least in this reign, they did not display any hostility to the other marks of difference – the mise and conciliar rule – which remained between them and the king's English subjects. Prince Charles sat in the Lords during the readings of the bill of grace and acted as a mediator during the final stages of its passage.[36] He was not to visit his principality or gain experience in government at Ludlow, but a number of Welsh gentlemen, such as Sir Richard Wynn of Gwydir, had served in his household as prince. Most significantly of all, perhaps, as a member of the upper house Charles had observed at first hand the extent to which his father had been prepared to cede any attribute of his prerogative. Charles I's accession was greeted with acclamation in Wales, and in 1630 William Vaughan voiced what was now a common sentiment, at least among his fellow countrymen: 'Rejoice that the memorial of Offa's Ditch has been extinguished with love and charity. . . . God gave us grace to dwell together without enmity, without detraction.'[37]

IX

The reputation of the Council in the Marches deteriorated during Charles I's personal rule, and the king himself allowed its authority to be undermined even as it acted as the instrument of his will. Through Charles's personal intervention both the Puritan Sir Robert Harley of Herefordshire and the Catholic Earl of Worcester were able to overturn judgements unfavourable to their interests. When the Court of Arches challenged the Council's right to try cases of sexual immorality, this lucrative part of its business was suspended, and the matter had not been resolved by 1642. In 1637, it was said, Archbishop Laud himself 'doth tickle in the business'. The Lord President, the Earl of Bridgewater, found that with the levying of the forced loan and ship money, and the raising of troops for the Bishops' Wars, the Council was tarnished with the unpopularity of the policies it implemented. 'While it was attacked at Court by the agents of personal rule, its association with that rule made it unpopular in Wales and the Marches.'[38] From this period date the major grievances of the Welsh against the Council: unprecedented allegations of its injustices, corrupt practices and oppressive methods abound in the records.

The bill introduced into the Long Parliament for the abolition of the Court of Star Chamber also extinguished the criminal jurisdiction of the Council in the Marches. A special committee set up by the Commons, with Sir Edward Hyde as chairman, sat at intervals between December 1640 and June 1641 to review the remaining powers of the prerogative courts at York and Ludlow. Among its members were the knights and burgesses for Wales, who were now given a voice in deciding the fate of the Council, just as their predecessors had been present in the Commons in 1543 when it had received its statutory recognition. The committee resolved that the present jurisdiction was a grievous burden to the subjects in Wales and should be abolished.[39]

A last-minute attempt to rescue the Welsh jurisdiction of the court at Ludlow was made in an unsigned memoir addressed to Bridgewater which has been attributed to the King's Attorney in North Wales, Richard Lloyd of Esclus. These 'Propositions' recommend that a court of common law and equity be established to provide a convenient access to justice for poor Welsh litigants, who would be deterred by their inability to speak English from resorting to the Westminster Courts. Experience had proved that the presence of such a tribunal in the past had checked the oppressions of the poor commons by the great and had contributed to the 'reducing and civilizing' of the king's subjects in Wales. With its removal, it was argued, the country was in danger of falling into its old disorder. In thus recognising the peculiar needs of the Welsh, the scheme was reminiscent of the 'effectes devised for Wales', with its provision for a Welsh chancery, advanced exactly a century previously. The opponents of the Council were now dismissed as gentlemen and great men 'eclipsed in the firmament', and their objections were represented as rather an argument for its continuance, 'by so much the more it will behove the Prince and Common People respectively to assert it'. The author evidently believed in Charles's benevolent paternalism, and yet no such reform had been contemplated during the personal rule, the years when the locusts had eaten, as far as the probity of the legal establishment at Ludlow was concerned. Though the new court was to be a judicial rather than an administrative body, it was justified in this memoir on the grounds that devolution of authority – of 'several distribucions of the Government' – brought benefits to the subjects, besides welcome relief to an over-populated capital. Since the new court would replicate the jurisdiction of the Westminster Courts, it would be free from the criticisms levelled against the Council as an instrument of arbitrary rule. Moreover, under this dispensation Ludlow would be accounted part of the principality and its castle would provide a permanent seat for the Prince of Wales.[40]

There is no evidence that the 'Propositions' reached either Parliament or the king, for whom in any case the fate of the Council was inextricably bound up with that of Star Chamber. It was too late to salvage any remnant of their criminal jurisdiction from the onslaught on the prerogative courts in an assembly that was not disposed to compromise. The discredited Council lingered on with its civil jurisdiction more or less intact until May 1642, when the bill to exempt the four shires completed its passage in Parliament. A bill to repeal the vital clause in the Act of 1543, which would have given force to the recommendation of Hyde's committee, seems to have been abandoned in August 1641.[41] Had the former bill received the royal assent, an attenuated court in the form of a 'Council for Wales' might have emerged from the wreckage. As it was, this became one of the first casualties of civil war.

6. James VI, James I and the Identity of Britain*

JENNY WORMALD

From the moment of his accession to the English throne on 24 March 1603 to the day of his death on 27 March 1625, James VI and I conceived of himself as King of Great Britain – or rather, more accurately, since even this most enthusiastic of Britons could not swallow up the adjacent island of Erin into the bulk of mainland Britannia, King of Great Britain and Ireland, with France still euphemistically thrown in. That is well known; and so is the irritation which it aroused, most notably in his English subjects. What is much more obscure is what King James meant by it, and it is actually very doubtful if even he quite knew. As in any case he manifestly failed to achieve any sort of 'British' kingship, and as the visible hostility of his subjects led him increasingly to tone down the 'British' language which he employed so enthusiastically in the early years of his reign, it might be argued that his early enthusiasm was no more than a huge political miscalculation, a phantasmagorical addition to the very real and complex burdens of his composite kingship. Conversely, it is just possible that opposition to a concept may serve not only to block its immediate realisation, but also to heighten awareness of that concept, and create therefore a subtle shift in mental perceptions which in the long term would have its effect; in that sense, men may not have liked King James's Britain, but they were quite unable to forget about it.

Therein lies a fundamental problem, however. 'Britain' might appeal to, or outrage, the imagination, but it totally lacked any clear and defined constitutional existence – as, it might be argued, given the difficulty that a 'British' Parliament at Westminster still finds in coping with separate Scottish and English law, it continues to do today. The early seventeenth-century problem began with King James. The old and very Anglocentric view of it was fairly straightforward: an insensitive

148

Scot was so crassly indifferent to his good fortune in becoming King of England that he arrived in London with a Scottish entourage and insisted that his new English subjects should embrace them, and even welcome union with his Scottish kingdom. This has been effectively demolished by Bruce Galloway.[1] Nevertheless, it remains something of a puzzle that James, brought up since childhood to regard himself as heir to the English throne, and with plenty of time, as Elizabeth's life dragged on, to think about what this would entail, came up with very little in the way of concrete proposals, and on the whole contented himself with sweeping generalisations. He was adept at the snappy phrase: 'as there is over both but *unus Rex* [one king], so there may be in both but *unus Grex* & *una Lex* [one people and one law]', for example.[2] How this was to be achieved, what it would actually mean in practice, was much less clear. He could make more elaborate and tortuous claims, such as 'I am the Husband and all the whole Isle is my lawfull wife. . . . I hope therefore that no man will be so unreasonable as to thinke that I that am a Christian king under the Gospel should be a Polygamist'; and as a man who tended to repeat phrases and ideas which appealed to him, he could rework this metaphor as 'you [the English] are to be the husband, they [the Scots] the wife'.[3] Neither version, however, advanced the cause of Britain; indeed, the second positively retreated from it. He much desired a union of hearts and minds, although all this really came down to was the suggestion that the English and the Scots should stop disliking one another. His accession medal depicting him as 'Emperor of the Whole Island of Britain' might be a visual symbol of unity, but in fact the words only raised rather than resolved problems; for the English had already grabbed 'British Empire' in Elizabeth's reign, invoking it to signify England's maritime sovereignty, only to reassert 'the absolute Imperial Monarchy' of England, in Thomas Wilson's phrase, in anticipation of 1603.[4]

These were all designed to create an impression of new harmony, a single people under a benign king and an overarching law. They failed to do so. The British atmosphere which James seemed so determined to emphasise in the early years of his reign only served to suggest that he was causing insoluble problems for his old and his new subjects by showing that he could not conceive of himself as a single king ruling over two (or

more) distinct peoples. This was in effect a denial of the idea
of composite monarchy. Yet James VI and I was no fool. He
was well aware that the union of Scotland and England was
only a belated example of the composite monarchies of sixteenth-century Europe: the vast Spanish *monarchia*, the Scandinavian monarchies of Denmark and Norway, and Sweden and
Finland, the union of Poland and Lithuania, the short-lived
unions of Poland and France, and Poland and Sweden, in the
1580s and 1590s, and England itself, with Wales and Ireland.
These were well known to the king, and provided the major
examples which informed the flood of Anglo-Scottish tracts about
union of 1603–7.[5] Yet only one offered any sort of model for
the British kingship which James apparently wanted: Poland
and Lithuania, who first came together in personal union in
1386 with the marriage of Jadwiga, Queen of Poland, and Jagiello,
Grand-duke of Lithuania, and then moved to the incorporating union created by the Treaty of Lublin in 1569. In view of
he opposition to the treaty, and the conflicting assertion of
the separate sovereignty of the duchy of Lithuania, under the
Third Lithuanian Statute of 1588, even this was not a particularly encouraging example for the would-be British King. But
the examples of composite monarchies were hardly encouraging either. The dynastic union of Aragon and Castile, begun
in 1474, still looked very solid in 1603; the cracks which were
visibly opened up by Olivares in the 1620s did not yet show.
But the extension of that monarchy was much more uncertain.
The northern Netherlands, sloughing off Spanish rule, showed
what could happen to a remote and hated monarch; Portugal,
taken over by Philip II in 1580, had little love for or loyalty to
a Habsburg king who pressed his dynastic claim with troops at
his back. On a smaller scale, the dual monarchy of Sigismund
Vasa ended, somewhat ironically, with the loss of Sweden, leaving
him only his new Polish kingdom. What James was up against,
therefore, was the paradox that there were many composite
monarchies, but not one which offered a satisfactory model.

If European composite monarchies did not help, even more
problematic was the one closer to home. The Tudor Crown
had tried to apply both solutions to its dependent and conquered territories, incorporation in the case of Wales, and separate royal rule for Ireland. The example of Wales would have
offered an acceptable solution for Scotland as far as the English

were concerned, but manifestly not for King James and his Scottish subjects; Scotland was an independent and sovereign state, an equal partner with England. Presumably the English would also have been satisfied with the Irish model, which would have left James as King of England, Scotland and Ireland, with England as the main centre of interest and power. Again, that was blocked by the Scots, who in 1607 emphatically rejected the idea of being ruled by a deputy; they cited Spanish practice, but undoubtedly Ireland was also in their minds.[6] To that extent, the only course open to James, in adding Scotland to the English composite monarchy, was to leave Ireland and Wales where they were, and create a single kingdom of Britain by uniting Scotland and England.

It was a high-risk policy, and yet one which made a certain amount of sense. There was, after all, a veneer of similarity, in language, religion and government institutions; and there was the appeal of geography, for the uniting of two peoples living in close proximity within a single island suggested a neatness and cohesion which offered a hope of unity denied to the other composite monarchies of Europe or even to the sprawling territories of Poland–Lithuania. The king certainly spoke as if he believed in it. In his first English Parliament, in 1604, he put the point with admirable succinctness: 'one worship to God; one kingdom intirely governed; one uniformity in laws'. His proclamation of the same year, declaring that his title would be 'King of Great Brittaine, France and Ireland', was a sustained comment on his perception of the island, which had 'but one common limit or rather Gard of the Ocean Sea, making the whole a little world within it selfe', with 'A communitie of Language, the principall meanes of Civil societie, An unitie of Religion, the chiefest band of heartie Union, and the surest knot of lasting Peace.' There is here a strong, if rather flat, echo of Shakespeare's 'scept'red isle'

> This precious stone set in the silver sea
> Which serves it in the office of a wall . . .
> This blessed plot, this earth, this realm, this England.[7]

Therein lay the flaw. James's version, which included Scotland in his 'little world' guarded by the sea, has the merit of greater geographic accuracy. But it had infinitely less emotive power than Shakespeare's invocation of England, the 'demi-paradise', written only seven years before the proclamation. It takes little imagination to appreciate which imagery, British or English, would appeal to King James's English subjects. Indeed, *Richard II* had already been successfully censored by one English monarch, Elizabeth, who ensured that the abdication scene was cut. Perhaps the British monarch, who was clearly not in the least troubled by the abdication scene, should have seen the dangers in this profoundly English eulogy.

In one respect, however, James did raise the stakes for his British island. Shakespeare's was a 'fortress built by Nature for herself'. For the king, it was God who had brought together the two great nations within Britain, formerly at war, now at peace. Moreover, Britain was

> the true and ancient Name, which God and Time have imposed upon this Isle, extant and received in Histories, in all Mappes and Cartes, wherein this Isle is described, and in ordinary Letters to Our selfe from divers Forraine Princes . . . and other records of great Antiquitie . . .

God, history and contemporary rulers: it was an impressive trio to underwrite Britain. And the sheer simplicity of a single kingdom with its ancient name was sharply and tartly contrasted with the complexity of composite monarchies; by using the style 'King of Great Brittaine', James ensured that

> no man can imagine Us to be led by an humour of Vaineglory or Ambition, because wee should in that case, rather delight in a long enumeration of many Kingdoms and Seignories (whereof in Our Inheritance We have plentie enough, if Wee thought there were glory in that kind of Stile).[8]

So much for the pretensions of a king of Spain.

It was, however, the pretensions of James VI and I which disturbed his south-British subjects. The proclamation itself was necessary precisely because the Commons in 1604 has not been in the least impressed by God or history or foreign princes, and refused to sanction the title. And when, in 1607, James returned for the last time to his theme of common ground between England and Scotland, in his speech to the English

Parliament, it was the despairing last throw of a man who had already lost. Or had he?

It has been too readily assumed, not least by myself, that James VI and I did believe – even believed passionately – in a British identity. But there may be a greater significance in the lack of precision with which he attempted to create it than has been realised, which suggests a very different way of looking at the intense Britishness of the early years of his dual monarchy. He certainly gave out strong 'British' signals. But if he did not know exactly what he meant by them, then no-one else was in the least likely to do so. Lack of precision therefore led to a deal of confusion. James's Scottish Privy Council and Parliament made friendly noises, but their real feelings were better articulated in the mutterings of 1603–4, which grew into a full-throated roar in 1607 about their own independent and free kingdom.

In England, flattering poets, scholars and politicians settled down in the early years of the reign to extol the 'British' idea, without being very clear what it was. The great antiquary Sir Robert Cotton, proud of his Scottish connection with the house of Bruce – which he paraded by calling himself Robert Cotton Bruceus – was in a huge hurry to advance the concept, producing within two days of Elizabeth's death a treatise advocating the ancient name of Britannia as the most appropriate for the two kingdoms now united under one king. Cotton's theme, grounded in a wealth of examples ranging from the smaller kingdoms within England which came to form the kingdom of England itself to the same developments within France and Spain, was the inexorable process whereby smaller parts drew together into a greater whole; and James certainly used this lesson of history when it suited his purpose. Jonson obligingly devised British imagery for the king's entry into London in 1604, anticipating the 'little world' of the king's 1604 proclamation with his 'world divided from the world'; but the considerable trouble he got into only a year later for his part in the play *Eastward Ho*, with its satires on the Scots, hardly suggests wholehearted commitment. Other poets – the English Michael Drayton and Samuel Daniel, the Scottish Alexander Craig – extolled the re-creator of Britain. Bacon played around with the notion. Cecil worried about it. Lord Chancellor Ellesmere paid lip-service to it in public, but his private feelings show up all too clearly in his endorsement to a letter from Bacon advocating a history of Britain: 'Sir Francis Bacon touching the story of England'.[9]

What this surely amounts to is that when James came south, his new English subjects faced the fact that they had to deal with a lunatic visionary, with grandiose ideas about being King of a mythical and undesirable thing called Britain, and those closest to him, or anxious for notice, did their best to humour him – as they had to, when the lunatic visionary was their king. The Scots, who knew the lunatic visionary rather better, simply concentrated on reminding him that new preoccupations should not be allowed to crowd the old ones out. Two of the Scottish tracts on union, by Robert Pont and John Russell, were very explicit on the point. Pont dealt with the problem by skimming over it, and advancing the optimistic view that his 'magnanimous and princely disposition', derived from his English as well as Scottish ancestors, would ensure that he would be 'indifferent to all the Britons'; and he went on to support the king's idea of *unus grex* in claiming that 'a commixtion of the commonwealth and blood of both nations' would mean 'that a Scot in time will not be knowen from an Englishman'. We are still waiting. Russell, by contrast, sounded a sinister warning note that it was the king's responsibility not to forget Scotland; 'wtheruyis his Grace in end will loss the heartis of his people heir'.[10] This was more genuinely prophetic. In life, James did not lose the hearts of his people. But to later generations, unaware of the scene in his bedchamber in 1617 when his English servants knelt by his bed, vainly imploring him to call off the visit to Scotland from which he was at last not going to be deflected, he did become the king who had turned his back on his first kingdom, in the interests of the fleshpots of his second.

The king's own contribution to this wholly conflicting situation was by no means as clear-cut as has been thought. Certainly he made great claims for Britain. But when he added to his accession medal the even more dramatic visual symbol of the British flag, the Union Jack, which united the flags of England and Scotland (although not Ireland), he was not actually showing total and bull-headed commitment to the creation of a British identity. For although he used the right language in his proclamation of 1606 ordering the use of the new flag for royal and merchant shipping, referring to 'our Subjects of South Britaine . . . and our Subjects of North Britaine', this most public symbol was undermined by the fact that, although all British ships must fly it, the South Britons still flew the cross of St George, the North Britons the cross of St Andrew.[11] His British flag, therefore, far from symbolising Britain, flew as a symbolic reminder of the confusion which surrounded the notion of the kingdom of Britain. His British message was not only imprecise. It was, perhaps deliberately, confusing.

It does not, after all, take later historians to pose the question which was clear enough to King James: was there, in fact, any chance whatever of imposing a British 'identity' on the four component parts of the British Isles, each with its own sense of identity, and none of whom liked one another? The obvious answer is, and was, no. Indeed, in the search for a *modus vivendi* for the composite monarchy which now embraced the whole of the British Isles, the idea of a composite identity was simply an irrelevance. What mattered was that that there already was a composite monarchy, that of England, Ireland and Wales. It was now faced with the novel difficulty of incorporating the separate and independent Scotland, while Scotland had to find some way of assimilating the new situation into her political experience. But such need for adjustment did nothing to dent the existence of four 'national' identities. And as the self-styled King of Great Britain was well aware, there was little enthusiasm for being 'British', not only among the English, who responded by becoming ever more fearfully English, but among the subjects of his ancient kingdom of Scotland, whose immediate response was a mixture of Scottish pride and Scottish concern about their future, making them more aggressively Scots; the Welsh can hardly be said to have bothered, or for the matter to have had their opinion particularly sought; and the Irish, whatever they may have felt, were certainly too exhausted by the Nine Years War and the position in which it had left them to worry about the greater whole.

None of this offered much chance to implement *una lex* or *unus grex*, impossible and infinitely vague concepts as they were. Both King James and his English subjects, for example, entirely agreed with the idea that the creation of national unity did indeed involve *una lex*. But there was a complete clash of ideas about what that meant. For the English, it was not a new idea, and what it meant was English law, as it had been imposed on Wales by the Act of Union of 1536; and it was the rejection of 'the civil and honourable laws and customs of England' which was advanced by Sir John Davies as the reason for Irish and English colonial barbarism in 1612.[12] If the identity of 'Britain' depended on *una lex*, therefore, it was doomed from the beginning. The king's woolly ideas about codifying the laws of England and Scotland were acceptable to neither English nor Scots lawyers. There were, to begin with, obvious problems about trying to reconcile English common law and Scots Roman-based law. Moreover, the English were deeply satisfied with their law, and saw little need for improvement, let alone full-scale change. The Scots, by contrast, had only just begun the process of codifying theirs, which hardly provided a reasonable basis for international codification; and even the pro-unionist Sir Thomas Craig of Riccarton, who sought to find common ground between the two legal systems, came out against any immediate attempt to create a single law.[13] From the English point of view, James's ideas only underlined the problem which a Scottish king had brought them; they interrupted and complicated their own solution to their composite kingdoms, which was the extension of English law, by bringing into the picture a kingdom which manifestly would not accept such an extension. For Scottish lawyers, there began the pride in their law which would prompt Craig to assert its advantages over English law, and which would lead in the later seventeenth century to the great treatise of Stair, which built on the work of Craig and his contemporary Sir John Skene to provide a philosophical basis for Scots law, and to the determination of the Scots that the union of the Parliaments would not involve a union of the laws.

If *una lex* offered no solution to 'the British Problem', neither did *unus grex*. For a king seeking assimilation, the only way forward was to bring the English and the Scots together, and desperately hope that they might like one another. Of course they did not. As Keith Brown has shown, those things which might have led in time to a greater sense of unity, cultural contacts and intermarriage, hardly happened;[14] and even at the end of the seventeenth century, the *apogèe* of Scots baronial, Glamis Castle, stands as a triumphant reminder of determined

Scottishness. What did happen was that at every level of society, from the Courts of king and queen to the streets of London, at social gatherings such as the theatre or sporting ones like the 1611 Croydon horse races, there were clashes of style and personality which produced not better relations but verbal and physical violence, as well as an out-pouring of scurrilous anti-Scottish literature from the bitter pens of men like Anthony Weldon and Francis Osborne and even from the more moderate Bishop Goodman.[15]

Thus the initial attempt to give equal numbers of English and Scotsmen place in the Bedchamber, that most important inner sanctum, was very quickly revealed as a non-starter. In May 1603, the English whom James had appointed on his way south were cleared out, leaving the new King of England surrounded by his Scots; and for over a decade, the Bedchamber remained as an exclusively Scottish enclave, the source of vast English resentment, until 1615, when the new favourite George Villiers was admitted – an act which would not, in the second half of the reign, necessarily make excluded Englishmen feel any happier. Only in the Privy Chamber was there a balance; and that, being more remote from the king, offered less in the way of access, the key to advancement and success.[16] A mere two Scotsmen were given important office: George Hume, later Earl of Dunbar, was briefly Chancellor of the Exchequer (1603–5), and Edward Bruce, Lord Kinloss, Master of the Rolls. James was fairly cautious about trampling on English toes over offices of state and places in the judiciary. Nevertheless, the extension of Household positions, now that there were the three royal Households of King James, Queen Anne and Henry, Prince of Wales, rather than the single Elizabethan one, meant that it was not only in his Bedchamber that he could satisfy Scottish demand, so that the English Court did take on a genuinely Anglo-Scottish flavour.[17] Indeed, it took on more. As Sir Henry Wotton had observed on his visit to Scotland in 1600–1, James's preference had been for the French style, which was less ritualistic and hide-bound than the English under Elizabeth. Dinner at James's Scottish Court, for example, was the occasion for conversation, argument and wit; and he continued this practice in England, using the Privy Chamber as the venue. It was in marked contrast to the previous monarch, always formal and, in her last years, the 'lady shut up in a chamber from her subjects and most of her servants', or, as it would become under Charles I, the boring spectacle of a monarch silently feeding himself under the gaze of suitably reverential courtiers.[18] English style, for twenty-two years, was replaced by Scottish substance. Inevitably, it was a cause for criticism.

If the English complained bitterly about the intrusion of the Scots at Court, they were equally hostile to the king's other solution to satisfying his northern subjects: money. This became the subject of furious complaint in the English Parliament of 1610, spearheaded by the outspoken Sir John Hoskins, in his pointed, if inelegant, speech 'The royal cistern hath a leak . . .'. James's general extravagance and his bounty to the Scots was the target. But perhaps especially offensive was his habit of assigning old Crown debts to Scotsmen; the appearance of a man on the doorstep demanding repayment of money lent by, for example, Edward VI would be in any event unwelcome, but how much more so when the demand was made in a Scottish accent.[19]

None of this advanced the cause of *unus grex*. All it did was to underline the impossibility of achieving it. Yet only from the most blinkered Anglocentric viewpoint could James's actions be seen as insensitive and tactless. The 158 Scots who found places in his government and Household did not actually do so at the expense of great numbers of Englishmen. It was English perception, not reality, which caused the squeals and the howls, like that of Sir John Holles, writing in 1610 about the Scots who stood 'like mountains between the beams of his grace and us'. After his initial and over-enthusiastic appointment of Kinloss, James honoured his agreement with the English lawyers and union commissioners in 1604 not to give the Scots legal office or place in Parliament;[20] and there was no second Dunbar. Until his death in 1611, Dunbar played a unique part, as the king's greatest Anglo-Scottish servant, moving readily between London and Edinburgh. It was a workable and intelligent arrangement. Yet it was not repeated. The Increasingly shrill complaints of 1610–12 persuaded the king to separate the leading politicians in his two kingdoms; lesser Scots remained in London, but Dunbar's successors, Alexander Seton, Earl of Dunfermline, and Thomas Hamilton, Earl of Melrose, stayed in Edinburgh. To that extent, determined Anglo-centricity might be seen to have won – on points.

Yet (if one can use a word which is, interestingly, much less familiar than Anglo-centric) from the Scoto-centric point of view, their Scottish king had protected their interests to a remarkable degree, given the hostility to his policy. And considering what he was prepared to hold out for, what he was willing to concede, and perhaps above all what he did not attempt, brings us back to the question of how genuinely James saw himself as a British king. In 1604, Francis Bacon, writing 'not as a man born in England, but as a man born in Britain', ruminated on the possibility of a single Parliament, and asked 'whether it will not be more convenient for your Majesty, to have but one Privy Counsel about your person, an idea taken up in the same year in two of the union tracts, one Scottish, one English. In both cases, what was under discussion was purely Anglo-Scottish; but there was also a plea from Ireland that the Irish might be included. Yet this very obvious idea, which just might have been possible in 1604 when there was still something of the honeymoon period left, was not taken up by the king. All he did was to keep some Scots on the English Privy Council; and it is a nice paradox that the highest number of Scots on the English Council, and the appointment of Englishmen to the Scottish one, were to be found not in the reign of the British James, but under his much more Anglo-centric successor Charles I.[21]

One again, therefore, there are grounds for doubting the extent of James's commitment to a British identity. The vast clouds of Britishness with which he surrounded his arrival and early years in England might better be seen as a vast smokescreen; and the explanation for that approach lies in the fact that, throughout his life, he was a Scottish king, and in his approach after 1603 to the addition of both the English and the Irish to his ancient kingdom of Scotland.

Lurking on in the recesses of the debate about King James is the idea that his reason for wanting to be 'King of Great Britaine' owes something to his own overweening conceit, an idea which derives from the misunderstanding that 'Great' was equated with power, when in fact it was a purely geographic term, to distinguish this Britain from Lesser Britain, which was Brittany. In any event, as the English said at the time, King of England should have been enough to satisfy him. What has had far less attention is his description of what 'Britain' meant: the com-

ing together in unity of 'two mightie Nations'.[22] It is all to
easy to assume that he used the phrase because he had to –
he could hardly insult the inhabitants of his original kingdom
by describing them in any other way – but that in fact he shared
the attitude of Englishmen such as Ellesmere and Bacon who
were prepared to pay lip-service to the equal standing of England and Scotland; it was mere tact and no more. That is profoundly wrong. When King James talked of 'two mightie nations',
he did so because he absolutely meant what he said. Scotland
was indeed 'a mightie nation': a nation which, unlike those
victims of imperialist England, Ireland and Wales, had over
the previous three centuries fought off English attempts to
intrude an English king, and could now offer the other 'mightie
nation', which had so significantly failed to bring England and
Scotland together, the compliment of recognition of greatness
by its new Scottish king.

It was precisely because of his Scottish experience that he
could so confidently depict Scotland and England in this way.
For all the apparent troubles of sixteenth-century Scotland –
and a country 'cursed' (to use King James's unfilial word)[23] by
Mary Queen of Scots was certainly not short of troubles – it
was in fact infinitely more confident and outward-looking than
the worried and fraught kingdom to the south. James inherited
from his Stewart predecessors the belief that Scotland and her
monarchy had an important place in Europe. They undoubtedly exaggerated that importance, although they had been
remarkably successful, through sheer persistence, in reminding the great powers of Europe that they existed, in diplomatic
dealings and, spectacularly in the case of James V, in the European marriage market. It was no bad attitude for the northern part of an offshore island to adopt, and it was that
self-perception which underpinned the Scottish pride which
was a matter of comment at home and abroad; _fier comme ung
Escossoys_ [proud as a Scot]', the French said.[24]

The most notable feature of that Scottish pride was that it
did not derive from the normal medieval and early-modern
yardstick of military renown and achievement. Scotsmen might
have a reputation for being brave fighters, but Scotland never
ranked, nor tried to rank, as a mighty nation at war. Their
only enemy was England; and as they habitually lost battles
with the English, they had, during three centuries of intermittent

hostility, done their best to avoid them. But their one spectacular success, at Bannockburn in 1314, came to be seen as the
crucial and decisive victory, thus giving it an aura which great
English victories such as Crécy, Poitiers and Agincourt, or the
Armada, could not have. And that, combined with repeated
English failure to move from winning the occasional battle against
the Scots to annexing Scotland, created the paradox that this
militarily weak kingdom could still feel considerable confidence
in its legacy of success in war against its much stronger
neighbour.

Three savage defeats of the Scots by the English in the first
half of the sixteenth century might have dented that confidence. Yet only one, Solway Moss in 1542, was followed by
something of a move towards closer ties with England. But that
was less a reaction to the battle than the offshoot of the Protestant ideology unleashed by the death of James V; and in terms
of Anglo-Scottish relations, it was extemely short-lived. The Rough
Wooing of 1544–5 and the massive English victory at Pinkie in
1547 hardly encouraged Scottish enthusiasm for union with –
or, more accurately, annexation by – England. The most notable aspect of this period was its *déjà vu* quality; Protector
Somerset had no better idea than Edward I about how to go
beyond victory in battle and the garrisoning of Lowland strongholds, while the Scots reacted exactly like their medieval
predecessors and turned emphatically to France. In these
circumstances, the main exponent of union was Somerset, continuing the ambitions of Edward I, Edward III, Henry VIII, to
control Scotland, and adding reforming zeal to the same old
reason.[25] Since the outbreak of Anglo-Scottish hostility in the
1290s, England had always been much more fearful of Scotland's alliance with France than the Scots had been of occasional
English victory, and it was therefore far more in English than
Scottish interests to seek, by violence or by negotiation, to bring
the two countries closer together. The Scots, by contrast, had
every reason to maintain their European links, for they under-
wrote Scottish independence and achievement. Even the advent of Protestant reform after 1559–60 only meant for the
Scots grounds for greater friendship with England. Not until
1603 was there any point in more. It would be a very different
matter in the mid-seventeenth century, when defeat at Dunbar
and Worcester in 1650 and 1651 hammered home to the

Covenanters the astonishing fact that God was not on the side
of Scoto-British upholders of Charles II. But that was after half
a century when Anglo-Scottish relations had come to overlie
Scotland's European perceptions.

Before 1603, however, it was these European perceptions which
provided the main *raison d'être* for Scottish pride. And it was
not only kings, but the scholars who flocked to, and were sometimes luminaries of, the universities of Europe, who sustained
that self-image. And if that was an approach with three centuries of history behind it, it was enhanced in the sixteenth
century by two things: first, the prominence of Scots intellectuals
and theologians in the European Reformation movement, and
secondly, the vitality of the reformed Scottish Kirk. There was,
in Scotland, a violent row throughout the 1580's and 1590s
between the king and the radical leadership in the Kirk, the
extreme Presbyterians headed by Andrew Melville, over relations between Church and state; James sought, and ultimately
won, an authority which the Melvillians utterly denied him But
both sides were absolutely agreed on the trumpeting of purity
of their Kirk, and the importance of its place in the international Reformed Church. To the Melvillians, the Elizabethan
Church was a pale, insular and wishy-washy compromise by
comparison. King James took a less harsh view. To him, it offered a compromise – Calvinist doctrine in the main and episcopal polity – which made it more soothing and manageable
than the more radical Scottish Kirk, and left him only with the
puzzle that it appeared to give Elizabeth, Archbishop Whitgift
and Bishop Bancroft such paranoid nightmares.[26]

That agonising was only one element in the visible loss of
morale in late fifteenth and sixteenth-century England. In 1453,
final defeat in France meant that England ceased to be a European power, and shrank into the southern part of an offshore island. Its inability to come to terms with this, as the
Scots had done, showed up dramatically in the pathetic desire
of the bombastic Henry VIII to get a papal title which would
put him on a par with the kings of France and Spain, and his
attempt to see himself as Henry V, in his military exploits of
the 1510s and 1540s. More generally, if the Scots' most noted
characteristic was pride, the English counterpart was obsession
with the superiority of the English. Even God become English,
according to John Aylmer, future Bishop of London, in 1559 –

an excessive response to the uneasy awareness that England was no longer able to sustain the image created for it by Bede, of being God's chosen people.[27] It was all too obvious that England was neither the great power she had been in international terms, nor the most advanced and successful kingdom in domestic ones. The loss of France was succeeded by the late fifteenth-century mayhem created by too many 'heirs' to the throne, a mayhem which contrasted sharply with the stability of England's northern neighbour derived from the secure hold of the house of Stewart, dynastically unchallenged even if two individual kings came to grief. And if exhausted Englishmen after 1485 might optimistically respond to Tudor propaganda about the blessings of the new dynasty, this was increasingly undermined by the lack of heirs, as that most macho of kings, let alone a sickly child, an aging woman and a relentless virgin, failed to guarantee future security.

By the 1590s, when the relentless virgin was still clinging infuriatingly to life, the contrast between the two kingdoms could not have been more stark. Both England and Scotland suffered from the economic distress of that decade. But for Scotland, the present was good and the future golden. For England, economic distress only compounded the fact that present and future were bleak. The hard reality was that England was no longer a 'mightie nation'. Whatever was to happen in the long term, at that moment 'the mightie nation' was Scotland, still independent, visibly successful, and about to send England a king. In his equation, therefore, James was indeed flattering not the Scots but the English. And he was quite correct. It was the replacing of the Tudor spinster with the Stewart dynasty which was to give early seventeenth-century England a major role in European politics which the late sixteenth-century version had not had.[28]

This is not to say that James did not realise that, in becoming King of England, he had moved up in the world. He did. He acquired another kingdom, and came to it with all the confidence of an experienced and successful ruler, not, as Englishmen like Nicholas Fuller MP or Robert Cecil, Earl of Salisbury, would have liked, as a schoolboy to be taught his craft.[29] Thus from the moment he crossed the border – indeed, even in the period between Elizabeth's death and his departure from Scotland – he imposed his authority without hesitation or doubt.

He resisted Cecil's suggestion that he should travel south in-
cognito as far as Burghley House in Northamptonshire, where
he would be recognised, welcomed and ushered into London
by Cecil and his cronies, on the grounds that he was not going to deny York, the second city of his kingdom, the chance
to greet their king and have a party. He wrote directly to the
Lieutenant of the Tower, commanding the release of Essex's
ally the Early of Southampton.[30] He brought new men onto
the Council, extending the number of Englishmen, and adding his five Scots. An immediate assertion of authority was expected from 'native' English monarchs. It was a good deal less
palatable when demonstrated by a foreigner and a Scot – or,
as James perceived it – an Anglo-Scot.

What all this makes clear is that it is not only the extreme
view of King James which sees him as regarding Scotland as
the stepping-stone to England – a mistake made by his mother,
but never by him – which is unsustainable. Even the more
moderate line, which acknowledges that he could not turn his
back on his Scots and therefore had to risk upsetting the English, is unconvincing, especially if one views the problem not
from the London to which he came, but from the Edinburgh
which he left. James did not maintain his Scottish entourage
just because of past loyalties. His view was infinitely more positive. His Scottish servants had shared with the king the successful governing of Scotland in the 1590s. Some inevitably,
had to remain in Scotland to continue that governing. Others
could come south and become part of the English political
establishment because they, like the king himself, had much
to offer the English. The fact that it would not be easy to persuade the Brito-sceptics in 1603, ancestors of the Euro-sceptics
of today and cast in very much the same mental mould, to
widen their horizons was well known to a European-minded
Scottish king. But any skilled negotiator begins not with his
final bargaining position, but with an extreme one which al-
lows him room for maoeuvre. That, surely, was what all the
noise about Britain was about. Anything less than the creation
of the British identity which the king appeared to desire so
ardently would look like gain to its English opponents. In fact,
the gainer was the king. He might not have Britain. But he
could keep Scotsmen scattered throughout his Court and government, as a very real and undeniable presence. And above all,

he could maintain a Scottish Bedchamber, which was itself a far more remarkable achievement than has been recognised. Seen from the English point of view, it was a menace and a block to English aspirations; and a king primarily anxious to please his English subjects would not have created it. That the political heartbeat of the English establishment was wholly Scottish is, in British, or at least Anglo-Scottish, terms, a revealing comment on the political balance which the king really wanted. This was not failure. It was very considerable success against the odds.

It was of course the case that King James was committed to some level of integration of Scots and English. It was also the case that he could react with frustration and angers to the siren voices of those in England who did pay lip-service to the union project – men such as Ellesmere, with his 'blessed worke the Union'[31] – as much as to the determined Englishness of MPs who in 1604 and 1607 so strenuously opposed either 'Britain' or any move towards incorporating union. But if he was an idealist, he was also a political realist. The slide down from the strident British claims of the early years to the more soothing assurances to the English in his Star Chamber speech of 1616 that

> my desire was to conforme the Lawes of Scotland to the Law of England, and not the Law of England to the Law of Scotland . . . my intention was alwayes to effect union by uniting Scotland to England, and not England to Scotland

was not in fact the retreat which it appears.[32] He could afford to soothe, having achieved not his ideal but all the reality he had striven for. He did not create Britain; on his death in 1625, there was still *unus rex*, but *unus grex* and *una lex* were as unimaginable as they had been in 1603. But he was much more than 'king of all and king of each'. Scotland might still remain Scottish. But England – or, more specifically, the English Capital and the English Court as well as, to an extent, the English government – had been made Anglo-Scottish.

James was not only an Anglo-Scottish king. He was also King of Ireland. And if the arrival of a Scottish king had a marked impact on England, it was equally true of Ireland, where James's approach differed markedly from the traditional ideas of the

London government. Once again, it can only be fully understood in Edinburgh rather than London terms. James had a concern for Ireland, and certainly Ulster, which was greater than that of many English politicians, to whom it was a conquered province, full of barbarians who certainly did not qualify for integration but only had to be kept on the leash. To that extent, Ireland benefited from having a Scottish king on the English throne; the Scottish king who looked west with a wary eye towards his Gaelic Scots who had been 'conquered' long enough ago to be regarded as an integral, if difficult, part of his Scottish kingdom, was rather more subtle in his dealings with the Irish, more likely to allow them some place among his *unus grex*, than the English who had so recently had the real fright of the Tyrone rebellion.

It was not that James was an enthusiast for Scottish Gaelic culture. In partnership with Andrew Knox, Bishop of the Isles, he made great efforts to bring the Highland chiefs more closely into line, linguistically and culturally, with his Lowland subjects, as signified in the Statutes of Iona of 1609, which demanded that the heirs of the chiefs should be sent to the Lowlands for education, and that the chiefs themselves should from time to time appear before the Privy Council; and these were re-issued in 1616 with the additional demand that only those who could speak, read and write English could inherit land. And as a forerunner to the ambitious Anglo-Scottish Plantation of Ulster, if an inauspicious one, he encouraged gentry from Fife to settle in Lewis, although the two attempts they made to do so in 1602 and 1605 were disastrous and bloody. In the following decades, however, by working through Archibald, Earl of Argyll, he had rather more success in Kintyre and Inveraray, and in the north, through the Mackenzies of Kintail, who were rewarded by the earldom of Seaforth.[33] In the Scottish case, use of Highland magnates of powerful local influence, whose interests matched those of the Crown and, notably in the case of Argyll, who saw themselves as having an important place in the Scottish political nation, was the key to at least a measure of success. And indeed, his relations with the former rebel Hugh O'Neill, Earl of Tyrone, suggest that he might well have used him in a similar role, had Tyrone not complicated both religious and secular considerations in Ireland by his sudden flight in 1607.

Nevertheless, despite the loss of Tyrone, the Plantation of Ulster, which was carried through extensively from 1610, contrasts very sharply in both planning and execution with the cultural imperialism as expressed by Sir John Davies, which saw the solution to Ireland in terms of the imposition of Englishness. It was a policy which was visibly different from the English Crown's approach to the Irish, especially when one of the greatest of Tudor rebellions, led by Tyrone and otherwise known as the Nine Years War, had terrified the English in the closing years of Elizabeth's reign; and it clearly owed much to a king who could conceive of a mix of cultures, which would add civility to the Irish, as to the Highland Scots, precisely because it did not violently destroy all vestiges of their native traditions. The difference was simply one of scale: it was an international venture, by Scots, English and Irish. To that extent it was at odds with the reluctance of the Lord Deputy, Sir Arthur Chichester, to allow too many 'British' settlers – and particularly Scots – to displace 'deserving Irish', and the insistent anglicising of his successor, Davies. The king's more 'British' approach, however, sat readily with the very practical consideration of material gain, and English and Scottish undertakers did indeed co-operate in the Plantation after 1610.[34]

James's Irish policy has been criticised on the grounds that by setting up the Protestant Plantation of Ulster, while failing to deal with the problem posed by the resentful Old English Catholics and the considerable number of Irish Catholics, he created the modern Irish problem. This of course is quite untenable. One might as well say that the modern Irish problem was created by Henry II and his English successors, who insisted on laying claim to Ireland without deploying the manpower and resources to annex it as Edward I was eventually to do in Wales. The problem lay in the fact that the Plantagenet kings had ambitions in Ireland, as they did in Scotland. But as ambition, at its highest point in the mid-fourteenth century, stretched to the creation of an English empire which ran from the Pentland Firth to the Pyrenees, it is easy to see why Scotland eluded their grasp altogether, and the question about what to do with the Ireland was left on the sidelines; up until the mid-fourteenth century the English had failed to consolidate and advance their control, and thereafter they were in retreat.[35]

In that context, the attempt to extend 'British' influence in

Ireland by planting English and Scottish landowners who might – and especially in the case of the Scots did – find sufficient economic incentive to work for, rather than against, the interests of the King of Scotland, England and Ireland, was a somewhat happier policy than had hitherto been devised, not least because it went beyond the level of institutional control, itself a problem which had been endlessly and, in the case of Henry VIII's decision to make himself King of Ireland, dramatically tampered with, but never resolved. Moreover, recent research has shown that it is an oversimplification to see the Jacobean Plantation as an English Lowland-Scots and Protestant one. The creation of the Protestant Ulster which is supposed to be the root of present troubles lay in the future, after 1641. Not only did those Jacobean Protestant Scots planters, the Earl of Abercorn and Sir George Hamilton of Greenlaw, settle Catholics extensively in Strabane, but the success of Scottish border and southwest planters, themselves from a still partially Gaelic area, contrasts favourably with that of the purely Lowland Scots.[36] What James presided over was a very genuine religious and cultural mix.

This highlights the second way in which the Scottish king showed himself more confident, less fearful, in his Gaelic dealings, than his English predecessor. In general terms, he was far less frightened of Catholics than the late-Elizabethan establishment. This was clear enough from his treatment of the northern Catholic earls, which provoked Elizabeth's famous outburst, 'Methink I do but dream'. His sharp exchange of letters with Cecil in 1601–2 contained the same message; he utterly rejected Cecil's defence of persecution. It was he who refused to extend villainy of the Gunpowder Plotters to the Catholics of England in the hysterical aftermath of the discovery of the Plot. Earlier, in the 1580s and 1590s, missionary priests in north-east Scotland did not suffer the horrific fate of their counterparts in England, 129 of whom were butchered between 1577 and 1603; and towards the end of his reign, James was to outrage Knox's successor as Bishop of the Isles, Thomas Knox, whose appeals for help against the Jesuits in Argyll were met with the sardonic comment that anyone – even if papist – who could civilise the Highlanders could go ahead with the King's blessing.[37]

No wonder, then, that the Old English and Irish Catholics

were not regarded as a major threat, to be crushed by force in military terms; nor did the king share the view that theologically the very fact that they were Catholic meant that a Calvinist God had undoubtedly ordained for them eternal damnation. Indeed, if the English government did not necessarily appreciate it, the Old English Catholics could regard themselves as beneficial because of their civilising force, thus playing the same role as James's Jesuits in Argyll.[38] There were certainly periods when recusancy fines were strenuously levied, just as in England, and for the same reason; the exchequer lost too much from James's intermittent willingness not to pursue his Catholic subjects through their purses. That is only to say that, in somewhat more extreme form, James clashed with his English government over the treatment of Irish Catholics just as he had clashed with them over English Catholics when he immediately reduced the recusancy fines between 1603 and 1605. More generally, he was pursuing exactly the flexible religious policy, if again in more extreme form simply because of the sheer number of Catholics, which he did in both England and Scotland for much of his reign: as far as possible, his intention was to depress, rather than to stir up, religious differences and their likely consequences. The only significant departure from that general rule was his imposition of the Five Articles on the Scottish Kirk, in a strenuously fought battle between 1617 and 1621. But this was designed to increase the common ground between the Churches of England and Scotland, and it involved the kingdom in which his interest had been engrained since birth, which was not the case with Ireland. There, his occasional lurches into a hard line with the Catholics were sufficiently inconsistent and unenthusiastic to make it clear that English hardliners did not have the sympathy of the king. The mid-seventeenth-century Irish crisis would overtake an English monarch not because James, King of England, failed as King of Ireland to stamp out Counter-Reformation Catholicism, but because Charles I, King of England, failed as King of Ireland to deliver the Graces. Meanwhile, what better symbol is there of a Scottish king's approach to the English problem of Ireland, with its numerous Old English and Irish Catholics along with a faltering Protestant Church, than the translation of that doughty Scots co-operator in his Scottish Highland policy, Andrew Knox, Bishop of the Isles, to the Irish bishopric of Raphoe.

What James did, in his Irish policy, was to introduce a new dimension to Anglo-Irish relations, on an Anglo-Scottish level. It did not give much comfort to the Old English, although one could hardly say that they were visibly content with what was happening to them before 1603. It did not resolve the problem of Ireland's place in the English hegemony at any fundamental level. But seen in his terms, and not in terms of what was done later by very different men, it was a policy which reduced and reversed the mounting tensions of late Elizabethan Ireland. Just as in his 'British' activities, it was the policy of inspired fudge.

Between 1603 and 1625, in both Church and state, England, Scotland and Ireland were presided over by a ruler who did not see security in precision and conformity. His genius was to recognise that the drive for a precision and conformity which could never be achieved was only a breeding ground for resentment, dissent and ultimately rebellion. This was a highly individualistic approach. It was far more usual for early-modern kings to meet the complexities and uncertainties of a world torn by religious division and political conflict with an insistence on definition and clarity, in both the making and the implementing of policy. But as Elizabeth and, to an infinitely greater extent, Charles I found, clarity was not the answer to the religious and political unease and confusion of their day. In James's reign, the search for clarity over the creation of a British identity, or the settlement of Ireland, is fruitless. It did not exist, because the king did not want it to exist. This did not mean that there were not plenty of malcontents and grumblers in his new kingdoms of England and Ireland, and even in his ancient kingdom of Scotland. That, of course, is the perennial problem for any government, of whatever complexion. The point about the Jacobean malcontents is that it was never made clear enough to them what exactly they had to grumble about; and surly muttering rather than outright opposition can be regarded as a happier condition for kings, and for their kingdoms.

And in the long run King James's vague and undefined 'Britishness' did have its effect, where a more precise blue-print would undoubtedly have failed. In the centuries since his reign, the idea of 'Britain' has never gone away. Inhabitants of the northern kingdom were always careful to make clear the distinction between 'the British' and 'the Scots' who formed part of Britain – or, in the very different circumstances of the eighteenth century, when identification with 'Britain' suited them very well, 'the North Britons'. The English, with considerable offence to other parts of the British Isles, settled down to use the terms interchangeably. Nevertheless, considering the total hostility of Jacobean Englishmen to the very idea of Britain, the fact that their successors have been prepared to do as much as this must surely rank as a notable triumph for the king who talked enough about it to push it into an enduring place in their very reluctant minds.

7. The Atlantic Archipelago and the War of the Three Kingdoms*

J. G. A. POCOCK

This paper will seek to develop a position, on the history of the Atlantic Archipelago in early modern times, which I originally took up in articles published nineteen and eleven years ago.[1] Since those times a good deal has happened, and we have all gone on thinking about what is no longer 'the unknown subject' – though it would not be true to say that we have a governing paradigm for treating it. In developing these earlier positions, I wish to select, however tendentiously, a few positions away from which I think there has been some movement, and see if I can employ that pattern in an attempt to define where we are now.

In the first place, there is the phrase 'Atlantic archipelago' itself. One book has been published with that title, by an American scholar, Richard S. Tompson of Utah;[2] on the other hand, Hugh Kearney's book is entitled *The British Isles: A History of Four Nations*.[3] I offer the term in an attempt to get away from inappropriate pan-national language; Irish historians – though not Kearney – object, or so I have been told, to the term 'the British Isles' for reasons with which I can sympathise. The problem lies less with the term 'British Isles' than with the term 'British history', a concept to which there are or might be objections on various nationalist grounds, but which we have been employing speculatively and aggressively in the attempt to overcome a writing of history so Anglocentric that 'British history' itself has in the past denoted nothing much more than 'English history' with occasional transitory additions.

* This essay differs from the others in that it was commissioned not for this volume, but as a 'keynote address' to a workshop of the other authors. Its appeal was so great that the editors conscripted it – bearing the livery of a lecture rather than a paper bristling with footnotes, and publish it much as it was delivered.

I will cautiously defend the new use of 'British history' to de-
note archipelagic history in general on the following grounds.
This history in the early modern and modern periods has been
dominated by the attempt to construct a 'British' kingdom,
state and nation embracing the archipelago as a whole, and
even the great antithesis furnished by the largely successful
secession of the Irish Republic is part of 'British history' to
the extent that it is dominated by the struggle to escape from
it. That struggle, in turn, is not the whole of 'Irish history',
which must be and is being written within parameters of its
own, but means that 'Irish history' can be viewed as part of
'British history' in the larger sense: the fortunes and vicissi-
tudes of the attempt, and the reactions against the attempt, to
create a multi-national 'Britain' which has a past and may have
a future. Similarly – at the risk of extending the term 'Atlantic
archipelago' to include Piedmont and tidewater North America
– one can include 'American' within 'British history' through
the War of Independence, until the formation of the federal
republic when it becomes 'United States history', and a field
of study self-affirmed in its own terms.

'British history', then, is located within 'the Atlantic archipelago', an expression partly geographically and partly politically defined, so that it includes the Shetland but not the Faroe
Islands, the Channel Islands but not the adjacent coasts of
Normandy and Brittany. An archipelago is a group or collection of islands, and the effect aimed at in using this term is to
remind ourselves and our readers that we are writing a history
pelagic, maritime and oceanic, into which an extraordinary
diversity of cultural and other movements have penetrated deeply
after making their way from the adjacent extremities of the
Eurasian landmass. Here we reach the point of employing the
tendentious and aggressive term 'Europe', an expression once
again both geographic and cultural; it denotes in the first place
a peninsula (or strictly speaking two, one Europe proper and
the other Scandinavia) extending from the landmass into the
inland seas and the ocean, and in the second place a civilisation, Latin in its origins and exceptional in its expansiveness,
which made its way into the Scandinavian peninsula, the Atlantic archipelago, and many other parts of the planet. This
combination of meanings renders 'Europe' a term dynamic,
indeterminable and hegemonic; it can be used to include hu-

man societies or to exclude them, depending on how it is employed by those who have appropriated the power to define it, and as I have found myself both included and excluded by those who use it to instruct me as to who I am, I look on its employment with a certain critical concern. In using the term 'Atlantic archipelago', therefore, we encounter the term 'Europe'; and we affirm that the history of 'Europe' can either be confined to that of a continental peninsula, or include a history of islands and mountains and a waste of seas, in which case it is a different history from that it would be if it did not.

The notion of an archipelago invites us to let our mental vision travel out into a diffusion of pelagic cultures lying beyond the frontiers of 'Europe' and 'civilisation' as conventionally imagined. This is of course a way of thinking full of dangers, which have to be resisted if they cannot be evaded, and one has to challenge it as soon as one has embarked upon it. But there are senses in which one cannot avoid embarking on it; a real sense, for instance, in which the archipelago takes us beyond the territories of the Roman Empire and the papal, feudal and royal monarchies which succeeded it. The expansion of this barbaro-Latin civilisation is what creates 'Europe' as we know the term, and it expanded west as well as east, into the further islands of the archipelago and Scandinavia, as well as into the Saxon and Slavonic lands at the heart of the European peninsula. This expansion was still going on in early modern times, when it took the form of the consolidation of the English and British monarchies in control of the Atlantic archipelago; and very complex and intricate interactions developed over centuries between governments based on the control of land tenure defined as 'property' through written redactions of customary, statute and punitive law, and cultures where similar ends were attained through the obligations of kinship backed by various forms of partly ritualised violence. This is one of the more important frontiers in Atlantic, European and indeed world history, because mutual incomprehension between the two systems reached a height where each regarded the other as altogether alien and barbaric, and the writ-governed culture set out to establish its control of the kin-governed culture by means of conquest. We are expected to deplore this state of affairs, but we have to study it; and it is a circumstance to which we must constantly return that the English and Scottish monarchies in the archipelago were distinguished among those in the west of Europe by their conviction that they existed on a barbarian frontier, and by the existence of a frontier on either side of which peoples did regard one another as barbaric.

It was this chain of considerations which led me, in those articles which I mentioned earlier, to make much of the distinction between kingdom and march, between the zone of government, in which the written law operates normally and minimises its resorts to violence, and the zone of war, in which the writ has to impose its authority on the kindred by a more frequently visible employment of the sword. A good deal has been written about the extent to which these two zones penetrate one another and are hard to tell apart, and this has been a theme of Anglo-Irish historiography, for instance, since there began to be such a thing. There is Hiram Morgan's monograph on the outbreak of Tyrone's rebellion,[4] in which the queen's men and the chiefs, the men of law and the men of the sword, behave in ways between which there is singularly little to choose; but let me recall Sir John Davies's Jacobean apologia for conquest, in which the point is repeatedly made that this is precisely the problem which the rule of the kingdom needs to overcome – even though the problem might not exist if the kingdom were not there. We should also consider the point made by several Scottish historians, Jenny Wormald among them,[5] that in blood-feud societies the level of private violence is high but containable, whereas in societies governed by king and law the level of public violence is occasionally explosive and devastating. It is in the latter that we find armies fighting pitched battles in pursuit of dynastic and civil war; and the *Problematik* of what constitutes civil war should now receive the attention of historians.

Nevertheless, it may still be useful for some purposes to retain the model of kingdom and march, and keep in mind the extent to which Mountjoy and Cromwell and Ginkel, and Wade and Cumberland far into the eighteenth century, were engaged in the ancient imperial pursuit of reducing provinces to obedience. Eliga Gould has written a most persuasive doctoral dissertation,[6] in which 1745 and 1759 emerge as significant moments in the reorganisation of Anglo-Hanoverian empire between the Elbe and the Ohio, not without bearing on the American Revolution. But to say this is to pass from the model of kingdom and march to the model of multiple monarchy, and perhaps the ascent of the latter model to its present paradigmatic authority is the most important change in the construction of 'British history' since the time when I began proposing the latter subject in those early articles.

It was J. C. Beckett who seems first to have used the phrase 'the War of the Three Kingdoms' – or was it 'the Wars'? – but the phrase has gone on growing since it first became known, and we are now in a position where we must borrow a term from our Chinese peers and speak of an 'Age of the Three Kingdoms' in British history and the history of the Atlantic archipelago, lasting from 1534 or 1603 to 1707 or 1801. Within it might be located a sub-period of the 'Wars of the Three Kingdoms', datable from 1637 to 1691, in which the concepts of wars of conquest, social wars and civil wars skirmish to command our attention. The 'Age of the Three Kingdoms', in the larger sense, is that in which sovereign or imperial kingdoms in England and Scotland, and a subject kingdom established by conquest and legislation in Ireland, come first under a single dynasty, constituting a multiple monarchy, and then under a common parliamentary sovereignty, constituting or never quite constituting a unified parliamentary state. It is succeeded by an 'Age of Union' lasting from 1801 to 1921, and beyond that the enterprise of periodisation by nomenclature had perhaps better not go. This conference must necessarily focus predominantly on the problems of multiple monarchy, and perhaps on the Wars of the Three Kingdoms in particular; but it is possible to carry on beyond the seventeenth century, and in conjunction with Scottish, American, and now and then English colleagues, I have found myself discussing the American Revolution as growing out of the problems of multiple monarchy,[7] while J. C. D. Clark is prepared to go further and examine it as the last (or not the last?) of the British wars of religion.[8]

The model of kingdom and march presents an image of sovereignty and its spatial limitations, but that of multiple monarchy presents that of the relations between modes of sovereignty when several are exercised by the same crown or person. But this is tricky language; James VI and I once complained that he could not be the husband of two wives, the more so because to find oneself in that situation is really to find that one is trying to be two husbands, and the head of a plural monarchy has several mystical or political persons met together in one natural body. And if the King of Scots who became King of England could not merge his three bodies in that of an Emperor of Great Britain, what person had he as King of Ireland, where his sovereignty was acquired by conquest and Ireland was perhaps not a body politic incorporate at all? It was worse for George III, when his colonial subjects invited him to maintain a harem of some twenty independent bodies politic; but this demand was so absurd that the king may not have noticed it. From these abstract and symbolic, but not for that reason insignificant considerations, we move to consider the problems of plural majesty: that is to say of 'The Causes of the English Civil War' and 'The Fall of the British Monarchies'.

There is a historiographical, linguistic and political problem here, which I want to consider without laying it all at the door of Conrad Russell. Are we substituting the War, or Wars, of the Three Kingdoms for the English Civil War, in spite of Russell's choice of a title for his Ford Lectures? If so, why and with what effect? Let me generalise by saying that the thrust of his argument is to deny that there was anything wrong enough with the English kingdom as a whole to break its structure apart, to divide its ruling elites into opposing camps, to furnish them with opposed and irreconcilable patterns of religions and political belief, or to need explanation in terms of the long-range operations of social change. What happened was rather that the strains imposed on the monarchy by the need to govern three kingdoms led to its breakdown, and that the English, like the other, ruling elites fell apart in consequence of this failure of leadership. The British problem caused the dissolution of government, and the dissolution of government caused the war.

This is a simplistic account of Russell's complex narrative, but I have no difficulty in accepting his argument in this simplified form. I accept all that is said about the need to escape from Whig constitutionalist or Marxian socialist explanations, though when we have escaped from them I want to go back and look at both, and see what may be left of them. What does trouble me is the presence of a state of mind which I know Russell does not share, but which is sufficiently widespread all the same: a prevailing climate of national defeatism and snarling self-dislike, a conviction that we live in a time of the breaking of nations and the unmaking of states, which impels many opinion-makers and not a few academics to deny that English history makes any kind of sense, or contains within itself any of the motors of its own dynamic or the causes of its own crises. With these intentions some of our contemporaries inject the Civil War of 1642 into a British context or the revolution of 1688 into a European context; not because we learn more about English history when we realise that it was not the whole of the story, or because there are other stories needing to be told, but because we want to deny that the English were ever the makers of their own history in any degree whatever. It was not with intentions like these that I broached the idea of a 'British history' in a lecture to the New Zealand Historical Association in 1973. I hasten to add that the revisionist debate, of which the British reading of seventeenth-century history has been part, has not had these insanitary effects; rather, it has rendered the national sovereignty and the national history tougher because more fragile, because more exposed to external and internal contingencies than we used to realise.[9] But in this perspective, the result of absorbing the English Civil War into the War of the Three Kingdoms should be to illuminate the former, not to make it disappear.

Let me ask two questions: was there an English Civil War, and was there a War of the Three Kingdoms? I have already suggested my answer to the second question, and I want now to put forward for consideration the still rather abstract proposition that there was a confluence of several wars, which arose separately but had to be fought together for the reason that they could not be pursued, much less brought to a conclusion, separately. This proposition opens up a problem. Can we construct a holistic explanation of the War of the Three Kingdoms, or must we concede that a multiple monarchy cannot have a single or holistic history? The issue turns on the extent to which the single dynasty ruling several realms had created a single polity, or a complex of polities centred on itself, which had its own life and within which a series of things could go wrong; an entity which engendered or suffered its own crises, in short, and – above all – which had its own history. There is, as we have seen, a sense in which Conrad Russell is denying that English history engendered the English Civil War, and John Morrill can be read as accepting this, but asserting that Russell's explanation is still insufficiently 'British' or 'Britannic' in the sense that Scottish and Irish history figure in it only as the external forces which impelled the unwilling but still central English into a civil war they did not want. Russell has characterised the English role in this crisis as that of 'the pig in the middle'; the victim of external forces, but still in the middle. It is a temptation to see in this a reflection of the British self-image in the 1980s and 1990s.

If a 'holistic' account of the crisis could be put forward, it would be because the multiple monarchy had created a unity of structure somewhere, within which a crisis could develop and a breakdown could take place. This unity would have a history of its own, and we should have found *a* 'British' or 'Britannic' history within which we could situate *a* War of the Three Kingdoms. But what would be the architecture of the structure of which this was the history? Of what institutions or conventions or relationships would it consist? In one projection intelligible to seventeenth-century minds, it would consist solely in the natural person of the King who was head of all Three Kingdoms, and there is much latitude for explaining the crisis as the effect of the natural personality of Charles the First – even when, with Russell, one thinks he did not do badly all the time. But it was equally well understood that a king's natural person could not be finally separated from his political person, which he enjoyed or endured as the head of a body politic; and it was of the essence of multiple monarchy that one natural person might find himself, or herself, endued with two or three political persons – the predicament so accurately expounded by James VI and I. In the historicist language I am deliberately, and I hope not blindly, employing, this might mean that such a king found himself acting in two or three histories at once – each political body having its own history, the effect of whatever social or cultural forces it had mobilised by existing as a political structure – and he might find his government, his court and his person the focal point at which all these histories converged, whether in confluence or in collision.

But to say only this leaves open the question of whether or not such a king, and any predecessors he might have as head of a multiple monarchy, had about him some set of institutions or conventions or usages for dealing with this convergence, or whether it was dealt with only by the king's natural person dealing with problems as they came along; was there a *jurisdictio* or was there only a *gubernaculum?* In the former case there would be a locus of politics complex, stable and unstable enough to have a history of its own; there would be a 'Britannic' history along with the English, Scottish and Irish histories, one in which the latter converged so as to form a whole, which must exist if a 'holistic' explanation is to be offered. But we shall not find ourselves pursuing this hypothesis to the point where the whole has absorbed the parts; it is simply *ex hypothesi* that there did not exist a 'Britannic' state or empire, or consequently a 'Britannic' history, in which the Three Kingdoms and their several histories were absorbed and swallowed up. We need not go so far as to say that there never has existed such an entity, and that consequently the search for a 'British history' is a search in vain. There is a British history in so far as its several components have converged in a shared political culture, and in so far as the attempt to make them do so has a continuous history. In that 'matter of Britain' which is the problem of the War or Wars of the Three Kingdoms, we appear to be faced with an opposition of extremes which are not absolutes. At one – let us call it Russellian – extreme, the central locus or focus is simply the place where the accidents go to happen, where the decisions of *gubernaculum* (the 'high politics') are made, wrongly made, or not made at all. At the other – let us call it Morrillian – the central place has a structure and a history of its own, and may in some measure have reshaped the Three Kingdoms by drawing them to itself. There is clearly plenty of room – the more so as we are dealing with a breakdown of government, both central and local – for both readings to be right and to exist together; we do not even have to synthesise them.

I am moving towards the reopening of the first of the two questions I proposed earlier, by setting up the implication that in a history of the Three Kingdoms each kingdom has its own history, no matter how much it converges, or interacts by refusing to converge and instead colliding, with the histories of others; particular histories do not cease to exist when it is seen that they cannot be written in isolation. Before I turn to the particular case of the English, however, I ought to emphasise that one did not have to be a kingdom in order to have a history, and that we must avoid falling into some Central European error of distinguishing between peoples that have histories and peoples that have none; though it seems not unreasonable to add that for an entity to have a place in political history, it needs a political structure of some kind with which to receive and respond to the actions of others. There is the case of Wales, which was never a kingdom and no longer a principality or a collection of marcher lordships but had been shired and incorporated within the kingdom of England, while retaining a cultural and social distinctiveness with a capacity for response; there is even the case of Cornwall, for a long time no more than an English county but possessing a certain cultural personality of its own.

There would not have been an English civil war – I show my hand by saying this – if the King had not found an army willing to fight for him; and it is my understanding that initially he found it at Shrewsbury rather than at Nottingham, and that it consisted in significant measure of men from Wales and the Welsh Marches. At a somewhat later date there were the Cornish regiments, who for a while fought with a determination that suggests they may have had something on their minds. This is a war in which it is possible to know something about the common soldier's point of view, and I could wish to know more than I do about what these Welsh and Cornish regiments thought they were doing and who they thought they were. I am not over-impressed by the tendency of historians of the left to ascribe a merely 'traditional' consciousness – whatever that is – to the royalist rank and file, as opposed to the enhanced religious and political awareness of godly Londoners and East Anglians; any more than I am overwhelmed by Charles Carlton's perfectly true contention that most soldiers in most wars are too much preoccupied by thoughts of pay, food, loot, sanitation, and survival to have much time for significant discourse. The remarkable thing about this among the early modern wars is that some of the soldiers did develop their own political awareness, and one would like to know more about how far it went and what forms it took.

If the King had found no Englishmen willing to fight for him in 1642, the pig in the middle would never have fought a civil war; but he did, and we are no longer pursuing the suggestion – fruitful though it was – that England was a collocation of county communities, who acted out of their own local considerations and not as members of an English realm at all. The reason why it cannot be pressed further is that the county communities did not wish to fight one another, still less to fight within themselves, but nevertheless did because they found they had to; from which one may conclude that the English realm possessed such unity that even in its breakdown it could oblige its subjects to engage in the public quarrel against their wills and against their strenuous opposition, and that this was not a relapse into some Hobbesian anarchy – though often it looked very like that – but a public quarrel or civil war. The bitter unwillingness of the English to fight one another – which of course increased the bitterness with which they did so – is used, as we all know, to demonstrate that nothing had so far divided them into hostile camps motivated to engage in civil war; but I am suggesting that it can and should be used, with equal force, to demonstrate that it was a civil war they found themselves engaged in. It is not exactly news, after all, that the war in England was a conflict between people who had thought themselves, and to that extent had been, in a condition of profound consensus. Harrington and Clarendon both premised this in the seventeenth century, and David Hume thought so in the eighteenth. Harrington and Hume both went in search of profound changes, occurring in the historical world, which had converted consensus into conflict. At present we do not want to follow that line of enquiry – it may be revealing to ask why not – but we do not have to follow it in order to perceive that the English war was fought between people who supposed themselves to belong to the same political culture, and that this may be the definition of what a civil war is. To say this may be to turn Russell's interpretation on its head, and at the same time to endorse Harrington's dictum that the dissolution of the government caused the war, not the war the dissolution of the government.

That famous dictum, however, can always be turned around once more: Russell's British war causes the dissolution of the English as well as the British government, Harrington's dissolution of the government causes the English civil war. I am revealing my answer to both the questions I posed. There was a War of the Three Kingdoms but it was several wars going on together. There was an English Civil War, but where Harrington and nearly all his successors thought its origins lay deep in English history, Russell invites us to consider it a product of the War of the Three Kingdoms; that is to say, of a rebellion in Scotland followed by a rebellion in Ireland, with which Charles I's headship of a multiple monarchy was so far unable to cope that it broke down as a government of each of the Three Kingdoms, so that war followed both among the three of them and within each of them severally.

Russell further invites us to suppose that there was nothing going on in English history which necessitated this process, so that it should not be considered as an English-generated civil war, but as something else. Be it so; but I have two further questions. Does it follow that there was nothing going on in Scottish or in Irish history either, so that the origins of the conflict must be located in the history of another entity, which might be called 'Britain', 'the British monarchies', 'the Three Kingdoms', or whatever? I have already considered this possibility, and I am fairly certain that Russell is not proposing it; in which case it must follow, I think, that under any one of these names we are looking at a field of action in which at least three histories – there may have been more – impinged upon one another, and the task in which Stuart government failed was that of managing their interactions. The Three Kingdoms acted in one another's history, we begin to say; from which it follows that each had a history which others could act in, but which could also react against those interventions.

I am beginning to ask – this is still an extension of the first of my two questions – how the word 'history' is being used in the discourse before us; and one implication my question rather disturbingly bears is that history may still be, among other things, the memory of the state. A body politic conducting its own affairs will have institutions, discourse and memory; it may discover for itself, or leave for historians to discover, complex processes defined by its structure and modifying it. This is what we mean by speaking of 'English', 'Scottish', or 'Irish' history – terminology which is certainly contingent and contestable; but if we abandon this way of putting it altogether, we will end by abandoning the concept of Three Kingdoms in its turn, and the problem is that these entities, and their capacity to act and suffer, may have existed as *verità effettuali* in early modern history, and may refuse to disappear when we try to exorcise them. There may therefore have been an English history, a Scottish history, an Irish history, at other levels a Welsh or a Cornish, an Argyll or an Ulster history, in which the War of the Three Kingdoms happened and became different wars, or from which it arose as well as arising from the interactions between them; it depends on where people have history and what sorts of history they have. My second question bears on the problem of how many of these *verità effettuali* we are compelled to discover.

I have been insisting that the English experience in the Wars of the Three Kingdoms was an experience of civil war. I do so from the standpoint of a historian of discourse, who studies what people said was happening around them and how they tried to affect what was happening by what they said. The English of the period we are discussing possessed an enormously articulate print culture, in which an enormously complex discussion occurred; and what this tells us is indeed that they did not wish to fight one another – they insisted with one voice that the war in which they were engaged was 'unnatural' – and that it was a new idea to them, though one which they were compelled to explore, that there might be deep-seated fissures and processes within their culture which had got them where they were. We might say, as they might, that these issues had not obliged them to fight each other, but once they were so obliged they had to give them their attention; the great debate over political and religious issues had not caused the dissolution of government or the war, but once dissolution and war had happened the great debate had to occur, because the war could not be comprehended or resolved without it. We may say that the crisis was not resolved in 1660 because the issues had been resolved, but because 1660 was an imperfect resolution the debate had to continue; and what I am seeking to say is that these are the characteristics of an intensely integrated and articulate society, in which violence when it occurred did not mean the disappearance of these characteristics, but would be conducted between people who had a great deal, including a capacity for complex discussion, in common. This is the profile of conflict within consensus, which is to say, of civil war.

I propose therefore that the impact on England of the War of the Three Kingdoms was such as to produce the English

Civil War, which was as it was because England was the culture it was. By civil war I mean that the English found themselves fighting each other over the nature of the English polity. Their disagreements about its nature may have been the effect rather than the cause of their civil war; I suspect that this is the case; but this may be a problem of chicken and egg. The break-down in their government may have been thrust upon them by actions originating among Scots and Irish; but once they realised that this was so, they went out and eliminated these interferences at source by such actions as Drogheda and Dunbar; some pig, we might say with Winston Churchill, and some middle. War within England could not be other than civil war, because of the intensity of English ecclesiastical and governmental in-tegration; and the difficult question which I shall now raise is that of whether civil war, in this sense, can be said to have occurred in the other kingdoms of the Atlantic archipelago, and if not, what other kinds of war can be said to have been going on within the concept of the War of the Three Kingdoms.

The Scots, it appears to me, did not fight each other very much, and if this is correct the concept of a Scottish civil war is out of place. The most obvious exception, perhaps, is Montrose's war of 1644–5, in which Montrose could contend that he and Argyll were fighting out a conflict over the mean-ing of a Covenant both had subscribed to, and were therefore engaged in a civil war within the Scottish polity. But in so far as his following consisted not of dissident Covenanters but of men of the house of Gordon, these were fighting out the poli-tics (partly religious) of the north-east Highlands, while the men of clan Donald – some of whom came from Antrim – were fighting out those of an archipelagic marchland extend-ing from Argyll to Antrim, on the maritime borders of two of the Three Kingdoms. Did Montrose not succeed in converting his war of the frontiers into the civil war within the Scottish polity he desired to make it? There were armed clashes be-tween Engagers and non-Engagers at the time of the Second English Civil War; but were they enough to constitute a Scot-tish Civil War?

The crucial war in which that polity was engaged was not a war with itself, but an attempt to maintain the British charac-ter of the War of the Three Kingdoms by containing the Eng-lish civil war within it and ensuring that the latter could have only a British solution. In this the Scots failed; the English, engrossed in their civil war, regarded the Scottish intervention as essentially an interference, and ended by conquering Scotland itself, less to annex it than to eliminate it as an actor in events. But what character shall we assign to the Scottish war in England? It was only at moments in 1648 a civil war among Scotsmen, and in so far as the English made it marginal to a civil war among Englishmen they repudiated the thesis that it was a civil war among inhabitants of any single polity. It was a war among (not between) the kingdoms composing a multiple monarchy, and to find an appropriate label we should turn, I suggest, to the ancient Roman distinction between *bellum civile* and *bellum sociale*; I retain the Latin because the English term 'social war' suggests a war between members of the same social system, which is not the relevant issue. A *bellum civile* was a war between *cives*, citizens of the same polity; a *bellum sociale* war a war between *socii*, polities associated in a system comprising a multiplicity of states. The great *bellum sociale* of antiquity turned on the eligibility of Italian *socii* to be treated as *cives Romani*; it has a formal similarity with the Scottish endeavour to establish by military means that English and Scots should be members of a uniform ecclesiastical polity. Something converse yet similar may be said of the next great war between polities subject to a British monarchy, the War of the American Revolution; the concept of a *bellum sociale* appears to have its uses to historians of multiple monarchies and confederations. At the risk of inadvertently hoisting a Confederate flag, I will say that a War Between the States is not the same thing as a Civil War, and that a war may be fought to determine what kind of war it is. Are we trying to reverse a military decision which subjected the War of the Three Kingdoms to the English Civil War?

There remains the third kingdom of Ireland, of which I know least and am therefore at greatest risk of speaking imperceptively. There is a suggestive essay by Hiram Morgan,[10] in which he challenges what he calls a 'colonialist' model of Irish history. In this model Ireland is treated as extra-European, as an alien and what would be called (as Ireland was called) a barbarous culture, on which history is inflicted by way of conquest and colonisation and which does not share a history with its invaders. Repudiation of this model can, of course, take place in situations till recently more unqualifiedly colonial; Amerindians,

Africans and Polynesians are learning to mobilise a history of
their own, out of which they acted and reacted before and
after colonisation took place. But the argument in the case of
Ireland goes further; non-Roman Ireland became Christian just
as soon as did the ex-Roman provinces which were its neighbours, and can be said to have shared their Christian or European history – though there is the new work by Robert Bartlett,[11]
in which 'Europe' is shown as an explosion of Latin and Frankish
aggression against Christians in the archipelagic west, Muslims
in the Mediterranean south, Slavs and pagans in the continental east. In addition, there are the important contentions put
forward by Brendan Bradshaw, for whom Tudor structural reforms amounted to an 'Irish constitutional revolution', as a
result of which Ireland became one of the Three Kingdoms
and capable of contributing to their history – though one has
to add that it was held to be a kingdom by conquest and was
a kingdom in which conquest was still going on. How then is
the model I have begun to elaborate to be applied to the third
of the Three Kingdoms?

Readers will have observed that my taxonomy of wars so far
has made no use of the conceptual category of 'wars of religion', so energetically developed by John Morrill.[12] This is
not because I reject or even modify it; on the contrary, I take
it as self-evident that all of the wars with which we have to do
were wars of religion, and that these continued in the archipelago after the year 1648, in which such are conventionally
held to have ended in the Franco-Netherlandish-German region. I tend therefore to suspect that the archipelagic Wars of
Religion differed somewhat in character form the continental.
I adopt, however, a perspective on all such wars extremely
common among participants and observers in the sixteenth and
seventeenth centuries – though adopting it does hold out the
temptation to exaggerate the secularity of their thought. According to such commentators, the predominant character of
a war of religion was its appalling capacity to disrupt government and civil order, so that humans found themselves fighting
for religious reasons within a structure of government it was
their first desire to maintain. We are in the world depicted in
the frontispiece to Hobbes's *Leviathan* – though as that work
remains Anglican to the extent that it is directed against Catholicism and Calvinism with equal vigour, it reinforces the be-

lief that it was the disruption of the Tudor unity of church and kingdom which was at the centre of the stories we are retelling. 'War of religion', in short, is a category which interacts with others that have been used in attempting to establish a taxonomy of those wars which together made up the War of the Three Kingdoms. The English civil war was fought within the Church of England, within the unitary monarchy or 'empire' in Church and state established by the Tudors. The Scottish *bellum sociale* was fought within the multiple monarchy over several Churches and kingdoms established since 1603, which the Scots were trying to bring to greater homogeneity if not unity. How may this complex taxonomy best be applied in the history of Ireland, or of three kingdoms of which Ireland was one?

That there was an Irish *bellum sociale* seems established beyond much doubt. The Old English and Old Irish aristocrats involved in the rebellion of 1641, the leaders of the Confederation which some of them became, possessed a clear image of their role in the structure of a multiple monarchy, and of Ireland as one of the kingdoms constituting that monarchy; and they resorted to the sword as a means of re-asserting and redefining that role. Even if there were those who reached the point of demanding an independent Catholic monarchy in Ireland – and this one understands to be doubtful – they would not compel us to abandon the notions of multiple monarchy and *bellum sociale* since it would be from that system that they desired to secede; and there appears no anticipation of the startling success enjoyed by the American rebels of 1776 in transforming a *bellum sociale* into a war between unconnected states. The programme of placing the Irish kingdom under Spanish or French protection aimed no higher than involving foreign kingdoms in the affairs of the Stuart monarchy, and I am not quite able to accept Jane Ohlmeyer's contention that French and Spanish subventions, aimed largely at the recruitment of Gaelic mercenaries, transformed a War of Three Kingdoms into a War of Five.[13] Ormonde and his Old and New English following, Inchiquin (that Protestant Gael) and his New English, were engaged in the Irish *bellum sociale* as champions of the authority of the English king and Parliament respectively, over what was to remain a subject kingdom; though one might at the same time regard both, and Monro's Scottish army as well, as establishing an Irish theatre for the English Civil War and the Scots attempt to Britannicise it, at which point the concept of a War of the Three Kingdoms approaches completeness of meaning. Montrose's campaign now begins to appear a re-exportation of the War of the Three Kingdoms to Scotland, but not to England.

We are not yet forced out of the paradigm of *bellum sociale* in accounting for the wars in Ireland, but phenomena may be found which will produce that effect. The paradigm in question depends upon that of multiple monarchy, and to a large degree on the concept of Ireland as a kingdom subject to that of England. If there were Irish who resorted to war to make Ireland a sovereign kingdom under the Stuart or any other crown, and Irish or English or Scots who fought to keep it subject, still that would be *bellum sociale* as the term is being used here. *Bellum civile* – an Irish civil war categorically identical with the civil war going on among the English – could exist only if there were Irish who agreed that Ireland was or should be a sovereign civil polity, but fought each other to determine what kind of laws and polity there should be. The present writer confines himself to asking whether such a war among Irishmen can be found.

An alternative model – which need not exclude the foregoing but might exist side by side with it – would be stated by supposing Ireland at this period to have been not only a kingdom subjected by conquest, but a zone of settlement and resistance in which wars of conquest were still going on; and a war of conquest is generically distinct from a *bellum* either *sociale* or *civile*. This is to reinstitute the 'colonial model' to which Dr Morgan takes exception; but it may be one thing to deny that Irish history as a whole should be subjected to this model, another to deny that the model has some place in the interpretation of Irish history. If we think of Ormonde as a royalist leader of (mainly) the Old English, Inchiquin or Jones or in the end Cromwell as parliamentary leaders of the New, we can go on to credit the latter with an agenda of conquest and settlement, of which Cromwell made use in pursuing the English objective of eliminating Ireland, along with the rest of Britain, as an actor in the English Civil Wars; while the English and Scottish adventurers in Ireland retained their agenda of conquest.

There remains, not unrelated to this question but at a distance from its main theatre, the war carried on by Clan Donald in Ulster, the islands and Kintyre, of which Montrose's war was in some ways an extension; and there remain the recent studies of the Marquis of Antrim by Jane Ohlmeyer and of Alasdair MacColla, the most famous of his captains, by David Stevenson.[14] The latter's Alasdair is exactly what the writers of empire mean by a barbarian; he appears out of the world of another culture and momentarily imposes its military superiority. The 'Highland charge' intrudes the antique tactics of sword and buckler on those of pike and musket, with startling if occasional success until both are superseded by those of the ring bayonet. I have observed Ohlmeyer's assertion that many of Antrim's men were veterans of pike and musket, schooled by mercenary service in the armies of Spain; and I do not know if the Highland charge figured in the battles in Leinster and Cork, where MacColla and most of his men ultimately perished. Yet I am not ready to give up the image of them as actors in a war along the borders of empire, which was among other things a clash between cultures alien to one another. This image, though it may smack of colonialism, is reinforced rather than weakened by Jane Ohlmeyer's portrait of Antrim as a genuinely hybrid figure, who had real reason for uncertainty whether he was a lord of the isles or a great Caroline courtier, and was consequently none too successful in either role. There were others like him in Anglian–Gaelic history; and if I am focusing my attention to Clan Donald, where I could and perhaps should be focusing it on the Catholic Confederation which Antrim briefly led, it is because I want to keep open, alongside the image of multiple monarchy and war among three kingdoms, that of empire and march in the Atlantic archipelago.

At the centre of my argument there remains the War of the Three Kingdoms as a great *bellum sociale*; but at one wing stands the English Civil War, so engrossing and agonising an experience that it was all that the English knew was going on, and at the other those aspects of war in Ireland – though not at this time in the Scottish Highlands – which were wars of empire and its frontiers, of conquest and colonisation, not without the accompanying phenomena of ethnic war and ethnic cleansing; though it is to be remembered that ethnic groups and their wars are not the simple product of cultural diversity, but arise out of the pressures of conquest on populations which find

themselves on its frontiers. In the year of Bosnia, it is important to get this right. The war by which Cromwell terminated
the First War of the Three Kingdoms (1637–51) was, in Ireland, as it was not in Scotland, a war of conquest and colonisation; and there was to be one more such conquest as part
of the Second War of the Three Kingdoms (1688–91), which
was also an aspect of a major war within the European states-
system[15] and, in a strange invisible way, the last of the English
Civil Wars brought about by disjunction within the headship
of the Tudor Church and state.[16] There is no circumscribing
these wars within a single dominant paradigm.

8. The English Republic and the Meaning of Britain*

DEREK HIRST

I

English historians have over the past decade or so engaged in a salutary exercise in self-criticism. With the erosion of old certainties about the manifest destiny of English constitutional history, scholars – like Westminster politicians – have been reminded that other inhabitants of the British Isles, be they Scots, Irish, or Welsh, have claims to be considered. Nowhere has the impact of the challenge to Anglocentrism been clearer than in explanations of the great upheaval of the mid-seventeenth century. Assumptions that analyses could be safely confined geographically, if not thematically or chronologically, are now generally in question as 'the war of the three kingdoms' begins to replace 'the English civil war' in academic parlance.[1] Yet the insensitivity of English historians to developments on what used to be deemed the periphery was truer to an important part of the historical record than is the new multiculturalism.

English chauvinism is, after all, not an invention of the twentieth century. English historians seeking English causes of an English civil war found ample warrant in the English sources they naturally enough studied. We have long been made familiar with the localism of seventeenth-century England, whose inhabitants often found it easier to think in terms of county than of kingdom. Nation, in its turn, with its familiar administrative and political boundaries, was a far more congenial concept than was that modern category 'multiple kingdoms', whose constitutional, let alone political, implications were scarcely

* An earlier version of this article was delivered to a conference title 'Multiple Kingdoms' at the University of Illinois at Urbana-Champaign in April 1990. I am grateful to those present, and especially to John Morrill, for their comments.

explored. Modern historians who ignore the world beyond the Tweed and the Irish Sea can find consolation in the observation of the first and greatest of their number, the Earl of Clarendon:

> The truth is there was little curiosity either in the court or the country to know anything of Scotland or what was done there, that when the whole nation was solicitous to know what passed weekly in Germany and Poland and all other parts of Europe, no man ever inquired what was doing in Scotland, nor had that kingdom a place or mention in one page of any gazette, so little the world heard or thought of that people.[2]

Even when the advent of a logistically sophisticated army brought improved communications in its wake, political as well as physical geography still limited horizons. Seizing the chance offered by a passing army messenger, one senior officer in the south-west wrote breathlessly in 1650 to a friend in southern Ireland, 'at as great a distance as sea and land can make'.[3] If uncertainty encompassed even the army command, the incomprehension elsewhere must have been all the greater – especially since few maps of the neighbouring territories were available.[4]

Indeed, our Olympian vantage, offering all the consolations of hindsight and a perspective that is at least potentially pan-British, risks obscuring the sense of their world held by Clarendon's contemporaries. We may think we know what the term 'Britain' means; but we should pause a little – as successive rules were forced to do – before requiring our forebears to think supranationally. Historians of early modern Ireland have expended considerable energy in pursuit of an Irish identity within a British state.[5] However different its role, England was no less a part of a larger British whole; what meaning that status had in the seventeenth century has yet to be studied. One answer is suggested by the ability of Shakespeare's John of Gaunt to see 'this England', standing alone, as 'this sceptred isle'.[6] Indeed, Clarendon's castigation of the myopia of those around him points to the prevalence in the prewar years of a similarly complacent Anglocentrism. But in the Republic, conquest and forcible union brought the relations among what had been the more or less discrete political units of Britain unavoidably into the view of politicians, of newsbook readers, and of those in the way of the marching armies. The process and the consequences of unification, and English responses to it, offer an unparalleled opportunity to study the sense of place held by those who inhabited the core state of 'the Atlantic archipelago'.[7] In the middle of the seventeenth century England came close to experiencing a genuinely British moment; that moment shows that if Britishness appealed little to those south – if not, significantly, north – of the border with Scotland, they were by no means immune to its effects. If the Scots and the Irish suffered from union, so too in other ways did the English. Indeed, the British problem was to prove as damned an inheritance for the Republic as it had been for Charles I, whom it had done so much to destroy.

II

The Commonwealth's eventual solution to that problem was a formal union of the three states of England, Scotland, and Ireland. Yet the shaping of the policy of union, far from pointing to some coherent and supranational vision in the fledgling Republic, in fact adds one more chapter to the familiar story of contingency and crisis. If empire was eventually acquired in a fit of absence of mind, so too was a united Britain.[8]

The pressure of circumstance is particularly clear in the shifting of policy towards Ireland. The domestic peace that came to England with the close of the so-called second civil war of 1648 – whose 'civil' dimensions were belied by Scottish invasion – was bound to signal major changes in relations with Ireland. The massacre of Protestant settlers in Ireland in 1641 and the near loss of the whole island to the forces of the Catholic Confederacy in the ensuing was ensured that England would, once it was freed from its internal distractions, pay closer attention to its western neighbour. Yet however turbulent and dangerous Ireland's recent history, there was little in Anglo-Irish relations in the 1640s – still less in republican ideology – to push England into its eventual course of formal union with what had so long been a dependency. The very antiquity of England's engagement in Ireland, and the cultural and religious differences involved, ensured that thinking rarely passed beyond a visceral determination to extirpate any remnants of rebellion.[9] The verdict of one newsbook early in 1652, that 'the only way to save that Land, is to destroy it', reminds us how easy Englishmen found it to avoid constitutional reflection when they thought of Ireland.[10] A correspondent of the journalist Marchamont Nedham reflected what was probably the English consensus when he hoped, as Irish resistance crumbled that year, that 'a short time will bring them all upon their knees, and make way for the doing Justice upon the bloody part of them that Englishmen may once more live in peace in Ireland'.[11] There is something typical too in Cromwell's utter certainty, expressed in his angry letter to the Catholic hierarchy at Clonmacnoise during the 1649 campaign, that the English presence in Ireland was in large part a matter of property rights, triable at law: 'Remember, you hypocrites, Ireland was once united to England. Englishmen had good inheritances, which many of them purchased with their money; they or their ancestors, from many of you and your ancestors.'[12] Such confidence is apparent as well in the repeated insistence – an insistence that wilfully ignored those so recently expropriated and suppressed – in Richard Cromwell's Parliament that the Irish 'are all English' and 'born free'.[13] The conviction – born of nearly five hundred years of involvement as well as of recent conquest – of the straightforwardly 'English' status of Ireland was widespread, though more complicated with bitter resentments, it was probably no more conducive to constitutional reform than a later conviction of the English status of colonists across the Atlantic Ocean was to prove. Only at the very end of the republic were English voices heard speculating on the proper constitutional relationship of Ireland to England. And when a few English MPs serving for Irish constituencies in the Protectorate's last Parliament argued vainly for a separate Irish assembly on the grounds of Ireland's distance from Westminster, they testified merely to problems that had arisen in the working out of union and the provisions of the Cromwellian Instrument of Government, and not to any recognition of a longer-standing dilemma.[14] Indeed, when Englishmen formulated what might be called a British policy, they did so towards Scotland and then applied it as an afterthought to Ireland.[15]

It is in the complicated dealings with Scotland that English assumptions and expectations about Britain must be sought. An independent unitary state in a way that Ireland had never been, Scotland had been linked to England primarily through the dynastic tie of the shared Stuart monarchy.[16] Although that tie was severed with the king's head in January 1649, the question remained whether a dynastic tie must be replaced with something else. The Republic's brutal assertion of its power against the Scots in 1650 and beyond has, in hindsight, assumed an air of inevitability. Yet at the end of his 1648 campaign against Scots royalists Cromwell seems to have hoped to leave the northern kingdom in the hands of the Earl of Argyll and his radical Presbyterian allies, whose animosity to the supporters of Charles I showed itself in that remarkable exercise in proscription, the Act of Classes.[17] In such calculations, the English army and its civilian allies would then presumably have been left free to pursue in England and its dependency, Ireland, a settlement without Charles I.[18] But these hopes, difficult enough of achievement, were rendered unattainable when, on news of Charles I's execution, Argyll promptly had the younger Charles Stuart proclaimed King of Great Britain, rather than merely King of Scotland.[19] The Rumpers, who during the last ten years might have been expected to have recognised the Covenanters' deep commitment to a shared British ecclesiastical – and hence political – destiny, were appalled. The likely consequences of the Scottish proclamation were not lost even on Scottish observers. Robert Baillie, who had been one of the Scottish deputation in London in the 1640s, despaired, 'One Act of our lamentable Tragedy being ended, we are entering again upon the scene'; one of his correspondents, equally gloomy, predicted, 'Let Scotland chuise what syde they please, that poor land sal be the seat of war, by al appearance, this summer.'[20] The prophecy missed by twelve months, since both the Rump and the young king judged Ireland more urgent. Yet even then the march of the English sword from conquests in Ireland to conquests in Scotland was by no means as inexorable as it is made to seem in the most famous depiction of these months, Andrew Marvell's 'An Horatian Ode upon Cromwel's Return from Ireland'.[21]

The Rump's posture towards what it declared to be the aggression of Scotland's proclamation of Charles II was at first firmly limited. The government's decision in the summer of

1650 to embark on a preemptive strike against the Scottish kingdom – a decision that drove the lord general, Fairfax, into resignation – may have been unusually assertive for a regime whose habitual posture was simply reactive.[22] But the Republic was by no means casting expansionist eyes northward. The declarations issued by both Parliament and army that summer insisted that England only sought punishment of the guilty, security against yet another Scottish invasion of her soil, and reparations for the last[23] – indeed, Cromwell himself continued to sing that tune long after the dramatic victory at Dunbar, up to the very eve of the Scots' collapse in August– September 1651.[24] The English authorities left the matter of Scotland's precise constitutional shape studiously vague. Not until its declaration of June 1650 – and then almost as an afterthought – did Parliament propose 'the furthering of a just Freedom, where God shall minister the opportunities.[25]

Such vagueness amounted not simply to a failure of thought but rather to a positive evasion of the issue. As late as October 1650, more than a month after Dunbar, the posture of the council of state remained fundamentally non-expansionist. The council then responded to a stalemate in the north that was constitutional almost as much as it was military by suggesting that the Scots go their own, monarchist, way – though with a king who would be less threatening to England than was Charles Stuart. The Council's preferred candidate for the Scottish throne was Charles's younger brother, the Duke of Gloucester. Cromwell for his part warned that the price for Scotland's retention of its independence and its crown would have to extend beyond the promises of non-intervention in England that the Kirk's leaders offered, to include the banishment or perpetual imprisonment of Charles.[26] Such plans came to nothing, for the Kirk no longer held the initiative in Scotland as it had before Dunbar, and in the following years the Republic formulated a bold solution to the old problem of the existence in the British Isles of three separate states.[27] Yet the reluctance with which the Rump and its successors developed a policy towards Scotland is unmistakable.[28] The English regime had far too many problems to risk plunging vaingloriously into a Scottish morass. The Scottish proclamation of Charles Stuart as a 'British' king, a proclamation that can only be seen as the fruit of intense Scottish commitment to a British ideal, therefore provoked an English invasion that would not otherwise have happened. Argyll's must have been one of the most fateful gestures in all the long and sorry history of Anglo-Scottish dealings.

Though the English authorities certainly had abundant interest in lulling their opponents by concealing hidden agendas, their protestations of disinterest were in line with what can be sensed of opinion in the country. In 1650 Thomas Violet, addressing the committee on trade, warned correctly of the economic and financial dangers of foreign military entanglements, that all would be 'carried away into Scotland'. A year later, in the immediate aftermath of Worcester, the Essex minister Ralph Josselin was performing similar calculations, writing worriedly in his diary, 'To destroy the nations were barbarous, to plant them with English colonies is very hard and unlikely, and Scotland will not invite our men, and yet this must be done besides good garrisons.'[29] English sources in fact reveal singularly little enthusiasm for the Scottish venture in its early months. The Herefordshire grand jury encouraged the Rump in its twin aims of security and reparations, since the Scots had 'for many ages heretofore bin infesters and Invaders of this Commonwealth, to the great impov'rishment of it'.[30] But the unusual nature of such an expression doubtless accounts for its airing in the press.

What the Rumpers heard more generally was a chorus of denunciation of the Scots – in itself grist enough to the regime's mill – coupled with calls that they be left well alone. Hostility from English Presbyterians towards moves to subordinate their co-religionists to the north was to be expected;[31] but there were less partisan grounds for doubt too. Though the author of *The False Brother*, one of the most impressive publications of 1650, began irenically, wishing that the Scots 'may . . . live as happily without us, as we can do without them', his consciousness of 'the disproportion between our Nation and Scotland, in our enjoyments, and priviledges' led him to the forceful conclusion that 'we can get nothing worth our labour and cost in Scotland'. In no way, he argued, could 'power and domination' be the English aim in invading Scotland, 'seeing it would cost us more to gain such a power, than ever we could get by the most intire communion in it; and it would be a sad exchange for English men to remove from such a fertile and flourishing Nation, to make a plantation of the fag end of the Creation'.[32]

As late as November 1651 Col. John Jones agreed, writing from Dublin that the English demand for reparations would require the payment of 'a greater account than all Scotland is worth'.[33] The diatribes against the barren, inhospitable land to the north and against the brutality, bestiality, and hypocrisy of its inhabitants, which run as an unceasing refrain refrain through all the newspapers from the moment the army crossed the border, could have left the Rumpers in little doubt of the sentiments in articulate quarters about a closer approach to the Scots.[34] It is no wonder, then, that the first mention in the press of wider war aims should have been so hesitant and apologetic. Four months after Dunbar an army spokesman in Edinburgh pleaded for support for 'the subduing of this People, who have so often prejudiced the People of England by making Inroads, and spoiling the Inhabitants; what say you, if their necessities and our own carry us on so far, as to see the necessity of making this a Province to England ... there being little hope of security upon other Terms?'[35]

And indeed, the initial response of the republic to its next great victory, in the late summer of 1651, was simply to seek to dismember its helpless neighbour. England would, as the aborted bill put it that autumn, appropriate 'so much of Scotland as is now under the Power of the Force of this Commonwealth', presumably in the confidence that internecine feuding and strategic garrisons would neutralise any danger from the Scots in the remaining portion. When the newspapers had stressed that for the most part of countryside 'to Edinburgh' – the region firmly under English control – 'is as fertile for Corn as any part of England', such a decision was rational enough.[36] It was also entirely consistent with a strategic vision that had tantalised in turn Edward I, Edward III, and Edward IV, and with the Rump's earlier insistence that England's war aims were security and reparations. As Cromwell had found to his cost in the demoralising months both before and after Dunbar, the line between the two Firths, of Forth and Clyde, by way of Stirling, was eminently defensible; and the rich lands south of it would, once they had recovered from the devastation wreaked on them, amply repay England for what any Scots forces had done to the northern counties between 1640 and 1648. But by November the Rump's plans had changed decisively.[37]

The Rump in the winter of 1651– 52 opted for an incorporating union of Scotland with England, instead of annexing it as a conquered province, and in so doing wrote one more chapter into the Scots' catalogue of English hypocrisies.[38] The decision, taken under Cromwell's prompting,[39] has been plausibly presented as a response to the realisation that only such a policy would block Charles Stuart's efforts to reorganise in what he sought to make his northern kingdom. Incorporation was also urged at the time as cheaper in the long run than forcible annexation.[40] And in the threatening climate of the 1650s, with its recurrent fears of a Franco-Spanish alliance against republican England, even the most phlegmatic could see the defensive advantages of union. In union lay security, as the Lord Chief Justice was to remind the Norfolk assizes in 1657[41] and as speaker after speaker intoned in the debates in Richard Cromwell's Parliament. Thomas Scot the commonwealthsman, though opposed then to the continued sitting of the members for Scotland and Ireland, was nevertheless able to observe that at most a single voice had been heard raised in the Rump against the principle of union.[42] But however powerful the defensive arguments, the new policy also had more positive appeal.

Paradoxically, incorporation affirmed the English sense of themselves, and in particular of their generosity. What might be called the orthodox self-image of he English was proclaimed by the solicitor-general at the treason trial of the Presbyterian minister Christopher Love in the summer of 1651: Love had intended that 'the free, and noble, and magnanimous people of England, should be made vassals and contributaries to the Scots Nation'. Love's proved an unpardonable offence, for, as a pamphleteer wrote, 'they are our inferiors, and we a free people'.[43] The subtlety of the Spanish in devising forms of subjugation and subordination was something of a byword.[44] But, judged one commentator, 'if we look on the English as Conquerors, we find them herein also generous, and that in all places where they have been Masters, they have shown the truest effects of commendable and noble dispositions'. In contrast to Spanish conduct in the Indies, 'Where shall we find a People Conquered by Arms, used with more moderation and gentleness, then the Scots are at this time by the English? If these have overcome them, they have recompenced it, with introducing more Liberty and greater Priviledges then they had before.'[45] The argument of benevolence formed a central element in England's 'British' ideology just as it was to do when Britons later developed the theme of 'the white man's burden'.[46]

Assumptions of English paternalism arose easily enough when the objects of English attentions were the Gaelic-speaking Catholic Irish, for whom even confinement in proximity to English settlements was – if it was not foolhardy – an act of kindness and betterment.[47] But the English had had unwelcome experience during the 1640s of Scots 'blue-bonnets' too. Impressions formed in the earlier wars were only confirmed by repeated news stories during the early stages of the conquest of the sheer credulity, superstition, and backwardness of the Scots – especially in face of the eclipses of 1652 – and of the 'peevish insolent obstinacie' of those who inexplicably preferred to be shot on the spot rather than be marched captive into England. The English programme in Scotland could therefore also be presented as one of 'Civill proceedings against Incivillity'.[48] Such a representation was doubtless all the more convincing after 'many thousands of tatterd Scots', the remnants of the 'Barbarians' defeated at Worcester, had been paraded through the city in September 1651.[49] Concession to such a people could only be an act of magnanimity, to be expected of the liberal English. The applause of the soldiers gathered around the Mercat Cross in Edinburgh to hear the reading of Parliament's declaration of union in 1652 was a token of the army's 'complying with the parliament in their free conferring of liberty uppon a conquered people'. Rather more pointed was the demand of the governor of Ruthven Castle, urging the leaders of the Badenoch region to submit in 1653: 'is not the State of England immediately about to incorporate and make yow one free Commonwealth with themselves, and what greater favour could they cast upon yow?'[50] Those involved in the conquest of Scotland, from Cromwell down, certainly prided themselves on the philanthropic aspects of that overthrow of Scottish Kirk and nobility whose strategic advantages were so plain to see;[51] but the very act of incorporation was a token that English hearts were in the right place.

Union, however, did more for the English than simply affirm their self-esteem. The suddenness and the scale of the Scottish collapse in the late summer of 1651 – with the seizure of its government at Alyth proving as decisive as the destruction of its remaining army at Worcester – took Englishmen by surprise.

What Cromwell saw as the 'crowning mercy' others read more enthusiastically. Peter Sterry, one of the Cromwell's favourite divines, preached – under the patronage of one of Cromwell's close allies, Sir Gilbert Pickering – the 5 November sermon to Parliament in 1651, at just the time when the republic's policy was beginning to change. In this sermon Sterry held forth the union of the English and Scots Churches as the necessary reformation of a north from which Christ would ride in his chariot, as foretold in Ezekiel and Revelations.

> Is this then the Age? Is this the Land, in which our Lord Jesus ascends from the North? Doth he now call up the cloudes, and winds to minister to him? Doth he now from hence begin, as a Bridegroom to come forth from his Chamber, as a Giant, or Warriour refresht with Wine, to run his race, unto the Ends of the Earth? . . . It is so. The Lord is upon his white-horses of divine discoveries.

The time for winnowing, for the destruction of the old world, had come.[52]

Sterry was not alone – as indeed the invitation to him to preach and publish his sermon would suggest – in so typing the times. Henry Parker, who had been the most astute parliamentarian propagandist of the 1640s, recognised the appeal of the Commonwealth's conquests in the north to 'the Chiliasts'.[53] And in the country, Ralph Josselin's long years of millennialist excitement began, not with the execution of the king, which so aroused the Fifth Monarchy men, but rather with England's expansion the following year. Though he lacked the animosity of Cromwell, of Sterry, of Pickering, for the Presbyterianism of the Scots, he was convinced of the religious significance of the reshaping of Britain. It was in the autumn after Dunbar that he suspected 'that god was beginning to ruine the kingdome of the earth, and bringing christs kingdome in, and wee English should bee very instrumental therein'. As the young Charles Stuart's last strongholds in the Channel Islands fell at the end of 1651 Josselin foresaw the fall of the earthly city, 'except wee say its not compleate untill all he appendices of this crowne in Ireland and Scotland are reduced which wee expect shortly'.[54]

The case for unification was therefore driven by a powerful religious imperative. Although others were soon to put their own, secular, gloss on matters, the Rump's committee for Scottish affairs, which drew up the policy and the Tender by which it was offered to the Scots, was composed not of the classical republicans who might have been thought the natural constituency of a programme of expansionism,[55] but overwhelmingly of Independents and army officers.[56] In September 1651 Cromwell indicated his own preference 'for making it on[e] nation' rather than 'a conquest',[57] and this, with the composition of the English commission appointed in late October to go to Scotland to set union in train, points still more clearly to a policy conceived by the saints and the soldiers.[58] Those on the receiving end of the new policy had few doubts, hearing religious notes in the commissioners' explanation of their mission. Thus, John Nicoll, Glasgow's agent in Edinburgh, excoriated the conquerors who hoped 'that the name of a Nationall Churche may perische fra under Hevin and Britane'; he seems also to have detected millennial undertones to the terms in which the Tender of Union was offered to his compatriots:

> So excellent a blessing of God, as, since the world was, our predicessouris in this yland nevir tasted the lyke; and though the present generatioun do smart and suffer in this chaynge, yit the efter ages sall blis the Maker of heavin and earth, quho in his appoynted tyme hes brocht this great work to ane happie period.[59]

Union in the 1650s had a religious appeal, just as it had had for James VI and I, with his dreams of Christian unity. Indeed, for all James's eloquence, union received perhaps its finest accolade in the republican years, in the Shakespearian tribute paid by the deeply spiritual Sussex ironmaster Samuel Gott during the debate on the sitting of Scots and Irish representatives in Richard Cromwell's Parliament: 'The four seas do environ this happy island, as the four rivers did the garden of Eden.... This Union must be preserved by natural means, and not by force.'[60]

Although the religious radicals had fostered it, and although Gott and others might vest it with spiritual significance, union was nevertheless inseparably associated with the sword, in its potential as well as its origins. Those elemental forces that Marvell saluted in his 'Horatian Ode' on the forward march of 'restless Cromwel'[61] are evident in the cry of one of William Clarke's equally restless army correspondents in the spring of 1652: 'Wee shall rust heere for want of action, but this summer will bee spent in setling the 3 nations[;] against the next summer wee may thinke of action elsewhere.'[62] Similar confidence resounds in the posturings of armchair warriors in the 1650s, who pointed to Rome's failure to conquer Scotland as evidence of England's superiority to that empire, and as the warrant for their own predictions of glory.[63] The domestic as well as the external possibilities of the moment are apparent in the hundred pages of panegyric written in 1652 by Thomas Manley to the 'Lord Generall of Great Brittaine', entitled *Veni; Vidi; Vici.*

In the history of the revolution that spread from Whitehall to engulf the highlands and islands, the excitement born of the British conquests formed the matrix for a major ideological innovation – an imperialism rooted in the new British policy.[64] This was compounded of the British concerns of the saints and of the rather more expansionist outlook of the classical republicans. Indeed, even the army of saints, as it moved beyond the border, seems to have had a Roman model partly in view.[65] But the most systematic thought occurred elsewhere. Marchamont Nedham, the unsaintly editor of the government's newspaper, *Mercurius Politicus*, first conjured 'that prodigious Empire' of the Roman republic in the New Year of 1651– 2, in the aftermath of the battle of Worcester.[66] Admittedly he found little glory in such poor opponents as the Scots; rather, the particular excellence of the founders of Rome, 'that wondrous Empire that overshadowed the World', had been the fact that 'their first Conquests were laid in the ruin of mighty Nations, and such as were every jot as free as themselves'. Nedham then went on to glance unmistakably at the Dutch, a new Carthage, as suitable victims for this second imperial Roman republic.[67] Yet however much Nedham despised the Scots, they proved crucial to the classical republicans' vision. The edition of John Selden's *Mare clausum* that Nedham brought out in 1652 to justify the Commonwealth's war with the Dutch – an edition that, as has recently been shown, provided the founding text for the new maritime empire – made the point graphically, for its frontispiece trumpeted Cromwell's first, British, conquests on which Britannia's rule of the seas was to be based.[68] The gesture was repeated time after time, if less elegantly, in the following years.[69]

The most famous of all classical republican texts, James Harrington's *Oceana*, published in 1656 at the height of the controversy over the meaning of Cromwell's Western Design, most clearly reveals the role of the union of the commonwealths in the new imperialism.[70] The book begins, in its introduction, with an account of the present situation of Marpesia (Scotland) and Panopea (Ireland) and the contribution they could make to Oceana. Marpesia is 'the dry nurse of a populous and hardy people'; now, with 'the yoke of the Nobility . . . broken by the Common-wealth of Oceana' – a reference to what became the cornerstone of English policy in Scotland after 1650 – it will be 'an inexhaustible Magazeen of Auxiliaries'. The theme is taken up yet more emphatically in the Lord Archon's closing speech to his council, which heralds the Marpesian auxiliaries as a 'greater revenue unto you then if you had the Indies'.[71] Harrington here seems to be looking to Scotland's recent role as a furnisher of armies for repeated invasions of England and Ireland, and of regiments too in the service of every European Power.[72] And if the fate of Scotland may have done much to shape Harrington's outlook, the same can be said for Ireland. Of course, the settlement of Ireland by emigrants, and particularly by soldiers, from the mainland after 1652 was central to Harrington's theme of an expansionist republic of citizen-soldiers; but there is a still greater topicality in the introduction's discussion of Ireland. Here Ireland/Panopea is linked to the admission of the Jews, so lively an issue in 1655; Harrington laments that the occasion was not taken to turn the country over to that people who above all would have made of it 'an inestimable treasure' and of Oceana a true 'Common-wealth for increase'.[73] The pressure of such topical themes in the text suggest that the union of Britain, and the problem of what to make of it, was as important a stimulus to Harrington as the domestic context, the inception of the Cromnwellian protectorate.[74]

The imperial claims were scarcely the preserve of doctrinaire Harringtonians. Even in Scotland, hardly the beneficiary, Robert Baillie could note that Cromwell's expansionist foreign policy, with the 'high and advantageous designes' of Blake and Penn in distant oceans, 'did much please the spirits of the vulgare'.[75] Another convert was James Howell, formerly a devoted royalist, who had in 1650 dedicated his *Instructions and directions for forren Travell* to the young Charles Stuart in the hope that he would see 'Brittain . . . by a Charles be made Imperiall'. In his very successful *Som Sober Inspections* of 1655 Howell by no means abandoned his partisan past, for he congratulated Oliver through-out on his dissolution of the Long Parliament; but he went on to salute 'his Highness, whom all Nations cry up for the Hero of the times' and whose victories over the Scots 'did more than Roman Emperours, or after them, the Saxon, Danish, Norman, or English Kings cold ever do'.[76] George Wither began one of his most successful works with a paean to Oliver, 'Lord, of the noblest of all Soveraign Stiles, / Of Britain's Empire, Provinc-es, and Isles,[2] and though we might think few would have been converted by his execrable verse, the Protector at least seems to have taken him seriously.[77] Scholars have usually concen-trated on the conservative appeal of a new Cromwellian mon-archy; yet many at the time hankered also after imperial greatness. In 1655 the corporation of Harwich sent a petition of congratulations to the Lord Protector of the 'British Jerusa-lem',[78] and the rumours that Oliver would be made 'Emperor of Great Britain'[79] speak to what contemporaries took to be a leading feature of the new regime. The potential was certainly not wholly lost on those who held power. In his closing speech at the treason trial of Gerard, Vowel, and Fox in June 1654 Lord Commissioner Lisle sought to heighten the guilt of the accused by pointing to the implications of the plot for the approaching Parliament, 'never the like Parliament heard of for the interest of England, a Parliament for England, Scot-land, and Ireland'. And the Protector himself ranked the achieve-ments in Ireland and Scotland first among his government's merits when appealing to his second parliament.[80] No remind-er is needed that Cromwell passed by the opportunity to link his name, and a new style, with the new Britain; more remark-able is the failure of the republic in general to make more of the ideological and propaganda openings that its British con-quest had created.[81]

III

Both commonwealth and protectorate governments have often and justly been criticised for their ideological lameness; but their failure to exploit more purposively the new order can surely be traced to something other than mere pressure of events. English affectations of Britishness – then as, surely, now – were shallow, and the formalities of union and the glories of conquest did little to undermine a rooted English chauvinism. It is not insignificant that while Argyll proclaimed Charles II King of Great Britain, Oliver was proclaimed Lord Protector of the commonwealths of England, Scotland, and Ireland.[82] Like his compatriots, Oliver showed no willingness to follow an earlier Protector, Somerset, in offering the name of England as a sacrifice on the altar of union.[83] However much the state deemed itself a multiple commonwealth, policy remained strictly English;[84] and when most Englishmen spoke of 'Great Britain' they unapologetically intended 'England'.[85]

Indeed, the tendency to exclude neighbours increased in many quarters as contacts grew. Perhaps the classic example of the way familiarity bred distinction is provided by the dealings of the various inhabitants of the British Isles on the complicated terrain of Ulster. Newspaper reports and even government pronouncements made a point of separating English settlers from the 'British' – that is, Scottish – Protestants also found there.[86] More predictable, but perhaps more troubling, was the way national prejudices had rooted themselves deeper in the troubles of the 1640s. There were those who could recognise that others had claims to rights; and when he read of the remorseless work done by the English army against Scots as well as Irish, Ralph Josselin asked gloomily, 'What probability is their of continuing their command over them, for surely the seed of liberty will remaine in those nations'[87] But such scruples were rare. If the struggles of the 1640s were as much a war of three kingdoms as they were an English civil war, that may cast light on the relative politeness of the fighting among the English; but it also suggests that those struggles may have intensified national hostilities. The widespread slur against the Scots, which likened their handing over of Charles I to Parliament in 1647 to Judas's sale of Christ,[88] like the scale of the Cromwellian settlement of Ireland, speaks to the political consequences. The human consequences are evident in the notorious brutality shown to Irish prisoners of war; and as the squalid aftermath of the Battles of Preston and Worcester showed, the Scots were not immune to such prejudice.[89] Many in England would have sympathised with the complaint of a soldier indicted in the West Riding in 1651: 'They charge me with the killing of a woman, and she was but a Scotch woman ... the women in Scotland had murdered many Englishmen, and ... he would kill more of them if they came in his way.'[90] Indeed, even the relatively sensitive Colonel Lilburne could, when quartered in Scotland, refer as easily to 'these kinde of cattell'[91] as officers of a more recent age spoke of 'gooks'.

Other distinctions were less visceral but perhaps as influential in giving firmer shape to an English sense of identity. While the roots of Scottish affections for 'Great Britain' have recently been traced to defences against earlier English claims to overlordship,[92] English counterarguments grew increasingly articulate as the prospect of union loomed with the dynastic juncture of 1603.[93] Claims to nationhood were contestatory then, and they remained so.[94] One major product of the earlier controversy, A Restitution of Decayed Intelligence, in Antiquities, by Richard Verstegen, who has been called 'the ancestor of the Gothicists in England', was printed twice in the 1650s for an audience well primed to appreciate its case for the Teutonic origins and excellences of England.[95] The challenge posed by Scottish arguments ensured that even such unlikely bedfellows as John Milton and the Presbyterian lawyer William Prynne could in the middle years of the century make common cause in appropriating 'Britain' to England.[96]

English exclusiveness thus became increasingly self-conscious in these years, in part at least under the pressure of 'British' competition. The title of 'Free-born Englishman' which John Lilburne the Leveller accorded to himself in the later 1640s had a wider normative appeal than is often appreciated. He was not simply setting himself up against 'the Norman Yoke' of lordly power; he also had in view the Scots, the chief proponents of the religious tyranny he despised. His rhetoric was widely adopted. One distinctly non-Leveller attack on the Scots in 1650 denounced the northern kingdom for its long-standing conspiracy 'to enslave and abase this Free-born Nation'.[97] At the end of the decade, Col. John Jones in Ireland trumpeted 'the spirit of an army of Freeborne Englishmen', while the Norwich election address of the fervent commonwealthsman John Hobart early in 1659 is a long blend of Lilburne and Colonel Blimp, a promise 'to breake every Yoke from off our

Neckes, and to restore and establish agayne the auncient Government, Rights and Libertyes of this English Nation'. The implications of Hobart's position for Britain are apparent in his passionate appeal to 'the old English jealousy' when he challenged the sitting of Scots and Irish MPs in Richard Cromwell's Parliament.[98]

While the occasions for friction grew, little was published that might have engendered more informed and tolerant relations between the neighbours. The newspapers are full, at least until the collapse of Glencairn's revolt in late 1654, of military reports from Scotland, larded with haphazard efforts at recapturing Scottish place names and personal names – efforts that must have been all but incomprehensible to most readers who lacked maps. The newspapers are full too of partly gleeful, partly horrified, accounts of the endless bickering of the Scottish Presbyterian factions. But little of what might now be called 'background' came off the presses. As the work of conquest proceeded in the summer of 1652 a few descriptive sentences appeared;[99] and the newly reduced Orkneys earned one derisive travelogue, written, revealingly, not just to gratify curiosity but 'to provoke the appetite towards our government, whose bounds extend to above 150 miles' beyond the Scottish coast.[100] More ambitious was the carefully detailed account of the economic state of the Scottish coast produced for fiscal purposes for Broghill's council.[101] But even such pragmatic considerations left Scotland at a disadvantage. Wide-open spaces and the prospect of profit seem to have been needed to shift the reading public's gaze from its traditional preoccupations on the European mainland. Even Jamaica, which like Ireland had land up for grabs[102] (and where face needed to be saved after the Hispaniola disaster), was the subject of a number of descriptive pieces.[103] In Scotland, though senior army officers in the early days of conquest seem to have evaluated the range of Scottish landed estates pretty thoroughly, little profit was likely.[104] The daily contacts of the marketplace did little to increase familiarity, for English trade with Scotland was small in scale.[105]

The only major exception to the journalistic silence on things Scottish came in a spate of reporting on Scottish law, occasioned by the descent on Scotland of the English commissioners for the administration of justice in 1652. This unusual press attention might, however, have hindered rather than helped the

cause of understanding. The journal began by reporting more
than a little hopefully that 'There is little difference betwixt
our Lawes, save only in the Terms and Forms; they imitate us
English in most things.'[106] But they continued by fixing – in
tones whose air of studied superiority is unmistakable only on
the most salacious aspects of the Scottish taste for cases of
buggery, bastiality, witchcraft, adultery, and murder, 'the natural
crimes of the Country . . . though by the Scot looked upon as
venial sins', as one newspaper reported unctuously.[107] Such cover-
age, while provocative enough, was only temporary. Once the
initial phase of upheaval, and attention, was over, newsbook
discussion of Scotland – even more than of Ireland, where the
dynastic interest could be gratified by accounts of the progresses
of Henry Cromwell – settled into brief reports of the regime's
ceremonial.[108] Those reports may have been intended to reassure,
but scarcely to inform, an English audience.

    Journalistic and epistolary conventions were obviously involved
in such silences. As one correspondent from Edinburgh put it
in 1655, 'the peaceable and quiet condition of these parts, (doe
most justly and willingly) put a frequent stop to my pen, which
(otherwise) would be oftner imployed, though to your trouble.'[109] But such conventions cannot explain the general bar-
renness of the English presses.[110] That profit-hungry royalist
wordsmith John Taylor the water poet brought out a list of
Scottish kings in 1650.[111] But these seem to have been only
two real works on Scottish history published in London in the
1650s, both written by Scots and both posthumous. One, Archbishop Spottiswood's ecclesiastical history, was published not
as a contribution to an understanding of the union but rather
as an element in the Anglican polemic and memorialising of
the 1650s.[112] The other, less partisan and a classic of humanist
historiography, was by William Drummond of Hawthornden,
and its way through the London presses was paid for the by
another Scot, Sir John Scot of Scotstarvet.[113] It was not that
educated Englishmen were intellectually oblivious to Scotland.
While his council contemplated the commissioning of a history of the army's conquest of Scotland, Cromwell himself
treasured Drummond's work for what could be gained from it
for the cause of religious toleration;[114] and Milton and others
regularly mined the writings of James VI's tutor George Buchanan
for arguments for resistance to kings. But there was little sign

of any readiness to take Scotland on its own terms.[115] Perhaps the most telling evidence of English unconcern is the silence on Scotland – in contrast to the treatment of Ireland, whose helplessness invited speculation – in the overflowing correspondence of the Hartlib circle.[116] Apart from some patchy discussion of prospecting for precious metals,[117] the only sign of anyone looking north of the Tweed is a 1649 approach to the town council of Edinburgh – on the recommendation of a weary English council of state'. – by some Hartlibian projectors who had for three years been failing to interest the English Parliament in their proposals for improved herring fishing; to their distress, they were laughed out of the Edinburgh council chamber.[118]

The contrast between the English and the Scottish records of interest in a British identity is striking. One critic, castigating the Scots' constant 'thirst after the power and priviledges of this Commonwealth', warned that they had never loved Charles Stuart 'as King of Scotland, but of Great Britain'; he exaggerated, but in singling out the long-standing Scottish interest in a wider polity he had a point to make.[119] Certainly the Scottish equivalents to the Englishmen who meant only 'England' when they said 'Great Britain' can be found.[120] But on the other hand, probably nowhere can there be found a commitment to a wider British culture equalling that of Scot of Scotstarvet, who not only funded the publication of Drummond's works in London but also, and more signally, organised and paid for the printing of Blaeu's elaborate British maps. Urging Scot's case for support to the Lord Protector, Colonel Lilburne revealed English priorities when he noted, 'I finde the said mappes might be very useful to the army.'[121] Almost as impressive is the record of Sir Thomas Urquhart of Cromarty, one of the many European searchers after a universal language in the 1650s, who was taking his voluminous plans in the royal baggage train to have them printed in a conquered London when he had the misfortune to be plundered with the rest of the king's army at Worcester. Undaunted, he urged the example of England's treatment of Wales, and the authority of Virgil's 'divisos orbe Britannos'. in a plea for a glorious union.[122] Indeed, even the arch-fanatic Johnston of Wariston may not have been quite as purblind as he is usually thought, for he can be found reading Speed's *Chronicles* as well as the more predictable English controversialists.[123] Similarly, the network of English correspondents maintained during the 1650s by Robert Baillie, and Baillie's own passionate interest in a wider world, hint – as did the agents retained by the Scottish boroughs in London – at a society that could adapt to its British position.[124]

The pattern of individual and small-scale contacts a Scottish emotional or intellectual investment in Britain that does not square with the cynical interpretations usually put on the Scots' readiness to intervene in England in the 1640s and to proclaim Charles II King of Great Britain in 1649. Most early modern Englishmen assumed the sheer rapaciousness of the Scots; most modern English historians assume that the Scots aimed mainly at the protection of the Presbyterian Church order. Materialism and fear for he Kirk obviously cannot be discounted.[125] Yet the language of some of the replies[126] to the Tender of Union in early 1652, language uttered in quite unpromising circumstances and by no means always forced by the English sword onto those who vented it, suggests that even if many shires and burghs found the manner of the proffered union abhorrent, the principle still held considerable attraction, just as it had for Argyll. The embattled nature of the Scottish Reformation had worked on a long-standing interest in themes British – a response to English feudal claims on Scotland – to give Scottish apocalyptic thought, especially as manifested in the writings of John Knox, a peculiarly British character. Myopic the Covenanters of the 1640s may have been in their dealings at Westminster; but they were also seeking to realise the dreams of Knox.[127] True to that tradition, the deputies of Stirlingshire urged Parliament's commissioners to 'procure a speidie and happie union, that may maik the Nation inseperable, and so insuperable'. The 'gentlemen and heretors' of Morayshire objected forcefully enough to the Tender; yet they professed themselves eager otherwise

> to bee incorporated and made one with England, they being of all Nations dearest to us and cheife in our Affeccions and respect and with whom wee would Associate and take part against anie or all the Nations of the Earth . . . and being as it were naturally devidit from the rest of the world or in ane unseperable Contiguity so imbodied togeather as one of us cannot bee well without the other. This is that Designe which our fathers aimed at, as foreseeing how much Confusion and

blood might thereby bee avoidit and how much happines by the attainement thereof would accrue to the present and Generacions to Come.[128]

Just as some English millenarians could see in union a matter for exultation, so some Scots could see in it matter for hope despite the horror of conquest.

IV

Few of those hopes were borne out, it scarcely needs to be said. What closer ties with England meant in practice to Scotland and Ireland has been well surveyed by Lesley Smith and T. C. Barnard – the legal and institutional reforms petered out, and not even the Quakers had much energy to spare for evangelism elsewhere when there was so much to be done in England.[129] When a similar reckoning of the impact of union is attempted for England it yields a balance sheet scarcely more favourable. In no field, economic, ecclesiastical, or political, did union provide a clear record of the imposition of England's priorities and needs; nor did it bring England unmitigated gains.

The union was too short-lived for its economic effects to become clear; but the few visible signs were mixed. The economic recovery of the later 1650s brought the revival of irish agricultural exports to England[130] – a revival that was to incur much animosity from English landowners and politicians in the 1660s – and the advent of free trade with Scotland probably helped lower livestock prices somewhat as the path south for Scottish drovers was eased. But the limited contacts between and English merchant circles, the small tonnage of the shipping in Scottish harbours, and the fact that part of the Scottish distance trade was still channelled through a staple, at Veere in Zeeland, all suggest that Scotland's impact on England's economy was limited.[131] Scotland did not strike English observers as a land of opportunity, especially after the devastation cause by the recent wars. A handful of English tradesmen settled at Leith, the main supply port in the shadow of army headquarters, but Scottish borough regulations and the pessimism of serving army officers discourage any inrush of English profit seekers. As the

Receiver of the Scottish Exchequer reported gloomily late in 1655, 'Here is no encouragement as yet for any to come hither for trading.'[132] The direct repercussions of union were almost certainly localised, and limited to England's far north. There, controversy developed over the threat of Scottish salt, which thrived on lower wage rates, to the Tyneside salt pans, though tariffs did give some protection to its coal industry against the Scots.[133] Berwick-upon-Tweed, on the other hand – along with King's Lynn – boomed in the 1650s as a staging post and supply point for troops bound for Scotland.[134]

One indirect economic consequence of the closer integration of Britain was undoubtedly more significant than the petty gains in trade. Historical demographers have calculated that in the 1650s England experienced, proportionately, its highest rate of emigration until the later nineteenth century. The bulk of these unfortunates travelled not to the New World but to Ireland in search of subsistence on the lands and in the houses of that still more unfortunate group, the Catholic victims of the Republic's reconquest.[135] The churchwardens' and overseers' accounts of parishes in western England abound, especially in the bad years of the early 1650s, with records of petty doles paid to paupers of all sorts on their way to the Irish Sea ports.[136] In that sense Ireland played a valuable role as a safety valve – less politically, for any danger of popular insurrection was by then over, than economically, in allowing England to recover from the terrible hardships of the later 1640s.

If Ireland's suffering contributed to England's unsteady progress in the later seventeenth century towards economic growth, so the peripheries played an unwitting and an unwilling part in the growth of a colonial empire too. Until the full development of the African slave trade, the colonies from Virginia southward into the Caribbean remained perennially short of labour. In the early seventeenth century various ad hoc and unsystematic addresses to the problem had been made. To meet the needs of the Virginia Company, physical coercion was sometimes added to the economic constraint of indentured servitude, as City magistrates sought to off-load helpless paupers, with the occasional blessing of the privy council. The policing element in such a response to labour shortage became more apparent as it briefly enveloped English felons and Irish troublemakers around 1620.[137] The sudden and dramatic increase in the numbers of prisoners under English control at the end of the 1640s – at a time when turncoats willing to enlist in parliamentarian regiments were no longer needed – dramatically changed the dimensions of policy. English and Welsh prisoners from the 1648 fighting transported 'beyond the Seas . . . to America, Venice, or as they shall be appointed', were early victims of what became the regularised practice of penal transportation.[138]

The extension of transportation to Scotland and Ireland affected both the numbers and the quality of the victims. The losers in war in Ireland and Scotland had long paid the penalty for their mistakes, for their religion, or for their clan name by emigration; the 'flight of the earls' from Ulster in 1607 is only the most famous episode in a history that had provided mercenary regiments for most of the belligerents in Europe. The victor of course watched happily as potential troublemakers were removed to fight and die abroad. Accordingly, capitulation agreements during the wars of conquest and reconquest from 1649 to 1654 often contained clauses permitting the vanquished to take their men into the service of a foreign power, provided that power was not hostile to the Commonwealth.[139] But complications arose. At least until 1652 or 1653 there were few powers which were not hostile to the Commonwealth; furthermore, after Dunbar in particular the sheer number of prisoners, and the impossibility of returning them to a still-belligerent Scotland, precluded an orderly recruiting effort. Despite Cromwell's denial that he intended 'to make merchandize of men, or to get a gain to our selves',[140] the Rump was driven to seek a way out of its embarrassment by allowing the northern potentate Sir Arthur Hesilrig to draft captives from Dunbar into the Tyneside coal mines; Cromwell's concern for the Protestant interest in Ireland, but very soon private enterprise had to be co-opted and the Rump's friends among the City merchants were shipping them off to New England.[141] Another flood of prisoners in the following year, from Worcester, set the Council of State looking again, if only briefly, to the New World.[142] The progressive collapse of resistance in Ireland, coupled with the danger of renewed instability during the transplantation of Catholics into its western provinces, gave a new urgency to this solution, and in April 1652 Parliament referred to the Council of State the matter or transportation

of Irish prisoners abroad. Soon, transportation to the plantations of Barbados was in full swing.[143] Within a year the council, on the familiar assumption that idleness was the raw materials
of political dissidence, had extended the penalty of transportation from those taken in arms to the idle poor in conquered
areas; in the view of the Venetian resident, England was thus
approaching a solution to the problems of Catholicism in Ireland and of labour supply in the colonies.[144]

The outbreak and then the quelling of Glencairn's revolt in
1652–4 occasioned the extension to Scotland of a method of
pacification whose appeal was a much social as political. The
singling out there of 'idle rogues' as well as belligerent clansmen
underlines the connection between methods of control in the
conquered territories and those that were in 1655–6 to be applied
against potential troublemakers in England during the rule of
the major generals.[145] The systematic transportation to the colonies of reprievable English convicts began with a warrant to
the magistrates of Surrey in August 1655.[146] The need to deal
with the subjugated peripheries, first by disposing of the surplus
of prisoners and then by forcibly pacifying discontented and
impoverished regions, had thus set a pattern for the use of
human resources throughout Britain for an overseas empire.

But such an imperial posture could not be without its costs.
However much the acquisition of empire affirmed providentialists'
sense of divine mandate, it may conversely have helped sap
the self-confidence of a regime whose ideological origins could
be traced back to the Self-denying Ordinance of 1645. Misgivings
naturally centred on Ireland: there was little for the fortune
hunter in Scotland apart from opportunities for advance up
the army's career ladder[147] and petty shakedowns and poaching
for the common soldiers.[148] But Ireland offered opportunities
aplenty to the covetous. It was no accident that Colonel Fenwick,
commanding in Edinburgh, dreamed of sending Johnston of
Wariston, perhaps the greatest single obstacle to the smooth
exercise of his command, to Ireland; there, Fenwick told him,
he 'might maik a fortune'.[149] Lord Deputy Fleetwood would
have been appalled, for he urged Secretary Thurloe in 1654
that only such officers be sent to Ireland who were 'fearing
God, able, and hateing covetousnes the great temptation of
Ireland which most that comes if not impowred with a very
selfe denying spirit wil fall into'. Indeed, the English officers

in Ireland saw settlement as in all likelihood a moral disaster, and petitioned for the total displacement of all Catholics, not so much to avoid religious contamination or physical danger but rather to save the English from themselves, by removing 'those temptations . . . as in reference to gifts, rewards, and other advantages; as also in usurping and exercising of Dominion over them in waies of oppression'.[150] Empire, with all its trappings, could prove unsettling to the truly godly,[151] as one admiralty official affirmed when he denounced 'the vaine pomp' of the stately funeral of Henry Ireton, Lord Deputy of ireland, finding it 'very offensive to many a gracious soule that desired to walke slowly with the Lord'.[152]

The conquered lands exacted toll from England in ways that were central to the self-definition of the republic. Self-denial was one element in the ethic of godly republicanism; the other was of course moral discipline and reformation. And here the impact of the periphery on the centre is clear, if unexpected. The high point in England's moral campaign is often taken to be the 1650 Act against fornication and adultery, an Act which is usually described as in part a response to Ranter excesses and in part the culmination of a century or more of moralist impulse.[153] But in Scotland in 1649 the search for a cause of that divine displeasure that had brought political and military disaster, combined with the growing fears of sectarian contamination from England, produced a remarkable series of moralist statutes, even fiercer than England's adultery Act.[154] The possibility that the latter was to some extent a reply to the former is suggested by the fact that some in the two nations were quite literally playing holier-than-thou.[155] When the doomed Scottish Parliament in 1650 enacted that for the 'doun bearing of sin and filthines' no woman should sell ale or wine in Edinburgh, the Leith garrison soon responded with a similar order for its confines; and English military punishments on dissolute soldiers were, as Scots approvingly noted, harsher than the already harsh punishments of the Kirk.[156] But the clearest evidence that one party looked at the other through its moral programme is provided by the English commissioners for the administration of justice in Scotland. At their first session one of their number

made an elegant speech concerning the occasion of their

meeting and to take off some aspersions which were laid upon the parliament by the Ministers of Scotland as to the tolerating and countenancing of Heresies and Blasphemies whereas the parliament of England had by severall Acts declared against all Evills of that Nature and more particularly against swearing, breaking the sabboth and the like and gave directions for reading the Act against Heresies etc.[157]

In its constitutional form as well as its dominant ethic the Cromwellian regime was, paradoxically, shaped by its British subjects. The confusion over the revision of the protectoral constitution in the Humble Petition and Advice occasioned an interminable and acrimonious debate in Richard Cromwell's Parliament over the sitting of the members for Scotland and Ireland. Time and again English members observed that since the quorum for business in the Commons was forty, the combined group of sixty members from the peripheries could – given the prevailing but of course unacknowledged absenteeism – sway the House. For as members pointed out as frequently, the Humble Petition had itself been passed by only three votes in a House whose Scottish and Irish members were overwhelmingly governmental loyalists. To the commonwealthsmen who so opposed the protectorate, the very constitution had in a sense been imposed by the peripheries on the centre.[158] As John Hobart graphically put it, 'They have fully morallised that Fable of the Pigg that having by squeaking first got in his nose not onely soone got in his wholl body, but crowded away the Children from the fyre.'[159]

But it was in the dynamics of politics that the making of Britain had the clearest impact on England. More than perhaps anything else, the union underlines the fundamental dilemma of the republic. Facing Stuart challenges in both Ireland and Scotland, the Rump in 1649–52 determined to subjugate or destroy its enemies; but, as Marvel so presciently warned, the sword once drawn must remain erect.[160] In December 1654, 42,000 out of Commonwealth's total establishment of over 53,000 troops were serving outside England and Wales.[161] Force, so necessary for survival, itself undermined the regime, for the armies cost money: even though both Ireland and Scotland were taxed at, proportionately, considerably higher rates than was England,[162] the regimes there never broke even.[163] Maurice

Ashley estimated that 'the net cost of the union [with Scotland] to England was at least £130,000 a year', a figure that represents, roughly, 10–20 per cent of the varying level of the monthly assessment on England during the protectorate.[164] The impact of Ireland on the government's budget was similar. Clarendon regarded Ireland as 'the great capital out of which all debts were paid', and it is true that in the short term the availability of Irish lands to satisfy the arrears of unpaid troops helped stabilise the republic.[165] Yet in the longer term the verdict must be very different, since the Dublin administration ran constantly at a sizable deficit.[166] Taxation in England therefore remained at politically unacceptable levels, which in turn required a larger military establishment within England. The anger shown in the assessment debates in Parliament in 1657 suggests members' consciousness of the imbalance: more far-sighted observers recognised as well the hidden economic costs of the diversion of so many resources to the task of holding down hostile populations.[167] The Republic's failure to normalise its position in the core state, to gain a greater measure of acceptance, thus owed much to the fiscal consequences of its projection of its might. The misgivings of all those who had in 1650 warned against the conquest of Scotland were borne out. When the largest part of a hugely expensive army was committed to sustaining that rule beyond England's borders, it can be argued that the British Problem brought down the republic almost as surely as it did the early Stuart monarchy.

Successive attempts to deal with the British Problem during the revolutionary years had a longer-term significance. Not only did the costs of too close a relationship provide an object lesson for the future; the group identifications that the episode inspired – not only among the Scots and the Irish[168] but among the English too – shaped future choises. While republicans, whether classical or providentialist, might have found England's British rule consoling, the number Englishmen who had anything positive to say for their British neighbours had been vastly reduced. Yet there was a symmetry in the final outcome. If the Scots and the Irish gained little beyond bloodshed and fiscal exactions, much the same can be said of the English.

9. Divergence and Union: Scotland and England, 1660–1707

MARK GOLDIE

I

The Anglo-Scottish Union of 1707 used to be regarded as a preordained element in the building of the modern British state. The union of crowns in 1603 and the Stuarts' exercise of government from London made the fuller incorporating union of parliaments seem the logical next step. And the flourishing of Great Britain for more than two centuries after 1707 offered the comfort of hindsight. Consequently, an old series of books recounted the history of the Union as a 'natural consummation' or 'natural evolution' which mature statesmanship had brought to pass. Several of these books coincided with demands for Scottish Home Rule, which grew up in the 1880s and rumbled on until after the Great War. Most were hostile to devolution, emphasising the good sense and mutual benefits of 1707. They also tended to be burdened with three articles of late Victorian faith: the destiny of the British Empire, the Darwinian evolution of strong nation-states, and the doctrine known as legal positivism – the idea that statehood requires a single, untrammelled source of legislative sovereignty, and that that source must lie at Westminster. The Union was thus seen as an historical and juridical necessity.[1]

In the Europe of the 1990s orderly federal devolution and disorderly break-up of multi-national states proceed apace. The fusion of ancient independent nations which had occurred in many of the centralising states of early modern Europe no longer seems predestined.[2] In 1992 polls recorded three-quarters of the Scottish electorate favouring a Scottish Parliament of some sort. In a television debate a studio audience hooted down the English presenter who remarked that 'Scotland agreed to the

Act of Union in 1707.' In this debate there seemed no oddity about drawing parallels between Scotland and Lithuania or Catalonia. Equally it was no surprise that a Conservative former Secretary of State for Scotland intoned the old Unionist dogmas: that the Scots derived enormous benefits from the Union and that autonomy would be fatally destructive to the sovereignty of Westminster.[3]

A devolutionary impetus has been vigorous in Scotland since the 1960s and has made its mark on the historiography of the Union.[4] This is not to say that historians simply follow political impulses, rather that nobody can now readily speak of a high road to Union. Recent accounts persuasively contend that the supposed unfolding destiny of Union cannot be sustained. The starting point is an insistence on difference and divergence. Before 1560 England and Scotland were two of the most hostile nations in Europe; between 1639 and 1652 Scottish armies invaded England four times and an English army crushed the Scots at Dunbar and imposed a military occupation. Despite the regal union of 1603 the two nations remained politically, socially, culturally and religiously distinct. Moreover, it is plausible to claim that they were growing further apart during the seventeenth century.

This is apparent if we compare the two union proposals made a century apart. When James I and VI attempted a union in the early 1600s its terms were more extensive than those achieved in 1707. He sought a union of law and religion as well as of parliaments. It is crucial to appreciate that in 1707 there was a union of parliaments and economies, but not of law or religion or education. The Scottish courts, the Presbyterian Kirk and the educational system remain distinctive to this day. During the great flowering of intellectual life in the Scottish Enlightenment of the eighteenth century the mental and institutional fabric of the law and the Church sustained an autonomous polity and national identity even without a Parliament. Whereas the Hanoverian government closed down the troublesome Convocation of the Church of England, it never dared to interrupt the General Assembly of the Church of Scotland. The paradox remains that, for all the vaunted legislative omnicompetence of Westminster, metropolitan governments have had to respect what the Union officially was: a free treaty between two nations, circumscribed by limits and conditions. The

Union has accordingly never been as complete as that of, say, Brittany with France or Aragon with Castile.

Moreover, the Union did not achieve overnight the homogenising of two distinct social and economic structures. That came gradually during the eighteenth century, through the intermingling of elites – the anglicisation of the nobility and the lairds – and the application of political management. It came more rapidly with the deliberate crushing of Highland clan society in the aftermath of the last Jacobite Rebellion of 1745–6. Rarely has a project of social engineering been so deliberately undertaken, to create a 'polite' and 'commercial' society out of a 'rude' and 'barbarous' one. One legacy of the successful redirection of loyalties was the disproportionate presence of Scots in the British army. The putting of Scots into uniform and sending them on imperial missions abroad was a masterful instrument of assimilation. By the 1770s even Scotland's Roman Catholic bishop was ready to ship his popish and erstwhile Jacobite Highlanders to North America to fight the rebellious colonists.[5] It reminds us that there is a complex and lengthy social history to union as well as a legislative one.

During the eighteenth century Scottish intellectuals gradually sloughed off the old patriotic rhetoric of a proudly independent kingdom and began to see pre-Union Scotland as a backward periphery badly in need of modernisation. The remedy for Scotland's incivility lay in getting copies of the *Tatler* and *Spectator* from London coffee-houses into Scottish parlours. It became fashionable to speak not of Scotland but of 'North Britain'. At the extreme, it could be argued that Scotland experienced a radical failure of nerve that led to a severe case of 'retarded nationalism' in the nineteenth century, when other European nations experienced an ebullient self-assertion. It was at least the case that Scotland acquired a complex dual identity, a civic Britishness overlying a Scottish cultural identity.[6]

II

The Union sponsored convergence: it was not sponsored by it. We need now to explore the evidence for divergence before 1707. The experience of the Covenanter Revolution of the mid-seventeenth century and of the subsequent restoration of the

Crown and episcopal Church after 1660 drove a wedge between the two nations in five ways.

First, the memory of the Cromwellian union of 1654, achieved by conquest and more complete than that of 1707, left deep scars. This cut two ways: it led to a fear of being forcibly absorbed by English institutions, but also to a fear that English aggression was the price to pay if Scotland chose to go its own way. At Dunbar and Worcester in 1650–1 Cromwell punished Scotland for setting up Charles Stuart as an independent monarch in his ancient kingdom, a situation which, as we shall see, was echoed in the crisis of the early 1700s.

Secondly, the Covenanter Revolution had entrenched Presbyterianism more deeply in Scotland's religious consciousness, at least in its strongholds south of the River Tay. The Scottish Reformation had already followed a more radical path than England's, although its dismantling of episcopacy was incomplete and a degree of semi-episcopalian compromise had been achieved in the Jacobean period. The Covenanters had abolished episcopacy altogether, and in the 1640s the ideology of the National Covenant entailed the exportation of Scotland's purer Reformation to England. For some Scots a demand for union flowed from an apocalyptic vision of Scotland's God-given destiny as a new Israel, a chosen instrument of a perfected Reformation. In a weaker form this idea was kept alive in James Kirkton's *Secret and True History of the Church of Scotland* (1678), which demonstrated that Scotland had been less corrupted by the papacy than England. Conversely, English churchmen became fearful that union threatened an expansionist Calvinism intent on destroying episcopacy and the Book of Common Prayer. Talk of union in 1689 provoked the Anglican William Beveridge to denounce it as a Trojan horse designed to spread Presbyterianism south of the border.

During the Restoration the Covenanter tradition in Scotland became hardened and incorrigible under persecution. Episcopacy was reimposed in 1661, no General Assembly was permitted, ministers were humiliated by being forced to re-enact their ordination, and the appointment of parish ministers was put into the hands of lay patrons. Two-thirds of parish ministers acquiesced in the settlement, but one-third were ousted – many more in Ayrshire and Galloway – leaving congregations unministered or resentful of the new men intruded. Despite the Act against Conventicles of 1662, which outlawed non-parochial gatherings for worship, illegal 'field conventicles' flourished.

It is true that many Scots, especially the nobles, combined the remnants of a Covenanting faith with support for bishops as a counterweight to the theocratic and populist radicalism of the 1640s. But, in contrast to England, episcopacy had neither deep roots nor social power, and the Scottish liturgy (or rather lack of it) remained alien from Prayer Book Anglicanism. Some of the ousted clergy utterly repudiated the Restoration regime, denouncing Charles II for apostasy to the Covenant he had signed, and castigating the restored episcopate as a Babylonish and papistical tyranny. The new bishops were seen to be turn-coat Presbyterians or doctrinaire prelatists, malleable to royal will. The hardline Covenanters staged two rebellions, in the Pentlands in 1666 and in the south-west in 1679, both bloodily suppressed. The second uprising led to ferocious military policing of the south-west during the 1680s which has gone down in Presbyterian martyrology as the 'Killing Times'. The record of fines, imprisonments, the seizure of horses and arms, and summary executions, was preserved by Robert Wodrow in his *History of the Sufferings of the Church of Scotland* (1722). In Scottish historiography all too much has hung upon quarrels over the authenticity of Wodrow's catalogue of atrocities. A bitter flurry of pamphlets in Victorian times debated the evidence for the Wigtown Martyrs: were a widow and a maid really tied to stakes on the shoreline and left to drown in the rising tide?

A signal event was the assassination in 1679 of the Scottish primate, Archbishop James Sharp, by a group of Covenanters alleged to have sung psalms as they thrust swords of Godly righteousness into him. Sharp had once been a Presbyterian; he had turned to episcopacy and the suppression of dissent. English Tory propagandists trumpeted the murder as proof that Presbyterianism bred fanatical anarchism and that the English Whigs were heirs and neighbours to revolutionary Calvinism. This ploy of using Scottish religious extremism to frighten the English was an old one: Bishop Bancroft had used it against the Puritans in the 1590s.

The third disparity between the two nations was the greater extremity in the character of Scotland's political regimes. The constitutional revolution of 1641 limited the Scottish Crown

more than the English, while the Royalist counter-revolution
of 1660, and its reinforcement in the 1680s, rendered Scotland more demonstrably an absolute monarchy. Parliament had
never mattered as much in Scotland as in England, and the
use of the same word 'parliament' disguises significant dissimilarities. The Scottish Parliament had only a single chamber;
commoner representation from the shires and burghs was er-
ratic; its business was rigidly controlled by the Lords of the
Articles; and (in contrast to the appellate jurisdiction of the
House of Lords) it had no right to hear legal appeals from
the Court of Session. It was closer to the sort of extended conciliar court that the English Parliament had originally been.
Although it developed legislative autonomy and constitutional
weight with remarkable rapidity in the 1640s and again in the
1690s, it was not a body upon which could readily be grafted a
theory of an Ancient Constitution, in which Parliament provided the historic counterbalance to monarchy – the Whig historical doctrine which nourished the English parliamentary
tradition.

Through their resistance to Mary Stuart and to Charles I
the Scots had come to see their polity as a monarchy regu-
lated by the nobility. In humanist rhetorical guise, provided
by the scholar George Buchanan in the late sixteenth century,
this was glossed as the wise patriotic counsel which the *primores
regni* gave their king. Scotland was thus akin to the Continental pattern of a shifting relationship between an absolutising
Crown periodically opposed by a *thèse nobiliaire*. It was a doctrine of aristocratic rather than parliamentary balance. And
whereas the English wrote histories of Parliament, the Scots
wrote histories of magnate families. Gilbert Burnet's way of
expressing a Whiggish history was to recount *The Lives of the
Dukes of Hamilton* (1677).

During the Restoration, however, the nobility offered no coherent threat to the Crown. Demoralised, divided, and heavily
indebted after the failure of the Revolution, and fearful of the
theocratic pretensions of the radical clergy whom they had unleashed, they either unflinchingly served the Crown or withdrew into political quietism. Practically all Charles II's Scottish
ministers – Lauderdale, Middleton, Rothes, Tweeddale – were
old rebels who had turned their backs on the Covenant. The
Covenanting preachers of 1638 had echoed Buchanan's ideal

of an aristocratic commonwealth, but after the nobles deserted them the rebel preachers of the Restoration became populists, lashing out against oppressive landlords and servile courtiers. Tracts such as *Naphtali* (1667) and *A Hind Let Loose* (1687) voiced the most radical utterances of the time, explicitly defending the right of any godly individual to engage in terrorism. Only in the Earl of Argyll's rebellion in 1685 did a magnate take arms, and he did so in forlorn and incompetent isolation.

Into the vacuum left by the demise of the Covenanter Revolution stepped an absolute monarchy. In England there was a vigorous ideology of absolutism and some of its political instruments, but the civil and social infrastructure made for an ambiguous polity. In Scotland a purer form was possible. In 1661 the Act Rescissory annulled all legislation since 1633, imagining away the whole Revolution, and the Act Concerning Religion placed ecclesiastical power directly in the Crown's hands. The key text of Covenanting revolution, Samuel Rutherford's *Lex Rex* (1644), was publicly burnt. For most of Charles II's reign Scotland was in the grip of his viceroy Lauderdale, who boasted that 'never was king so absolute as you are in poor old Scotland'.[7]

In the early 1680s Scotland became a Royalist laboratory for James, Duke of York, the Catholic heir to the throne. When the English Whig opposition tried to exclude James from the succession, Charles sent him to Edinburgh, where he contemplated establishing his future reign and dissolving the dynastic union, should his southern kingdom repudiate him. The Scottish Parliament of 1681 was used to stage an ideological refutation of the claims of the Whig-dominated English Parliament. The Succession Act declared the inviolability of divine hereditary right. The mythology of Stuart hereditary succession was revived: whereas the English Crown had often been usurped and violently overthrown, the Scots had ever been loyal. The 1685 Excise Act proclaimed that 'this nation hath continued now upwards of two thousand years in the unalterable form of our monarchical government, under the uninterrupted line of one hundred and eleven kings'. The iconographic representation of this line is visible at Holyrood House in Jacob De Wet's fanciful paintings of 1684–6 depicting those one hundred and eleven kings, by turns valiant and pious, but all exhibiting the Stuart physiognomy. The flourishing circle of absolutist episcopalians, led by the Lord Advocate Sir George Mackenzie (who founded the Advocates Library, and was known by his enemies as 'Bluidy' Mackenzie for his part in the Killing Times) and Sir Robert Sibbald (who founded the Royal College of Physicians), offered a viable independent culture for James should England turn Whig.

The fourth divergence of Scotland from England during the Restoration years lay in the formalisation of the distinctive tradition of Scottish law. This was partly Mackenzie's doing: his *Treatise Concerning Matters Criminal* (1678) became the standard authority on criminal law. But it was mainly the work of James Dalrymple, Viscount Stair. Like many others, Stair was a soldier of the Covenant turned Restoration royalist. However, his loyalism had bounds in that he fled abroad in the 1680s, leaving his son Sir John to serve James II and VII – their enemies alleged that father and son connived to hedge their political bets. Stair's *Institutes* (1681) provided a massive synthesis of Scots law. He showed how the Scottish legal mind was more philosophical and systematic than the pragmatic and piecemeal mode of English common law, and he revealed the debt of Scots law to the European tradition of Roman or Civil Law. Stair extolled the virtues of flexibility and inventiveness in the historical evolution of customary law, while brilliantly demonstrating how the clutter of case law precedents could be intellectually organised on rational principles. He showed how Scottish law could be shown to reflect divine and natural law, and how it could be reformed by selective importation of Civil Law principles. One legal historian has judged that Stair's *Institutes* 'to a substantial extent created modern Scots law', and that without it, Article 18, guaranteeing Scottish law, might have been absent from the Union Treaty.[8]

Fifthly and finally, there were dissimilarities of social structure. Scotland was much poorer than England. It was dominated by a small magnate elite, who controlled vast territories – 'petty principalities' in Adam Smith's phrase – and who had inordinate power over their benighted tenantry. This resolution of social power into a few hands – the dynasties of Hamilton, Queensberry, Buccleuch, Athol, Gordon, Tweeddale and Argyll – had had no parallel in England since the close of the Middle Ages. There were only about fifteen hundred people who might be called gentry – the entire shire electorate amounted only to two thousand – and most of those were Lowland 'bonnet lairds', the equivalent of an English yeoman farmer. The gradual emergence in the century after 1660 of an autonomous gentry class is a phenomenon scarcely yet investigated. Scotland's condition was the object of English contempt, given colour by xenophobic caricature. *A Modern Account of Scotland* (1670) described Scotland as 'one large waste', where the nobility treat their tenants 'worse than galley slaves', keep a gibbet near their houses, conduct 'butcheries . . . in their feuds', and exercise that most notorious of patrimonial privileges – that cynosure of a primitive society – the right to 'first board all the young married women within his lairdship'. The author of *Scotland Characterised* (1701) remarked that when the devil offered Christ the kingdoms of the world he put his thumb over Scotland as offering no temptation.[9]

To dwell on Anglo-Scottish divergences is, in one important respect, misleading, for gradually the disjunction came to lie less in the contrast between England and Scotland, than in that between the Highlands and Lowlands within Scotland. Increasingly the tendency of Lowlanders was to emulate English economic and social developments. In the eighteenth century the Highlands represented everything contrary to civilisation: they were a byword for Jacobitism, backwardness, superstition and popery. In the 1770s, Adam Smith's sharp perception of how capitalism produces a radically novel and preferable social and moral order had much to do with a Lowland Scotsman's keen awareness that a poor, pastoral, pre-modern and dangerous world lay not far to the north. Given the dependence in turn of Karl Marx's treatment of the transition from feudalism to capitalism on Smith's idea of social stages, one is tempted to say that the modern world's most famous theses about modernisation stemmed from reflection on the Highland/Lowland divide. Even Sir Walter Scott, who gave to Highland Jacobitism the romantic glow which still warms it, emphatically shared the Enlightenment view that Highland society was an anachronism, the dying voice of a primitive society on the margins of modernity. This treatment of the Highlands as an underdeveloped periphery of the British Empire began early. In the 1680s the godly scientist Robert Boyle sent bibles to the American Indians, the Irish and the Highlanders. Writing of the Highlands in 1700 a Scots Presbyterian minister complained, 'has not Britain laid out much greater sums on colonies abroad of not half the importance of civilising and improving this part of Britain itself that has been so long a nuisance and reproach to the nation?'.[10]

This kind of fearful condescension towards the Highlands can be deceptive. It is true that some events served to confirm an impression of feudal barbarism. The Keppoch murders of 1663 offered the spectacle of two Catholic brothers riddled with stab wounds, and then of their avengers displaying the murderers' severed heads. The Highland Host of 1678 saw the use of Highland military units to terrorise the Covenanting farmers of the south-west. Yet changes in architecture bear witness to the successful pacification of Scottish society: after 1660 fortified tower houses were no longer built. Recently historians have been keen to point out, in an anthropological spirit, that the equation of social difference with barbarism should not always be taken at face value. The 'civilising' imperative often amounted to the imposition of rackrenting landlordism in place of clan patriarchy, which was grounded in local personal allegiances and hereditary kinship obligations. The Highland system of settling disputes in independent courts and by private bonds and treaties could be effective in keeping the peace, even if it offended against projects for bureaucratic and judicial centralisation. In any case, clan chiefs frequently lived double lives: they were peers and courtiers, perhaps with a French education, as well as warriors with kilted retinues. The main agents of 'civilising' the Highlands on behalf of British overrule, the Argyll dynasty, were themselves ruthless clan chiefs.

Scotland's decentralised polity and distinctive social system had not posed serious threats to the stability of the medieval monarchy, whereas in England between 1399 and 1485 the crown changed hands violently six times. That polity only became a threat after the Covenanting period, as Scotland was drawn into the dynamics and imperatives of pan-British reckonings. The ferocious campaign against the Covenanting cause waged by the Marquis of Montrose and Alasdair MacColla in the 1640s embroiled the Highlands in strategies that spanned all three kingdoms. MacColla's atrocities marked the importation of the savagery of the Irish Counter-Reformation wars, and in so far as his cause exploited clan hatred against the Argyll fiefdom, which provided the backbone of Covenanting, he created the tradition of Highland Royalism and resistance to militant Protestantism which later inextricably linked the Highlands with the Stuart and Jacobite cause.[11] By temporarily suppressing Argyll in the 1680s the Duke of York inherited Highland support even before he became king. Thereafter, the dynastic issue ensured that the solution to the Highland 'problem' lay in the imposition of Britishness.

III

Given all these divergent tendencies, we cannot presume that there was a long-term gravitational pull towards the Union. Instead we must look to specific circumstances which arose after the Revolution of 1689. The Union did not emerge from a withering away of differences, but as a result of particular crises, in fact from an increasingly dangerous conflict brewing between the two nations.

During the 1960s and 1970s a series of books and articles greatly expanded our knowledge of the precise configurations of Anglo-Scottish politics after the Revolution. William Ferguson, on the one hand, was deeply hostile to the Union, his account vividly anti-English. Patrick Riley, on the other, believed that the Scottish Parliament deserved its abolition, for it had degenerated into a corrupt tool of magnate faction: Scotland was 'well rid of it'. Yet both had in common a grimly Namierite view of history: they were preoccupied with factional intrigue, personal ambition and chicanery. The Union, on both views, was marked by bribery, arm-twisting, devious manoeuvre and hypocritical propaganda. Ferguson called it 'probably the greatest political job of the eighteenth century'. For Riley, 'the Union was made by men of limited vision for very short-term and comparatively petty, if not squalid, aims'. Christopher Smout has criticised both positions as overblown. He reminds us of the powerful contemporary perception of the need for economic union in order to save the Scottish economy. Scotland's medieval trade had mainly been with the Continent, but after 1560 it was increasingly dependent on England. Trade crises in 1667, 1670, 1681 and 1689 led the Scots themselves to make overtures for a commercial union. Free trade was always the Scots' fundamental desideratum for union, and in 1707 they achieved Europe's largest free trade area.[12]

The worst legacy of the prevailing historical approach is that it negates the role of political ideology – the arguments of principle which raged within and between the two nations. A modern bibliography of the Union controversy runs to 535 items.[13] These include treatises, pamphlets, sermons and poems, on the constitution, the Church, the succession, the fishing industry, the malt tax, and economic growth. There were the melodramatic – *Scotland's Tears*; the portentous – a tract on the providential appearance of whales at Kirkcaldy; the utopian – schemes to unite all the British Protestant Churches; and the antediluvian – assertions that the Covenant forbad the Union. The debate drew upon the talents of Daniel Defoe, and produced a political theorist of significant stature, Andrew Fletcher of Saltoun. It will not do to dismiss the Union debates as empty talk and cynical window-dressing, yet because of the hold of such a view the intellectual history of Scotland in this period is only just beginning to be explored. None the less, the modern wave of scholarship has crucially stressed what we must now explore more closely: that out of long-term divergence came a contingent political and economic crisis which made it imperative to secure a union.

In the decade after the Williamite Revolution, Scotland, and specifically its Parliament, became unmanageable, and the Scots came to have profound reasons for dissatisfaction with any kind of union, even that of Crowns. William III was deeply resented and his ministers proved incapable of working with Parliament. In pragmatic terms we might see this as a classic instance of the failure of Court management of political elites. In constitutional terms we can identify a conflict between two models of the polity. On the one hand, the Court or executive point of view, which held that there can be no stability unless the Crown secures its will in Parliament: assemblies are instruments of government and must in the end co-operate with government. On the other hand, there stood the Country, or Patriot, or quasi-republican view. This held that assemblies embody the political nation at large, and have a right to act independently of Court interference, and to legislate free from executive interference. In the context of multiple kingdoms, this doctrine took on a federal complexion, asserting the rights of provinces against the metropolis. The idea of a radical separation between legislative and executive powers, and of the autonomy of periphery from centre, eventually found expression in the American constitution. Whenever it reared its head within the Thee Kingdoms, however, it was successfully slapped down by the imperial power. This occurred, in conditions of near secession, in the Anglo-Scottish Union of 1707; and in a parallel way, after the constitutional revolution of 1782 and, in conditions of actual rebellion in the 1790s, in the Anglo-Irish Union of 1800.

The Scottish version of the ideology of devolution burst forth in the remarkable Parliament of 1703. But we first need to examine the three components, parliamentary, religious and economic, of Scottish dissatisfaction and of Anglo-Scottish breakdown during the 1690s.

The parliamentary revolution of 1689 took a more aggressive form in Scotland than its equivalent in England. It is true that the Claim of Right[14] was, like the English Declaration of Rights, a recitation of ancient rather than novel or abstract rights, and true that it was not imposed on William and Mary as a formal condition of their crowns. But the terms of James's deposition were more forthright: he was said to have forfeited his crown because he had 'invaded the fundamental constitution of the kingdom and altered it from a legal limited monarchy, to an arbitrary and despotic power'. There were only five dissentient voices; the Jacobite Party under its leader, Viscount Dundee, had withdrawn, and soon launched the first of the Jacobite rebellions. The Convention, contrary to William's wish, abolished the Lords of the Articles, the committee which had hitherto controlled parliamentary business, and debarred officers of state (unless nobles) from voting. This created a political vacuum, for there had been little need hitherto for the development of the English practice of informal management through the building up of Court placemen and spokesmen. The Scottish Parliament began to exercise extensive independence in calling to account ministers and policies. This was the work of the 'Club', led by Sir James Montgomerie of Skelmorlie, who, after eagerly advocating the deposition of James, soon turned to inflict humiliation on William and his ministers, seeking to trammel as many of the royal prerogatives as possible. Paradoxically, Montgomerie's republican distaste for the absentee and authoritarian Dutch king drove him towards Jacobitism, thus inaugurating a strong political tradition of Whig Jacobitism.

From a Country or Patriot point of view, the Club had created an opportunity for a free and uncorrupt Parliament, able to secure the liberties of the nation. This project had parallels in England, in Sir Robert Harley's Country Party, which put limitations on the Crown into the Act of Settlement of 1701, and later in Viscount Bolingbroke's campaign against the executive tyranny of prime minister Sir Robert Walpole. But in Scotland its appearance was more dangerous. As the case of Montgomerie illustrates, the Patriot ideal attracted a combustible mixture of ill-matched causes: downright republicans, like Andrew Fletcher, who would reduce the Crown to a cipher; Jacobites, who wanted to restore the Catholic house of Stuart; radical Presbyterians, who despised English episcopacy and still hoped to export the Calvinist reformation; and powerful magnates dangerously detached from government influence.

From the Crown's point of view, and that of Unionist historians, an uncontrolled Parliament became a scene of chaotic factionalism, in which Country principles were seen as ideological posturings designed to raise the stakes in magnate jockeyings for the spoils of office. Four great dynasties contended: Hamilton, Queensberry, Argyll and Atholl. On their coat-tails were political families who zigzagged between office and petulant withdrawal. There was an inexhaustible supply of time-serving Dalrymples active in Scottish politics for decades. Certainly the magnates bargained for high stakes. A spectacular case occurred in 1705, when Argyll, chosen as the English government's plenipotentiary for securing the Union, demanded a dukedom and generalship for himself and a peerage for his brother, the latter of whom threw a tantrum when he was refused the provocative title of Dundee. Yet 'magnate factionalism' can be an unhelpful catch-all: it is the argument of those who see the Union as saving Scotland from its own squalid incompetence, and who detect political immaturity in any system other than the Westminster and executive model.[15] In 1698 an angry Country Party demanded action on the famine and trade crises, but courtiers prevented votes on these issues: it is not obvious that the former should be described as irresponsible wreckers. As Bruce Lenman has remarked, Scotland's unique achievement of parliamentary independence, in the face of Williamite centralisation, marked 'a temporary reversal of the sustained attempt by the British government to deprive the events of 1688 of any long term significance'.[16]

William III had little understanding of Scottish politics and allowed himself to be advised by a narrow group, dominated by returned exiles: Carstares, Melville, Burnet and Dalrymple. The keenest symbol of the king's ineptitude was the massacre of Glencoe in 1692, ostensibly a disciplining of Jacobite rebels, committed on the order of Sir John Dalrymple, but long carrying the suspicion of a retribution wrought by Campbells upon Macdonalds.

A second type of disruption in the Scottish polity lay in the Church settlement of 1690. The General Assembly was summoned for the first time since 1653. It was dominated by a clique of Presbyterian ministers, the remnant of those who had been ejected in the purge of 1660–2, together with some who had been in exile in the 1680s. Chief of them was William Carstares, who had been put to torture in Edinburgh, had plotted in Holland, and whose grip on the post-Revolution Church earned him the sobriquet 'Cardinal Carstares'. The Assembly declared itself to be the established Church of Scotland, and the parliamentary Convention acted in tandem with it. King William had hoped to mollify both religious parties, but the refusal of the entire episcopate to acknowledge his rule left the way open for the Convention's abolition of bishops as 'a great and insupportable grievance'. It went on to abolish lay patronage: the right of nobles and gentlemen to appoint parish ministers. In the following years, by a mixture of violent 'rabbling' and dubious legal measures, episcopalian ministers were driven from their parishes. About half of all incumbents were purged. In 1697, in order to demonstrate the greater godliness of Scottish religion compared with the laxity of England, a young theology student, Thomas Aikenhead, was hanged for heresy, the last such execution in Britain. Likewise sermons on the occasion of the burning of the Renfrew witches were an opportunity to assert Scottish superiority against the pollution of unbelief and immorality that infected England.[17] In 1698 the Assembly reaffirmed, at least verbally, one of the fundamental tenets of the Covenanter tradition, the independence of the Church from the state. Its declaration that 'Jesus Christ is the only Head and King of his Church' was a rebuff to William and to erastian Anglican notions of the civil supremacy.

After their 'rabbling' the episcopalians became an untolerated sect, and, often together with the nobles to whom they were chaplains, became instinctive Jacobites. Some engaged in skilful polemics against the new religious order. *Scotch Presbyterian Eloquence* (1692), regularly reprinted until the nineteenth century, offered a 'gallimaufry of enthusiastic zeal, fun and nonsense of the Presbyterian preachers'. The intolerant settlement of 1690 was not only a source of instability in Scotland, but also enraged English high churchmen, who had been forced to concede toleration in England to Presbyterians and other Protestant dissenters. After the Union, the high Tories did their best to spite the Kirk through legislation at Westminster. The Toleration and Patronage Acts of 1712 were a deep affront and amounted to a breach of the guarantees to the Kirk embodied in the Union. The restoration of lay patronage – abolishing the right of the Church to select its own ministers – was to be the cause of sectarian disruption in the Scottish Presbyterian Church well into the nineteenth century: it was England's bitterest legacy to Scotland.

The third crisis for Scotland in the 1690s lay in economic disaster. After 1660 Scotland had only a limited share in England's commercial prosperity. Her trade, like Ireland's, was discriminated against by the Navigation Act of 1651, which prevented Scottish ships from carrying English goods, by several Restoration statutes, and especially by the wartime embargoes imposed in the 1690s. The Scots pinned high hopes on the herring industry as a key to commercial wealth. Though they could not match the Dutch factory ships, which packed and salted herring without touching land, they at least prided themselves on having a technical superiority over the English. England's closure of the French market after 1689 was catastrophic. Even worse were the harvest failures between 1695 and 1700, leading to a famine in which, through starvation and emigration, Scotland lost between 5 and 15 per cent of its population. Among desperate remedies proposed was Andrew Fletcher's for the revival of slavery on the ground that paternalist protection was preferable to the immorality of a failed marketplace. Economic pamphleteers began to say that since the Crown inevitably put England's economic interests above Scotland's, the Crown's influence must be removed from the conduct of affairs. But they also castigated the callous landlordism of the magnates and urged an emulation of the English system of tenant farmers and freeholders. Convergence with England was as plausible a remedy for social ills as independence from her.

In an effort to revitalise Scotland's economy, by borrowing the English model of colonial merchant adventures, the Company of Africa was launched, massively capitalised by a large segment of the Scottish elite. In 1698 the company established a colony on the isthmus of Darien in Panama, and with some foresight envisaged a canal joining the Pacific and Atlantic Oceans. But Spanish territory had been violated at a time when England was in alliance with Spain against France. The English ambassador in Madrid was forced to repudiate the Darien scheme in the name of the Crown. By 1700 the colony had failed appallingly, with considerable loss of life from disease and Spanish attack, and with massive financial loss. As much as one-sixth to one-quarter of Scotland's liquid capital had been thrown away by an English betrayal.

IV

These dislocations form the background for the Scottish revolt against English rule in the 1703 Parliament. The immediate prelude to the crisis was the problem of the succession. In 1700 Queen Anne's only surviving son, the Duke of Gloucester, died. In 1701 the English Parliament passed the Act of Settlement which placed the Crown in the House of Hanover; it did so without consulting the Scottish Parliament. In 1702 William III died and Louis XIV of France recognised James II and VII's son, the Old Pretender, as King of England and Scotland. The war being fought with France was therefore as much the War of the British Succession as it was the War of the Spanish Succession. The Scottish succession remained unresolved, and Scotland was unavoidably a player in the international contest. The Highland Jacobite rising of 1689–92 had made Scotland a threat to the new dynasty and a tempting locale for diversionary military expeditions by Louis XIV. A year after the Union, in 1708, a French naval force was to sail into the Firth of Forth in expectation of a Jacobite rising.

From 1701 until 1705, when it was finally brought to accept the Union, the Scottish Parliament went its own way. Far from declaring for the Hanoverian succession, the 1703 session passed a series of hostile Acts directed against English authority. The

Act of Security asserted that unless England granted free trade with Scotland, including freedom to trade with the colonies, then Scotland reserved the right to settle the Crown differently from England after Queen Anne's death. The Act Concerning Peace and War awarded Parliament control over foreign policy after Anne's death. And the Wine Act snubbed the war blockade by allowing the import of French wine.

The government in London accepted the second two, and in 1704 even conceded the first. It was desperate for money to fund the Duke of Marlborough's campaigns, and the Scottish Parliament made supply conditional on capitulation to their terms. The royal prerogative and the power of the metropolitan executive had been drastically curtailed. One commentator said Scotland was now like Poland, Europe's most notoriously enfeebled monarchy, where the Diet did what it liked. Gilbert Burnet wrote that 'a national humour of rendering themselves a free and independent kingdom did inflame them'.[18]

Indicative of the degeneration of Anglo-Scottish relations was the Worcester affair of 1704. An English ship of that name was seized in the Forth for alleged customs offences. Its cargo was impounded, and its officers tried on a flimsy charge of piracy and sentenced to death. The Edinburgh crowds bayed for blood; the government in London demanded a reprieve; the Scottish administration would not, or dared not, act; and the captain and two officers were executed.

The politics of these years consisted of complex manoeuvres and alliances, involving much chopping and changing of political tactics. Unstable ministries were patched together by Godolphin and other English ministers. We need not get entangled in their byzantine complexity, but we should note the essence of it. The Court appointed a commissioner for each parliamentary session who was meant to secure a majority for the government. In 1703 the Duke of Queensberry tried and failed. Against him stood a rainbow coalition of at least five distinct causes: the Jacobites, of whom the best known is George Lockhart (whose memoirs are a major source of evidence); the 'Patriots', the doctrinaire republicans led by Fletcher; a pragmatic Country Party, led by Tweeddale, soon called the Squadrone; diehard Presbyterians; and magnate factions who would not truck with Queensberry, including the duke of Hamilton, who half-heartedly entertained a claim of his own to the Scottish throne. This affinity of strange bedfellows was not only a political expedient, but had become a characteristic of Scottish cultural life. (In 1700–3 Sir Robert Sibbald, Jacobite and episcopalian, worked closely with Presbyterian virtuosi on a scheme to establish a Royal Society of Scotland: his membership list is a tally of Country Party leaders, especially the Hamilton and Tweeddale connections, as well as Darien directors and subscribers.[19]) After Queensberry's abject failure, Tweeddale took office, with a show of being a Patriot who would be uncorrupted by office, and who would secure the succession by embracing schemes of limitations on the prerogative. But the Tweeddale session of 1704 failed too.

When the succession question first became pressing, in 1701–2, William III made tentative overtures for a fuller union. The Patriot victory of 1703–4 was therefore achieved as a self-conscious rebuff to union. The huge pamphlet controversy which erupted was explicitly concerned with the cases for and against a union.

The Patriot position was not republican in a literal sense: rather than abolish the monarchy it aimed to reduce the Crown to a figurehead. Nor did it propose total separation of the kingdoms, but a federal relationship. These ideas were expressed in purest form by Andrew Fletcher, who, if regarded as a marginal visionary by political historians, remains both a signal intellectual influence on the Scottish Enlightenment and a keystone in the Scottish nationalist tradition – today the Scottish National Party's discussion society is called the Andrew Fletcher Society. The French philosopher Rousseau contemplated writing a life of Fletcher, in which the Union would be shown to be one of the classic evidence of the corruption of modern civilisation, the servile sacrifice of a once vigorous small nation to a monstrous empire. Fletcher was a powerful orator, a religious sceptic, and a professional rebel. He had had soldiers quartered on him for his opposition to the Duke of York in the early 1680s; he fled to the Continent; took arms in the Monmouth Rebellion in 1685; was condemned to death in absentia; and sailed with William of Orange. Then, like so many of the Revolution radicals, he became disillusioned with William's rule. His early publications condemned the standing army as an instrument of Courty tyranny, and proposed instead a national citizen militia. He won the applause of the Jacobite

Lockhart, who called him the Cicero of the Country Party. 'The indignities and oppressions Scotland lay under galled him to the heart . . . he exposed them with undaunted courage and pathetical eloquence.'[20] Although it has been easy to describe Fletcher as a precursor of modern liberal nationalism, he was profoundly 'antique' in his commitments, a product of the Renaissance obsession with the ancient and austere civic virtue of the Greek and Roman city states. The Spartans, he noted, had a free state for eight hundred years, and the Swiss cantons were the happiest and freest states in the world.

Fletcher pronounced that Scotland had become 'more like a conquered province than a free independent people', and must liberate herself from 'perpetual dependence upon another nation'. He constantly condemned the 'horrid corruptions' of the English Court, and the bleeding dry of Scottish pockets since 1603. His own scheme of limitations on the Crown was drastic indeed, and reflected the platform of the Covenanting Parliament of 1641. There were to be annual Parliaments, electing their own president; for every new peerage creation there was to be a new commoner MP; all officers of state and judges were to be chosen by Parliament; the royal veto on legislation was to be abolished; in between the meeting of Parliaments a council chosen by Parliament would govern; Parliament was to have a veto over foreign policy; there was to be no standing army without Parliament's permission; a citizen militia was to be created; and no general pardons were to be issued without parliamentary consent. The final clause was the trump card: if the monarch broke these rules, the crown was to be declared forfeit. Such a scheme, Fletcher said, would make Scotland's Parliament 'the most uncorrupted senate in Europe'.[21]

For Fletcher this reconstruction of civic institutions would be the prelude to social and economic regeneration. He did not, like other celebrants of ancient virtue, resort to an arcadian sentimentalism and deplore trade and market economics as harbingers of decadence and oppression. He roundly condemned feudal Scotland and the rackrenting by idle noblemen, and hoped for the promotion of commerce. But equally he thought that the hankering after a stake in England's commercial system was naive. His *Account of a Conversation* (1703) is a profound analysis of the position of subordinate provinces in such a system. Poor countries suffer more than they gain from a rich metropolis: they have the advantage of low wage costs, but the disadvantages of underdeveloped expertise and of the immobilities of a rigid pre-modern social structure. A union, he said, would lead to England draining Scotland of its resources, and the Scottish elite becoming absentee riders on the metropolitan gravy-train. He used to the full the parallel of Ireland's plight. In the 1690s the English Parliament, with West Country textile interests to the fore – represented no less by Whig philosophers like John Locke as by high Tories like Sir Edward Seymour, one of the interlocutors in Fletcher's semi-factual *Conversation* – had, in the passage of the Irish Woollen Act, dismantled one of Ireland's key industries. As one modern historian has put it, 'the casual brutality of England's destruction of the Irish woollen trade' was plain for any Scot to see.[22]

In his utopian moments, Fletcher dreamed of a pan-European federation of small, free and non-expansionary republics. Within the British Isles, London, Bristol, Exeter, York, Norwich, Edinburgh, Stirling, Dublin, Cork and Londonderry would be regional capitals. It was a vision grounded in the Greek polis ideal, of city-states with their agrarian hinterlands, autonomous but associated in a commonwealth. His vision belongs to a tradition that can be traced back to Dante's celebration of city-states, independent and at peace under a benign and nominal universal emperor. It was also a riposte to two rival models of international relations in his own time: the Counter-Reformation aspirations of Spain and latterly France to a universal tyrannic Catholic empire, and the theory of a balance between major superpowers who engrossed small states under their supposedly protective wings.

Other writers on the anti-Unionist side explored the historical and constitutionalist case for Scotland's independence. This debate was in part an off-shoot of a quarrel in the late 1690s about the position of Ireland. In 1698 William Molyneux's *Case of Ireland* had denied England's right to legislate for Ireland. It quoted John Locke's *Two Treatises of Government*, which argued, in defence of the overthrow of the Stuarts, that a people are only subject to a regime to which they have given their consent. Molyneux's was the first of several occasions when the English were to be embarrassed at the unintended uses to which Locke could be put. Molyneux was answered by an English Whig lawyer, William Atwood, who asserted England's right of conquest over Ireland. The Scottish parallel to Molyneux was a Presbyterian journalist called George Ridpath, who in 1703 published *An Historical Account of the Ancient Rights and Powers of the Parliaments of Scotland*. He tried to manufacture a Scottish Ancient Constitution grounded in a parliamentary tradition. He also published Sir Thomas Craig's contribution of 1603 to the Jacobean debate on union, *Scotland's Sovereignty Asserted*, which, among other things, celebrated Scotland's martial glory in comparison with England's proneness to foreign conquest by Romans, Danes and Normans. Ridpath added to his constitutional case the suggestion that a Union would be an affront to the Covenant and would open the Scottish Church to being taken over once more by episcopalians. Atwood answered Ridpath with *The Superiority and Direct Dominion of the Imperial Crown of England over the Crown of Scotland*, which argued that Scotland was merely a province of England, its Church part of the jurisdiction of the Archbishop of York. It was burnt in Edinburgh by order of Parliament. Locke's friend James Tyrrell similarly argued that the Lothians had been part of the Saxon kingdom of Northumbria. Ridpath was not alone: Jacobites like Sibbald, Pitcairne and Ruddiman endorsed Country principles and likewise dwelt, in Sibbald's title, on *The Liberty and Independence of the Kingdom and Church of Scotland*.

The pro-Union case is generally regarded as less intellectually absorbing, but it was no less compelling. Daniel Defoe, the prodigious propagandist, journalist and novelist, was hired by the London government to convince the Scots of Union. He relentlessly extolled the economic virtues of free trade, warned of the imminent collapse of the Scottish economy, and promised commercial and agrarian regeneration as the fruit of Union. The choice lay between 'peace and plenty' and 'slavery and poverty'. He argued that the rhetoric of Scottish independence was an empty fantasy: Scotland was a bankrupt backwater in need of a firm dose of English commercialisation. The truest patriotism, echoed Sir John Clerk of Penicuik, lay in the pursuit of economic improvement. William Seton of Pitmeddon agreed: 'this nation, being poor, and without force to protect its commerce, cannot reap great advantage by it, till it partake of the trade and protection of some powerful neighbour nation'.[23] Queen Anne's episcopalian physician, John Arbuthnot, said that union would liberate the Scottish tenantry from the

petty tyranny of the nobles. Although historians find it hard to
dispute the economic case in the long term, there is no doubt
that Defoe offered an overly sanguine analysis. Inequitable taxes,
the myrmidons of the customs and excise bureaucracy, and a
deliberately curtailed wool trade were the stuff of resentment
for a long time to come. They spilled over in the Porteous
Riots in Edinburgh in 1736 (which formed the basis for Scott's
novel, *The Heart of Midlothian*).

It is mistaken to assume that the only Unionist card was economic. Seton and the Earl of Cromartie offered a political analysis
also. They extolled the virtues of unitary parliamentary sovereignty and a strong executive: liberty did not lie in the chaos
of a government hamstrung by checks and balances. They urged
that imperfect federal unions did not flourish: in the unions
of Denmark with Sweden, Aragon with Castile, and Portugal
with Spain, the weaker party always suffered. Only full integration with the metropolis dissolved the disadvantages suffered
by unequal partners. Cromartie delivered a lesson on the European balance of power, on Bourbon aspirations to universal monarchy, and on the nonsense of Little Scotlander ideology amidst Great Power politics. His cry was 'May we be Britons,
and down go the old ignominious names of Scotland, of
England.'[24]

V

The mystery is not why the Scots took a tough stand in 1703,
but how they came within a very short time to accept the incorporating Union. In September 1705 the key vote for Union
was passed. Argyll (in tandem with Queensberry) succeeded
where Queensberry (alone) and Tweeddale had failed, and they
reaped their reward by dominating Scottish politics for the next
generation. So dramatic was the *volte face* that historians' attempts to provide explanations seem scarcely satisfactory. It
certainly eased matters that guarantees were given for the independence of the Church, the courts, the universities, and
the burghs. The Act of Security for the Church in 1706 guaranteed the Kirk 'in all succeeding generations'. But more material considerations weighed heavily too.

The importance of political management cannot be denied.

The English government administered large doses of patronage: peerages showered from London, including dukedoms for Queensberry and Roxburghe. Secret offers to Hamilton were suspected: his last-minute switch of sides provokes one historian to remark that it was 'one of the most unscrupulous but successful acts of treachery in the whole of political history'.[25] There is a long tradition holding that Scottish politicians sold their country for lucre, and even the most ardent Unionists among historians have conceded a certain lack of 'pecuniary disinterestedness'.[26] In 1711 the English prime minister Robert Harley frankly said, 'we bought them'.[27] Three financial settlements were offered: 'the equivalent', a sum of £400,000 credited to the Scottish revenue to offset liability for a share of the English national debt; a lesser 'equivalent' to buy out creditors who had suffered in the Darien disaster; and about £20,000 in cash for 'expenses' and arrears of payment to office-holders. Once Union came to seem inevitable, the further temptation to jockey for position to control Scottish seats in the united Parliament became irresistible. The allocation of seats in the new House of Commons was generous: Scotland's forty-five constituted one-twelfth of the total, despite the fact that her land tax assessment was one-forty-fifth of England's. As for the Lords, the Scottish nobility were allowed to select sixteen representative peers; soon there was much vying to be among them. In future years the representative peers were to prove remarkably compliant ministerial fodder.

A second reason for the swing to Union in 1705 was that a fair proportion of the Country politicians of 1703 had no fundamental objection to Union. Some perhaps were raising the stakes as a gambit for place and influence: Belhaven complained of those 'undertakers and pragmatic statesmen' who will serve the Crown 'upon their own terms'.[28] (Similarly, after the Union, loss of office could be as important as deep conviction in producing Jacobites: John, Earl of Mar, became the leader of the rebellion of 1715, yet he had voted for Union, sat in the post-Union British Parliament, and served as Secretary of State for Scotland.) In so far as the votes of 1703 amounted to sabre-rattling, there was a deeper point behind it: the aim was to force England to make concessions. The assertion of Scotland's autonomy and of its capacity to make matters awkward for England served to show that what was envisaged was a bargain between equals. This paradox had also been present in James I and VI's time: Sir Thomas Craig had attacked English overlordship in the name of Scottish sovereignty, but he was pro-Union – a union between equal kingdoms. Moreover, for those who were above all anxious to secure the Hanoverian succession a scheme of limitations seemed tactically the best way to win over waverers: if there were to be a pan-British monarch, then it was as well to prevent that monarch putting English interests first.

Consequently, positions on Union proved cross-grained. With some, the desirability of Union was a matter of a fine balance of judgement: devout Presbyterians feared a Catholic Jacobite succession but also loathed the English prelatists. Carstares thought the Kirk safest under Union, but in *The Smoaking Flax* (1706) a Presbyterian argued that a Stuart king was a lesser evil than English and Hanoverian rule. Defoe found that his chief service, as an English Presbyterian himself, was to calm Presbyterian nerves. Equally, while some English churchmen opposed Union as threatening Presbyterian contamination, others, like James Drake, argued bullishly in favour, in order to promote Anglican values north of the border. His book *Historia Anglo-Scotica* (1703) so alarmed Presbyterians that it was ordered to be burnt in Edinburgh.

The third factor was that Defoe's economic case was persuasive, not least because England turned the screw by passing the Aliens Act in 1705, by which, if a treaty of union were not entered into, all Scots in England would be declared aliens, and all imports of cattle, linen and coal would be banned.

The final consideration was that, without Union, some dire consequences of 1703 might have to be endured. By failing to settle the succession, the Scots had threatened restoration of the House of Stuart. Some single-minded Jacobites such as Patrick Abercromby even proposed that Scotland throw in its lot with Catholic France by reviving the 'Auld Alliance'. The result of dynastic irresolution would, almost certainly, be a Scottish civil war and invasion and conquest by England. The English minister Godolphin made noises about an invasion, and in 1706 troops were sent to the border. The Duke of Marlborough, in the wake of his victories at Blenheim and Malplaquet, might be called upon to open a new theatre of the European war, across the Tweed. Pamphlets appeared with such titles as *The*

Reducing of Scotland by Arms and Annexing it to England as a Province Considered (1705). Nobody seriously doubted that England would win a war against Scotland. In weighing up every factor, Roxburghe's summary of Scottish motives is often quoted: 'trade with most, Hanover with some, ease and security with others, together with a general aversion to civil disorders' – but he immediately went on to accent a visceral fear of an English invasion to forestall a Jacobite succession.[29]

The parliamentary session of 1706 was given over to such forlorn proposals as that the new British Parliament should meet in Edinburgh every three years, and to threnodies of regret by the diehards. Belhaven gave his famous 'Mother Caledonia' speech: the Union was 'an entire surrender', 'we are slaves for ever'. He likened the Scottish Parliament's murder of Scotland's independence to Caesar's assassination by his own senators. 'I see our ancient mother, Caledonia, like Caesar, sitting in the midst of our senate, ruefully looking round about her, covering herself with her royal garment, attending the fatal blows, and breathing out her last, with a *Et tu quoque mi fili* [and you also my sons]?'.[30] With that speech the Scottish nationalism of Andrew Fletcher's generation faded. In the ensuing century there would be no middle way between Westminster and Jacobitism: the question of dynasty settled the question of sovereignty.

On 1 May 1707 the Scottish Parliament ceased to exist. In the 1970s a former high school on a prominent site in Edinburgh was refurbished for a new Scottish assembly. It is still empty.

10. The Communities of Ireland and the British State, 1660–1707

JIM SMYTH

In 1682 the old Cromwellian survivor Colonel Richard Law-rence argued that 'if the majority of proprietors may give the denomination to a country, which usually it doth, Ireland is become *west England*'. Those Protestant proprietors were 'governed by English laws enacted by English parliaments and administered by English judges, guarded by an English army, and governed by English ministers of state . . . and all this administered by the absolute commission from the king of England'. Moreover, the Protestants in Ireland were 'not only English by privilege, as Paul was a Roman, but English by blood, and many of them English by birth'. Sixteen years later another pamphleteer wrote, simply, that Ireland was now 'an English Protestant country'.[1] Yet the provincial identity to which Law-rence and others laid claim is called into question by the pol-emical context in which the claim appears. Similarly, when seventeenth-century Scots used the term 'North Britons', the political context cannot be ignored. Yet the inhabitants of eastern or southern England did not need to insist upon their English identity: who would dispute it?

In fact, Lawrence testified to the essentially colonialist charac-ter of the settler community of the Restoration period in two ways. First, he had an acute awareness of belonging to a min-ority group, the 'governing party' or English Protestant inter-est, planted amidst, and sharply differentiated from, the hostile Catholic natives. Thus he advocated Protestant solidarity, ex-tending to dissenters, against the common popish enemy. He also recommended the concentration of Protestants in walled towns, and laws designed to increase the Protestant birth rate by encouraging earlier marriage.[2] Secondly, he recited a litany of grievances, and proposed remedies, which any eighteenth-century Irish Protestant patriot would have recognised and applauded. Lawrence complained that the English in Ireland forfeited some of their rights as Englishmen, particularly in relation to overseas trade; that too many public offices were held by non-residents; that the Protestants were too often perceived by the English as 'an Irish Interest' – as the conquered rather than as the conquerors. This treatment he considered unjust, impolitic and shortsighted. The Protestants of Ireland were entitled to all the rights and privileges of free-born Englishmen. Furthermore, only by upholding the English interest there could the Catholic threat, domestic and foreign, be contained. This objective, argued Lawrence, could best be obtained by lifting restrictions on Irish trade – enriching the 'mother country' in the process; by leaving the conduct of local affairs to the local elite; and, above all, by appointing an 'Irish Protestant chief governor'.[3] A central tension of the colonial predicament was dual allegiance, to the metropolis and to the adopted homeland. In this respect the inconsistency of Lawrence's terminology is as instructive as his proposed solutions to settler grievances. On the one hand he rebuked the English for denigrating the Protestants as 'Irish', on the other he called for the installation of an 'Irish chief governor'.

If Lawrence cuts an unlikely figure as an early Protestant nationalist, nevertheless, between the 1650s and the 1680s, it has been claimed, he made the journey from 'English stranger to Anglo-Irishman'.[4] Increasingly during the late seventeenth century the formation of an 'Anglo-Irish' identity found political expression through denials of the English Parliament's right to legislate for Ireland, and through an insistence upon Ireland's status as a distinct kingdom under the British Crown.[5] It is not difficult to discern in these positions the 'origins' of eighteenth-century Protestant nationalism. However, the process of settler differentiation from the mother country was protracted, uneven and equivocal. In Lawrence's time and later, Protestant senses of English, or occasionally British, identity, coupled with the conviction that their security and fortunes depended on the British connection, are just as striking as any signs of local patriotism. Ireland's constitutional status was disputed, but many Protestants were prepared to acknowledge its subordination – as a conquered country, or as a colony or province of the English 'empire'.[6] And, if the Protestants saw themselves as unequal partners in that relationship, they were as likely to seek equality, or redress, in closer union with England (and eventually Great Britain) as in greater constitutional autonomy.[7] One pamphleteer looked forward to the day when

> the king, and an English parliament . . . will consider us as their own flesh and blood, a colony of their kindred and relations, and take care of our advantages with as little grudging . . . as Cornwall does at Yorkshire: there are instances in several islands in the East Indies, as far distant as Ireland is from England, that make up but one kingdom, and governed by the same laws.[8]

Sir William Petty considered the union of England and Wales wholly successful and advocated its extension to Ireland as the best means to dismantling those trade barriers which hindered economic growth. William Molyneux dismissed the propositions that Ireland was either conquered or a colony, yet in his celebrated defence of legislative independence, *The case of Ireland being bound by acts of parliament in England, stated*, he described union as 'an happiness we can hardly hope for'.[9]

The relationships, perceived and actual, of the English Protestant Interest to the 'British state' were crucial. As the chief beneficiary of confiscation, and belonging to the Church by law established, land, wealth and power in Ireland were largely concentrated in its hands. Seventeenth-century Englishmen readily assumed that Ireland was a conquered country, but they still needed the Protestants to police it. The Protestants, as they liked to remind their English co-religionists, represented a 'bulwark' in Ireland against the ever-present danger of Catholic insurgency. But as the settler community was in turn reminded, particularly after their Williamite 'deliverance' from Catholic and Jacobite ascendancy, their own security ultimately rested on English arms. Ireland's grim sectarian arithmetic ensured that an aggrieved 'Anglo-Irish' patriotism fell short of demands for outright independence.

Irish unionist advocacy rested upon arguments for greater security and prosperity and on the right to representation. As Bishop William King put it in 1697, if Ireland was to 'be governed by the parliamentary law of the English parliament we shall like it very well, provided we be all represented in the English parliament. . . . I take all power that is not with consent of the subject to be arbitrary.'[10] Molyneux claimed the right of representation and consent as inherent in all mankind, except Catholics. Others limited the claim to Englishmen. Theirs was a rhetoric of entitlement, based on identity and on an equal share in the liberties and protections of the ancient constitution. For the English Parliament, however, reason of state – and the power to enforce it – easily outweighed mere opinion. The Westminster Cattle Acts (1663 and 1667), the Woollen Act (1699) and the Resumption Act (1700) all violated the sovereignty of the kingdom of Ireland, subjecting the English Protestant interest, along with everyone else, to laws to which they had not consented.

Disregarded by Westminster in practice, protests based on a common English identity were also flawed in logic. English-born Catholics and English-born Protestant dissenters were denied full civil rights in England. Full membership of the 'British' state depended upon conformity to the state Church. Ultimately, all state–individual and state–community relationships were defined by religious confession.

The sharp political reconfigurations of 1660 rapidly entrenched an Anglican ascendancy in Irish society and politics. But that dominance was neither preordained nor uncontested. No bishops sat in the Dublin convention which negotiated the Restoration settlement, whereas several of the convention's 137 members, including its chaplain, Samuel Cox, were Presbyterian. Presbyterians, and at least one 'independent', were also represented on the advisory committee of ministers appointed by the convention as consultants on ecclesiastical policy.[11] That Presbyterian presence reflected the real religious pluralism of post-Cromwellian Protestant Ireland and helps explain expectations of an inclusive ecclesiastical settlement. In the event the force of Anglican reaction against religious radicalism proved unstoppable.

The bishops and their political supporters were well-motivated and well-placed to impose an exclusive, narrowly-based settlement. Unlike those of England or Scotland, the Church in Ireland, although it had ceased to exercise episcopal authority, had never been formally disestablished. Eight Irish bishops survived into the interregnum. Charles II's subsequent record suggests that he inclined towards toleration, and according to the seventeenth-century historian of Ulster Presbyterianism,

Patrick Adair, two Presbyterian delegates who obtained an audience with the king in 1660 received 'good words'.[12] However, they were hopelessly out-lobbied at Court. Throughout the summer of 1660 and into 1661 John Parker, Bishop of Elphin, Michael Doyle, Bishop of Cork, Gilbert Sheldon, Bishop of London (afterwards Archbishop of Canterbury), the Marquis of Ormond and the Duke of Clarendon, kept up the pressure for a rigorously Anglican state Church.[13]

Bishops were nominated to vacant sees in the summer of 1660. A royal declaration of 30 November promised to restore all church lands held before 1641. On 24 January 1661, the lords' justice issued a proclamation banning all meetings of 'Presbyterian, independents and Quakers' and three days later two archbishops and ten bishops were consecrated in an elaborate ceremony in St Patrick's Cathedral, Dublin.[14] The Irish Parliament met in May. The opening address to the House of Commons was delivered by Jeremy Taylor, Bishop of Down and Connor, and an implacable enemy to dissent. The primate, John Bramhall, Archbishop of Armagh, served as Speaker in the House of Lords, one of the first acts of which was a declaration requiring religious conformity. Ministers had to submit to episcopal ordination or reordination, and had to use the Book of Common Prayer. Preachers, were licensed. Those who refused to conform were expelled from their livings; some even faced imprisonment. The solemn league and convenant was burned by the public hangman.

The Restoration episcopal bench which secured and enforced this ecclesiastical regime was formidable, vigorous and talented; English in origin or by extraction, royalist in politics and high church in ethos. They did not, of course, faithfully reflect the views of their subordinates, and historians often stress the distinctiveness and Calvinist inclination of the seventeenth-century Church of Ireland. R. F. Foster, for example, detects puritan continuities in Restoration Trinity College, yet two of the great luminaries of the English non-juring movement in the 1690s, Charles Leslie and Henry Dodwell, were graduates of the College in this period. Dodwell has been described as 'a disciple of Jeremy Taylor', a bishop noted for the 'Catholicity' of his views.[15] Bramhall's Laudian apprenticeship was equally evident. And although the Erastian mentality which these men shared might countenance differences of religious opinion –

or 'tender consciences' – it could never admit the legality of religious *organisation* outside the Church.

Taylor purged 36 Presbyterian ministers in a single day, although that figure may reflect the Presbyterian concentration in his east Ulster diocese of Down and Connor, as much as it does his hardline attitude towards dissent. Significantly, these predominantly Scots ministers were generally replaced by Englishmen, underscoring the ethnic identities of the two major Protestant Churches in Ireland.[16]

The centrality of the relationship between the two Churches emerges forcefully from a Presbyterian standpoint in Adair's *True Narrative*. Adair's account of the fortunes of Ulster Presbyterianism during the 1660s focuses almost exclusively on 'the yoke of prelacy'.[17] Popery scarcely rates a mention. Yet it is clear, even from such a blatantly partisan witness, that after the initial crackdown of 1661 the story of Presbyterianism during the Restoration era is not simply one of unrelenting, unmitigated persecution.[18]

By insisting upon conformity, bishops such as Bramhall, Taylor, George Wilde of Derry, or Robert Leslie of Raphoe, merely applied the letter of the law. The law was not always so strictly interpreted, however. The laxness or zeal of individual bishops varied, and for dissenters good years followed bad. In his attitude to dissent, Bramhall's successor as primate, James Margetson, adopted a more eirenic, or perhaps unconcerned, posture than his predecessor. Just as importantly, the Restoration state did not possess the coercive resources needed to fully enforce the law.[19] For Presbyterians, civil disobedience, often with the connivance of their local gentry, was always an option. Nothing more vividly demonstrated the virtual impotence of the authorities when confronted by widespread nonconformity than the activities of itinerant preachers in their 'field conventicles'. During the 1660s young ministers from the Covenanter stronghold of south-west Scotland preached in the large barns and open fields of east Ulster. These illegal gatherings drew huge crowds, undeterred by bishop or magistrate, or by the disapproval of the local Presbyterian clergy, who feared that open defiance might provoke a punitive reaction by the Church or secular authorities.[20]

Some historians have read the covenanting movement of Restoration Scotland as an early expression of Scottish nationalism. According to that view the Covenanters adhered to what they believed were peculiarly Scottish forms of Church government, in opposition to the impostion of English episcopacy from London.[21] Even if true that interpretation cannot automatically be extended to the Scottish 'Presbyterian colony' in Ulster. Although the Presbyterian ministers there were entirely Scots in origin, just as the prelatical clergy whom they confronted were mostly English, in Ireland the dissenters, as a minority, could not and did not aspire to the status of a national Church. Rather the Ulster ministers sought accommodations within the *status quo*.

As we have seen, working accommodations might be reached at local level, but tacit compromises of this kind were exposed to shifts in the political climate. Virtually the entire Presbyterian clergy in Ulster was imprisoned in the wake of the thwarted 'Blood plot' of 1663. While it is clear that the great majority of these men were not implicated in the conspiracy, the episode illustrates the firm links which existed, in the official imagination, between political radicalism and religious dissent.[22] It also underlined the vulnerability of nonconformists to a hostile and suspicious administration. Small wonder Adair and his colleagues did not share in the laity's enthusiasm for field conventicles. Distrust of the Presbyterians resurfaced in the mid-1670s when east Ulster was garrisoned by troops assembled for the purpose – for which they were not, in the end, used – of helping to suppress the anticipated Convenanter rebellion in the adjacent region of south-west Scotland.[23] More strikingly, as the writings and anxieties of William King, Bishop of Derry, indicate, that distrust had not abated by the 1690s when, following their display of solidarity against the Catholic James, Presbyterians might reasonably have expected more generous attitudes from their fellow Protestants.

The sensitivity of local accommodations to the vagaries of politics was not always negative. For example, the appointment in 1669, of Lord Robartes, a lord lieutenant sympathetic to dissent, made life easier. Similarly. Robartes' successor, Berkeley, was well-disposed towards Catholics. Thus, before 1673, when an English Parliament-inspired British-wide reaction set in, Presbyterian meeting houses and a few Catholic schools enjoyed a brief, open, legally ambiguous existence. The politically contingent position of all the Churches, including the established Church, was dramatically revealed between 1686 and 1689 when the Catholic Earl of Tyrconnel, first as lieutenant general of the army and then as Lord Deputy, abruptly reversed government policy in favour of his co-religionists. Presbyterians likewise benefited from high-level political decisions, notably the declarations of indulgence by Charles II and James II and VII in 1672 and 1687. More enduringly, ministers were granted a royal stipend, the *regium donum*, also in 1672. Doubled by William III and II, and temporarily suspended by Queen Anne's high church Tory administration, the *regium donum* had a symbolic importance in so far as it conferred semi-official legitimacy.

The fluctuations in Presbyterian fortunes reflect the complexity of that community's relationships with the 'British state'. Constitutional theory upheld the indivisibility of Church and state; the king stood at the head of the Church and the bishops represented royal authority. But, while it conceded royal authority in secular affairs, there was no place for kings or for apostolic succession in the Presbyterian doctrine of Church government. Like the Old English Catholics before them, Ulster Presbyterians distinguished between loyalty to the Crown and conformity to the established Church. Unfortunately for them, in a pre-pluralist society neither the civil nor the ecclesiastical authorities could allow that distinction to be made.

Official distrust and suspicion was readily matched by Presbyterian resentment. But Anglican–Presbyterian rivalry did not ignite into open confrontation before the late eighteenth century for precisely the same reason that Protestant nationalism did not proceed to separatism before then either. The Protestant community as a whole was locked into the British connection, and into a loveless solidarity, by the pressure of the Catholic threat. Protestant unity was strongest, between 1688 and 1691, when the Catholic threat was greatest. It is revealing, too, that the term 'British' was used in these years to embrace both the 'English' and the 'Scots' in Ireland.[24] However, almost as soon as the Jacobites were defeated, the Churchmen reverted to type, once more reserving 'British' for the Scots in Ulster. The Church party thus distanced themselves on the mercenary assumption that no matter how shoddily they were treated, the Presbyterians had no choice but to close ranks with their fellow Protestants when confronted by the common Catholic foe.

If anything, Anglican hostility to dissent increased after the revolution of 1688/9. Viewed from the episcopal bench, Presbyterianism appeared more dangerous than ever. Presbyterianism became established in Scotland. An Ulster synod – the first dissenting synod in the British Isles – met in 1690, and the *regium donum* was doubled by a sympathetic, Dutch Calvinist king. Later in the decade Ulster hosted a major influx of immigrants fleeing the collapse of the Scottish rural economy. As Bishop of Derry during the 1690s William King had direct experience of a thriving – and expanding – northern dissenter community. He considered the Presbyterians to be clannish and doctrinally misguided, and in 1695 he turned his pen on them in a polemic, *The inventions of men in the worship of God.* One of the many reasons which pamphleteers advanced against the proposed Woollen Act in 1697 and 1698 was that since the woollen 'interest' was an 'English interest', the destruction of the wool trade would devastate the English Protestant community. Just as damagingly, it would boost the 'Scottish interest' by clearing the economic field for the largely Ulster-based linen industry. Similarly, in the run-up to the Anglo-Scottish Union, high church Tories such as the attorney general, Sir Richard Cox, pressed for the inclusion of the kingdom of Ireland on the grounds that the prospective Union would enhance Presbyterian influence in the new British Parliament and, by extension, strengthen the position of the 'Scots' in Ulster. *The story of the injured lady,* Jonathan Swift's first Irish pamphlet, not published at the time, is a protest at Ireland's exclusion from the Union, fired by savage indignation at this boon being bestowed upon faithless, Presbyterian Scotland.[25]

Opposition to dissent had practical as well as rhetorical consequences. In 1695 the bishops, a cohesive and effective voting *bloc,* sank a government-sponsored toleration bill in the House of Lords. In 1704, with Anne on the throne and the 'Tory' 2nd Duke of Ormond in Dublin Castle, an 'act to prevent the further growth of popery' was returned by the English Privy Council which, using the procedures of Poynings' Law, had tacked on a sacramental test clause. That clause effectively debarred dissenters from public office and provoked a stinging pamphlet from Daniel Defoe, *The Parallel, or persecution of Protestants the shortest way to prevent the growth of Popery in Ireland.* Sean Connolly has recently argued that the impact of the penal laws directed against Catholics in this period has probably been overestimated. If the laws had not been in place, he suggests, the composition of the ruling landed elite would have looked little different.[26] And if this is true for the Catholics it is also true for the Presbyterians. Parliament and the political nation were dominated by land-owning grandees who were overwhelmingly Anglican. Nevertheless, the psychological impact of exclusion can be guessed.[27] what, for example, must the Presbyterian merchants of Belfast have thought of the fact that they could not sit on the corporation which returned the town's two MPs?

Not surprisingly, the wound did not quickly heal. Whereas William was (and is) commemorated for delivering the Protestants of Ireland from 'brass money, popery and wooden shoes', the memory of Queen Anne continued to rankle in the Ulster Presbyterian imagination. As late as 1792 a correspondent of the radical paper the *Northern Star* complained of how, since Anne's reign, Presbyterians had 'severely suffered . . . under the galling restraints of a proud ascendancy'. *Plus ça change*: the same year an MP remarked of the northern dissenters that they were 'a turbulent, disorderly set of people, whom no king can govern or no God could please'.[28]

Between 1660 and 1685 the legal and political predicament of Irish Catholics roughly resembled that of the Presbyterians. Catholics loudly proclaimed their loyalty to the Crown but, like the Presbyterians, refused to concede royal authority in Church affairs. Catholics were excluded from public life. For instance, the membership of the Restoration Parliament (1661–5) was entirely Protestant. There were also important contrasts in Presbyterian and Catholic relations with the state. First, and obviously, Presbyterians were a minority and they curbed their ambitions accordingly. Catholics formed the majority community in Ireland. They also constituted the indigenous population of the island, the Church of Ireland's appropriation of Saint Patrick notwithstanding. Even the 'Old English' had been around much longer than the Protestant newcomers. History, tradition and denominational arithmetic thus reinforced Catholic aspirations, openly touted in the late 1640s and again in the late 1680s, to be the established Church. However, the numerical advantage depended upon the unit of measurement. If Catholic claims seem compelling in an Irish context, they appear less so in a

British one. From a British perspective, Catholics – Irish, English and Scottish combined – were a minority. Furthermore, how could the Crown straddle different Churches, professing different doctrines and adhering to different rites? Quite easily is the answer, as the Presbyterian settlement in Scotland in 1690 would demonstrate. But that was far from obvious before it happened.

The second major contrast between Presbyterians and Catholics concerned papal jurisdiction. Dissent was politically suspect in the eyes of the churchmen because of its anti-hierarchical ethos and because the role played by the Convenanters in the 'fall of the British monarchies' was not soon forgotten. Catholics were suspect because, in the Pope, they had an alternative, extraterritorial, focus of loyalty superior to their king. This was a serious matter: popes reserved the 'right' to depose princes and to release subjects from their allegiance. Indeed, it was this submission to a 'foreign jurisdiction', more than any theological dispute or seventeenth-century Protestant prejudices about popish servility, zealotry or superstition, which kept Catholics locked outside the gates of the political nation.

The Catholic community itself, or at least certain members of it, first confronted the problem. In late 1661 over 100 prominent laymen, a number of priests and one bishop issued a declaration of political principles or remonstrance, which conceded absolute authority to the king in the temporal sphere. In politics timing is all, and for the guardians of Catholic orthodoxy – the Pope, the Irish hierarchy and the divinity faculty of Louvain – the remonstrance offered too much too soon. By detonating public controversy, among Catholics, and between Catholics (represented by the prominent remonstrant and Franciscan, Peter Walsh), and Protestants (represented by the hardline Earl of Orrery), the remonstrance succeeded only in underlining the predicament faced by Catholics in an early modern Protestant state.

The lord lieutenant, the 1st Duke of Ormond, responded positively to the remonstrance initiative, and in 1666 allowed a congregation of Catholic clergy to meet in Dublin to settle the dispute. When the assembly failed to ratify the original formula the Ormond administration moved quickly, imprisoning known anti-remonstrant priests. Ormond's motives are hard to interpret. Compared with his political rival, Orrery, his attitude to Catholicism was moderate. Whenever he held office, Catholics, provided always that they remained unobtrusive, had little to fear from the civil authorities. He refused to license Dublin reprints of Sir John Temple's *History of the Irish Rebellion*, presumably on the grounds that that lurid account of the 1641 massacres would only inflame sectarian hatreds.[29] Equally revealing was that Ormond, although he ordered the closure of mass houses, effectively shielded Ireland – in Protestant demonology a nest of popish disaffection – from the worst excesses of the 'Popish plot'. Oliver Plunkett's 'trial' and execution were orchestrated in an English context. Orrery, on the other hand, called for the immediate expulsion of all Catholics from the towns. Perhaps in 1666 Ormond hoped for a resolution of the Catholic dilemma of divided allegiances favourable to the state. Yet it is hard to avoid the conclusion that the outcome of the congregation, Catholic disunity and the confirmation of Protestant suspicions, was predicted. Having dug themselves into a hole, the Catholics were handed a shovel by Ormond with which to dig it deeper.[30]

Even if the Catholic community as a whole had supported the remonstrance, any consequent attempt to change their status would surely have met resistance. Protestants harboured a profound mistrust of Catholics. Memories of 1641 were fresh. Orrery – or Colonel Lawrence – was almost certainly more representative of Protestant opinion than Ormond. Indeed, Protestant opinion and government policy, far from coinciding, more often pulled in opposite directions.

Tensions were generated in the triangular relationship between Protestants, administration and Catholics, by the Restoration land settlement. Charles II promised to restore the property of royalists and 'innocent papists' as well as to confirm the titles of Protestants in possession of recently confiscated lands. Neither the Act of Settlement (1662), the Act of Explanation (1665) or the Court of Claims, which sat until 1669, could reconcile the irreconcilable. Stuart stalwarts, like Ormond himself and the Catholic Earl of Antrim, recovered large estates by royal *fiat*. Incumbent landowners had to surrender as much as one-third of their property, creating a sort of 'land bank' for redistribution by the Court of Claims. Catholic proprietorship rose in these years from under one-tenth of the total land in Ireland in the late 1650s to approximately one-quarter. Land changed hands, then, on nothing like the scale of the Cromwellian confiscations. A classic political fudge, the land settlement alarmed Protestants by surrendering too much and angered Catholics for ceding too little.

The Blood Plot, in which at least eight MPs were involved, grew out of fears that the Protestant near-monopoly in land was about to be overturned. And if that episode stands out as the extreme reaction of former Cromwellian radicals, it none the less crystallised a sense of insecurity among Protestants which persisted. William Petty caught that mood of uncertainty in 1672: 'why should men endeavour to get estates' he asked, 'where the legislative power is not agreed upon, and where tricks and words destroy natural right and property?' There was thus for Petty a rational basis for Catholic truculence: 'tricks and words' alluded to the influence wielded at Court by the Catholic agent, Richard Talbot, and helped explain Catholic expectations that 'they shall shortly be restor'd'. For Orrery matters were simpler. 'Irish papists rebel', he wrote, 'every time the opportunity presents.'[31] Of course, the duplicity of 'evil councillors' as the source of kingly misgovernment was virtually a political axiom in the seventeenth century. Free from constraint, and from the vantage-point of the mid-1690s, the Jacobite exile Hugh Reilly condemned the 'wicked acts of settlement' as 'plaine and palpable injustice'. Although Charles II was not blameless, and would answer to God, the real culprits, in Reilly's view, were crafty courtiers 'buzzing night and day in his majesty's ear'.[32]

How volatile were the unresolved interdenominational tensions so close to the surface of Restoration society? If the civil war of 1689–91 is viewed as the outcome of that friction, then in retrospect Restoration Ireland appears structurally unstable. But this is to ask perhaps the wrong, and certainly not the only, question. Sean Connolly poses a different one: how did the Protestant landed elite which dominated Irish politics and society for 200 or more years after 1660 sustain its hegemony?[33] Approached from that angle, Restoration Ireland is remarkable for its stability and the Catholic *revanche* under James, 'a counter-revolution that failed', dwindles in significance to a temporary reversal of Protestant power. It is a bold and arresting thesis, but it underestimates both the consolidation of Protestant power in post-revolution Ireland and the trauma experienced by Protestants who lived under the Jacobite regime.

Only with hindsight can be contemporary impact of James's accession, and of his Irish deputy's Catholic policies, be reduced. Those at the sharp end of these policies could not predict that their misfortunes were temporary and reversible. On the contrary, Protestant army officers, purged as suspected 'Cromwellians' – and replaced by Catholics; dismissed magistrates – likewise replaced by Catholics; or Protestant burgesses, obliged to cohabit with Catholics in remodelled corporations, were more likely to predict that their dire situation would deteriorate further. In England and Scotland James's infiltration of Catholics into public life constituted a high-risk strategy, certain to arouse powerful political opposition and with only a limited chance of achieving more than cosmetic change. In Ireland the prospects for achieving major and enduring changes were more realistic. Catholics remained in a majority and more than one hundred years of confiscation, proscription, transplantation and military defeat had so far failed to completely eradicate the Catholic elite. The remarkable regenerative capacity demonstrated by the Catholic nation after 1685 has clear implications for its resilience before that date.

Protestants in Ireland were therefore deeply alarmed by the progress of the Catholic 'counter-revolution'. And alarm turned to panic or flight when, following James's expulsion from the throne in November 1688, Ireland became a Jacobite redoubt. The Catholic resurgence assailed a beleaguered Protestant community on every flank. According to Bishop King, himself a prisoner in 1689, Protestant gentlemen were the victims of a social revolution, conducted by 'cowherds and footmen'.[34] Deference-based social control collapsed, undermined by political instability, and by the widespread belief that the Old Catholic proprietors were about to recover their estates. Armed bands of Catholic irregulars, or 'rapparees', roamed the countryside as law and order, always a nagging problem in Restoration Ireland, finally broke down. But it was the spectre of a Catholic Parliament and the overturning of the Act of Settlement which, more than anything else, shattered Protestant morale.

Admittedly, none of this came remotely near to repeating the horrors of 1641; nevertheless it is a mistake to underestimate the impact of the events of the late 1680s on the Protestant pysche. King's *The state of the Protestants of Ireland under the late king James government* defended Irish Protestant resistance to the 'late' king on the grounds that, as a people, they were about to be 'extirpated'. He emphasised Catholic infamy, Protestant suffering and the role of divine providence in delivering the Protestants from persecution and near-extinction. *The state of the Protestants* exercised immense influence as it helped to shape as well as to express the unyielding Protestant mentality of the 1690s and early eighteenth century. The trauma of the late 1680s, and King's widely-read account of it, can be seen as justifying, in Protestant minds, the anti-Catholic legislation, known collectively as the 'Penal Laws', the core of which were enacted by the Irish Parliament between 1695 and 1709.[35]

There are good reasons for seeing 1691 as 'Year One' of the 'Protestant nation'. Catholic Ireland 'surrendered' at Limerick in October, although the completeness of the capitulation was unclear to both Catholics and Protestants at the time. In the years immediately after 1691 'the king over the water' and the progress of French arms kept alive Catholic hopes of restoration. Protestants felt that the articles of Limerick were to generous to the defeated. Anthony Dopping, Bishop of Meath, who, like his colleague King, had been imprisoned by the Jacobites, was expelled from the Privy Council for denouncing the Limerick 'treaty' in a sermon preached in Christchurch Cathederal. Protestants also suspected that William's government was soft on popery. The Parliament which met in Dublin in the autumn of 1692 was nevertheless entirely and vociferously Protestant. Moreover, whereas technically Catholics could still sit in the Restoration Parliament, though none did so, they were now explicitly debarred from taking seats.

It is significant that the Act effectively excluding Catholics from the Irish Parliament, by prescribing an oath for MPs which no Catholic could take, was passed not by the Parliament itself, but by Westminster in 1689. This pointed to the dual political inheritance of the revolution for Protestants in Ireland. The substance of the Act was welcomed by them and anticipated over twenty years of anti-Catholic measures enacted by the Dublin legislature. If the status of Catholics after 1660 remained legally ambivalent and politically contingent, from 1695 onwards a body of laws reached the statute books which secured the monopoly of public office and near-monopoly in rights of citizenship on which the 'Protestant nation' rested. But, although Protestant power was consolidated in relation to the Catholic population, in relation to England it has weakened.

In the first instance, no matter how much they insisted upon the verdict of providence or upon the heroism of their country-men who had shut the gates against James, the Protestants of the 1690s owed their 'deliverance' to William's armies. They had been rescued by England. This contrasted sharply with the Restoration settlement which owed so much to local Prot-estant initiative,[36] and gave English polemicists grounds to ar-gue that Ireland was a reconquered country, subject to Eng-lish parliamentary rule. Secondly, the doctrine that sovereignty now lodged in the Crown-in-Parliament created major diffi-culties for Irish constitutional theory. The traditional view, that Ireland was a distinct kingdom, with its own Parliament, con-stitution and courts, and with a king who also happened to be King of England, became increasingly anachronistic and unsustainable. In short, if the Crown was imperial, its jurisdic-tion extending to all the king's dominions, then the Parlia-ment from which it could not now be separated, was imperial too. Westminster's jurisdiction therefore extended to Ireland.[37] Ireland, perhaps, had never been anything other than a colony, yet the constitutional fiction that it was an autonomous king-dom packed considerable rhetorical force. As a result of the revolution, that fiction appeared increasingly threadbare; the colonial dependency more naked. There is a piquant, almost quixotic, quality to Molyneux's impassioned defence of Irish legislative independence. By the time he wrote, in 1698, the 'Protestant nation' for whom he spoke had been reduced to a querulous outpost of the English Parliament's empire.

Further Reading

1. THE BRITISH PROBLEM, *c.* 1534–1707

There is no textbook on this subject except for the very general one by H. F. Kearney, *The British Isles* (Cambridge, 1989), but there are now several collections of essays mostly covering longer periods than that covered by this book. The most important include R. Asch (ed.), *Three Nations – A Common History?* (Bochum, 1992); S. G. Ellis and S. Barber (eds), *Conquest and Union: Fashioning a British State, 1485–1720* (London, 1995); and A. Grant and K. Stringer (eds), *Uniting the Kingdom: The Enigma of British History* (London, 1995). Books which offer a comparative framework within which 'the British Problem' can be examined include M. Hechter, *Internal Colonialism* (London, 1975), and S. G. Webb, *The Governors General: The English Army and the Definition of Empire, 1569–1681* (New Haven, 1979). Monographs that take seriously the relationship of three or more of England, Ireland, Scotland and Wales include S. G. Ellis, *Tudor Frontiers and Noble Power* (Oxford, 1995); C. Russell, *The Fall of the British Monarchies, 1637–1642* (Oxford, 1991); and J. Ohlmeyer, *Civil War and Restoration in Three Kingdoms: The Career of Randall Macdonnell* (Cambridge, 1993).

S. G. Ellis, *Tudor Ireland* (London, 1985); B. Bradshaw, *The Irish Constitutional Revolution of the Sixteenth Century* (Cambridge, 1979); and N. Canny, *Kingdom and Colony: Ireland in the Atlantic World, 1500–1800* (Princeton, 1988) offer different perspectives on Anglo-Irish relations. K. Brown, *Kingdom or Province: Scotland and the Reginal Union* (London, 1992); J. S. Morrill (ed.), *The Scottish National Covenant in its British Context* (Edinburgh, 1991); R. Mason, *Scots and Britons* (Cambridge, 1994); and W. Ferguson, *Scotland's Relations with England to 1707* (Edinburgh, 1977) offer very different perspectives on Anglo-Scottish Relations. Most fundamental of all are the articles of John Pocock, and above all 'British History: A Plea for a New Subject', *Journal of Modern History* 4 (1975); and 'The Limits and Divisions of British History', *American History Review*, 87 (1982).

2. THE TUDOR REFORMATION AND REVOLUTION IN WALES AND IRELAND: THE ORIGINS OF THE BRITISH PROBLEM

The new British History as represented in this volume has yet to produce a survey covering the fifteenth century. However, the backdrop for the developments discussed here is excellently established in two recent studies of the preceding centuries: R. R. Davies, *Dominion and Conquest: The Experience of Ireland, Scotland and Wales* (Cambridge, 1990); and Robin Frame, *The Political Development of the British Isles, 1100–1400* (Oxford, 1990). For the history of fifteenth-century Wales, see two works by the *doyen* of Welsh early modern historians, Glanmor Williams: *The Welsh Church from Conquest to Reformation* (Cardiff, 1976); and *Wales c. 1415–1642* (Oxford, 1987), a work which summarises the material contained in the earlier book. Fifteenth-century Ireland is also well served in volume II of *The New History of Ireland: Medieval Ireland, 1169–1534*, ed. Art Cosgrove (Oxford, 1987) – see especially the later chapters by Cosgrove himself and by D. B. Quinn. A succinct introductory survey is also provided by Cosgrove in *Late Medieval Ireland, 1370–1541* (Dublin, 1981).

The security considerations which led to a significant shift in the perception from the centre of the English Crown's peripheral dominions during the fifteenth and early sixteenth centuries is provided in the seminal study of Steven G. Ellis, 'England in the Tudor State', *Historical Journal*, XXVI (1983). That dimension is further explored in the context of the developments of the later Tudor period by J. E. A. Dawson, 'Ireland in Anglo-Scottish Relations in the Middle of the Sixteenth Century' in R. A. Mason (ed.), *Scotland and England, 1286–1815* (Edinburgh, 1985); and the same author's 'William Cecil and the British Dimension of Early Elizabethan Foreign Policy' *History*, LXXIV (1989).

Finally, for the impact of the Tudor Revolution of the 1530s on Ireland and Wales respectively, see Brendan Bradshaw, *The Irish Constitutional Revolution of the Sixteenth Century* (Cambridge, 1979), esp. chs 4–6; Glanmor Williams, *Wales c. 1415–1642* (chs 11–12); and W. R. B. Robinson, 'The Tudor Revolution in Wales', *English Historical Review*, CIII (1988). See also S. G. Ellis and S. Barber (eds), *Conquest and Union: Fashioning a British State, 1485–1725* (London, 1995), chs 1–5; and other chapters in this book – especially ch. 3 (Hiram Morgan), ch. 4 (Ciaran Brady) and ch. 5 (Peter Roberts).

3. BRITISH POLICIES BEFORE THE BRITISH STATE

William Palmer, *The Problem of Ireland in Tudor Foreign Policy* (Woodbridge, 1994); Jane Dawson, 'William Cecil and the British Dimension of Early Elizabethan Foreign Policy', *History*, LXXIV (1989), 196–216; Philip Smith, 'On the Fringe and in the Middle: the MacDonalds of Antrim and the Isles', *History Ireland*, I, 2 (1994), 15–18; Hiram Morgan, 'Extradition and Treason-Trial of a Gaelic Lord: The Case of Brian O'Rourke', *Irish Jurist*, XXII (1987), 285–301; G. A. Hayes-McCoy, *Scots Mercenary Forces in Ireland, 1565–1603* (Dublin, 1937); R. Mason, 'The Scottish Reformation and the Origins of Anglo-British Imperialism', in R. Mason (ed.), *Scots and Britons: Scottish Political Thought and the Union of 1603* (Cambridge, 1994), ch. 7; and A. Hadfield,

'Briton and Scythian: Tudor Representations of Irish Origins', *Irish Historical Studies*, XXVIII (1993), 391–408.

4. ENGLAND'S DEFENCE AND IRELAND'S REFORM: THE DILEMMA OF THE IRISH VICEROYS, 1541–1641

The literature pertaining to the Irish viceroyalty in this period is hardly distinguishable from the general political history of Ireland in the sixteenth and early seventeenth centuries, and for this T. W. Moody et al. (eds), *A New History of Ireland*, vol. 3: *Early Modern Ireland, 1534–1691* (Oxford, 1976) remains the best introduction, though the work of Richard Bagwell, despite is old-fashioned approach and biases, is still indispensable: see his *Ireland under the Tudors* (3 vols, London, 1885–90) and the first volume of his *Ireland under the Stuarts*, 3 vols (London, 1909–16).

The general administrative and political context in which the viceroys worked is described in Steven Ellis, *Tudor Ireland: Crown, Community and the Conflict of Cultures, 1470–1603* (London, 1985), ch. 4; Ciaran Brady, 'Court, Castle and Country: the Framework of Government in Tudor Ireland', in Ciaran Brady and Raymond Gillespie (eds), *Natives and Newcomers: Essays on the Making of Irish Colonial Society, 1534–1641* (Dublin, 1986), pp. 22–49; Jon G. Crawford, *Anglicizing the Government of Ireland: the Irish Privy Council and the Expansion of Tudor rule, 1556–1579* (Dublin, 1993); Victor Treadwell, 'Irish Financial and Administrative Reform under James I: The Customs and State Regulation of Irish Trade' (PhD thesis, Queen's University of Belfast, 1960); Aidan Clarke, '28 November 1634: A Detail of Strafford's Administration', in *Journal of the Royal Society of Antiquaries of Ireland*, XCVII (1967), 161–7.

Sketches of all the major viceroys are provided in the *Dictionary of National Biography*, some (Strafford) are now seriously out of date but others (Fitzwilliam and Falkland) remain the best short introductions to their subjects, all provide very useful lists of primary sources for further research. Interpretations of the viceroyalties of Grey, St Leger, Sussex, Sidney and Perrot are provided in Ciaran Brady, *The Chief Governors: The Rise and Fall of Reform Government in Tudor Ireland, 1536–1588* (Cambridge, 1994). Brendan Bradshaw provides a sophisticated and original study of the government of St Leger in *The Irish Constitutional Revolution of the Sixteenth Century* (Cambridge, 1979), pt iii; Nicholas Canny has fitted Sidney, in a somewhat procrustean manner, into *The Elizabethan Conquest of Ireland: a Pattern Established, 1565–76* (Hassocks, 1976). Hiram Morgan has devoted a chapter each to Perrot and Fitzwilliam dealing largely with their conduct in Ulster in *Tyrone's Rebellion: The Origins of the Nine Years War in Ulster* (Woodbridge, 1993). For Mountjoy there are two older studies: Cyril Falls, *Mountjoy: Elizabethan General* (London, 1955), and F. M. Jones, *Mountjoy, 1563–1606: The Last Elizabethan* (Dublin, 1958). Chichester has now been carefully studied in John McCavitt's admirable

Queen's University, Belfast, PhD thesis: 'The Lord Deputyship of Sir Arthur Chichester in Ireland, 1605–1616' (1988), which is shortly to be published by the Institute of Irish Studies at Belfast. Oliver St John is the subject of a Master's thesis by Vera Rutledge, 'The politics of reform in Ireland under Oliver St John, 1616–22' (MA, McGill University, 1976), and a related article, 'Court–Castle Faction and the Irish Viceroyalty: the Appointment of Oliver St John as Lord Deputy in 1616', in *Irish Historical Studies*, XXVI (1988–9), 233–49. Viceregal politics in the late 1610s and 1620s must as yet be approached obliquely through studies concerned with other issues: see, for instance, the early chapters of Aidan Clarke, *The Old English in Ireland, 1625–42* (London, 1966); and the later chapters of Terence Ranger's doctoral thesis, 'The career of Richard Boyle, First Earl of Cork in Ireland, 1588–1643' (DPhil, Oxford, 1958), are the most valuable. But our knowledge of the complexities of the period will be greatly enhanced by the appearance of Victor Treadwell's as yet unpublished study of 'Buckingham and Ireland', 1616–28'. Wentworth has given rise to much distinguished work: in addition to H. F. Kearney's classic study *Strafford in Ireland, 1633–1641* (2nd edn; Cambridge, 1989), at the relevant chapters of Clarke's *Old English*, see Terence Ranger, 'Strafford in Ireland: a Revaluation', reprinted in Trevor Aston (ed.), *Crisis in Europe, 1560–1660* (London, 1965), pp. 271–93; and Michael Perceval-Maxwell, *The Outbreak of the 1641 Rebellion in Ireland* (Dublin and Kingston, Ontario, 1994).

5. THE ENGLISH CROWN, THE PRINCIPALITY OF WALES AND THE COUNCIL IN THE MARCHES, 1534–1641

There is no comprehensive history of Wales which takes into account the changing nature of the principality as concept and territory, though the question of the shifting nature of national identity is addressed in Gwyn A. Williams, *When was Wales?* (London, 1985).

Sir Goronwy Edwards, *The Principality of Wales, 1267–1269: A Study in Constitutional History* (Caernarfon, 1969) is a short survey by way of commentary on enacted legislation which does not take into account the alternative proposals considered in the process of policy-making. Francis Jones, *The Princes and Principality of Wales* (Cardiff, 1969) is a heraldic history, mainly of the English Princes and their investitures from 1301 to 1969.

Recent studies by Madeleine Gray on the Crown lands in sixteenth-century Wales, and by Graham Haslam on the duchy of Cornwall in the reigns of Elizabeth and James, indicate the extent to which the early Stuart principates became increasingly funded out of the proceeds of the Cornish estates, *The Estates of the English Crown, 1558–1640*, ed. R. W. Hoyle (Cambridge, 1992), chs 3, 4, and 10. Except for the work of Rhys Robinson on the early Tudor Earls of Worcester and that of T. B. Pugh on the Staffords, Dukes of Buckingham as lords marcher, there has been little research done on the nobility in

Wales in this period, W. R. B. Robinson, 'Early Tudor Policy towards Wales, part 3: Henry, Earl of Worcester and Henry VIII's Legislation for Wales', *Bulletin of the Board of Celtic Studies*, XXI (1966), 334–62; *The Marcher Lordships of South Wales, 1415–1536: Select Documents*, edited by T. B. Pugh (Cardiff, 1963).

The present writer has reinterpreted the legislation of union and its constitutional and cultural significance for early modern Wales in the articles referred to in the notes. For a fuller exploration of the main themes of this chapter, see in particular P. R. Roberts, 'Wales and England after the Tudor "Union": Crown, Principality and Parliament, 1543–1624', in *Law and Government under the Tudors: Essays Presented to Sir Geoffrey Elton on his Retirement*, ed. Claire Cross, David Loades and J. J. Scarisbrick (Cambridge, 1988), pp. 111–38; and P. R. Roberts, 'The Welsh Language, English Law and Tudor Legislation', *Transactions of the Honourable Society of Cymmrodorion* (1989), 19–75.

Penry Williams is the authority on the history of the Council in the Marches in this period. See his *The Council in the Marches of Wales under Elizabeth I* (Cardiff, 1958); and his 'The Elizabethan Borderlands', *Welsh History Review*, 1 (1960)

A. H. Dodd's analysis of 'the principles of Welsh government' outlined in 'The Pattern of Politics in Stuart Wales', *Transactions of the Honourable Society of Cymmrodorion*, 8–91, needs to be revised in the light of recent critiques of the writings of Sir John Neale and Wallace Notestein. But Dodd's *Studies in Stuart Wales* (Cardiff, 1952) is still invaluable.

G. Dyfnallt Owen, *Elizabethan Wales* (Cardiff, 1962) and *Wales in the Reign of James I* (Woodbridge, 1988) are both narratives in social history which contain interesting materials on Welsh customs; however, the sources are not analysed so as to present distinctive interpretations. Glanmor Williams, *Recovery, Reformation and Reorientation: Wales c. 1415–1642* (Oxford and Cardiff, 1987) is an extensive work of synthesis for the whole history of Wales during these years. His *Wales and the Act of Union* (Bangor, 1992) is a useful general introduction to the subject.

6. JAMES VI, JAMES I AND THE IDENTITY OF BRITAIN

Only a proportion of the ever-increasing literature on this subject can be mentioned here; so crucial advice is: use the footnotes and bibliographies for suggestions for further reading. The best starting points are K. M. Brown, *Kingdom or Province? Scotland and the Regal Union, 1603–1715* (London, 1992); and B. P. Levack, *The Formation of the British State: England, Scotland and the Union, 1603–1707* (Oxford, 1987), lively and informative both. The more detailed study by R. R. Galloway, *The Union of England and Scotland, 1603–1608* (Edinburgh, 1986), was a path-breaking example of 'British' history, going far beyond the traditional and misleading concentration on English attitudes; and it should be read alongside the excellent edition of tracts on the union, in B. R. Galloway and B. P. Levack (eds), *The Jacobean Union* (Scottish History Society, Edinburgh, 1985). Two very stimulating collections of essays have recently appeared: R. G. Asch (ed.), *Three Nations – a Common History? England, Scotland, Ireland and British History, c. 1600–1920* (Bochum, 1993) and R. A. Mason (ed.), *Scots and Britons: Scottish Political Thought and the Union of 1603* (Cambridge, 1994). Other article literature includes S. T. Bindoff, 'The Stuarts and their style', *English Historical Review*, 60 (1945), 192–216; K. M. Brown, 'The Scottish Aristocracy, Anglicanization and the Court', *Historical Journal*, 36 (1993), pp. 543–76; B. P. Levack, 'Towards a More Perfect Union: England, Scotland and the Constitution', in Barbara C. Malament (ed.), *After the Reformation: Essays in Honor of J. H. Hexter* (Manchester, 1980); B. W. Henry, 'John Dee, Humphrey Llwyd and the Name "British Empire"', *Huntington Library Quarterly*, 35 (1971–2), 189–90; Neil Cuddy, 'The Revival of the Entourage: the Bedchamber of James I, 1603–1625', in D. Starkey (ed.), *The English Court from the Wars of the Roses to the Civil War* (London, 1987), pp. 173–225; Jenny Wormald. 'The Creation of Britain: Multiple Kingdoms or Core and Colonies?', *Transactions of the Royal Historical Society*, 6th series, 2 (1992), 175–94. On Wales, P. R. Roberts, 'Wales and England after the Tudor "Union": Crown, Principality and Parliament, 1543–1624', in C. Cross, D. Loades and J. J. Scarisbrick (eds), *Law and Government under the Tudors: Essays presented to Sir Geoffrey Elton* (Cambridge, 1988), pp. 111–38; and for essential European context, J. H. Elliott, 'A Europe of Composite Monarchies', *Past and Present*, 137 (November 1992), 48–71.

There is now a lot of exciting work on Jacobean Ireland; again, only a selection can be given here. There is an excellent discussion by Aidan Clarke, with R. Dudley Edwards, 'Pacification, Plantation and the Catholic Question, 1603–23', in T. W. Moody, F. X. Masters and F. J. Byrne (eds), *A New History of Ireland*, vol. III: *Early Modern Ireland, 1534–1691* (Oxford, 1976), pp. 187–232; and a brief but illuminating account by N. P. Canny, *From Reformation to Restoration Ireland, 1534–1660* (Dublin, 1987), especially ch. 5. On the Plantation, M. Perceval-Maxwell, *The Scottish Migration to Ireland in the Reign of James I* (London, 1973) can rightly be regarded as a classic. Also R. Gillespie, *Colonial Ulster: The Settlement of East Ulster, 1600–41* (Cork, 1985); P. S. Robinson, *The Plantation of Ulster* (Dublin, 1984); and J. Michael Hill, 'The Origins of the Scottish Plantations in Ulster to 1625: a Reinterpretation', *Journal of British Studies*, 32 (1993), 24–43. There is also the wide-ranging work by N. P. Canny, *Kingdom and Colony: Ireland in the Atlantic World* (Baltimore and London, 1988); and the splendid collection by Ciaran Brady and Raymond Gillespie (eds), *Natives and Newcomers: Essays on the Making of Irish Colonial Society, 1534–1641* (Dublin, 1986). The problems inherited from the Tudor period are tellingly analysed by C. Brady, 'The Decline of the Irish Kingdom', in M. Greengrass (ed.), *Conquest and Coalescence: The Shaping of the State in Early Modern Europe* (London, 1991), pp. 94–115; the tinge of sadness here can be compared with the robust discussion by M. Perceval-Maxwell, 'Ireland and the Monarchy in the Early Stuart Kingdom', *Historical Journal*, 34 (1991), 279–95. One mysterious episode, and perhaps missed opportunity, is elucidated by N. P. Canny, 'The Flight of the Earls, 1607', *Irish Historical Studies*, 17 (1971), 380–99. The struggles of the Protestant Church are ably dealt with by A. Ford, *The Protestant Reformation in Ireland, 1590–1641* (Frankfurt, 1985). And the struggles of Lord Deputy Davies are the subject of H. S. Pawlisch, *Sir John Davies and the Conquest of Ireland* (Cambridge, 1985).

Finally, the point of view of the man who presided over it all can be discovered in C. H. McIlwain (ed.), *The Political Works of James I* (reprint, New York, 1965), J.P. Sommerville (ed.), *King James VI and I, Political Writings* (Cambridge, 1994), and J. F. Larkin and P. L. Hughes (eds), *Stuart Royal Proclamations I* (Oxford, 1973). His accession began the problems; its consequences are still being debated, and indeed vigorously fought over, in the wealth of scholarly writing indicated above.

7. THE ATLANTIC ARCHIPELAGO AND THE WAR OF THE THREE KINGDOMS

It is difficult to provide a tentative and exploratory essay in re-conceptualisation with much in the way of a supportive critical biography. David Mathew's, *The Celtic Peoples and Renaissance Europe* (London, 1933), whatever its shortcomings, was a *tour d'horizon* unforgettable for the scope of the horizons it revealed. J. C. Beckett's *The Making of Modern Ireland* (New York, 1966) is the source from which I drew the term 'War of the Three Kingdoms'. Arthur H. Williamson's *Scottish National Consciousness in the Age of James VI* (Edinburgh, 1979) remains a pioneer study in the Scottish perception of both Scotland and the matter of 'Britain'. D. C. Stevenson's *The Scottish Revolution, 1637–44: The Triumph of the Covenanters* (New York/London, 1973), and *Revolution and Counter-Revolution in Scotland* (London, 1977) opened up a contemporary understanding of the National Covenant's place in Three Kingdoms history. Richard F. Helgerson's *Forms of Nationhood: The Elizabethan Writing of England* (Chicago, 1993), is by far the most valuable (at least to present purposes) of the 'new historicist' analyses of literature's role in the formation of national identity. My own studies of the comparable role of the common law have been brought up to date by Glenn Burgess's *The Politics of the Ancient Constitution: An Introduction to English Political Thought, 1603–1642* (London, 1992); and the light shed by William Haller's *Foxe's Book of Martyrs and the Elect Nation* (London, 1963) is best re-focused by William M. Lamont's *Marginal Prynne, 1608–1669* (London; 1963), and *Godly Rule, 1603–1660* (London, 1969). The best demonstration that what the English underwent in the Wars of the Three Kingdoms was a civil war, irresistibly thrust upon bitterly unwilling combatants, remains Anthony Fletcher's *The Outbreak of the English Civil War* (London, 1980).

For how the process ended in the largest of the kingdoms, see Ronald Hutton, *The Restoration: A Political and Religious History of England and Wales, 1658–1667* (Oxford, 1985). Post-Covenant Scotland and post-Cromwellian Ireland await their revisionist historians, as on the whole does the Second War of the Three Kingdoms that broke out in 1688, though the literature which accompanied the less than glorious commemoration of the Glorious Revolution's tercentenary will supply useful insights. For the rest, this volume supplies its own bibliography.

8. THE ENGLISH REPUBLIC AND THE MEANING OF BRITAIN

D. Stevenson's essay on 'Cromwell, Scotland and Ireland', in J. Morrill (ed.), *Oliver Cromwell and the English Revolution* (London, 1990), is the essential starting-point. Political, religious and administrative developments in Scotland and Ireland are well outlined in T. C. Barnard, *Cromwellian Ireland* (Oxford, 1973); F. D. Dow, *Cromwellian Scotland* (Edinburgh, 1979); and in P. J. Corish's essay on 'The Cromwellian Regime', in T. W. Moody, F. X. Martin and F. J. Byrne (eds), *A New History of Ireland*, vol. III: *Early Modern Ireland, 1534–1691* (Oxford, 1976). R. Hutton, *The British Republic, 1649–1660* (London, 1990), does provide a British dimension in a generally English survey. K. S. Bottigheimer, *English Money and Irish Land* (Oxford, 1971), discusses the 'Cromwellian' confiscations in detail. There has been more far-reaching work recently on British themes in the Scottish field than in either the English or the Irish. Several essays in J. Morrill (ed.), *The Scottish National Covenant in its British Context* (Edinburgh, 1990), trace the themes of Presbyterian imperialism, or of commitment to a British Church, up to 1651. Much the same can be said of R. A. Mason (ed.), *Scots and Britons* (Cambridge, 1994); K. M. Brown's essay in that volume, 'The Vanishing Emperor: British Kingship and its Decline, 1603–1707', is illuminating in the longer term. R. Mitchison and P. Roebuck (eds), *Economy and Society in Scotland and Ireland, 1500–1939* (Edinburgh, 1988), contains suggestive essays by R. Gillespie, D. Stevenson, and A. MacInnes on, respectively, the effects of revolution and conquest on landed society in Ireland and Scotland, Scottish political structure, and Scottish Gaeldom. The manipulation by English politicians of Scotland's place in the political structure is examined by E. D. Goldwater, 'The Scottish Franchise: Lobbying during the Cromwellian Protectorate', *Historical Journal*, 21 (1978), 27–42, and J. Buckroyd, 'Bridging the Gap: Scotland, 1659–1660', *Scottish Historical Review*, 66 (1987), 1–25; for English encounters with the Scottish Church, see J. Buckroyd, 'Lord Broghill and the Scottish Church, 1655–1656', *Journal of Ecclesiastical History*, 27 (1976), 359–68; and especially L. M. Smith's essay on the survival of the Presbyterian Kirk sessions in Cromwellian Scotland in J. Dwyer, R. Mason and A. Murray (eds), *New Perspectives on the Politics and Culture of Early Modern Scotland* (Edinburgh, 1982). The only systematic discussion of the economic consequences of conquest is T. M. Devine, 'The

Cromwellian Union and the Scottish Burghs', in J. Butt and J. T. Ward (eds), *Scottish Themes* (Edinburgh, 1976). Finally, H. R. Trevor-Roper's essays on 'Scotland and the Puritan Revolution' and 'The Union of Britain', in his *Religion, the Reformation and Social Change* (London, 1956), are still worth reading for their verve if not always for their balance.

9. DIVERGENCE AND UNION: SCOTLAND AND ENGLAND, 1660–1707

Useful surveys are: K. M. Brown, *Kingdom or Province? Scotland and the Regal Union 1603–1715* (London, 1992); G. Donaldson, *Scotland, James V to James VII* (Edinburgh, 1965); W. Ferguson, *Scotland, 1689 to the Present* (Edinburgh, 1968); W. Ferguson, *Scotland's Relations with England: A Survey to 1707* (Edinburgh, 1977); R. Mitchison, *Lordship to Patronage; Scotland, 1603–1745* (London, 1983); D. Szechi and D. Hayton, 'John Bull's Other Kingdoms: the English Government of Scotland and Ireland', in *Britain in the First Age of Party, 1680–1750*, ed. C. Jones (London, 1987). There are review essays by: K. M. Brown, in *Journal of British Studies*, 31 (1992), 415–25; J. H. Burns, in *History*, 70 (1985), 46–59; B. Lenman, in *Historical Journal*, 25 (1982), 217–28; and J. Wormald, in *Comparative Studies in Society and History*, 27 (1985), 767–74.

The question of Scottish identity is discussed in: D. Allan, *Virtue, Learning and the Scottish Enlightenment* (Edinburgh, 1993); M. Ash, *The Strange Death of Scottish History* (Edinburgh, 1980); L. Colley, *Britons: Forging the Nation, 1707–1837* (New Haven, 1992); C. Harvie, *Scotland and Nationalism: Scottish Society and Politics, 1707–1977* (London, 1977); C. Kidd, *Subverting Scotland's Past: Scottish Whig Historians and the Creation of an Anglo-British Identity, 1689–c. 1830* (Cambridge, 1993); M. Pittock, *The Invention of Scotland: The Stuart Myth and the Scottish Identity* (London, 1991). For a modern perspective see T. Nairn, *The Break-Up of Britain* (London, 1977).

On religion in Scotland: C. G. Brown, *The Social History of Religion in Scotland since 1730* (London, 1987); J. Buckroyd, *Church and State in Scotland, 1660–1681* (Edinburgh, 1980); J. Buckroyd, *The Life of James Sharp, Archbishop of St Andrews, 1618–1679* (Edinburgh, 1987); I. B. Cowan, *The Scottish Covenanters, 1660–1688* (London, 1976); A. Drummond and J. Bulloch, *The Scottish Church, 1688–1843* (Edinburgh, 1973); A. I. Dunlop, *William Carstares and the Kirk by Law Established* (Edinburgh, 1967); W. R. Foster, *Bishop and Presbytery: The Church of Scotland, 1661–1688* (London, 1958).

On Restoration Royalism: A. Lang, *Sir George Mackenzie* (London, 1909); W. C. Mackenzie, *The Life and Times of John Maitland, Duke of Lauderdale* (London, 1923); H. Ouston, 'York In Edinburgh: James VII and the Patronage of Learning in Scotland, 1679–1688', in *New Perspectives on the Politics and Culture of Early Modern Scotland*, eds J. Dwyer et al. (Edinburgh, 1982); S. Bruce and S. Yearley, 'The Social Construction of Tradition: the Restoration Portraits and the Kings of

Scotland', in *The Making of Scotland*, ed. D. McCrone et al. (Edinburgh, 1989). The opposing ideology is discussed in I. M. Smart, 'The Political Ideas of the Scottish Covenanters, 1638–88', *History of Political Thought*, 1 (1980), 167–93. On Scotland's legal tradition: G. Donaldson, 'Stair's Scotland: the Intellectual Heritage', *Juridical Review* (1981), 1456–60; D. M. Walker (ed.), *Stair Tercentenary Studies* (Edinburgh, 1981); D. M. Walker, *The Scottish Jurists* (Edinburgh, 1985).

The Highland and Jacobite dimensions are explored in: E. Cregeen, 'The Changing Role of the House of Argyll in the Scottish Highlands', in *Scotland in the Age of Improvement*, eds N. T. Phillipson and R. Mitchison (Edinburgh, 1970); E. Cruickshanks and J. Black (eds), *The Jacobite Challenge* (Edinburgh, 1988); P. Hopkins, *Glencoe and the End of the Highland War* (Edinburgh, 1986); B. Lenman, *The Jacobite Risings in Britain, 1689–1746* (London, 1980); B. Lenman, *The Jacobite Clans of the Great Glen, 1650–1784* (London, 1984); A. I. MacInnes, 'Repression and Conciliation: the Highland Dimension, 1660–1688', *Scottish Historical Review*, 65 (1986), 167–95; F. McLynn, *The Jacobites* (London, 1985); D. Stevenson, *Alasdair MacColla and the Highland Problem in the Seventeenth Century* (Edinburgh, 1980); C. W. Withers, *Gaelic Scotland: the Transformation of a Culture Region* (London, 1988); J. Wormald, 'Bloodfeud, Kindred and Government in Early Modern Scotland', *Past and Present*, 87 (1980), 54–97.

Several books marking the tercentenary of the Revolution of 1688 include the Scottish aspect: essays by B. Lenman in *The Revolutions of 1688*, ed. R. Beddard (Oxford, 1991); and in *The Revolution of 1688–1689*, ed. L. G. Schwoerer (Cambridge, 1992); I. B. Cowan, in *The Anglo-Dutch Moment*, ed. J. I. Israel (Cambridge, 1991); and in *By Force or by Default?: The Revolution of 1688–1689*, ed. E. Cruickshanks (Edinburgh, 1989). An important earlier essay is J. Halliday, 'The Club and the Revolution in Scotland, 1689–1690', *Scottish Historical Review*, 45 (1966), 143–59.

The literature on the Union is huge. Some key items are: W. Ferguson, 'The Making of the Treaty of Union of 1707', *Scottish Historical Review*, 43 (1964), 89–110; T. I. Rae (ed.), *The Union of 1707* (Glasgow, 1974); P. W. J. Riley, 'The Scottish Parliament of 1703', *Scottish Historical Review*, 47 (1968), 129–50; T. C. Smout, 'The Road to Union', in *Britain After the Glorious Revolution, 1689–1714*, ed. G. Holmes (London, 1989). For greater detail: P. W. J. Riley, *King William and the Scottish Politicians* (Edinburgh, 1979); P. W. J. Riley, *The Union of England and Scotland* (Manchester, 1978). D. Szechi is preparing a new study of George Lockhart. On the ideological debates surrounding Union, see J. Robertson, 'Andrew Fletcher's Vision of Union', in *Scotland and England, 1286–1815*, ed. R. A. Mason (Edinburgh, 1987); and J. Robertson (ed.), *A Union for Empire: Political Thought and the Union of 1707* (Cambridge, 1995); *Andrew Fletcher of Saltoun: Selected Writings*, ed. D. Daiches (Edinburgh, 1979); P. H. Scott, *Andrew Fletcher and the Treaty of Union* (Edinburgh, 1992); B. P. Levack, *The Formation of the British State: England, Scotland, and the Union, 1603–1707* (Oxford, 1987). A new edition of Fletcher is in preparation (ed. J. Robertson, Cambridge). Also: W. Ferguson, 'Imperial Crowns: A Neglected Facet of the Background to the Treaty of Union of 1707', *Scottish Historical Review*, 53 (1974), 22–44; J. Robertson, *The Scottish Enlightenment and the Militia Issue* (Edinburgh, 1985). The economic aspect is explored in: T. C. Smout, *Scottish Trade on the Eve of Union, 1660–1707* (Edinburgh, 1963); T. C. Smout, 'The Anglo-Scottish Union of 1707: the Economic Background', *Economic History Review*, 16 (1964), 455–67; C. A. Whatley, 'Economic Causes and Consequences of the Union of 1707', *Scottish Historical Review*, 68 (1989), 150–81; I. Hont, 'The "Rich Country – Poor Country" Debate in Scottish Classical Political Economy', in *Wealth and Virtue: The Shaping of Political Economy in the Scottish Enlightenment*, eds I. Hont and M. Ignatieff (Cambridge, 1983).

Primary source material can be found in P. H. Scott, *1707: The Union of England and Scotland in Contemporary Documents* (Edinburgh, 1979); W. C. Dickinson and G. Donaldson, *A Source Book of Scottish History*, vol. III: *1567–1707* (Edinburgh, 1961); D. Reid (ed.), *The Party-Coloured Mind* (Edinburgh, 1982); and in Fletcher's writings, mentioned above. One of the best roads to an imaginative understanding of Scotland is through the novels of Sir Walter Scott: *Old Mortality*, *Rob Roy*, *The Bride of Lammermoor*, *The Heart of Midlothian*, *Waverley*, and *Redgauntlet*. Hugely popular in the nineteenth century, they are today difficult to approach, but worth perseverance.

10. THE COMMUNITIES OF IRELAND AND THE BRITISH STATE, 1660–1707

The basic narrative accounts of the period 1660–1707 (and 1707 is not seen as either a terminus or a starting point in Irish history) can be found in the last chapters of T. W. Moody, F. X. Martin and F. J. Byrne (eds), *A New History of Ireland*, vol. III: *Early Modern Ireland, 1534–1691* (Oxford, 1976), and in the early chapters of T. W. Moody and W. E. Vaughan (eds), *A New History of Ireland*, vol. IV: *Eighteenth-century Ireland, 1691–1800* (Oxford, 1986); but by far the best introduction is Sean Connolly's brilliant, argumentative *Law, Religion and Power: The Making of Protestant Ireland, 1660–1760* (Oxford, 1992). David Dickson demonstrates by example the case for a 'long eighteenth century' in his *New Foundations: Ireland, 1660–1800* (Dublin, 1987); this volume transcends its textbook format and is particularly illuminating on the workings of the Restoration government in Dublin. Patrick Corish's *The Catholic Community in the Seventeenth and Eighteenth Centuries* (Dublin, 1981), sheds many shafts of light on the Catholic experience – Connolly's devastating criticism of the book (*Irish Economic and Social History*, 1983) notwithstanding. Phil Kilroy's *Protestant Dissent and Controversy in Ireland, 1660–1714* (Cork, 1994) examines the many faces of Irish nonconformity, not just – the usual focus – Ulster Presbyterianism.

Notes and References

1. THE BRITISH PROBLEM, *c.* 1534–1707   *John Morrill*

* I am grateful to Brendan Bradshaw, Steven Ellis, John MacCafferty and David Smith for their forthright, constructive and frequently conflicting advice on earlier drafts of this chapter.

1. Discussion of this point is deferred until the end of the introduction: see below, pp. 20–38

2. J. G. A. Pocock, 'The Limits and Divisions of British History', *American History Review*, 87, no. 2 (1982), p. 318.

3. J. S. Morrill, 'The Fashioning of Britain, 1534–1660', in S. G. Ellis and S. Barber (eds), *Conquest and Union: Fashioning a British State, 1485–1725* (London, 1995), pp. 8–39.

4. This is a paraphrase of the conclusion to Morrill, 'Fashioning', pp. 38–9.

5. This is based on the calculation that the population of England was 2.3 million (J. Hatcher, *Plague, Population and the English Economy, 1348–1530* [London, 1982], p. 71), of Wales 0.25 million (G. Williams, *Renewal and Reformation: Wales 1415–1642* [Oxford, 1987], p. 90), of Scotland 0.5 million (R. A. Houston and I. D. Whyte (eds), *Scottish Society, 1500–1800* [Cambridge, 1989], p. 3), and Ireland 0.75 million (R. Foster (ed.), *The Oxford History of Ireland* [Oxford, 1991], p. 110). The proportion of English speakers being 95 per cent (to allow for Cornish and some borderers of Wales), 40 per cent, 30 per cent, and 65 per cent.

6. There was, in addition, an effectively independent additional dominion – the Lordship of the Isles in the Scottish south-west and tip of north-east Ireland, controlled by the MacDonalds but with the most nominal recognition of Scottish overlordship.

7. For this general point see now S. G. Ellis, *Tudor Frontiers and Noble Power: The Making of the British State* (Oxford, 1995).

8. G. W. J. Wilkins, *Gaelic in Scotland, 1698–1981* (Edinburgh, 1984), pp. 1–41; T. W. Moody, F. X. Martin, F. J. Byrne, *New History of Ireland*, vol. III: *1534–1691* (Oxford, 1978), ch. XX; G. H. Jenkins, *Foundations of Modern Wales, 1642–1789* (Oxford, 1987), pp. 219–23 and passim.

9. I argue this, perhaps too trenchantly, in 'The English, the Scots and the British', in P. S. Hodge (ed.), *Scotland and the Union* (Edinburgh, 1994), pp. 76–86; but note how often the world 'bluff' occurs in the more scholarly J. Robertson, *A Union for Empire: Political Thought and the Union of 1707* (Cambridge, 1995), pp. 203–6.

274   NOTES AND REFERENCES

10. C. Moreland and D. Bannister (eds), *Antique Maps* (1983), at p. 201 (for Abraham Ortelius's map of 1576, which bears the legend *'Angliae, Scotiae et Hiberniae sive Britannicar: Insularum'*) or at p. 211 (Magini's map of 1590 bearing the title *'Britanicae Insulae'*).

11. D. Kendrick, *British Antiquity* (London, 1950).

12. R. Mason, 'Scotching the Brut', in R. Mason (ed.), *Scotland and England, 1286–1815* (Edinburgh, 1985), pp. 60–82.

13. For confirmation of this for a slightly later period, see D. R. Woolf, *The Idea of History in Early Stuart England* (Toronto, 1991), pp. 55–61 and passim.

14. For a general review of this issue, see D. M. Head, 'Henry VIII's Scottish Policy: a Reassessment', *Scottish History Review*, 61 (1982), pp. 1–24. For Henry VIII's recital of the precedents in 1544, see his *Declaration, Conteyning the just causes and consyderations of this present warre* (1542), reprinted in J. A. H. Murray (ed.), *The Complaynte of Scotland* (Early English Text Society, 1872), pp. clvii–clxi.

15. J. S. Morrill, 'A British Patriarchy?: Ecclesiastical Imperialism under the Early Stuarts', in A. Fletcher and P. Roberts (eds), *Religion, Culture and Society in Early Modern Britain* (Cambridge, 1994), pp. 209–37.

16. This account will eschew the words 'nation' and 'nationality' while being influenced by many works on the subject including B. Anderson, *Imagined Communities* (2nd edn; Berkeley, 1992); P. Sahlins, *Boundaries: The Making of France and Spain* (Berkeley, 1989); and – less noticed, but more influential to my thinking – H. Seton-Watson, *Nations and States: An Enquiry into the Origins of Nations and the Politics of Nationalism* (London, 1977).

17. R. R. Davies, 'The Peoples of Britain and Ireland: I, Identities', *Transactions of the Royal History Society*, 6th series, vol. 4 (1994), pp. 1–20.

18. Ibid., and R. R. Davies, 'The Peoples of Britain and Ireland: II, Names, Boundaries, and Regnal Solidarities', *Transactions of the Royal Historical Society*, 6th series, vol. 5 (1995, forthcoming). I am grateful to Rees Davies for showing me a typescript of this important paper.

19. S. Anglo, *Images of Tudor Kingship* (London, 1992), esp. chs 2 and 5.

20. P. Jenkins, 'Identities in Seventeenth-century Wales', paper delivered to a Trevelyan Fund colloquium in Cambridge in July 1994 and to be published in 1996.

21. Davies, 'The Peoples of Britain and Ireland: II', forthcoming.

22. A. Grant, 'Aspects of National Consciousness in Medieval Scotland' in C. Bjorn, A. Grant and K. Stringer (eds), *Nations, Nationalism and Patriotism in the European Past* (Copenhagen, 1994), pp. 68–72.

23. Davies, 'The Peoples of Britain and Ireland: I and II', forthcoming; Grant, 'Aspects', pp. 68–95.

24. This paragraph owes much to the tension between the work of G. Barrow and A. Duncan (see Grant, 'Aspects', pp. 68 n. 1, 69 n. 1, 70 n. 1); and D. Broun, 'The Origin of Scottish Identity', in Bjorn et al., *Nations, Nationalism and Patriotism in the European Past* (Copenhagen, 1994) pp. 35–55.

25. R. R. Davies, *Conquest, Coexistence and Change: Wales 1066–1415* (Oxford, 1987), pp. 19–20; T. Charles-Edwards, 'Some Celtic Kinship Terms', *Bulletin of the Board of Celtic Studies*, XXIV (1970–2), 117, 122.

26. Davies, 'The Peoples of Britain and Ireland: II', forthcoming.

27. Ibid.

28. D. ó Corráin, 'Nationality and Kingship in Pre-Norman Ireland', *Historical Studies*, 2 (1978); F. J. Byrne, *A New History of Ireland: II Medieval Ireland, 1169–1534* (Oxford, 1981), pp. 7–13, 37–42.

29. K. Simms, *From Kings to Warlords: The Changing Political Structure of Gaelic Ireland in the Later Middle Ages* (Woodbridge, 1987), pp. 147–50 and passim.

30. S. G. Ellis, 'Nationalism and Historiography: the Gaelic Experience', forthcoming. I am grateful to Steven Ellis for showing this paper to me and for a discussion of its content.

31. Brendan Bradshaw strongly dissented from a less guarded version of this paragraph when he saw it in draft and is unlikely to be persuaded by this more cautious version, while John MacCafferty urged me to caution, speaking of this as a 'notoriously difficult area, littered with the whitened bones of Celticists'. But I can only report as I find.

32. Ellis, 'Nationalism and Historiography', forthcoming.

33. R. W. Leckie, *The Passage of Dominion: Geoffrey of Monmouth and the Periodization of Insular History in the Twelfth Century* (Toronto, 1981). I owe this reference to Rees Davies.

34. See below, pp. 45–53.

35. Jenkins, 'Identities in Seventeenth-century Wales' (forthcoming).

36. Pocock, 'Limits', p. 317.

37. Ibid., p. 318.,

38. J. G. A. Pocock, 'British History: a Plea for a New Subject', *Journal of Modern History*, 47 (1975), p. 619.

39. R. R. Davies, *Dominion and Conquest: The Experience of Ireland, Scotland and Wales, 1100–1300* (Cambridge, 1990); R. R. Davies (ed.), *The British Isles 1100–1500* (Edinburgh, 1989), esp. introduction and ch. 8.

40. J. H. Elliott, 'The Spanish Monarchy and the Kingdom of Portugal, 1580–1640', in M. Greengrass (ed.), *Conquest and Coalescence: The Shaping of the State in Early Modern Europe* (London, 1991), pp. 48–67.

41. In the 1530s, Thomas Cromwell seems to have favoured a unitary system: see B. Bradshaw, *The Irish Constitutional Revolution in the Sixteenth Century* (Cambridge, 1979), pp. 112–63, esp. 139–46.

42. For the general point, see J. H. Elliott, 'A World of Composite Monarchies', *Past and Present*, 133 (1992), pp. 48–71, the footnotes of which cite most of the relevant modern literature. I have discussed the implications of this important work for the Stuart composite monarchy in 'The Britishness of the "English" Revolution', in R. Asch (ed.), *Three Nations – A Common History?* (Bochum, 1993), pp. 83–116.

43. Morrill, 'Fashioning', pp. 14–26.

44. Steven Ellis urges me to add that this was 'only a re-run in the early modern period of what the English had done in Wales between 1100 and 1283'.

45. The best and liveliest introduction to this dimension of the British problem is probably N. Canny, *Kingdom and Colony: Ireland and the Atlantic World, 1560–1800* (Baltimore, 1988), esp. ch. 2. But he and others have written extensively on the subject.

46. Morgan has discussed Canny's book twice, in a review in *International History Review*, 13, 4 (1991), pp. 810–6, and in 'Mid-Atlantic Blues', in *Irish Review*, no. 11 (1991/2), pp. 50–5.

47. See below, pp. 165–6.

48. For example, J. Gillingham, 'Conquering the Barbarians: War and Chivalry in Twelfth-century Britain', *Haskins Society Journal*, 4 (1992), pp. 67–84 (I am grateful to Dr Daniel Power for a discussion of this article); C. Falls, *Elizabeth's Irish Wars* (1950); D. Stevenson, *Scottish Covenanters and Irish Confederates: Scottish–Irish Relations in the Mid Seventeenth Century* (Belfast, 1981); P. Lenihan, 'The Irish Confederacy, 1642–1649: an Irish State at War' (National University of Ireland, Ph.D thesis, 1995), esp. ch. 6.

49. This is, I take it, Jane Ohlmeyer's perspective, as revealed generally both in J. Ohlmeyer, *Civil War and Restoration in Three Stuart Kingdoms: The Career of Randal MacDonnell, Marquis of Antrim* (Cambridge, 1993), and in J. Ohlmeyer (ed.), *Ireland: From Independence to Occupation, 1641–1660* (Cambridge, 1995), chs 1 and 5. It will be the central thrust of Jonathan Scott's forthcoming book, *England's Troubles*. I am grateful to Dr Scott for many illuminating discussions of this question.

50. Seton-Watson, *Nations and States*, pp. 1–9.

51. J. Kirk, *Patterns of Reformation: Continuity and Change in the Reformation Kirk* (Edinburgh, 1989), esp. ch. 3.

52. A good introduction is C. Lennon, 'The Counter-Reformation in Ireland', in C. Brady and R. Gillespie (eds), *Natives and Newcomers: Essays on the Making of Irish Colonial Identity, 1534–1641* (1986), pp. 75–92.

53. See the admonitions of John Pocock, in 'Plea', p. 619; also J. G. A. Pocock, 'Two Kingdoms and three Histories: Political Thought in British Contexts', in Mason (ed.), *Scots and Britons*, pp. 293–311.

54. I have accused – perhaps a shade harshly – Conrad Russell of doing this in his *Causes of the English Civil War* (Oxford, 1990), and *The Fall of the Stuart Monarchies, 1637–1642* (Oxford, 1991): see J. S. Morrill, *The Nature of the English Civil War* (London, 1993), pp. 259–62. See also below, pp. 28–32.

55. K. Brown, 'British History: a Sceptical Comment', in Asch (ed.), *Three Nations – A Common History*, pp. 117–27.

56. Pocock, 'Limits', p. 318.

57. If 1453 saw the effective end of the continental empire of the Kings of England, 1534 saw the beginnings of the process by which the Tudors redefined their relationship to their various archipelagic dominions.

58. Elton's pithiest account of this is in G. R. Elton, *The Tudor Constitution* (2nd edn; Cambridge, 1982), pp. 233–40.

59. The literature on this is massive. An obvious cross-section would need to include G. R. Elton, *The Tudor Revolution in Government* (Cambridge, 1953), passim; G. R. Elton, *Reform and Renewal* (Cambridge, 1972); J. Guy, *Tudor England* (Oxford, 1988), esp. chs 6–7; P. Williams, *The Tudor Régime* (Oxford, 1979), esp. chs 1–4; C. Coleman and D. Starkey (eds), *Revolution Reassessed: Revisions in the History of Tudor Government and Administration* (Oxford, 1986), introduction and chs 1–2.

60. S. G. Ellis, 'Tudor State Formation and the Shaping of the British Isles', in Ellis and Barber (eds), *Conquest and Union*, pp. 52–8.

61. Ibid.; also Bradshaw, *Irish Constitutional Revolution*, pp. 231–57.

62. S. G. Ellis, *Tudor Ireland* ((London, 1985), pp. 137–48.

63. The classic statement is in Henry's *Declaration, Conteyning the just causes and consyderations of this present warre* (1524), reprinted in J. A. H. Murray (ed.), *The Complaynte of Scotland* (Early English Text Society, 1872), pp. clvii–clxi. There is an excellent short discussion in R. Mason, 'The Reformation and Anglo-British Imperialism', in Mason (ed.), *Scots and Britons*, pp. 167–71. See also more generally, M. Merriman, 'James Henrisoun and "Great Britain": British Union and the Scottish Commonweal', in Mason (ed.), *Scotland and England* (1987), pp. 85–112.

64. The English did not overlook the argument – see the Duke of Somerset's *Epistle or Exhortation to Unitie and Peace* (1548), reprinted in Murray, *The Complaynte of Scotland*, pp. 237–46, in abbreviated form. But it subsided before the onslaught of feudal and then protestant-eschatological arguments.

65. Probably the best recent account of the negotiations leading to the Treaty of Greenwich and its subsequent unravelling is in M. Sanderson, *Cardinal of Scotland: David Beaton, c. 1496–1546* (Edinburgh, 1986).

66. Except that there are hints of his future policy in his summons of James V to a meeting at York in 1541, which James backed out of at the last minute. But even then, Henry's 'hidden agenda' was probably no more than to exact yet another rather empty recognition of his overlordship, useful to Henry mainly in his propaganda wars with the Pope and the Emperor Charles V.

67. For a lively recent summary of these years from a Scottish angle, see M. Lynch, *Scotland: A New History* (1991) chs 12 and 13; for a cogent narrative, see R. K. Marshall, *Mary of Guise* (London, 1977), chs 7–10.

68. The best recent summaries include J. Wormald, *Mary Queen of Scots: A Study in Failure* (1989), chs 4–5; and (in contrast) M. Lynch (ed.), *Mary Stewart: Queen in Three Kingdoms* (Oxford, 1988), esp. chs 1 and 2.

69. The most important recent contribution to this debate is undoubtedly J. Dawson, 'William Cecil and the British Dimension of Early Elizabethan Foreign Policy', *History*, 74 (1989), pp. 196–216;

and more generally, J. Dawson, 'Anglo-Scottish Protestant Culture and Integration in Sixteenth-century Britain', in Ellis and Barber (eds), *Conquest and Union*, pp. 87–118.

70. C. Russell, 'The Reformation and the Creation of the Church of England, 1500–1640', in J. S. Morrill (ed.), *The Oxford Illustrated History of Tudor and Stuart Britain* (1996) pp. 280–4.

71. For the Latin service book, first produced by a Scottish exile – Alisius – for the benefit of continental reformers in the early 1550s and revised and issued under royal letters in 1560, see W. K. Clay, (ed.), *Liturgies and Occasional Forms of Prayer set Forth in the Reign of Queen Elizabeth* (Parker Society, 1847), pp. 299–434. Its provenance and content are discussed in the introduction, pp. xxiv–xxxiii. I am grateful to Professor William Tighe for long and exceptionally helpful discussions of this point.

72. For a preliminary analysis of the period 1559–1641, see Morrill, 'A British Patriarchy?', in Fletcher and Roberts (eds), *Religion, Culture and Society*, pp. 209–37.

73. The best recent discussions of the running dynastic crisis in the later sixteenth century are by Patrick Collinson. See his 'The Monarchical Republic of Elizabeth I', *Bulletin of the Rylands Library*, 69 (1987), and his 'The Elizabethan Exclusion Crisis and the Elizabethan Polity', *Proceedings of the British Academy*, 80 (1994).

74. Dawson, 'William Cecil and the British Dimension', pp. 196–216.

75. G. Donaldson, *The Scottish Reformation* (Cambridge, 1960), pp. 149–173.

76. 'A British Patriarchy?', in Fletcher and Roberts (eds), *Religion, Culture and Society*, pp. 215–20.

77. This is a theme fully explored by C. Brady in *The Chief Governors: The Rise and Fall of Reform Government in Tudor Ireland, 1536–1588)* (Cambridge, 1994).

78. His major study is entitled *Tyrone's Rebellion: The Outbreak of the Nine Years War in Ireland* (London and Dublin, 1993); but see also 'The End of Gaelic Ulster', in *Irish Historical Studies*, 26 (1988), pp. 8–32; and 'Hugh O'Neill and the Nine Years War in Tudor Ireland', *Historical Journal*, 36 (1993), pp. 21–37.

79. Morgan, 'Hugh O'Neill and the Nine Years War', p. 23.

80. Morgan, 'Hugh O'Neill and the Nine Years War', pp. 25–6.

81. Morgan, *Tyrone's Rebellion*, pp. 214–22; Morgan, 'Hugh O'Neill and the Nine Years War', pp. 27–34.

82. Cf. below, pp. 184–90.

83. The latest and authoritative study is by T. ó hAnnracháin, *The Mission of GianBattista Rinuccini to Ireland, 1645–49* (unpublished European University Institute, Ph.D dissertation, 1995); for a slightly contrasting view see P. Lenihan, *The Catholic Confederacy, 1642–9: An Irish State at War* (unpublished National University of Ireland, Ph.D dissertation, 1995), ch. 1. My own thoughts – which preceded my reading of these important theses, can be found in Morrill, 'Fashioning', pp. 28–38.

84. W. R. Foster, *The Church before the Covenant* (Edinburgh, 1975); D. G. Mullan, *Episcopacy in Scotland: The History of an Idea, 1560–1637* (Edinburgh, 1986).

85. I am currently trying to establish what word the English and Scots used to describe their movement of troops across the Anglo-Scottish border in both 1640 and 1643/4. So far my searches are incomplete and inconclusive, but it seems that the Scots do not see themselves as 'invading' England – entering a different polity. I will be reporting the conclusions of my study of the language of military intervention elsewhere.

86. C. Russell, *The Fall of the Stuart Monarchies, 1637–1642* (Oxford, 1991); C. Russell, *The Causes of the English Civil War* (Oxford, 1990); C. Russell, 'The Scottish Party in the English Parliament, 1640–2; or, The Myth of the English Revolution', *Historical Research*, 66 (1993).

87. I am grateful to Barbara Donegan for her informed discussion of this point, which is developed in her forthcoming book on the English at war in the 1640s.

88. In the same way, I am not convinced that the English fiscal system was unreformable in the early seventeenth century (*pace* Conrad Russell, *Causes*, ch. 7, and his wonderfully fresh and provocative Trevelyan Lectures in Cambridge in Lent Term 1995). There was no will to reform it but that will was present once war broke out. Within eighteen months of the outbreak of war, assessment and excise – the mainstay of government finance for 150 years – were introduced. It was civil war that produced the will to reform; but it need not have been civil war. A really nasty foreign (and preferably Catholic) enemy threatening invasion could have had the same effect. Or let us imagine that Charles had settled with the Scots in 1640 and then been faced by something like the 1641 rebellion in Ireland . . .

89. Morrill, 'A British Patriarch?', in Fletcher and Roberts (eds), *Religion, Culture and Society*, pp. 221–38. See also, Morrill, *Nature of the English Revolution*, pp. 91–177.

90. The most interesting and challenging recent discussion of these issues is in N. Canny, 'The Attempted Anglicization of Ireland in the Seventeenth Century: an Exemplar of British History', in Asch (ed.), *Three Nations – a Common History?*, pp. 49–82. The work of John Cooper, as gathered together in G. Aylmer and J. Morrill (eds), *Land Men and Beliefs* (London, 1983), chs 8–11, deserves reconsideration.

91. See the major recent discussion of all aspects of the Revocation in A. Macinnes, *Charles I and the Making of the Covenanting Movement* (Edinburgh, 1991), chs 3–5.

92. See my forthcoming article 'The Unplundering of the Church: Charles I and the Owners of Former Monastic Lands' (in a festschrift).

93. T. Ranger, 'Strafford in Ireland: a Revaluation', *Past and Present*, 19 (1961), pp. 26–45.

94. See, for example, C. Russell, *Unrevolutionary England* (London, 1991), p. 242; P. Donald, 'New Light on Anglo-Scottish Contacts in 1640', *Historical Research*, 62 (1989), pp. 221–9.

95. Russell, *Fall*, chs 12–13; and 'The Scottish Party', pp. 47–52.

280   NOTES AND REFERENCES

96. For two contrasting approaches to this issue, see K. Lindley, 'The Impact of the Irish Rebellion upon England and Wales', *Irish Historical Studies*, 18 (1972), and W. Lamont, *Richard Baxter and the Millennium* (Brighton, 1979), ch. 2.

97. For a fuller discussion of this, see M. Perceval-Maxwell, *The Outbreak of the 1641 Rebellion in Ireland* (1993), esp. ch. 7.

98. C. Hill, *God's Englishman* (1970), p. 176.

99. Morrill, 'Britishness of the English Revolution', pp. 93–115.

100. The standard account remains F. Dow, *Cromwellian Scotland* (Edinburgh, 1979).

101. Cromwell's *Declaration . . . for the Undeceiving of Deluded and Seduced People* (1649), printed in W. C. Abbott, *The Writings and Speeches of Oliver Cromwell*, 4 vols (1934–44), vol. II, p. 201.

102. Dow, *Cromwellian Scotland*, pp. 35–60, 195–210.

103. The basis of English policy, laid out in the Act of Union first drawn up in 1652, approved by the Protector in Council in 1654 and by the second Protectorate Parliament in 1657, was the abolition of the hereditable jurisdictions by which Scottish lords controlled much of the lives of their tenants, and the conversion of the tenures of those tenants into a form of freehold. The aim was to break the social and political power of the nobility and to create a new middling sort grateful to and dependent upon the English; but not to destroy the Scottish nobility in the way it was intended that the Irish nobility should be destroyed (for the text see S. R. Gardiner, *Constitutional Documents of the Puritan Revolution* (3rd edn; Oxford, 1906), pp. 418–23).

104. R. Gillespie, 'Landed Society and the Interregnum in Ireland and Scotland', in R. Mitchison and P. Roebuck (eds), *Economy and Society in Scotland and Ireland* (Edinburgh, 1988), pp. 38–57.

105. This is the gloomy phrase contained in the Rump Parliament's Act of Settlement for Ireland (1652). All were to suffer to a greater or lesser extent (mainly to a greater extent). The Act is most accessibly printed in Gardiner, *Constitutional Documents of the Puritan Revolution*, pp. 392–9.

106. See K. S. Bottigheimer, *English Adventurers and Irish Land: The Adventures in the Cromwellian Settlement of Ireland* (Oxford, 1971).

107. K. Brown, 'The Origins of a British Aristocracy: Integration and its Limitations before the Treaty of Union', in Ellis and Barber (eds), *Conquest and Union*, pp. 222–49.

108. Most recently studied by P. Kilroy, *Protestant Dissent and Controversy in Ireland* (Cork, 1994).

109. T. Barnard, 'Scotland and Ireland in the Later Stuart Monarchy', in Ellis and Barber (eds), pp. 250–75.

110. See especially, I. Cowan, *The Scottish Covenanters, 1660–1688* (London, 1976).

111. Ibid.

112. W. C. Dickinson and G. Donaldson, *A Source Book of Scottish History*, 3 vols (1954), vol. III, pp. 185–6.

113. Barnard, 'Scotland and Ireland in the Later Stuart Monarchy', in Ellis and Barber (eds), pp. 252–8.

114. The most recent summary is by T. Barnard, 'Settling and Unsettling Ireland', in Ohlmeyer (ed.), *Ireland*, pp. 265–80.
115. Kilroy, *Protestant Dissent and Controversy*, pp. 225–49.
116. See T. C. Barnard, 'Crises of Identity among Irish Protestants', *Past and Present*, 127 (1990); J. Smyth, '"Like amphibious animals": Irish Protestants, Ancient Britons, 1691–1707', *Historical Journal*, 36 (1993), 785–98.

2. THE TUDOR REFORMATION AND REVOLUTION IN WALES AND
IRELAND   Brendan Bradshaw

1. Glanmor Williams, *Wales c. 1415–1642* (Oxford, 1987), chs 12–13, especially pp. 330–1; Peter Roberts, 'The Union with England and the identity of Anglican Wales', *Transactions of the Royal Historical Society*, 22 (1972), 49–70.
2. Nicholas Canny presented a revisionist challenge to the view that the Reformation had failed in Ireland by the end of the Tudor period in 'Why the Reformation Failed in Ireland: *une question mal posée*', *Journal of Ecclesiastical History*, 30 (1979), 423–500. However, a number of subsequent studies showed that his case was unsustainable: Karl Bottigheimer, 'The Failure of the Reformation in Ireland: *une question bien posée*', *Journal of Ecclesiastical History*, 36 (1985), 196–207. Colm Lennon, 'The Counter Reformation in Ireland, 1542–1641', in Ciaran Brady and Raymond Gillespie (eds), *Natives and Newcomers* (Dublin 1986), pp. 75–92, C. Lennon, *The Lords of Dublin in the Age of the Reformation* (Dublin, 1989), chs 5 and 6; Alan Ford, 'The Protestant Reformation in Ireland', in Brady and Gillespie, *Natives*, pp. 50–74; Brendan Bradshaw, 'The Reformation in the Cities: Cork, Limerick and Galway, 1534–1603', in John Bradley (ed.), *Settlement and Society in Medieval Ireland* (Kilkenny, 1988), pp. 445–76; Steven G. Ellis, 'Economic Problems of the Church: Why the Reformation Failed in Ireland', *Journal of Ecclesiastical History*, 41 (1990), 239–65.
3. The confessional frame of reference was pioneered by R. Po-Chia, in *Social Discipline in the Reformation: Central Europe 1550–1750* (London, 1989), passim. It was taken up in the survey literature by Euan Cameron, *The European Reformation* (Oxford, 1991), ch. 20.
4. G. R. Elton, *England under the Tudors* (2nd edn; 1974), ch. 7 and pp. 479–85; cf. G. R. Elton, *The Tudor Revolution in Government* (Cambridge, 1969), passim.
5. M. E. James, 'English Politics and the Concept of Honour 1485–1642', in M. E. James, *Society, Politics and Culture: Studies in Early Modern Culture, 1485–1642* (Cambridge, 1986), pp. 308–415 (originally published as *Past and Present Supplement*, no. 3).
6. The quotations are in Roberts, 'Union and Identity', pp. 50 and 51; cf. Williams, *Wales*, pp. 245–6, 275–6; and J. Gwynfor Jones, *Wales and the Tudor State* (Cardiff, 1989), pp. 32–60.
7. These are surveyed in S. G. Ellis, *Tudor Ireland* (London, 1985),

pp. 124–9, 135–7, 228–74. See also N. Canny, *The Elizabethan Conquest of Ireland* (Hassocks, 1976), ch. 7.

8. C. Brady, 'Conservative Subversives: the Community of the Pale and the Dublin Administration, 1556–86', in P. J. Corish (ed.), *Radicals, Rebels and Establishments* (Belfast, 1985), 11–32, Canny, *Elizabethan Conquest*, B. Bradshaw, 'The Beginning of Modern Ireland', in Brian Farrell (ed.), *The Irish Parliamentary Tradition* (Dublin, 1973), pp. 68–87.

9. B. Bradshaw, *The Irish Constitutional Revolution of the Sixteenth Century* (Cambridge, 1979), ch. 9.

10. For an early analysis of European state formation within that frame of reference see N. J. G. Pounds and S. S. Ball, 'Core Areas and the Development of the European State System', *The Annals of the Association of American Geographers*, 54 (1964), 24–40. The place of the 'imperial idea' as an ideological force in the process has been strangely neglected. The seminal ideas of Figgis in that regard do not seem to have entered the mainstream of the subsequent discussion of Figgis's treatment of divine right theory, J. N. Figgis, *The Divine Right of Kings* (2nd edn; Cambridge, 1922), see especially chs 3–5. The seminal study of Frances Yates seems to have suffered a similar fate, *Astraea: The Imperial Theme in the Sixteenth Century* (London, 1975), passim. See also note 43 below.

11. Donal MacCartney, *The Dawning of Democracy: Ireland 1800–1870* (Dublin, 1987), pp. 1–25. An earlier revisionist interpretation had downplayed the element of bribery and bullying but see K. Theodore Hoppen, *Ireland since 1800: Conflict and Conformity* (London, 1989), 13–14.

12. This thesis, expressed from various standpoints, is found *inter alia* in G. V. Jourdan, 'The Breach with Rome', in W. A. Phillips (ed.), *The Church of Ireland*, vol. ii (London, 1934), pp. 235–6, 253–4; R. Dudley Edwards, *Church and State in Tudor Ireland* (Dublin, 1935), passim, but especially pp. xxxix–xliii, 195–202; Margaret MacCurtain, *Tudor and Stuart Ireland* (Dublin, 1972), p. 63.

13. R. R. Davies, *Domination and Conquest: The Experience of Ireland, Scotland and Wales* (Cambridge, 1990), pp. 73–84; Robin Frame, *The Political Development of the British Isles* (Oxford, 1990), pp. 35–9, 156–60. On Wales see Williams, *Wales, 1415–1642*, ch. 2; on Ireland see J. A. Watt, 'The Anglo-Irish Colony under Strain 1327–99', in Art Cosgrove (ed.), *A New History of Ireland*, vol. ii (Oxford, 1987), pp. 352–96, especially pp. 386–91; cf. James Lydon, *Ireland in the Later Middle Ages* (Dublin, 1973), pp. 94–7.

14. This orthodox account of the preconditions of the Tudor Reformation was provided by A. G. Dickens, *The English Reformation* (London, 1964), especially chs 3, 5 and 6. That these elements do not suffice of themselves to account for the success of the Tudor religious programme has been demonstrated by recent revisionist writing, most notably by Christopher Haïgh, *English Reformations* (Oxford, 1993), pp. 1–21 and part I; and Eamon Duffy, *The Stripping of the Altars* (New Haven, 1992), part I. However, it seems clear that they retain their validity as significant elements in moulding a *milieu* from which the

state-sponsored Reformation was enabled to draw crucial support for its successive campaigns: see A. G. Dickens, *The English Reformation* (second edn; 1989), pp. 9–24. On the absence of such preconditions in Wales see G. Williams, *The Welsh Church from Conquest to Reformation* (Cardiff, 1976), ch. 14.

15. G. R. Elton, *Reform and Reformation* (London, 1977), ch. 9 at pp. 203–5.

16. The act of Union is printed in Ivor Bowen (ed.), *Statutes of Wales* (London, 1908), p. 75; also in A. Luders et al. (eds), *Statutes of the Realm* (London, 1810–24), vol. iii, p. 563; see also Gwynfor Jones, *Wales and the Tudor State*, 1–38.

17. W. R. B. Robinson, 'The Tudor Revolution in Welsh Government', *English Historical Review*, 103 (1989), 1–20; Elton, *Reform and Reformation*, pp. 203–5.

18. Jones, *Wales*, ch. 1.

19. Williams, *Wales*, pp. 264–5; cf, Brady, Chapter 4 below, pp. 90–117.

20. Williams, *Wales*, pp. 249–50, 264–5; cf. Penry Williams, *The Tudor Regime* (Oxford, 1979), pp. 441–3.

21. Williams, *Wales*, pp. 78–9, 249–50, 264–5.

22. Ibid., ch. 2.

23. Ibid., pp. 242–3.

24. Robinson, 'Tudor Revolution', passim.

25. Williams, *Wales*, pp. 238–46.

26. Ibid., pp. 246–8; cf. Roberts, 'Union and Identity', pp. 49–51. Sydney Anglo persuasively argues that the implications of Henry Tudor's British descent received little attention outside of Wales, including from the Tudors themselves. See S. Anglo, *Images of Tudor Kingship* (London, 1992), ch. 2.

27. Elton, *Reform and Reformation*, pp. 203–5; Williams, *Wales*, pp. 262–4; cf. Penry Williams, *Tudor Regime*, pp. 441–3.

28. Williams, *Wales*, p. 274; Gwynfor Jones, *Wales and the Tudor State*, pp. 36–8.

29. Bradshaw, *Constitutional Revolution*, pp. 106–28.

30. Ibid.

31. Ibid.

32. Above, pp. 41–2.

33. Above, pp. 46–7.

34. Katharine Simms, *From Kings to Warlords* (Woodbridge, 1987), ch. 2; J. A. Watt, 'Gaelic Polity and Cultural Identity', in Art Cosgrove (ed.), *New History of Ireland*, vol. ii, (Oxford, 1987), pp. 319–24; Art Cosgrove, 'England and Ireland, 1399–1447', in *New History*, vol. ii, pp. 530–2; Art Cosgrove, 'The Emergence of the Pale, 1399–47', in *New History*, vol. ii, pp. 533–56; James Lydon, *Ireland in the Later Middle Ages* (Dublin, 1973), pp. 104–6.

35. Lydon, *Ireland in the Later Middle Ages*, ch. 4; D. B. Quinn, 'Aristocratic Autonomy, 1460–94', *New History*, vol. ii, pp, 591–6.

36. J. A. Watt, 'Approaches to the History of Fourteenth-century Ireland', in *New History*, vol. ii, pp. 303–13 at pp. 308–12.

37. Ibid., Quinn 'Aristocratic Autonomy', pp. 591–7; Simms, *From Kings to Warlords*, pp. 16–20, and chs 7 and 8; J. Lydon, 'The Years of Crisis, 1254–1315', in *New History*, vol. ii, pp. 179–204. R. R. Coss, 'Bastard Feudalism Revised', *Past and Present*, 33 (1989), 27–64; cf. K. B. MacFarlane, *England in the Fifteenth Century* (London, 1981, ch. 2.

38. Quinn, 'Aristocratic Autonomy', pp. 591–607; Lydon, *Ireland in the Later Middle Ages*, chs 5 and 6.

39. F. Martin, 'Overlord becomes Feudal Lord, 1172–85', *New History*, vol. ii, pp. 98–126 at pp. 110–126.

40. G. J. Hand, *English Law in Ireland, 1290–1324* (Cambridge, 1967), passim; A. J. Otway-Ruthven, *A History of Medieval Ireland* (London, 1968), chs 3 and 5.

41. Robin Frame, *The Political Development of the British Isles* (Oxford, 1990), pp. 179–87.

42. Quinn, 'Aristocratic Autonomy', *New History*, vol. ii, pp. 591–617; D. B. Quinn, 'The Hegemony of the Earls of Kildare', *New History*, vol. ii, pp. 638–60; Lydon, *Ireland in the Later Middle Ages*, chs 5 and 6.

43. J. R. Lander, *Crown and Community* (London, 1980), pp. 356–61.

44. The best recent studies of a neglected subject are John Guy, 'Thomas Cromwell and the Intellectual Origins of the English Revolution', in John Guy and Alastair Fox, *Reassessing the Henrician Age* (London, 1986), pp. 151–78; and Walter Ullmann, '"This realm of England is an Empire"', *Journal of Ecclesiastical History*, 30 (1979), 175–203; see also the perceptive treatment of G. R. Elton, *England under the Tudors*, pp. 160–2, and note 10 above; cf. the seminal classic, Frances Yates, *Astraea: The Imperial Theme in the Sixteenth Century* (London, 1975), part II.

45. See the Works of Guy, Fox and Ullmann, and in note 44.

46. Quoted in Guy, 'Intellectual Origins', p. 166.

47. Quoted in Bradshaw, *Constitutional Revolution*, p. 63.

48. P. G. Stein, 'Roman Law' in J. H. Burns (ed.), *The Cambridge History of Medieval Political Thought* (Cambridge, 1988) pp. 37–47. at pp. 45–7.

49. I am presently engaged on a study which extends the comparative analysis presented here down to the end of the Tudor period and which seeks to highlight, *inter alia*, the consequences in practice of the implementation of the Crown's programme of political and religious reform in Wales by the local gentry.

3. BRITISH POLICIES BEFORE THE BRITISH STATE
Hiram Morgan

1. A major influence in my approach to this chapter has been Ronald Robinson and John Gallagher, *Africa and the Victorians: The Official Mind of Imperialism* (London, 1981).

2. Roger Mason, 'The Scottish Reformation and the Origins of Anglo-

British Imperialism', in R. Mason (ed.), *Scots and Britons: Scottish Political Thought and the Union of 1603* (Cambridge, 1994), ch. 7; Andrew Hadfield, 'Briton and Scythian: Tudor Representations of Irish Origins', *Irish Historical Studies*, XXVIII (1993), 391–408.

3. David Buisseret, *Monarchs, Maps and Ministers: Cartography as a Tool of Government in Early Modern Europe* (Chicago, 1992), p. 2.

4. Quoted in Keith Brown, 'The Price of Friendship: the Well-Affected and English Economic Clientage in Scotland before 1603', in Roger Mason (ed.), *Scotland and England, 1286–1815* (Edinburgh, 1982), p. 142.

5. Quoted in J. J. Silke, *Kinsale: Spanish Intervention in Ireland at the End of the Elizabethan Wars* (Liverpool, 1970), p. 76.

6. Cambridge University Library, KK 1 15 61, ff. 126–7.

7. *Treasurers' Accounts, Scotland*, VI, pp. XXV, XXX–XXXVI.

8. Patricia Buchanan, *Margaret Tudor, Queen of Scots* (Edinburgh, 1985), pp. 246–7.

9. Steven G. Ellis, *Tudor Ireland: Crown, Community and Conflict of Cultures* (London, 1985), p. 108–18.

10. S. G. Ellis, 'A Border Baron and the Tudor State: the Rise and Fall of Lord Dacre of the North', *Historical Journal*, xxxv (1992), 253–77.

11. Ellis, *Tudor Ireland*, pp. 121–30.

12. David Head, 'Henry VIII's Scottish Policy: a Reassessment', *Scottish Historical Review*, LXI (1982), 12–13.

13. Glanmor Williams, *Recovery, Reorientation and Reformation: Wales, c. 1415–1642* (Oxford, 1987) pp. 264–78.

14. Ellis, *Tudor Ireland*, p. 133.

15. See G. R. Elton, *Reform and Reformation, England, 1509–1558* (London, 1977), pp. 203–11; Alan Smith, *The Emergence of a Nation State: The Commonwealth of England* (London, 1984), ch. 3; and B. I. Bradshaw, *The Irish Constitutional Revolution of the Sixteenth Century* (Cambridge, 1979), parts 2 and 3.

16. Philip Smith, 'On the Fringe and in the Middle: the MacDonalds of Antrim and the Isles', *History Ireland*, ii, 2 (1994) 15–18.

17. Bradshaw, *Irish Constitutional Revolution*, chs 7–8; see also Ellis, *Tudor Ireland*, pp. 136–44.

18. James Hogan, *Ireland in the European System* (London, 1920), pp. 65–73.

19. Donald Gregory, *The History of the Western Highland and Isles of Scotland from AD 1493 to AD 1625* (Edinburgh, 1881), pp. 156–76.

20. Mason, 'The Scottish Reformation', in Mason (ed.), *Scots and Briton*, p. 175.

21. Arthur Clifford (ed.), *The State Papers and Letters of Sir Ralph Sadler*, 3 vols (Edinburgh, 1809), vol. III, p. 326.

22. Gordon Donaldson, *Scotland, James V–James VII* (Edinburgh, 1979), pp. 75–9; M. H. Merriman, 'The Assured Scots: Scottish Collaborators with England during the Rough Wooing', *Scottish Historical Review*, XLVIII (1968), 10–34; M. H. Merriman, 'The Forts of Eyemouth: Anvils of the British Union', *Scottish Historical Review*, LXVII (1988), 142–55.

23. Ellis, *Tudor Ireland*, pp. 228–33.

24. David Potter, 'French Intrigue in Ireland during the Reign of Henri II', *International History Review*, V (1983), 161–80.

25. Ciaran Brady, *The Chief-Governors: The Rise and Fall of Reform Government in Ireland, 1534–1586* (Cambridge, 1995) p. 59–60.

26. My italics.

27. Quoted in Jane Dawson, 'William Cecil and the British Dimension of Early Elizabethan Foreign Policy', *History*, LXXIV (1989), 196–216.

28. Ibid., 196–216; Jane Dawson, 'Two Kingdoms or Three? Ireland in Anglo-Scottish Relations in the Middle of the Sixteenth Century', in R. Mason (ed.), *Scotland and England*, pp. 113–38.

29. *Calendar of State Papers, Ireland*, vol. I, pp. 141–2.

30. Ibid., 149–50.

31. *Calendar of Carew Manuscripts*, vol. I, p. 302.

32. Dawson, 'Two Kingdoms or Three', p. 126; *Calendar of State Papers, Ireland*; I, 298–9.

33. A. Collins (ed.), *Letters and Memorials of State* (2 vols, London, 1746), I, pp. 11–12; Calendar of State Papers, Ireland, I, p. 321.

34. See Ciaran Brady, 'The Killing of Shane O'Neill: Some New Evidence', *Irish Sword*, XV (1982). For evidence that Sidney and his client Sir William Piers were behind the assassination of Shane by the MacDonalds see 'Sir Henry Sidney's Memoir of his Government of Ireland, 1583', *Ulster Journal of Archaeology*, 1st series, III (1855), 91.

35. Collins (ed.), *Letters*, vol. I, p. 24.

36. Ellis, *Tudor Ireland*, pp. 262, 265.

37. Collins (ed.), *Letters*, vol. I, p. 32; N. P. Canny, *The Elizabethan Conquest of Ireland: A Pattern Established* (Hassocks, 1976), pp. 77–84; J. J. Silke, *Ireland and Europe, 1559–1607* (Dublin, 1966), pp. 9–12.

38. Canny, *Elizabethan Conquest*, pp. 84–92; H. Morgan, 'The Colonial Venture of Sir Thomas Smith in Ulster, 1571–75', *Historical Journal*, XXVII (1985), 261–75.

39. R. Garnett, 'Letter of Antonio de Guaras to the Irish Rebels, 1573', *English Historical Review*, VII (1893), 91–2; B. de S. de la Mothe Fenelon, *Correspondence Diplomatique*, ed. A. Teulet, 7 vols (London, and Paris, 1838–40), vol. IV, pp. 268, 339–40.

40. This section is based on the brilliant unpublished dissertation of Mitchell Leimon, 'Sir Francis Walsingham and the Anjou Marriage Plan, 1574–81' (Cambridge Ph.D, 1989). See also C. Brady, 'Faction and the Origins of the Desmond Rebellion of 1579', *Irish Historical Studies*, XXII (1981), 289–312.

41. PRO, SP 63/122, no. 94.

42. Bodleian Library, MS 30237 f. 51.

43. H. Morgan, *Tyrone's Rebellion: The Outbreak of the Nine Years War in Tudor Ireland* (Woodbridge, 1993), ch. 3; Donaldson, *Scotland*, pp. 182–3; *Calendar of Scottish Papers*, vol. VIII, pp. 43–6.

44. Conyers Read, *Mr Secretary Walsingham and the Policy of Queen Elizabeth*, 3 vols (Oxford, 1967), vol. I, pp. 57–8, 68–74.

45. *HMC Salisbury MSS*, XV, p. 2.

46. *Acts of the Privy Council*, XVIII, pp. xviii–xx; XXV, pp. xxix–xxxi.

47. *HMC Salisbury MSS*, IV, pp. 117–18, 145.

48. Morgan, 'The Fall of Sir John Perrot', in John Guy (ed.), *The Reign of Elizabeth I: Court and Culture in the Last Decade* (Cambridge, 1995).

49. Anne Chambers, *Chieftain to Knight, Tibbot Bourke, 1567–1629* (Dublin, 1983), pp. 60–66; Morgan, *Tyrone's Rebellion*, p. 60.

50. Morgan, *Tyrone's Rebellion*, chs 4, 7–9.

51. *Calendar of State Papers, Ireland*, vol. V, p. 457.

52. A. J. Sheehan, 'The Overthrow of the Plantation of Munster in October 1598', *Irish Sword*, XV (1982), 11–22.

53. Silke, *Kinsale*, chs 8–11.

54. G. A. Hayes-McCoy, *Scots Mercenary Forces in Ireland, 1565–1603* (Dublin, 1937), p. 193.

55. Ibid., p. 315.

56. Morgan, *Tyrone's Rebellion*, pp. 180–2.

57. Hayes-McCoy, *Scots Mercenary Forces*, chs 8 and 9.

58. Ibid., pp. 329–30.

59. Quoted in Brown, 'The Price of Friendship', in R. Mason (ed.), *Scotland and England*, p. 139.

60. Donaldson, *Scotland*, p. 183.

4. ENGLAND'S DEFENCE AND IRELAND'S REFORM: THE DILEMMA OF THE IRISH VICEROYS, 1541–1641 · Ciaran Brady

1. The formal powers of the Irish viceroy are set out and discussed in Steven G. Ellis, *Tudor Ireland: Crown, Community and the Conflict of Cultures* (London, 1985), ch. 4; Ciaran Brady, 'Court, Castle and Country: the Framework of Government in Tudor Ireland', in Ciaran Brady and Raymond Gillespie (eds), *Natives and Newcomers: Essays in the Making of Irish Colonial Society, 1534–1641* (Dublin, 1986), pp. 22–49.

2. A list of the most important viceroys of the period and their dates of service is supplied in the appendix to this chapter. The four attainted viceroys were Lord Leonard Grey, Sir John Perrot, Robert Devereux, Earl of Essex, and Thomas Wentworth, Earl of Strafford: three were executed, Perrot died in the tower.

3. Sir Anthony St Leger, Sir William Fitzwilliam, and Henry Cary, Viscount Falkland, all left office under a cloud of allegations concerning corruption and incompetence; Arthur Grey, Baron de Wilton, was forced to resign amidst charges of brutality.

4. Sir William Pelham and Thomas, Lord Burgh died while campaigning in Ireland; Sir Edward Belingham contracted a fatal illness and the Earl of Sussex's administration was paralysed by his illness in 1564.

5. On the circumstances at Court which led to the fall and in some cases ruin of particular viceroys see Ciaran Brady, *The Chief Governors: The Rise and Fall of Reform Government in Tudor Ireland 1536–1588* (Cambridge, 1994), pp. 20–5, 65–71, 102–7, 153–8; Hiram Morgan, 'The

Fall of Sir John Perrot' in J. A. Guy (ed.), *The Reign of Elizabeth I: Court and Culture in the Last Decade* (Cambridge, 1995); C. E. Pike, 'The Intrigue to Deprive the Earl of Essex of the Lord Lieutenancy of Ireland', *Transactions of the Royal Historical Society*, 3rd series, V (1911), pp. 89–104; H. F. Kearney, *Strafford in Ireland, 1633–1641: A Study in Absolutism* (Manchester, 1959), ch. 14; Conrad Russell, *The Fall of the British Monarchies* (Oxford, 1991), ch. 7.

6. For comparative perspectives on the evolution of Scotland and Ireland in the later Middle Ages see R. R. Davies, *Dominion and Conquest: The Experience of Ireland, Scotland and Wales, 1100–1300* (Cambridge, 1990); G. W. S. Barrow, *Scotland and its Neighbours in the Middle Ages* (London, 1992), esp., pp. 23–44; Roger Mason (ed.), *Scotland and England, 1282–1815* (Edinburg, 1987), esp. chs 1, 4–6.

7. On the different historical development of Ireland and Wales see Chapter 2 above; also Ciaran Brady, 'Comparable Histories: Tudor Reform in Ireland and Wales?', in Steven Ellis and Sarah Barber (eds), *Conquest and Union* (London, 1995), pp. 64–86.

8. Such anomalies are discussed at greater length in R. D. Edwards and T. W. Moody, 'The History of Poynings' Law: part I, 1494–1615', in *Irish Historical Studies*, II (1940–1), pp. 415–24; Brendan Bradshaw *The Irish Constitutional Revolution of the Sixteenth Century* (Cambridge, 1979), pt iii; Brady, 'Court, Castle and Country'; and Michael Perceval Maxwell, 'Ireland and the Monarchy in the early Stuart Multiple Kingdom', *Historical Journal*, 34 (1991), 279–95.

9. The best general introduction to such developments is K. W. Nicholls, 'Gaelic Society and Economy in the High Middle Ages', in Art Cosgrove (ed.), *A New History of Ireland*, vol. ii: *Medieval Ireland, 1169–1534* (Oxford, 1987), pp. 397–438; Nicholls, *Land, Law and Society in Sixteenth Century Ireland* (O'Donnell Lecture, Dublin, 1976); for more detailed studies see Katharine Simms, *From Kings to Warlords: The Changing Political Structure of Gaelic Ireland in the Late Middle Ages* (Woodbridge, 1987); Peadar Livingstone, *The Monaghan Story* (Enniskillen, 1980); Mary O'Dowd, *Power, Politics and Land: Early Modern Sligo, 1568–1688* (Belfast, 1991).

10. On Ireland's role in European international relations see, in general, William Palmer, *The Problem of Ireland in Tudor Foreign Policy 1485–1603* (Woodbridge, 1994).

11. On the Kildare rebellion and its ramifications see Laurence Corristine, *The Revolt of Silken Thomas: A Challenge to Henry VIII* (Dublin, 1987); Brendan Bradshaw, 'Cromwellian Reform and the Origins of the Kildare Rebellion', *Transactions of the Royal Historical Society*, 5th series, 27 (1977), pp. 69–93; and Steven Ellis, 'Tudor Policy and the Kildare Ascendancy in the Lordship of Ireland', *Irish Historical Studies*, XX (1976–7), pp. 235–71.

12. Brady, *Chief Governors*, pp. 13–25.

13. Bradshaw, *Irish Constitutional Revolution* pt iii; Brady, *Chief Governors*, pp. 25–44.

14. Brady, *Chief Governors*, pp. 45–71; Palmer, *Problem of Ireland*, ch. 4.

15. Brady, 'Court, Castle and Country', and *Chief Governors*, pp. 72–158, 291–300.

16. For Sussex's major statements of policy see his memoranda of 1560 and 1562 in *Calendar of Carew Manuscripts (1515–74)*, pp. 300–4, 330–44.

17. *Calendar of Carew Manuscripts (1515–74)*, pp. 300–4.

18. Brady, *Chief Governors*, pp. 101–7; James Hogan, 'Shane O'Neill comes to the Court of Elizabeth', in Seamus Pender (ed.), *Feil-Scribhinn Torna* (Cork, 1947), pp. 154–70.

19. Brady, *Chief Governors*, pp. 136–58; see also Nicholas Canny, *The Elizabethan Conquest of Ireland: A Pattern Established, 1565–76* (Hassocks, 1976), ch. 5.

20. The significance of Perrot's work in regard to composition awaits more detailed study: see Bernadette Cunningham, 'The Composition of Connacht in the Lordships of Clanrickard and Thomond', in *Irish Historical Studies*, XXIX (1984–5), pp. 1–14; and 'Natives and Newcomers in Mayo, 1560–1603', in Raymond Gillespie and Gerard Moran (eds), *A Various Country: Essays in Mayo History* (Westport, 1987), pp. 24–43.

21. Ciaran Brady, 'Faction and the Origins of the Desmond Rebellion of 1579' in *Irish Historical Studies*, XXII (1981), 289–312; Colm Lennon, *Sixteenth Century Ireland: The Incomplete Conquest* (Dublin, 1994), ch. 9.

22. With the benefit of hindsight, historians, myself included, have been inclined to emphasise the problems and failings of Perrot's administration – see David Mathew, 'The Fall of Lord Deputy Perrot', in D. Mathew, *The Celtic Peoples and Renaissance Europe* (London, 1933), ch. 11; Brady *Chief Governors*, pp. 291–300; but for a more positive view of Perrot's achievements see Hiram Morgan, *Tyrone's Rebellion: The Origins of the Nine Years War in Ulster* (Woodbridge, 1993), and H. Morgan, 'The Fall of Sir John Perrot', in Guy (ed.), *The Reign of Elizabeth I: Court and Culture in the Last Decade*.

23. The process of intermarriage between local families and legal and administrative newcomers is illustrated in the short biographies included in F. E. Ball, *The Judges in Ireland, 1221–1921*, 2 vols (London, 1926).

24. See Donald Jackson, *Intermarriage in Ireland, 1550–1650* (Montreal, 1970); Nicholas Canny, 'The Permissive Frontier: Social Control in English Settlements in Ireland and Virginia, 1550–1650' in K. R. Andrews et al. (eds), *The Westward Enterprise* (Liverpool, 1978); and 'Dominant Minorities: English Settlers in Ireland and Virginia, 1550–1650', in A. C. Hepburn (ed.), *Minorities in History, Historical Studies XII* (London, 1978). For Munster see Michael MacCarthy-Morrogh, *The Munster Plantation: English Migration to Southern Ireland, 1583–1641* (Oxford, 1986).

25. For contemporary accounts of his extraordinary behaviour towards his councillors, including a serious physical assault on the aged Marshal of the army, see *Calendar of State Papers of Ireland, 1586–88*, pp. 255, 350–54, 554–6.

26. Mathew, 'The Fall of Sir John Perrot'; Morgan, 'The Fall of

Sir John Perrot'; see also Pauline Henley, 'The Treason of Sir John Perrot', in *Studies: an Irish Quarterly* (1932), pp. 404–22.

27. For Perrot's dissatisfaction with the progress of the Munster scheme see *Calendar of State Papers, Ireland, 1586–88*, pp. 48, 91–2, 276, 388–9.

28. These factors are discussed in Henley, 'The Treason of Sir John Perrot' and most recently, Morgan, 'The Trial of Sir John Perrot'. For Lord Chancellor Halton's growing personal interest in Ireland see Eric St John Brooks, *Sir Christopher Hatton: Queen Elizabeth's Favourite* (London, 1946), ch. 12.

29. Fitzwilliam's administrations are more fully discussed in my forthcoming article 'Sir William Fitzwilliam and the Elizabethan Experience in Ireland'.

30. On the conduct of the wartime viceroys in general, see Cyril Falls, *Elizabeth's Irish Wars* (London, 1950), chs xiii–xxiii.

31. On the use and abuse of concordatums see Elizabeth's 'Instructions to the Earl of Essex, 25 March 1599', *Col. Carew Manuscripts (1589–1600)*, pp. 292–5; Privy Council to Sir George Carew, 14 July 1601, *Col. Carew Manuscripts (1601–3)*, p. 107; Elizabeth's 'Instructions to Lord Deputy and Council, June 1600', *Calendar of State Papers, Ireland 1601–3*, pp. 272–8; Chichester to Viscount Crambourne, *Calendar of State Papers, Ireland, 1603–6*, pp. 266–7; for a representative sample of concordatums see ibid., pp. 279–84.

32. For examples of this kind of writing see Nicholas Dawtrey's 'A Book of Questions and Answers', ed. Hiram Morgan, in *Analecta Hibernica*, no. 36 (1993); Hugh Mostyn's 'Plot for Ireland', Nov. 1598, PRO, S.P. 63/202 pt 3/185; Sir Henry Docwra, 'A Narration of Services Done by the Army', ed. John O'Donovan, in *Miscellany of the Celtic Society* (Dublin, 1849). The most convenient edition of Spenser is W. L. Renwick's (Oxford, reprt. 1970).

33. Compare Nicholas Canny, 'The Treaty of Mellifont and the Organisation of Ulster', in *The Irish Sword*, IX (1969–1970), pp. 249–62; 'The Flight of the Earls, 1607', in *Irish Historical Studies*, XVII (1970–1), pp. 380–99, with Devonshire to Cranbourne, 26 April 1605, and to Salisbury, June 1605, HMC, *Salisbury MSS*, xvii, pp. 159, 285–6.

34. The best study of Chichester's viceroyalty is John McCavitt, 'The Lord Deputyship of Sir Arthur Chichester in Ireland, 1605–1616' (unpublished PhD Queen's University, Belfast, 1988): a revised version of the thesis is due for publication shortly by the Institute of Irish Studies, Queen's University, Belfast.

35. McCavitt, 'Chichester', ch. 4 passim, and pp. 115–21, 128–30.

36. For Chichester's initial plans see *Calendar of State Papers, Ireland, 1606–8*, pp. 389, 404–6, 454–5, 606–7; and 'Ulster Plantation Papers' ed. T. W. Moody, in *Analecta Hibernica*, VIII, esp. pp. 281–6; on the development of the broader policy, Michael Perceval-Maxwell, *The Scottish Migration to Ulster in the Reign of James I* (London, 1973), pp. 82–90; on Chichester's reaction, see Chichester to Northampton, 31 October 1610, *Calendar of State Papers, Ireland, 1608–10*, pp. 521–2.

37. For the servitors' holdings, including Chichester's, see Philip

Robinson, *The Plantation of Ulster: British Settlement in an Irish Landscape, 1600–1670* (Dublin, 1984), appendix 2, pp. 196–9.

38. Aidan Clarke and R. Dudley Edwards, 'Pacification, Plantations and the Catholic Question, 1603–1623', in T. W. Moody et al. (eds), *A New History of Ireland, III: Early Modern Ireland*, pp. 219–21.

39. McCavitt, 'Chichester', pp. 318–19.

40. For a representative expression of this attitude see Chichester to Secretary May, 27 May 1612, in R. D. Edwards (ed.), 'Letter-book of Sir Arthur Chichester', in *Analecta Hibernica*, 8 (1938), pp. 27–8.

41. Linda Levy Peck, *Northampton: Patronage and Policy at the Court of James I* (London, 1982), pp. 89–94; see also Chichester's 'Letter-book', pp. 151–2.

42. Anthony Sheehan, 'Irish Revenues and English Subventions, 1559–1622', in *Proceedings of the Royal Irish Academy*, 90, Section C, no. 2 (1990), pp. 35–65.

43. 'Instructions' to Sir George Carew, 24 June 1611; James I to Sir Arthur Chichester, 24 June 1611, *Calendar of State Papers, Ireland 1611–14*, pp. 73–4; for Chichester's reaction to the 1613 commission see his 'Letter-book', pp. 143–7.

44. McCavitt, 'Chichester', p. 36.

45. Ibid., pp. 42–75.

46. T. W. Moody, 'The Irish Parliament under Elizabeth and James I', in *Proceedings of the Royal Irish Academy*, 45, Section C (1939), pp. 41–81, esp. pp. 58–61; Victor Treadwell, 'The House of Lords in the Irish Parliament of 1613–15', in *English Historical Review*, LXXX (1965), pp. 92–107.

47. On the character of Jacobean Court patronage in general, see Linda Levy Peck, *Court Patronage and Corruption in Early Stuart England* (London, 1990).

48. Peck, *Court Patronage*, pp. 43–5; Neil Cuddy, 'The Revival of Entourage: the Bedchamber of James I, 1603–1625', in David Starkey et al., *The English Court from the Wars of the Roses to the Civil War* (London, 1987), pp. 173–225; C. R. Mayes, 'The Early Stuart and the Irish Peerage', in *English Historical Review*, LXXIII (1958), PP. 227–51; for Chichester's continuing sensitivity to Scottish interests, see his 'Letter-book', pp. 20–2.

49. McCavitt, 'Chichester', pp. 304–19; Perceval-Maxwell, *Scottish Migration*, pp. 68–90.

50. McCavitt, 'Chichester', pp. 422–32.

51. Peck, *Northampton*, pp. 205–12; Roger Lockyer, *Buckingham: The Life and Political Career of George Villiers, First Duke of Buckingham* (London, 1981), pp. 16-35.

52. Compare McCavitt, 'Chichester', pp. 433–40, with Vera Rutledge, 'Court–Castle faction and the Irish Viceroyalty: the Appointment of Sir Oliver St John as Lord Deputy of Ireland in 1616', in *Irish Historical Studies*, XXVI (1988–9), 233–49.

53. On St John in general, see *Dictionary of National Biography*; and Vera Rutledge, 'The Politics of Reform in Ireland under Oliver St John' (unpublished MA thesis, McGill University, 1976).

54. Cuddy, 'The Revival of Entourage', in Starkey et al., *The English Court*, esp. pp. 214–25; Lockyer, *Buckingham*, pp. 53–75.

55. This paragraph is based upon Victor Treadwell's 'Buckingham and Ireland, 1616–1628: a Study in Anglo-Irish Politics', currently being prepared for publication by Irish Academic Press. I am grateful to Dr Treadwell for allowing me to see this valuable work in advance of publication.

56. Rutledge, 'The Politics of Reform', chs 2 and 6; the figures have been extracted from the 'Report of the 1622 Commissioners on revenues etc.', British Library, Add MSS 4756, fols 39, 50–1, 58.

57. See, in general, Conrad Russell, *Parliaments in English Politics, 1621–29*, (Oxford, 1979); Robert Zaller, *The Parliament of 1621: A Study in Constitutional Conflict* (Berkeley, 1971); the importance of the issue of Irish reform in the first session of this parliament is demonstrated by Treadwell in 'Buckingham and Ireland', ch. 4.

58. Treadwell, 'Buckingham and Ireland', chs 5 and 7; the commissioners' reports are contained in British Library, Add MSS 4756; a full edition is being prepared by Dr Treadwell for the Irish Manuscripts Commission.

59. H. F. Kearney, 'The Court of Wards and Liveries in Ireland, 1622–41', in *Proceedings of the Royal Irish Academy*, 57, Sec. C (1955), pp. 29–68.

60. Aidan Clarke, *The Old English in Ireland, 1625–42* (London, 1966), ch. 2, also pp. 238–54 for a full list of these concessions known as 'the Graces'.

61. For a vivid contemporary account of these negotiations see Sir James Ware's 'Diary', June 1627, *Calendar of State Papers, Ireland, 1625–32* pp. 244–6.

62. Clarke, *Old English*, ch. 3; and A. Clarke, 'The History of Poynings' Law, 1615–41' in *Irish Historical Studies*, XVIII (1972–3), pp. 207–22; J. P. Cooper, 'Strafford and the Byrne's Country', in *Irish Historical Studies*, XV (1966–7), pp. 1–20.

63. The classic study remains H. F. Kearney, *Strafford in Ireland, 1633–41: A Study in Absolutism* (Manchester, 1959; reprint Cambridge, 1989); but see also Terence Ranger 'Strafford in Ireland: a revaluation', in Trevor Aston (ed.), *Crisis in Europe, 1560–1660* (London, 1965), pp. 271–93; Aidan Clarke, 'The Government of Wentworth, 1632–40', in T. W. Moody et al. (eds), *A New History of Ireland: III, Early Modern Ireland*, pp. 242–69.

64. The significance of this spate of semi-officially inspired publications, which includes Sir James Ware's collected editions of chronicles and tracts (Dublin, 1633) and Thomas Stafford's publication of the Elizabethan memoir 'Pacata Hibernica' (London, 1633) has yet to be fully explored. The quotation is from Ware's preface (unpaginated).

65. Kearney, *Strafford*, chs 8, 14; Michael Perceval-Maxwell, *The Outbreak of the 1641 Rebellion in Ireland* (Dublin and Kingston, Ontario, 1994) chs 1, 7.

66. Kearney, *Strafford*, ch. 11.

67. J. P. Cooper, 'The Fortune of Sir Thomas Wentworth, Earl of

Strafford', *Economic History Review,* XI (1958), pp. 227–48; and 'Strafford and the Byrne's Country', *Irish Historical Studies,* XV (1966–7), pp. 1–20.

68. For a contemporary criticism of Wentworth's insensitivity to local interest see 'A Discourse between Two Councillors of State, the one of England and the Other of Ireland', ed. Aidan Clarke, in *Analecta Hibernica,* 26 (1970), pp. 159–75.

69. Clarke, 'The Government of Wentworth, 1632–40' in T. W. Moody et al. (eds), *A New History of Ireland: III, Early Modern Ireland,* p. 260.

70. For a full discussion see Perceval-Maxwell, *The Outbreak of the 1641 Rebellion in Ireland,* ch 7.

71. Perceval-Maxwell, 'Strafford, the Ulster Scots and the Covenanters', in *Irish Historical Studies,* XVIII (1972–3), pp. 24–51; and 'Protestant Faction, the Impeachment of Strafford and the Origins of the Irish Confederate War', in *Canadian Journal of History,* 16 (1982), pp. 235–55; Russell, *Fall of the British Monarchies,* pp. 274–89.

5. THE ENGLISH CROWN, THE PRINCIPALITY OF WALES AND THE
    COUNCIL IN THE MARCHES, 1534–1641   *Peter Roberts*

* I am grateful of Professor Ralph Griffiths for his helpful comments on a draft of this chapter.

1. For an example of a previous perspective on the subject, see J. F. Rees, 'Tudor Policy in Wales', in his *Studies in Welsh History* (Cardiff, s.a.). The question of a shifting identity through the ages is discussed in Gwyn A. Williams, *When was Wales?* (London, 1985).

2. Peter R. Roberts, 'The Welshness of the Tudors', *History Today*, 28 (1986), 7–13.

3. R. R. Davies, 'Colonial Wales', *Past and Present* 65 (1974), 3–23.

4. R. A. Griffiths, 'Wales and the Marches' in *Fifteenth-Century England: Studies in Politics and Society, 1399–1509,* ed. S. C. Chrimes, R. A. Griffiths and C. Ross (Manchester, 1972), pp. 145–72.

5. *The Marcher Lordships of South Wales, 1415–1536: Select Documents,* ed. T. B. Pugh (Cardiff, 1963); W. Ll. Williams, 'A Welsh Insurrection', *Y Cymmrodor,* XVI (1902); Ralph A. Griffiths, *Sir Rhys ap Thomas and his Family: A Study in the Wars of the Roses and Early Tudor Politics* (Cardiff, 1993).

6. For a statement of the view that the religious changes were already being implemented adequately in the older administrative units and within the dioceses, see Glanmor Williams, *Wales and the Act of Union* (Bangor, 1992), p. 25.

7. P. R. Roberts, 'The "Act of Union" in Welsh History', *Transactions of the Honourable Society of Cymmrodorion* (1972–3), 49–72; W. R. B. Robinson, 'The Tudor Revolution in Welsh Government, 1536–1593: its Effects on Gentry Participation', *English Historical Review,* 406 (1988), 1–20.

8. See Brendan Bradshaw, *The Irish Constitutional Revolution of the Sixteenth Century* (Cambridge, 1979), ch. 1.

9. P. R. Roberts, 'The Union with England and the Identity of

"Anglican" Wales', *Transactions of the Royal Historical Societies*, 5th series 22 (1972), 49–70.

10. For the text of the Act, see Ivor Bowen, *The Statutes of Wales* (London and Leipsig, 1908), pp. 75–93; William Rees, *The Union of England and Wales* (Cardiff, 1948), appendix (transcribed from the Chancery Roll), pp. 55–74.

11. P. R. Roberts, 'A Breviat of the Effectes devised for Wales, c. 1540–41', *Camden Miscellany*, XXVI (1975), pp. 37–47.

12. P. R. Roberts, 'The Tudor Princes of Wales', *The Historian*, 15 (1987), 3–8.

13. G. R. Elton, 'Wales in Parliament, 1542–1581', *Welsh Society and Nationhood*, ed. R. R. Davies, R. A. Griffiths, I. G. Jones and K. O. Morgan (Cardiff, 1984, pp. 108–21). Mises were to be levied again for James I and the princes Henry and Charles, though the brief delay in the collection, authorised in 1606, led to no remittances.

14. Ibid., Sir Geoffrey Elton counters the argument advanced by A. H. Dodd that the Welsh members organised themselves on a regular basis as a pressure group for Welsh causes. Dodd, 'Wales's Parliamentary Apprenticeship (1536–1625)', *Transactions of the Honourable Society of Cymmrodorion* (1942), 8–72.

15. Roberts, 'Union', 67–9.

16. B. G. Charles, *George Owen of Henllys: A Welsh Elizabethan* (Aberystwyth, 1973), p. 139. George Owen, 'The Dialogue of the Government of Wales' (c. 1594), printed in *The Description of Pembrokshire*, Cymmrodorion Record Series, no. 1, part iii (1906), pp. 56–7.

17. T. Jones Pierce, *Medieval Welsh Society: Selected Essays*, edited by J. B. Smith (Cardiff, 1972), pp. 61–85.

18. Cf. A. H. Dodd's entries on the Herberts and the Somersets in *The Dictionary of Welsh Biography*, ed. J. E. Lloyd et al. (Cymmrodorion, London, 1959), pp. 350–2, 916–19.

19. Simon Adams, 'Military Obligations of Leasehold Tenants in Leicestrian Denbigh: a footnote', *Denbighshire Historical Society Transactions*, XXIV (1975), 205–8.

20. *The Copie of a Letter, wryten by a Master of Arts of Cambridge, to His Friend in London* (?Antwerp, 1584), p. 86.

21. A. H. Dodd, 'An "Electioneering" lease of 1585', *English Historical Review* LXV (1950), 221–2.

22. *Calendar of Wynn (of Gwydir) Papers (1515–1690)*, ed. J. Ballinger (Aberystwyth, 1926), no. 99.

23. J. E. Neale, *The Elizabethan House of Commons* (London, 1949; 1963), chs 4 and 5, pp. 93–121.

24. Ibid., pp. 115–21.

25. J. G. Jones, *Concepts of Order and Gentility in Wales, 1540–1640* (Llandysul, 1992).

26. Lewis was a member of the Council, c. 1577–81. Penry Williams, *The Council in the Marches of Wales under Elizabeth I* (Cardiff, 1958), pp. 259–60.

27. Ibid., pp. 276–96.

28. *Calendar of Wynn Papers*, no. 170; T. Jones Pierce (ed.), *Calen-*

dar of Clenennau Letters and Papers (Aberystwyth, 1947), nos 48, 106.

29. A fragment, probably all that was printed, reproduced in facsimile (Cardiff, 1931), with bibliographical note by J. Ballinger.

30. G. D. Owen, *Wales in the Reign of James* (Woodbridge, 1988), pp. 2–3.

31. *Dictionary of Welsh Biography*, p. 352. The electoral and political patronage exercised by the 3rd and 4th Earls of Pembroke helped to integrate Welsh to English politics but lies outside the scope of this chapter. Cf. A. H. Dodd, 'Wales in the Parliaments of Charles I, 1625–29', *Transactions of the Honourable Society of Cymmrodorion* (1945), 16–49.

32. *Calendar of Clenennau Papers*, no. 204; *Dictionary of Welsh Biography*, 624.

33. P. Williams, 'The Attack on the Council in the Marches, 1603–1642', *Transactions of the Honourable Society of Cymmrodorion* (1961), part 1, 1–22.

34. For the contexts of the discussions summarised in the following paragraphs, and for the references to the sources quoted, see G. D. Owen, *Wales in the Reign of James I* ch. 1, pp. 8–63; P. R. Roberts, 'Wales and England after the Tudor "Union": Crown, Principality and Parliament, 1543–1624', in *Law and Government under the Tudors*, ed. Claire Cross et al. (Cambridge, 1988), pp. 111–38. P. R. Roberts, 'The "Henry VIII Clause": Delegated Legislation and the Tudor Principality of Wales', *Legal Record and Historical Reality*, ed. T. G. Watkin (London, 1989), pp. 37–49.

35. P. R. Roberts, 'Wales and England', pp. 123–4; G. D. Owen, *Wales in the Reign of James I*, p. 49.

36. P. R. Roberts, 'Wales and England', p. 137.

37. William Vaughan, *The Arraignment of Slander, Periury, Blasphemy, and other malicious Sinnes, showing sundry examples of Gods Judgements against the Offenders* (London, 1630), p. 322.

38. P. Williams, 'The Attack on the Council', 17.

39. *Commons Journals*, II, pp. 57, 210, 216–17, 242, 253; *The Journal of Sir Simonds D'Ewes from the beginning of the Long Parliament to the Opening of the Trial of the Earl of Strafford*, ed. W. Notestein (New Haven and London, 1923), p. 183. D'Ewes reports that the phrase 'Provincial Court' was in the Commons' order but that he had asked for it to be omitted 'because it [presumably Wales] was never reduced into the forme of a Province since the Roman time'.

40. Huntington Library, California, Ellesmere MSS., no. 7466; A. H. Dodd, 'A Lost Capital', in his *Studies in Stuart Wales* (Cardiff, 1952), pp. 66–7.

41. P. Williams, 'The Attack on the Council', 18.

6. JAMES VI, JAMES I AND THE IDENTITY OF BRITAIN
Jenny Wormald

* My thanks are due to John Morrill, model of editorial patience and helpfulness, and to Patrick Wormald, model of early medieval non-Anglocentricity.

1. Bruce Galloway, *The Union of England and Scotland, 1603–1608* (Edinburgh, 1986), pp. 15–18.

2. C. H. McIlwain (ed.), *The Political Works of James I* (New York, 1965), p. 292.

3. Ibid., pp. 272, 294.

4. F. J. Fisher (ed.), Sir Thomas Wilson, *The State of England* (1600), in *Camden Miscellany*, XVI (Camden Society, 1936), p. 1. S. T. Bindoff, 'The Stuarts and their Style', *English Historical Review*, 60 (1945), pp. 192–216. Jenny Wormald, 'The Union of 1603'; and R. A. Mason, 'The Scottish Reformation and the Origins of Anglo-British Imperialism', in R. A. Mason (ed.), *Scots and Britons* (Cambridge, 1994), pp. 22–4 and 161–86.

5. Six of the major tracts, and a list of others, are published in B. R. Galloway and B. P. Levine (eds), *The Jacobean Union* (Scottish Text Society, Edinburgh, 1985).

6. J. H. Burton and others (eds), *The Register of the Privy Council of Scotland* (Edinburgh, 1877–), VII, p. 536.

7. *Commons Journals*, I, p. 171. J. F. Larkin and P. L. Hughes (eds), *Stuart Royal Proclamations*, I (Oxford, 1973), pp. 94–7. W. Shakespeare, *Richard II*, Act II, scene i, ll. 46–7, 50.

8. *Stuart Proclamations*, I, pp. 96–7.

9. PRO, SP 14/1/3, 'A Discourse of the Descent of the K's Mty from the Saxons'. K. Sharpe, *Sir Robert Cotton, 1586–1631* (Oxford, 1979), pp. 114–15. Graham Parry, *The Golden Age Restor'd* (Manchester, 1981), p. 4. John Nichols (ed.), *The progresses, processions and magnificent festivities of King James the First...*, 4 vols (London, 1828), vol. I, pp. 121–34. Henry E. Huntington Library, Bridgwater and Ellesmere MSS, EL 126.

10. Galloway and Levine, *Jacobean Union*, pp. 28, 102.

11. *Stuart Proclamations*, I, p. 135.

12. Peter Roberts, 'Wales and England after the Tudor "Union": Crown, Principality and Parliament, 1543–1624', in Claire Cross, David Loades and J. J. Scarisbrick (eds), *Law and Government under the Tudors: Essays presented to Sir Geoffrey Elton* (Cambridge, 1988), pp. 111–38. Sir John Davies, *A Discoverie of the Trew Causes why Ireland was never entirely Subdued, nor brought under Obedience of the Crowne of England, untill the Beginning of his Maiesties happie Raigne* (London, 1612), p. 182.

13. Sir Thomas Craig of Riccarton, *De Unione Regnorum Britanniae Tractatus* (Scottish History Society, Edinburgh, 1909); B. P. Levack, *The Formation of the British State* (Oxford, 1987), pp. 68–101; and B. P. Levack, 'Law, Sovereignty and the Union', in Mason (ed.), *Scots or Britons*, pp. 213–37.

14. Keith M. Brown, 'The Scottish Aristocracy, Anglicanization and the Court, 1603–38', *HJ*, 36 (1993), pp. 543–76.

15. J. S. Brewer (ed.), Godfrey Goodman, *The Court of King James* (London, 1839). Francis Osborne, *Traditional Memoyres of the Raigne of King James the First*, and Anthony Weldon, *The Court and Character of King James*, in Walter Scott (ed.), *The Secret History of the Court of James I*, 2 vols (Edinburgh, 1811), vol. I, pp. 1–298; vol. II, pp. 1–20.

16. Neil Cuddy, 'The revival of the entourage: the Bedchamber of James I, 1603–1625', in David Starkey (ed.), *The English Court from the Wars of the Roses to the Civil War* (London, 1987), pp. 173–225. This excellent article is written from the point of view of the English and their reaction to the Scottish entourage.

17. Levack, *Formation*, pp. 59–61.

18. L. P. Smith (ed.), *The Life and Letters of Sir Henry Wotton*, 2 vols (Oxford, 1907), vol. I, p. 315. C. R. Markham (ed.), Sir John Harrington, *A Tract on the Succession to the Crown, AD 1602* (London, Roxburghe Club, 1880), p. 51. Kevin Sharpe, 'The Image of Virtue: the Court and Household of Charles I, 1625–1642', in Starkey (ed.), *English Court*, especially pp. 228, 232–3. The point is vividly illustrated in the painting of Charles I dining with Henrietta Maria, with Prince Charles at a suitable distance, painted in 1635, by Gerard Houckgeest.

19. Elizabeth Read Foster (ed.), *Proceedings in Parliament, 1610*, 2 vols (New Haven, 1966), vol. II, p. 344. BL, Add. MS 12,497, folios 150–3, 155–6.

20. Historical Manuscripts Commission, *Portland MSS*, vol. IX, p. 113. Levack, *Formation*, p. 60.

21. J. Spedding (ed.), *Lord Bacon's Letters and Life*, 7 vols (London, 1861–74), vol. III, p. 229. *Calendar of State Papers, Ireland, 1603–1606*, p. 238. Levack, *Formation*, p. 61.

22. *Stuart Proclamations*, I, p. 95.

23. J. Craigie (ed.), *The Basilikon Doron of King James VI*, 2 vols (Scottish Text Society, Edinburgh, 1944–50), vol. I, p. 125.

24. John Major, *A History of Greater Britain* (Scottish History Society, Edinburgh, 1892), p. 43.

25. R. A. Mason, 'Reformation and Anglo-British Imperialism', in Mason (ed.), *Scots and Britons*, especially pp. 170–8. Arthur Williamson, 'Scotland, Antichrist and the invention of Britain', in J. Dwyer, R. Mason and A. Murdoch (eds), *New Perspectives on the Politics and Culture of Early Modern Britain* (Edinburgh, 1983), pp. 34–58. M. Merriman, 'The Assured Scots: Scottish Collaborators with England during the Rough Wooing', *Scottish Historical Review*, 47 (1968), pp. 10–34. M. L. Bush, *The Government Policy of Protector Somerset* (London, 1975), ch. 2.

26. James Kirk, '"The Polities of the Best Reformed Kirks": Scottish Achievements and English Aspirations in Church Government after the Reformation', in J. Kirk, *Patterns of Reform* (Edinburgh, 1989), pp. 334–67. Jenny Wormald, 'Ecclesiastical Vitriol: The Kirk, the Puritans and the Future King of England', in John Guy (ed.), *The Reign of Elizabeth I: Court and Culture in the Last Decade* (Cambridge, 1995) pp. 171–91.

27. Aylmer is cited by P. Collinson, *The Birthpangs of Protestant England* (London, 1988), p. 4. P. Wormald, 'Bede, the *Bretwaldas* and the Origins of the *Gens Anglorum*', in P. Wormald (ed.), *Ideal and Reality in Frankish and Anglo-Saxon Society: Studies presented to J. M. Wallace-Hadrill* (Oxford, 1983), pp. 99–129.

28. S. L. Adams, 'Spain or the Netherlands? The Dilemmas of Early Stuart Foreign Policy', in H. Tomlinson (ed.), *Before the English Civil War* (London, 1983), pp. 79–101.

29. In 1610, Fuller claimed that the English Commons had the duty to teach the king: Foster (ed.) *Proceedings in Parliament*, II, p. 109; in the same year, Cecil complained that, unlike Elizabeth who listened mainly to him, James listened to many: 'Mr Henry Yelverton, his Narrative. . . .' *Archaeologia*, xv (1806), p. 51.

30. Bodl. Lib. Ashmole MS 1729, folios 55, 58, 62–3.

31. Huntington Lib. EL 162, f. 1r.

32. *Political Works of James I*, p. 329.

33. *Records of the Privy Council, Scotland*, IX, pp. 24–33; X, pp. 773–81. G. Donaldson, *Scotland: James V–VII* (Edinburgh, 1965), pp. 228–31.

34. M. Perceval-Maxwell, *The Scottish Migration to Ulster in the Reign of James I* (London, 1973); R. Gillespie, *Colonial Ulster: The Settlement of East Ulster, 1600–41* (Cork, 1985); Aidan Clarke with R. Dudley Edwards, 'Pacification, Plantation and the Catholic Question, 1603–23', in T. W. Moody, F. X. Martin and F. J. Byrne (eds), *A New History of Ireland, III: Early Modern Ireland, 1534–1691* (Oxford, 1976), pp. 196–208, 219–24. F. M. Jones, *Mountjoy, 1563–1606: The Last Elizabethan Deputy* (Dublin, 1958), ch. 18 and App. D; H. S. Pawlisch, *Sir John Davies and the Conquest of Ireland* (Cambridge, 1985).

35. For an excellent and thought-provoking discussion of medieval English attitudes to Ireland and Henry II's conquest, John Gillingham, 'The English Invasion of Ireland', in B. Bradshaw, A. Hadfield and W. Maley (eds), *Representing Ireland: Literature and the Origins of Conflict, 1534–1660* (Cambridge, 1993), pp. 24–42. More general and equally stimulating is the same author's 'The beginnings of English imperialism', *Journal of Historical Sociology*, 5 (1992), pp. 392–409.

36. J. Michael Hill, 'The origins of the Scottish Plantation in Ulster to 1625: a Reinterpretation', *Journal of British Studies*, 32 (1993), 24–43.

37. David Calderwood, *The History of the Kirk of Scotland*, 8 vols (Wodrow Society, Edinburgh, 1842–9), vol. V, pp. 7–8. J. Bruce (ed.), *Correspondence of King James VI of Scotland with Sir Robert Cecil and Others in England* (Camden Society, London, 1861), pp. 33, 36–8. John Morris (ed.), *The Condition of Catholics under James I: Father Gerard's Narrative of the Gunpowder Plot* (London, 1871), ch. VIII. Cathaldus Giblin, *Irish Franciscan Mission to Scotland, 1619–1646* (Dublin, 1964), pp. 45–7.

38. A. Ford, *The Protestant Reformation in Ireland, 1590–1641* (Frankfurt, 1985), pp. 222–8; Clarke and Edwards, 'Plantation and the Irish Question', pp. 225–6; N. P. Canny, *From Reformation to Restoration Ireland, 1534–1660* (Dublin, 1987), p. 182.

7. THE ATLANTIC ARCHIPELAGO AND THE WAR OF THE THREE
KINGDOMS   *J. G. A. Pocock*

1. 'British History: a plea for a new subject', *New Zealand Historical Journal*, VIII, 1 (1974), reprinted, *Journal of Modern History*, XLVII, 4 (1975); 'The Limits and Divisions of British History: in search of the unknown subject', *American Historical Review*, 97, 2 (1982). The present essay is one of a series in which I have recently returned to this enquiry; see 'Two Kingdoms and Three Histories? Political Thought in British Contexts', in R. A. Mason (ed.), *Scots and Britons: Scottish Political Thought and the Union of 1603* (Cambridge, 1994); 'Empire, State and Confederation: the War of American Indepedence as a Crisis in Multiple Monarchy', in John Robertson (ed.), *A Union for Empire: the Political Identities of Britain, 1688–1750* (Cambridge, 1995); and 'Political Thought in the English-speaking Atlantic, 1760–1790: Part I: the imperial crisis', in J. G. A. Pocock, Gordon J. Schochet, and Lois G. Schwoerer (eds), *The Varieties of British Political Thought, 1500–1800* (Cambridge, 1994).

2. Richard S. Tompson, *The Atlantic Archipelago: A Political History of the British Isles* (Lewiston and Queenston, 1986).

3. Hugh Kearney, *The British Isles: A History of Four Nations* (Cambridge, 1989).

4. Hiram Morgan, *Tyrone's Rebellion: The Outbreak of the Nine Years War in Tudor Ireland* (London, 1993).

5. Jenny Wormald, 'Bloodfeud, kindred and government in early modern Scotland', *Past and Present*, LXXX (1980), 54–97.

6. 'War, Empire and the Language of State Formation: British political culture in the age of the American Revolution', (Ph.D dissertation, Johns Hopkins University, 1992).

7. See note 1, above.

8. J. C. D. Clark, *The Language of Liberty: Political Discourse and Social Dynamics in the Anglo-American World, 1660–1800* (Cambridge, 1993).

9. See further, J. G. A. Pocock, 'History and Sovereignty: the historiographic response to Europeanisation in two British cultures', *Journal of British Studies*, XXXI, 4 (1991), 358–89.

10. 'Mid-Atlantic Blues', *Irish Review*, (Winter 1991), 50–5.

11. R. M. Bartlett, *The Making of Europe: Conquest, Colonisation and Cultural Change, 950–1350* (Princeton, 1993).

12. Most recently in *The Nature of the English Revolution* (London 1993).

13. Jane H. Ohlmeyer, *Civil War and Restoration in the Three Stuart Kingdoms: The Career of Randal MacDonnell, Marquis of Antrim, 1609–1983* (Cambridge, 1993), ch. 7.

14. David Stevenson, *Alasdair MacColla and the Highland Problem in the Seventeenth Century* (Edinburgh, 1980).

15. Jonathan I. Israel (ed.), *The Anglo-Dutch Moment: Essays on the Glorious Revolution and its World Impact* (Cambridge, 1991).

16. J. G. A. Pocock, 'The Fourth English Civil War: dissolution, desertion and alternative histories in the Glorious Revolution', *Government*

and Society, XXIII, 2 (1988), 151–66 (partly reprinted in Lois G. Schwoerer (ed.), *The Revolution of 1688–89: Changing Perspectives* (Cambridge, 1992); 'The Significance of 1688: some reflections on whig history', in R. A. Beddard (ed.), *The Revolutions of 1688: The Andrew Browning Lectures, 1983* (Oxford, 1991); Standing Army and Public Credit: the institutions of Leviathan', in Dale F. Hoak and Mordechai Feingold (eds), *The Revolution of 1688–89* (Stanford, forthcoming).

8. THE ENGLISH REPUBLIC AND THE MEANING OF
BRITAIN   *Derek Hirst*

1. Appropriately enough, the leading advocates of such a shift in terms have not been found at English universities. The first major proponent of the 'three kingdom' thesis was the Irish historian J. C. Beckett, in ch. 4 of his *Making of Modern Ireland, 1603–1923* (New York, 1966): his call was taken up and amplified by J. G. A. Pocock, an Antipodean transplanted to North America, in 'British History: A Plea for a New Subject', *Journal of Modern History*, 47 (1975), 601–24, and in 'The Limits and Divisions of British History: In Search of the Unknown Subject', *American Historical Review*, 87 (1982), 311–36; and it was given perhaps its most systematic application by the Scottish historian D. Stevenson, particularly in *Alasdair MacColla and the Highland Problem in the Seventeenth Century* (Edinburgh, 1980), and *Scottish Covenanters and Irish Confederates* (Belfast, 1981). See also the remarks of Arthur H. Williamson, 'From the Invention of Great Britain to the Creation of British History: A New Historiography', *Journal of British Studies*, 29 (1990), 267–76.

2. Edward, Earl of Clarendon, *History of the Rebellion*, ed. W. D. Macray, 6 vols (Oxford, 1888), vol. 1, p. 145.

3. MS. X.d.483, 50, Folger Library, Washington, DC.

4. *Calendar of State Papers, Domestic, 1650*, p. 328. Speed and Camden doubtless proved either unobtainable or too expensive: see R. Bird (ed.), *The Journal of Giles Moore* (Sussex, 1971), pp. 180, 181, 218, for some comparative costs. Some first-rate cartography was at last in progress by the late 1650s, albeit in the Netherlands: R. Hermannides, *Rutgeri Hermannidae Britannica Magna* (Amsterdam, 1661); I am grateful to Kathleen Colquhoun for this reference.

5. See esp. A. Clarke, 'Colonial Identity in Early Seventeenth-century Ireland', *Nationality and the Pursuit of National Independence*, ed. T. W. Moody (Belfast, 1978). pp. 57–71; N. P. Canny, 'Identity Formation in Ireland: The Emergence of the Anglo-Irish', in *Colonial Identity in the Atlantic World, 1500–1800*, ed. N. P. Canny and A. Pagden (Princeton, NJ, 1987), pp. 159–212; and T. C. Barnard, 'Crisis of Identity among Irish Protestants, 1641–1685', *Past and Present*, 126 (1990), 39–83.

6. *Richard II*, Act II, sc. i, lines 40–50.

7. The phrase is Pocock's, in 'British History', passim.

8. The Commonwealth was scarcely alone in its shortsightedness

and its chauvinism. The dealings of the restored Rump and the council
of safety with the Scots in 1659 were as one-sided, as cynical, as were
the negotiations of 1652–3; and the record of the restored crown in
the unhappy years after 1660 was to be no better. See esp. D. H.
Fleming and J. D. Ogilvie (eds), *The Diary of Sir Archibald Johnston of
Wariston*, 3 vols (Edinburgh, 1911–40), vol. 3, p. 127 (hereafter cited
as *Diary of Johnston of Wariston*). General Monck, at least, seems to
have had hopes of something more substantial (R. Spalding, *Contemporaries of Bulstrode Whitelocke, 1605–1675*, British Academy Records
of Social and Economic History, n.s. 14 [Oxford, 1990], p. 3).

9. Although the protests from the Leveller William Walwyn at the
prevailing eagerness to subodinate Ireland are famous, he was by no
means representative even the radicals; see Christopher Hill, 'Seventeenth-Century English Radicals and Ireland', in his *A Nation of Change
and Novelty: Radical Politics, Religion and Literature in Seventeenth-Century England* (London, 1990), pp. 133–51, esp. pp. 142–7.

10. *Weekly Intelligencer*, 13–20 January 1651–2, p. 327.

11. *Mercurius Politicus*, 15–22 April 1652, p. 1542.

12. W. C. Abbott, *The Writings and Speeches of Oliver Cromwell*, 4 vols
(Cambridge, Mass., 1937–47), vol. 2, p. 197 (hereafter cited as *Writings and Speeches*).

13. J. T. Rutt (ed.), *The Parliamentary Diary of Thomas Burton*, 4 vols
(London, 1828), vol. 4, pp. 114, 145, 230, 239 (hereafter cited as
Diary of Thomas Burton). That confidence undoubtedly increased in
the course of the 1650s with the dramatic extension of 'new English'
landownership and the reduction in the status of the 'old English',
the descendants of pre-Elizabethan settlers – for whom see A. Clarke,
The Old English in Ireland (Worcester, 1966) – whose Catholicism had
so complicated any analysis of Protestant England's relations to Ireland.

14. *Diary of Thomas Burton*, vol. 4, pp. 238–9, 241–2.

15. Symptomatic is the way the debates in Richard Cromwell's
Parliament on Scottish and Irish representation began fiercely with
Scotland and then trailed away when members turned to Ireland.
These debates, which seemed then and now almost interminable, take
up much of vol. 4 of *Diary of Thomas Burton*.

16. I say 'primarily' since there were, of course, linguistic bonds
between England and at least part of Scotland, and ties of geographic
proximity too; but the latter could lead to friction (and had for centuries) as much as to friendliness.

17. Cromwell may have pushed Argyll in the direction of proscription; yet proscription was hardly foreign to Scottish history in these
troubled years. For Cromwell's hopes of Argyll, see his letter to
Hammond, in *Writings and Speeches*, vol. 1, pp. 677–8; the letter is
quoted at some length in D. Stevenson, 'Cromwell, Scotland and Ireland', in *Oliver Cromwell and the English Revolution*, ed. J. Morrill (London,
1990), p. 154. Cromwell may have been willing to observe constitutional proprieties, for he warned the army council in March 1649
that though developments to the north were ominous, 'In the
Kingdome of Scotland, you cannott soe well take notice of what is

done': but he went on to predict that 'this their anger (though without any quarrelling of ours with them) will returne into their owne bosomes' (C. H. Firth (ed.), *Clarke Papers*, 4 vols [London, 1891–1901], vol. 2, p. 203).

18. Thus, the Rump's 1649 Act abolishing kingly power and prerogative spoke only of England and Ireland (C. H. Firth and R. S. Rait, *Acts and Ordinances of the Interregnum, 1642–1660*, 3 vols [London, 1911], vol. 2, pp. 18–20).

19. *Acts done and past in the Second Session of the Second Triennial Parliament of King Charles I . . . and in the First Parliament of our Sovereign Lord Charles the II* (Edinburgh, 1649), act 14, pp. 35–6: 'Proclamation of Charles the Second, King of Great Britain, France and Ireland'. For the long-standing Covenanter interest in the entity of Britain, see below, pp. 211–13. Argyll, as head of the Campbells, may have had his own ancestral axe to grind: see esp. Alexander Grant, 'Scotland's "Celtic Fringe' in the Later Middle Ages', in *The British Isles, 1100–1500: Comparison, Constrasts and Connections*, ed. R. R. Davies (Edinburgh, 1988), p. 122; see also Jane E. A. Dawson, 'Two Kingdoms or Three? Ireland in Anglo-Scottish Relations in the Middle of the Sixteenth Century', in S*cotland and England, 1286–1815*, ed. Roger A. Mason (Edinburgh, 1987), pp. 113–38.

20. D. Laing (ed.), *The Letters and Journals of Robert Baillie*, 3 vols (Edinburgh, 1881–2), vol. 3, pp. 66, 68 (hereafter cited as *Letters of Baillie*). It was doubtless with similar thoughts in mind that some prominent Scots urged that the young Charles Stuart be content with only a Scottish kingdom; his response was to threaten to hand them: see H. R. Trevor-Roper, 'Scotland and the Puritan Revolution', in his *Religion, the Reformation and Social Change* (London, 1967), pp. 415–16.

21. H. M. Margoliouth, *The Poems and Letters of Andrew Marvell*, 2 vols (Oxford, 1952, vol. 1, pp. 87–90.

22. See, generally, B. Worden, *The Rump Parliament* (Oxford, 1973).

23. *A Declaration of the Parliament of England upon the Marching of the Armie into Scotland* (London, 26 June 1650); *A Declaration of the Army of England upon their March into Scotland* (London, 19 July 1650); *A Declaration of the English Army now in Scotland* (London, 8 August 1650). Acceptance of the constitutional independence of the Scots probably accounts for the near universal readiness of Englishmen in Rumper circles to accord Charles Stuart the title 'King of Scots' in 1649–50 and even beyond. The English posture makes Argyll's determination to crown Charles Stuart something other than merely King of Scotland all the more remarkable; more than anything, perhaps, it reveals the depth of Scottish commitment to Britain, for which see below, pp. 207, 211–13. I am grateful to John Morrill for discussions on this point.

24. Clarke MSS, vol. 20, fol. 28, Worcester College, Oxford; *Writings and Speeches*, vol. 2, p. 350.

25. *A Declaration of the Parliament of England upon the Marching of the Armie into Scotland* (London, 26 June 1650), p. 9. Marchamont Nedham, by now ardently republican, surely went further in thoughts

of an imposed settlement than the Rump intended when he expressed the hope that 'the poor People will willingly shake hands with us, in defence of the two Commonweales of England and Scotland', *Mercurius Politicus* 17–25 July 1650, p. 111.

26. On 18 October 1650, the Rumper, Philip, Lord Lisle, a member of the Council of State, wrote to his father, the Earl of Leicester, 'This evening the Councell resolved to offer theire advice to the Parlement that the Duke of Glocester should be sent into Scotland, the Kirke now wanting a King' (*Historical Manuscripts Commission Reports, De L'Isle and Dudley*, 6 vols [London, 1925–66], vol. 6, p. 485: for Cromwell, see *Letters of Baillie*, vol. 3, p. 113). One republican seems to have found Charles Stuart particularly dangerous because of his tutor, who was of course Thomas Hobbes; even so, a mere two months before the Scots invaded in the summer of 1651 another radical republican could write of the king of the Scots, 'They have him, and have enthroned him, let them keep him to themselves' (*The False Brother; or, A New Map of Scotland* [London, 1650], p. 41 [hereafter cited as *The False Brother*]; R. F., *The Scot Arraigned* [London, 1651], p. 10 [The bookseller George Thomason dated his copy of this pamphlet to 16 June]).

27. That the Republic was aware of the continuities between its own hostility to the powers of the Scottish nobility and Kirk and the policies of the kings who preceded it is suggested by the remarks of Col. John Jones in Dublin (J. Mayer, 'Inedited Letters of Cromwell, Bradshaw, Col. Jones and other Regicides', *Transactions of the Historic Society of Lancashire and Cheshire*, n.s., 1 [1860–61] 192).

28. The tendency of the protector's council to leave law courts and councils inquorate in Dublin and in Leith and Edinburgh was interpreted by Scots as a considered policy of annexation, as evidence that they were seen as 'no nation' and not to be accorded their own government (T. C. Barnard, *Cromwellian Ireland* [Oxford, 1975], pp. 16, 19–22; F. D. Dow, *Cromwellian Scotland* [Edinburgh, 1979], p. 211; *Letters of Baillie*, vol. 3, p. 288). In fact, it was of a piece with the generally lethargic English response to Scotland and Ireland.

29. J. Thirsk and J. P. Cooper (eds), *Seventeenth-Century Economic Documents* (Oxford, 1972), pp. 58–9; A. Macfarlane (eds), *The Diary of Ralph Josselin* (London, 1976), p. 263.

30. *Mercurius Politicus*, 15–22 August 1650, p. 174.

31. See the report of the failure of attempts in July 1650 to raise an infantry regiment in Lancashire: 'the bold Dragoons of the Clergy are drawn up to oppose the Levy, crying out Heresie and Schism, the Covenant and Damnation' (*Mercurius Politicus*, [18–25 July 1650], p. 98; see also E. Axon (ed.), *Oliver Heywood's Life of John Angier of Denton* [Manchester, 1937], p. 67; R. Parkinson, (ed), *Autobiography of Henry Newcome*, 2 vols [Manchester, 1852], vol. 1, pp. 31, 33).

32. *The False Brother*, sig. A2 and pp. 35, 63.

33. Mayer, p. 192.

34. Virtually any issue of the nonroyalist press in 1650–1 tells the

same story; undoubtedly the finest version is the letter from an English soldier the week after Dunbar printed in *A Perfect Diurnal,* 16–23 September 1650, and reprinted in S. R. Gardiner, *Letters and Papers illustrating the Relations betwen Charles II and Scotland in 1650* (Edinburgh, 1894), pp. 136–40. This shows at great length how the Scottish nation regularly broke all ten of the Commandments.

35. *Mercurius Politicus,* 2–9 January 1650—1, p. 565.

36. *Journals of the House of Commons* (London, 1742–), 7, 14; *Mercurius Politicus,* 3–10 October 1650, p. 298.

37. The bill for the dismemberment of Scotland was still alive on 25 October 1651, Clarke MSS, vol. 20, fol. 28, Worcester College, Oxford.

38. The consent that union required, and that the Rumpers and Cromwell in turn professed to seek, accorded ill with political and military realities; that so few in England seem to have noticed the discrepancy is a telling reflection of unthinking English assumptions of superiority. Nowhere is the emptiness of English claims to consent better revealed than in the highly effective quartering of nine companies of troops on Glasgow, whose magistrates and ministers had had the temerity to reject the 'Tender' of union. The records of English policy and Scottish response at this time are generally collected in C. S. Terry (ed.), *The Cromwellian Union* (Edinburgh, 1902), passim, and esp. p. 35 and n. 118. One of the few Englishmen to challenge the myth was the commonwealthsman John Hobart, who pointed out in 1659 that Scotland had 'had no National Representment, nor as I humbly thinke was in a Condition to make Agreement, but to accept Conditions Our Army having wholly subdued them' ('Mr Hubbard's Speech in Parliament 21 March 1658[/9]', uncatalogued MSS, unfoliated, University of Illinois Libary). I am grateful to James Robertson for calling my attention to this document.

39. See below, pp. 200–3.

40. L. M. Smith, 'Scotland and Cromwell: A Study in Early-Modern Government' (D. Phil. thesis, Oxford University, 1987), p. 58; for Cromwell's role, see Dow (n. 28 above), pp. 30–1). For the argument of economy see, e.g., *The Antiquity of England's Superiority over Scotland* (London, 1652), pp. 3–4.

41. British Library, Additional MSS 25276, esp. fol. 15.

42. *Diary of Thomas Burton,* vol. 4, p. 136.

43. *The Whole Traill of Mr Love* (London, 1652: recte 1651 [Thomason dates this 1 September]), p. 17; R. F., *The Scot Arraigned* (n. 26 above), p. 11. The solicitor-general's outburst obviously from the same well of national passion that Cromwell had drawn on when he denounced those responsible for the war of 1648, who had sought 'to vassalise us to a foreign nation', (*Writings and Speeches* [n. 12 above], vol. 1, p. 691.

44. See, e.g., *Diary of Thomas Burton,* vol. 4, p. 131.

45. R[ichard] H[awkins], *A Discourse of the National Excellencies of England* (London, 1657), p. 192. The last argument echoed the retort of Marchamont Nedham to the hypothetical question whether

England would have accepted a union so tendered by the Scots: 'Yes, without doubt, and be glad of it too, if England could reap so much benefit by an Incorporation with Scotland, as Scotland will have by England', *Mercurius Politicus*, 22–9 January 1651–2, p. 1379.

46. See too the stress on England's generosity, its willingness to 'offre England', in an earlier unionist appeal, that of 1548: Edward Duke of Somerset, *An Epistle Exhortatoire . . . To the nobilitie, and counsailors, gentlemen and the commons, and all others the inhabitauntes of the realme of Scotland*, Early English Text Society, extra ser., 17 (London, 1872), pp. 238–46, esp. p. 241.

47. See Milton's contempt for the Irish who had so often in the past rejected the chance 'to improve and wax more civil by a civilizing Conquest' (*Observations upon the Articles of Peace* [1649]. in Don M. Wolfe et al. (eds), *Complete Prose Works of John Milton*, 8 vols [New Haven, Conn., 1953–82], vol. 3, p. 304).

48. Clarke MSS, vol. 24, fol. 25, Worcester College, Oxford. For examples of reports of the (Allegedly) universal Scottish credulity and superstition, see *Mercurius Politicus*, 18–25 March 1652, p. 1476, and 1–8 April 1652, p. 1520; for the suicidal 'obstinacie' of captives, see 26 September–3 October 1650, p. 279.

49. *Mercurius Politicus*, 11–18 September 1651, p. 1071. Disease quickly solved any problems of repartriation that might have arisen (H. F. Westlake, *St Margaret's Westminster* [London, 1914], p. 109).

50. Clarke MSS, vol. 22, fol. 80, Worcester College, Oxford; C. H. Firth (ed.), *Scotland and the Commonwealth* (Edinburgh, 1895), p. 269.

51. Stevenson, 'Cromwell, Scotland and Ireland', p. 164. Such benefits were, of course, not confined to Scotland: see Cromwell's determination 'to hold forth and maintain the lustre and glory of English liberty' to the Irish (*Writings and Speeches*, vol. 2, p. 205).

52. P. Sterry, *England's Deliverance from the Northern Presbytery Compared with its Deliverance from the Roman Papacy* (London, 1651), pp. 44–5, and also pp. 26–7, 32–3, 41–2.

53. Henry Parker, *Scotlands Holy War* (London, 1651), pp. 23, 65.

54. Macfarlane (ed.), pp. 220, 267 (for Josselin's sympathy for the Scots, see p. 217).

55. See Blair Worden, 'Classical Republicanism and the Puritan Revolution', in *History and Imagination*, ed. H. Lloyd-Jones, V. Pearl and B. Worden (London, 1981), pp. 182–200; and 'Andrew Marvell, Oliver Cromwell, and the Horatian Ode', in *Politics of Discourse*, ed. K. Sharpe and S. Zwicker (Berkeley and Los Angeles, 1987), pp. 147–80. Although they had not originated the policy of union, classical republicans may have taken it more seriously than others – thus, Henry Neville protested in 1659 at the government's practice of foisting its nominees onto Scottish parliamentary constituencies, which 'is absolutely to enslave and reduce them to a province' (*Diary of Thomas Burton*, vol. 4, 188).

56. The committee of thirty-six appointed on 9 September 1651, for drawing up a bill of annexation – a committee that was eventually to concoct a rather different measure – contained only three of

the committed classical republicans in the House. The proportion held in the new committee appointed on 24 December for better effecting one clause in the instructions for the commissioners to Scotland: the twelve were Lords Commissioners Whitelocke and Lisle, Marten, Sir Henry Mildmay, Nicholas Love, Strickland, Lord Grey, Vane, Carew, Major General Harrison, Alderman Allen (*Journals of the House of Commons*, 7, 14, 36).

57. After a year of campaigning in Scotland Cromwell at least seems to have worked out the options, for he then insisted that support from 'the honest party' in Scotland was essential to a policy of union: 'utherwayes they would gouverne us as Irland and a conquest' (*Diary of Johnston of Wariston*, vol. 2, p. 143).

58. The commissioners were Lord Chief Justice St John, Sir Henry Vane, Maj. Richard Salwey, Col. George Fenwick, Major General Lambert, Major General Deane, Alderman Robert Titchborne, Lieutenant General Monck (*Journals of the House of Commons*, 7, 30).

59. J. Nicoll, *A Diary of Public Transactions* (Edinburgh, 1836), pp. 63, 85. Such tones do not characterise the official documents of the Tender.

60. *Diary of Thomas Burton*, vol. 4, pp. 134–5. Gott made clear that he did not exclude Ireland from his earthly paradise, for he held that the one-sidedness of England's relations with Ireland accounted for 'the great tumults in Ireland'. The same debate called forth yet another poetic effusion: 'We are one clod of earth. Neptune kisses our shore on every side' (vol. 4, p. 145).

61. Margoliouth, *Andrew Marvell*, p. 87.

62. Clarke MSS, vol. 22, fol. 81, Worcester College, Oxford. Such energy was, of course, to find employment in Cromwell's 'Western Design', which he justified to his council in July 1654 in not dissimilar terms, of the 'work' to be done 'in the world' (*Writings and Speeches*, vol. 3, p. 370).

63. See, e.g., William Burton, *A Commentary on Antoninus his Itinerary* (1658); H[awkins], pp. 1–11, 77–8.

64. A strong case has recently been made for the origins in Cromwell's Protectorate, in 'the imperial moment' that extended from late 1654 to 1656 and encompassed the Western Design and the first flush of the Spanish war, of the concept and language of the British empire; as will be apparent, that argument overlooks developments during the Commonwealth. D. Armitage, 'The Cromwellian Protectorate and the Languages of Empire', *Historical Journal*, 35 (1992), pp. 531–55, esp. 533.

65. Thus, army headquarters at Leith in 1652 spoke of the soldiers 'tents or colony' (Clarke MSS, vol. 24, fol. 3, Worcester College, Oxford). On the whole, however, the army command in Scotland viewed its exploits in providential terms – see especially the discussions early in 1653 of a projected regimental history, and the suggestions for a similar effort in Ireland (Firth (ed.), *Scotland and the Commonwealth*, pp. 75–6; *Calendar of State Papers, Domestic, 1652–1653*, p. 194).

66. *Mercurius Politicus*, 25 December 1651–1 January 1652, p. 1304. The role of the battle in generating a new optimism is clear in his editorial of the week of 18–25 September, pp. 1077–9.

67. *Mercurius Politicus*, 15–22 January 1651–2, pp. 1350–1. The part played by the Dutch in the thought of the classical republicans casts an interesting light on Shaftesbury's famous 'Delenda est Carthago' rhetoric of the next reign; I am grateful to John Morrill for this suggestion. For another perspective on the relationship between the Dutch and empire, see Steven Pincus, 'England and the World in the 1650s', in *Revolution and Restoration*, ed. John Morrill (London, 1992), pp. 129–47.

68. Armitage, pp. 533–5. Furthermore, while Nedham had in the New Year of 1652 turned his gaze on the Netherlands rather than Scotland, it was in a Scottish context that he wrote grandly of 'the Parliament of Great Britaine', *Mercurius Politicus*, 22–29 January 1651–2, p. 1369.

69. See esp. H[awkins], pp. 232–3; Michael Hawke, *The Right of Dominion, and Property of Liberty* (London, 1655), pp. 86–7.

70. There can be little doubt of the imperialist fervour engendered during the period of the Western Design, or of the dreams spawned then of imperial status for Cromwell; but Armitage fails to consider the British element in the title 'first emperor of Greate Britaine, and the isles thereunto belonging, allways Caesar, etc.' that was accorded by rumour (Armitage, pp. 531–2).

71. J. G. A. Pocock (ed.), *The Political Works of James Harrington* (Cambridge, 1977), pp. 159, 257, 315. See also the similar claim of another classical republican, H[awkins] (pp. 129–30).

72. It was a role that Harrington might well have remembered from the negotiations in 1642 that sent a Scottish army off under English pay to suppress the Irish rebels, and that the Scottish deputies had themselves stressed when pleading with the Rump for milder terms in the negotiations for union in 1652 (*Calendar of State Papers, Domestic, 1652–1653*, PRO, p. 52, and see the remarks in R. Mitchison, *Lordship to Patronage: Scotland 1603–1745* [London, 1983], pp. 50–1).

73. Pocock (ed.), pp. 159–60.

74. For that context, see now Armitage, pp. 546–53, as well as Pocock's introduction to Harrington's *Works*. Pocock saw rather more straightforward roles for Scotland and Ireland, as, respectively, the object of English libertarian attentions and the source of material support for English citizen-soldiers (Pocock (ed.), p. 71).

75. *Letters of Baillie*, vol. 3, p. 291.

76. James Howell, *Instructions and directions for forren Travell* (London, 1650), and *Som Sober Inspections* (London, 1655), pp. 179–81, 141. The impact of this work, and its plea for change, was such that it drove Marchamont Nedham to publish his unfortunately timed plea for a republic, *The Excellency of a Free State*, in 1656, just as the Protectorate was about to move a little farther towards the old order.

77. G. Wither, *The Protector*, 2 edns (London, 1655, 1656), sig. A2; for a (perhaps hopeful) glimpse of his relations to Oliver, see Hartlib

MSS, 'Ephemerides, 1655' (Turnbull transcripts, p. 92), Sheffield University Library.

78. *Calendar of State Papers, Domestic, 1655*, PRO, p. 46.

79. Scotland's emissaries to Whitehall in the summer of 1654 clearly expected such a move (*Diary of Johnston of Wariston*, vol. 2, pp. 268, 273). For a discussion of the climate of opinion favouring it, see J. M. Wallace, *Destiny His Choice* (Cambridge, 1968), pp. 109–13; and now Armitage, passim.

80. *Calendar of State Papers, Domestic, 1654*, PRO, p. 240; D. Hirst, 'The Lord Protector', in Morrill (ed.), *Oliver Cromwell and the English Revolution*, pp. 122–3.

81. The laments of the commonwealthsmen in Richard Cromwell's Parliament for the lost glory of the Rump, while encompassing the Dutch war, suggest something of the emotive power of the British achievements (*Diary of Thomas Burton*, vols 3, 4, passim).

82. Stevenson, 'Cromwell, Scotland and Ireland', p. 180.

83. Protector Somerset had protested his willingness 'to leaue the name of the nacion. . . and to take the indifferent old name of Britaynes again' (*An Epistle Exhortatoire*, p. 241).

84. Both Protector and press saw foreign, colonial and economic policy as a strictly English affair see, e.g., *Mercurius Politicus*, 16–23 August 1655, pp. 5560–1; 1–8 November 1655, pp. 5738–40; 22–9 November 1655, pp. 5576–80.

85. Striking, because uncontestatory, examples are provided by Sir Ralph Maddison, who in 1654 pleaded for the sovereignty of 'the British-seas' by 'Great Brittany' with a set of wholly English precedents, and by the very ecumenical Samuel Hartlib, who also meant 'England' when he said 'Britain': R. Maddison, *Great Britains Remembrancer* (London, 1654), esp. pp. 40–2; [Samuel Hartlib], *A Plea for Gospel Communion . . . sued for by the Protestant Churches of Germanie, unto the Churches of Great Brittanie and Ireland* (London, 1654), preface and sig. a. Still more suggestive is the case of the future Charles II, who in 1654 styled himself 'Kinge of Great Britane and Scotlande' (C. H. Firth (ed.), *Scotland and the Protectorate* [Edinburgh, 1899], p. 31).

86. *Mercurius Politicus*, 3–10 August 1654, pp. 3671, 3672, 3673; see also Mayer pp. 184, 293. In other words, when Englishmen said 'British' they meant the Scots, but when they said 'Great Britain' they usually meant England.

87. Macfarlane (ed.), p. 263.

88. See Thomas Hobbes, *Leviathan* (London, 1651), ch. 3, for the most elegant version of that slur.

89. Barbara Donagan, 'Codes and Conduct in the English Civil War', *Past and Present*, no. 118 (1988), pp. 65–95, esp. pp. 93–5.

90. R. A. H. Bennett, 'Enforcing the Law in Revolutionary England: Yorkshire, 1640–1660' (Ph.D. thesis, London University, 1988), pp. 202–3; see also Smith, p. 141; and Gardiner, pp. 134–40.

91. Quoted in Dow, p. 80.

92. See esp. R. A. Mason, 'Scotching the Brut: Politics, History and National Myth in Sixteenth-Century Britain', in Mason (ed.), pp. 60–84.

93. Keith M. Brown, *Kingdom or Province? Scotland and the Regal Union, 1603–1715* (New York, 1992), pp. 79–81.

94. Thus, it seems likelier that James VI and I's dissolution of England's Society of Antiquaries in 1607 had to do with his dreams of Union, which received their final rebuff in that year, than with the antiquaries' research into parliamentary and feudal liberties, to which the dissolution has often been unconvincingly tied.

95. Samuel Kliger, *The Goths in England: A Study in Seventeenth and Eighteenth Century Thought* (Cambridge, Mass., 1952), p. 115. Verstegen's work was first published in 1605; it had new editions in 1628, 1634, and 1653, and was printed again in 1655.

96. The title of Milton's *History of Britain*, his history of England largely written in the late 1640s, is itself symptomatic: he made his assumptions more explicit elsewhere when he distinguished the feck-less 'Picts' from the 'true Britons' who of course lived in what was to become England (John Milton, *Pro Populo Angli Defenso* [1651 and 1658], in Wolfe et al. (eds), vol. 4, p. 509). Prynne's appreciation of Verstegen is made clear by Kliger, pp. 154–5.

97. *The False Brother*, p. 39. In a similar vein, the radical Lord Grey of Groby during the 1648 campaign against the Scots wrote an open letter to the Speaker of the House of Commons entitled 'Old Eng-lish Blood boyling afresh in Leicestershire Men' (J. Richards, 'The Greys of Bradgate in the English Civil War', *Transactions of the Leices-tershire Archaeological and Natural History Society*, 62 [1988], 45).

98. Mayer, p. 271; Bodleian MSS, Tanner 51, fols. 16–18, 32–3, and 35–9. That Hobart actually spoke some such words in Parlia-ment, rather than concocting an imaginary version on paper, is sug-gested by the account in *Diary of Thomas Burton*, vol. 4, p. 103.

99. See the excerpts printed in Firth (ed.), *Scotland and the Com-monwealth* (n. 50 above), pp. 362–3. James Howell's *Perfect Description of the People and Country of Scotland* (London, 1649) is, despite its title, full of predictable racist jokes and slurs.

100. *Mercurius Politicus*, 11–18 March 1652–3, p. 1470.

101. 'Report of Thomas Tucker upon the settlement of the rev-enues . . . 1656', *Miscellany of the Scottish Borough Records Society* (Edin-burgh, 1881), passim.

102. Thus, there were at least nineteenth different surveys of Ire-land between 1653 and 1660 (C. Webster, *The Great Instauration* [Lon-don, 1975], p. 436.

103. *Mercurius Politicus*, 23–9 July 1656, pp. 5593–6; see also the advertisement for *A General History of the Island of Barbados*, 23–30 April 1657, p. 7764.

104. It was reported of Lambert in mid-1654 that 'he knows them all now' (J. Y. Akerman (ed.), *Letters from Roundhead Officers* [Edin-burgh, 1856], pp. 69 and 56, 59, 60–1 [hereafter cited as *Letters from Roundhead Officers*]).

105. T. M. Devine, 'the Cromwellian Union and the Scottish Burghs: The Case of Aberdeen and Glasgow, 1652–1660', in *Scottish Themes*, ed. J. Butt and J. T. Ward (Edinburgh, 1976), pp. 7–8, 11. For a

comment on prewar Scottish overland trade, see Henry Best's 1641 reference to 'the poor Scottish merchants' trading with England, in Thirsk and Cooper (eds), p. 253. Cromwell did, however, receive a very precise assessment of potential coastal garrisons from someone who presumably had traded extensively with Scotland (J. Nickolls, *Original Letters and Papers of State* [London, 1743], pp. 62–4: the letter is misattributed to Samuel Chidley).

106. *Mercurius Politicus*, 10–17 June 1652, p. 1664; as usual with news from Scotland, most newspapers carried the same report. To be fair to that English reporter, while modern scholars may question his judgement, the greatest of all Scottish legal scholars, Sir Thomas Craig, writing at the turn of the century, would have agreed with him (A. H. Williamson, S*cottish National Consciousness in the Age of James VI* [Edinburgh, 1979], p. 8; see also W. David H. Sellar, 'The Common Law of Scotland and the Common Law of England', in Davies (ed.), pp. 82–99, esp. pp. 82, 94–5; and the remarks of W. Ferguson in his review of *The Formation of the British State*, by B. P. Levack, *Scottish Historical Review*, 68 [1989], 90).

107. *Perfect Passages of Every daies Intelligence*, 5–12 November 1652, p. 567; see also *Severall Proceedings in Parliament*, 28 October–4 November 1652, pp. 2535–6; *A Perfect Diurnall*, 1–8 November 1652, p. 2266; *Mercurius Politicus*, 26 June–3 July 1656, pp. 7061–6.

108. See, e.g., *Mercurius Politicus*, 14–21 June 1655, pp. 5416–18; 22–9 August 1655, p. 5565; 1–8 May 1656, pp. 6950–1.

109. *Mercurius Politicus*, 29 March–5 April 1655, pp. 5229.

110. The Scottish press at the time was largely monopolised by official declarations.

111. J. Taylor, *The Number and Names of all the Kings of England and Scotland* (London, 1650).

112. J. Spottiswood, *History of the Church of Scotland* (London, 1655).

113. William Drummond of Hawthornden, *History of Scotland* (London, 1655). Drummond's *Poems* were published in London the following year, thanks once again to the good offices of the Scottish 'Maecaenas', Sir John Scot.

114. Firth (ed.), *Scotland and the Commonwealth*, pp. 75–6; Hartlib MSS, 'Ephemerides, 1655' (Turnbull transcripts, p. 24), Sheffield University Library. Hartlib reported that Cromwell was much taken by 'the speech spoken to King James V recorded in the History of Scotland by William Drummond of Hawthornden': there is only one speech in the *History* to James V, and that (at pp. 210–14) is a speech put in the mouth of one of his councillors urging religious toleration.

115. Milton's nephew Edward Phillips did, however, think Drummond of Hawthornden not only the finest Scottish poet, 'a commendation not to be rejected', but as good as Tasso or 'even the choicest of our English Poets' (William Drummond of Hawthornden, *Poems* [London, 1656], preface). More signally, appreciation could even be found in Archbishop Usher's circle, for Gaelic Irish literary culture (Hartlib MSS, 'Ephemerides, 1649 [Turnbull transcripts, p. 65], Sheffield University Library).

116. Probably the most famous instance is the controversy over transplantation of Catholic Irish sparked by Vincent Gookin's measured pamphlet, *The Great Case of Transplantation Discussed* (London, 1655); but its intellectual high point is surely Gerald Boate's *Irelands Naturall History*, brought to the press in 1652 by Samuel Hartlib. The voluminous letters, drafts, and memoranda of Samuel Hartlib in Sheffield are full of schemes for particular and universal improvement, with many casting Ireland as the proving ground. Only a tiny portion of them got off the ground, even in Ireland (C. Webster, *The Great Instauration* [London, 1975], passim; and Barnard, *Cromwellian Ireland*, esp. pp. 213–48).

117. See Webster, pp. 395–6.

118. Hartlib MSS, 12/190, 55/10, Sheffield University Library.

119. *The False Brother*, pp. 35, 55. For a similar verdict, see *Mercurius Politicus*, 13–20 March 1650–1), pp. 656, 663.

120. See, e.g., Walter Forbes, *A Panegyricke to the High and Mighty Monarch Charles, King of Great Britaine, France and Ireland, etc.* (Edinburgh, 1633).

121. T. G. Snoddy, *Sir John Scot Lord Scotstarvet* (Edinburgh, 1968), pp. 23, 29. Had the money been available, the army's needs – whether for information or for esteem – in conjunction with the land transfers in Ireland and Scotland might in their turn have ushered in a new age of British cartography: some remarkably ambitious projects were being entertained in the mid-1650s – most notably, of course, Petty's Down survey – and it was presumably in a similar context that some English mapping of Scotland was under way at the end of the 1640s (Hartlib Papers, 'Ephemerides, 1656' [Turnbull transcripts, pp. 6–7]; 'Ephemerides, 1652' [Turnbull transcripts, p. 17]; 'Ephemerides, 1655' [Turnbull transcripts, p. 107]; Sheffield University Library).

122. Sir Thomas Urquhart of Cromarty, 'Discovery of a most exquisite Jewel' (London, 1652), pp. 2–5, 269–72.

123. *Diary of Johnston of Wariston* (n. 8 above), vol. 2, pp. 219, 229.

124. *Letters of Baillie*, vol. 3, pp. 198, 224–6, 226–7, 231–2, 235–6, 265–6, 291–4, 302–7, 309–10, 325–6, 328–31, 332–4, 344–6, 366–7, 391; Nicoll, p. 188; Firth (ed.), *Scotland and the Protectorate*, p. 222.

125. The evidence for the latter is so voluminous that it needs no rehearsing; the former is suggested by the list of economic demands made of the union by the Scottish burghs and, in a rather different way, by the emergence of London in the 1650s as a marriage market for the Scottish aristocracy (Terry (ed.), pp. xlv–lxvi, 54; *Letters of Baillie*, vol. 3, pp. 366–7).

126. Other of the replies were, it is true, more laconic, more formulaic, and sometimes more transigent.

127. See Mason, 'Scotching the Brut', pp. 60–84; Williamson, *Scottish National Consciousness in the Age of James VI*, pp. 10–12, 41–2; Brown, pp. 79–85; David Stevenson, 'The Early Covenanters and the Federal Union of Britain', in Mason (ed.), pp. 163–81. For the hereditary Argyll interest in British claims, see n. 19 above.

128. Terry (ed.), pp. 82, 112. To be fair, Colonel Birch insisted in

Richard Cromwell's Parliament that the English borderlands took the same view of the union – as an essential preservative – as some of the Scots claimed to: John Hobart, however, denied this claim (*Diary of Thomas Burton*, vol. 4, pp. 117–18; 'Mr Hubbard's speech in parliament 21 March 1658', at fol. 3, University of Illinois Library).

129. L. M. Smith, and Barnard, *Cromwellian Ireland*.

130. Barnard, *Cromwellian Ireland*, pp. 34–49.

131. Devine, pp. 7–8, 11; 'Report of Thomas Tucker upon the settlement of the revenues', passim; Mitchison, p. 103.

132. *Letters from Roundhead Officers*, pp. 122–3; Firth (ed.), *Scotland and the Protectorate*, pp. 239–40, 248–9; *Diary of Thomas Burton*, vol. 1, pp. 12–16.

133. *Calendar of State Papers, Domestic, 1657–1658*, PRO, pp. 286, 317–18; Firth (ed.), *Clarke Papers*, vol. 3, p. 81.

134. J. Scott, *Berwick-upon-Tweed* (London, 1888), pp. 211–14; H. J. Hillen, *History of King's Lynn*, 2 vols (Norwich, 1907), vol. 1, p. 380.

135. E. A. Wrigley and R. S. Schofield, *The Population History of England, 1541–1871* (London, 1981), pp. 219–21, 224.

136. This conclusion is based on reading of surviving parish accounts for the 1650s from a large number of counties.

137. Corporation of London Record Office, Precedent Book 2, fol. 57v; D. W. Galenson, *White Servitude in Colonial America* (Cambridge, 1981), pp. 3–15; *Analecta Hibernica*, 4 (1932), 159; I am grateful to James Robertson for the first citation and for pointing me towards the two latter sources. See also A. E. Smith, 'Transportation of Convicts to American Colonies in the Seventeenth Century', *American Historical Review*, 39 (1934), 232–7. For some further instances, see M. S. Gretton, *Oxfordshire JPs in the Seventeenth Century* (Oxfordshire, 1934), pp. xci–xciii; the governors of London's Bridewell in fact maintained the links with colonial merchants forged in James's reign through the Civil War (E. G. O'Donoghue, *Bridewell Revisited* [London, 1929], pp. 12, 18, 21, 90).

138. John Rushworth, *Historical Collections*, 8 vols (London, 1659–80), vol. 7, pp. 1145, 1250; H. M. Vaughan, 'Oliver Cromwell in South Wales, 1648–1649', *Transactions of the Honourable Society of Cymmrodorion* (1936), pp. 57–8. Welshmen suffered again in 1651: J. E. Auden, 'Shropshire and the Royalist Conspiracies', *Transactions of the Shropshire Archaeological and Natural History Society*, 3d ser., 10 (1910) p. 108 and n.

139. For example, Terry (ed.) pp. 276, 283; *Calendar of State Papers, Domestic, 1651*, PRO, p. 245.

140. *Mercurius Politicus*, 26 September–3 October 1650, p. 285; Cromwell was here denying any intention to sell captives for ramson. He had shown no qualms about putting Irish prisoners to – as he would have seen it – productive use in Barbados after Drogheda (*Writings and Speeches*, vol. 2, pp. 124, 204).

141. *Calendar of State Papers, Domestic, 1650*, PRO, pp. 333, 334, 340, 358, 375, 397, 402, 419, 438. Doubtless remembering the fate of Welsh captives in 1648, Marchamont Nedham had predicted this outcome even before the English army crossed the Scottish border (*Mercurius*

Politicus, 27 June–4 July 1650, p. 58). The Scots were not uniquely ill-treated as prisoners by being forced to work for their keep: prisoners taken in the Dutch war were set to help drain the Fens.

142. *Calendar of State Papers, Domestic, 1651–1652*, pp. 20, 44, 67, 120, 164, 267, 313, 500; and (for Welsh prisoners) *Mercurius Politicus*, 19–26 June 1651, p. 885. Many Scottish prisoners died in captivity; the rest were probably sent home, or to Ireland, as resistance in Scotland collapsed. See also Westlake, p. 109.

143. *Mercurius Politicus*, 15–22 April 1652, p. 1550; *Calendar of State Papers, Domestic, 1651–1652*, p. 432. For Cromwell's disposition of the Drogheda prisoners, see n. 140 above.

144. J. W. Blake, 'Transportation from Ireland to America, 1653–1660', *Irish Historical Studies*, 3 (1942–3), p. 269; *Calendar of State Papers, Venetian, 1653–1654*, p. 119.

145. *Mercurius Politicus*, 23 February–2 March 1653–4, p. 3302; and 13–20 April 1654, p. 3428; Firth (ed.), *Scotland and the Protectorate*, pp. 64, 65; *Letters from Roundhead Officers*, p. 88; *Calendar of State Papers, Domestic, 1655–1656*, p. 103. Many of those taken in Penruddock's Rebellion in the south-west in the spring of 1655 had been transported; furthermore, some of the English taken at Worcester in 1651 had been sold to Barbados (E. A. B. Barnard, 'Some Beoley Parish Accounts, 1656–1700', *Transactions of the Worcestershire Archaeological Society*, 25 [1948], p. 19).

146. A. E. Smith, p. 237.

147. *Letters from Roundhead Officers* is full of discussions of the pros and cons of a Scottish posting, in which the chance of action and recognition had to be set against the tendency of administrators in London to forget all who were at a distance from their door.

148. Firth (ed.), *Scotland and the Commonwealth*, pp. 141–2, 154–5; R. W. Ketton-Cremer, *Norfolk in the Civil War* (London, 1969), p. 268. The minister of Inverness, however, felt differently. Writing of the dismantling of the garrison in 1662, he observed, 'Never people left a place with such reluctancy. It was even sad to see and heare sighes and teares, pale faces and embraces, at their parting farewell from that town. . . . They made that place happy, and it made them so' (quoted in W. Ferguson, *Scotland's Relations with England: A Survey to 1707* [Edinburgh, 1977], p. 140).

149. Given the material complications of the rest of his career, Johnston's fear of being 'removed out of Scotland' at this time probably related as much to his fear of yielding to such temptation as to anything else (*Diary of Johnston of Wariston*, p. 262).

150. British Library, Add. MSS 4156, fol. 71v; *Mercurius Politicus*, 29 March–5 April 1655), pp. 5236–8. See also Col. Robert Bennet's warning to Sir Hardress Waller, newly returned to Ireland in 1650, of the dangers of prosperity: MS. X.d.483, 50, Folger Library, Washington, DC.

151. Especially when imperialism failed, as it did in the Western Design (see B. Worden, 'Oliver Cromwell and the Sin of Achan', in *History, Society and the Churches*, ed. D. Beales and G. Best [Cambridge, 1985], pp. 125–45; and Armitage, pp. 540–6).

152. Quoted in M. J. Seymour, 'Pro-Government Propaganda in the English Republic, 1649–1660' (Ph.D. thesis, Cambridge University, 1986), pp. 222–3.

153. K. Thomas, 'The Adultery Act of 1650 Reconsidered', in *Puritans and Revolutionaries*, ed. K. Thomas and D. Pennington (Oxford, 1978), pp. 257–82.

154. *Acts done and past . . .*, Acts 2, 11, 12, 18–20, 22–4, 26, 28, 30, 32, 33.

155. For some earlier examples of legislators in one country influencing those in the other, see Sellar, pp. 92–3.

156. Nicoll, pp. 5–6, 67, 69, 79; L. M. Smith, p. 42.

157. Clarke MSS, vol. 22, fol. 92, Worcester College, Oxford.

158. *Diary of Thomas Burton*, vol. 4, pp. 87–242, passim.

159. 'Mr. Hubbard's Speech in Parliament 21 March 1658', at fol. 2v, University of Illinois Library.

160. Margoliouth, p. 90.

161. H. M. Reece, 'The Military Presence in England, 1649–1660' (D. Phil. thesis, Oxford University, 1981), p. 287.

162. Monck estimated in 1657 that Scotland paid one-quarter of England's assessment on only one-sixteenth of its wealth, while the high level of the Irish assessment, at around one-eighth of England's, remained a perennial concern of Irish administrators throughout the decade (L. M. Smith, p. 90; Barnard, *Cromwellian Ireland*, pp. 28–30; *Calendar of State Papers, Irish, 1647–1660*, PRO, p. 660). Monck's figures for the Scottish assessment were only a slight exaggeration.

163. Thus, the 1659 Scottish assessment covered only one-quarter of the cost of the army in Scotland (Dow, p. 216).

164. M. P. Ashley, *Financial and Commercial Policy under the Cromwellian Protectorate*, 2d edn (London, 1962), p. 91.

165. Edward, Earl of Clarendon, *Life*, 3 vols (Oxford, 1888), vol. 2, p. 218.

166. Estimated in 1658 at £96,000 (Barnard, *Cromwellian Ireland*, pp. 26–7).

167. *Diary of Thomas Burton*, vol. 2, pp. 200, 208–12, 224, 246; Thirsk and Cooper (eds), pp. 58–9.

168. See J. H. Elliott, 'A Europe of Composite Monarchies', *Past and Present*, no. 137 (1992), p. 64.

9. DIVERGENCE AND UNION: SCOTLAND AND ENGLAND, 1660–1707   *Mark Goldie*

For commenting on a draft of this chapter I am grateful to David Allan, Keith Brown, John Coffey, Bernard Crick, Clare Jackson, Colin Kidd, Christine MacLeod, and the editors.

1. This tradition of histories of the Union includes books by Mackinnon (1896), Mathieson (1905), Lang (1907), Hume Brown

(1914), Dicey and Rait (1920), Trevelyan (1932), and Pryde (1950).

2. See J. H. Elliott, 'A Europe of Composite Monarchies', *Past and Present*, 137 (1992), 48–71.

3. BBC 1, *Panorama*, 17 February 1992. The Scottish edition of *The Sun* turned nationalist and gave its readers a history lesson under the headline, '1603 and all that... how the Scots got mugged' (23 January 1992).

4. See, for example, W. Ferguson, *Scotland's Relations with England: A Survey to 1707* (Edinburgh, 1977); P. H. Scott, *1707: The Union of England and Scotland* (Edinburgh, 1979).

5. M. Goldie, 'The Scottish Catholic Enlightenment', *Journal of British Studies*, 30 (1991), 36–7.

6. For diverse discussions on these matters see L. Colley, *Britons: Forging the Nation 1707–1837* (New Haven, 1992); C. Harvie, *Scotland and Nationalism: Scottish Society and Politics 1707–1977* (London, 1977); C. Kidd, *Subverting Scotland's Past* (Cambridge, 1993).

7. *The Lauderdale Papers*, ed. O. Airy, 3 vols (London, 1884–5), vol. II, p. 164.

8. D. M. Walker, 'The Importance of Stair's Work for the Modern Lawyer', *The Juridical Review* (1981), 161.

9. *Harleian Miscellany*, 10 vols (London, 1808–13), vol. VI, pp. 136–40; vol. VII, pp. 378–9.

10. Quoted in C. W. Withers, *Gaelic Scotland: The Transformation of a Culture Region* (London, 1988), p. 175.

11. D. Stevenson, *Alasdair MacColla and the Highland Problem in the Seventeenth Century* (Edinburgh, 1980).

12. W. Ferguson, 'The Making of the Treaty of Union of 1707', *Scottish Historical Review*, 43 (1964), 110; P. W. J. Riley, *The Union of England and Scotland* (Manchester, 1978), p. xvi; T. C. Smout, 'The Road to Union', in *Britain after the Glorious Revolution, 1689–1714*, ed. G. Holmes (London, 1969).

13. W. R. and V. B. McLeod, *Anglo-Scottish Tracts, 1701–1714: A Descriptive Checklist* (Lawrence, Kansas, 1979).

14. This title was borrowed for a new document in 1988 when the latest wave of devolutionists asserted their case.

15. In 1976 Hugh Trevor-Roper described the Scottish system before 1707 as 'political banditry'. See D. Stevenson, 'Professor Trevor-Roper and the Scottish Revolution', *History Today*, 30 (1980), 34–40.

16. B. Lenman, *The Eclipse of Parliament* (London, 1992), p. 258.

17. I. Bostridge, 'Debates about Witchcraft in England, 1650–1736' (D.Phil. thesis, Oxford University, 1990), ch. 3.

18. Quoted in Ferguson, 'Making of the Treaty of Union', p. 96.

19. R. L. Emerson, 'Sir Robert Sibbald, Kt, the Royal Society of Scotland and the Origins of the Scottish Enlightenment', *Annals of Science*, 45 (1988), 41–72.

20. Quoted in D. Daiches, *Scotland and the Union* (London, 1977), p. 62.

21. *The Political Works of Andrew Fletcher* (London, 1732), pp. 271, 289, 337, 342, 344.

22. I. Hont, 'Free Trade and the Economic Limits to National

Politics: Neo-Machiavellian Political Economy Reconsidered', in *The Economic Limits to Modern Politics*, ed. J. Dunn (Cambridge, 1990), p. 115.

23. Quoted in R. Mitchison, *Lordship to Patronage: Scotland 1603–1745* (London, 1983), p. 135.

24. Quoted in Scott, *1707*, p. 25.

25. Ibid., p. 38.

26. A. V. Dicey and R. S. Rait, *Thoughts on the Union* (London, 1920), p. 227.

27. Quoted in D. Szechi and D. Hayton, 'John Bull's Other Kingdoms: the English Government of Scotland and Ireland', in *Britain in the First Age of Party, 1680–1750*, ed. C. Jones (London, 1987), p. 253.

28. Quoted in P. W. J. Riley, 'The Structure of Scottish Politics and the Union of 1707', in *The Union of 1707*, ed. T. I. Rae (Glasgow, 1974), p. 8.

29. Quoted in Scott, *1707*, p. 27.

30. Quoted in Daiches, *Scotland and the Union*, p. 148.

10. THE COMMUNITIES OF IRELAND AND THE BRITISH STATE,
1660–1707   *Jim Smyth*

1. R. Lawrence, *The interest of Ireland in its trade and wealth stated* (Dublin, 1682), pt II, pp. 50–1, 118. [J. Hovell], *A discourse on the woolen manufacture of Ireland and the consequences of prohibiting its exportation* (Dublin, 1698), p. 8.

2. Lawrence, *The interest of Ireland*, pt. II, section II, ch. 2 unpaginated.

3. Lawrence, *The interest of Ireland*, pt. II, pp. 47, 51–3, 58, 96, 101, 104–5, 107, 118. Lawrence's condemnation of the treatment of the English in Ireland as 'foreigners' in respect of trade, and his call for Protestant unity, are reiterated in a pamphlet by 'WH', *Remarks on the affairs and trade of England and Ireland* (London, 1691), pp. 36, 63.

4. T. C. Barnard, 'Crises of identity among Irish Protestants, 1641–1685', *Past and Present*, 127 (1990), 68.

5. A. Clarke, 'Colonial constitutional attitudes in Ireland, 1640–1660', *Proceedings of the Royal Irish Academy*, vol. 90 (1991), pp. 357–75.

6. The Earl of Orrery argued that Ireland had been conquered by English Protestants' under 'royal authority': *An answer to the scandalous letter lately printed and subscribed by Peter Walsh* (Dublin, 1662), p. 10. Incidentally, Orrery's target, the Franciscan Peter Walsh, considered Irish Catholics members of 'the famous empire of Great Britain': *A letter to the Catholics of England, Ireland, Scotland* (1674), p. 1. In 1698 Hovell characterised the relationship between his fellow Protestants and England thus: 'We are a province of your empire': *A discourse on the wollen manufacture*, p. 10.

7. J. Smyth, '"Like amphibious animals": Irish Protestants, ancient Britons, 1691–1707', *Historical Journal* (1993).

8. *A letter from a gentleman in Ireland to a friend in London, upon the*

occasion of a pamphlet entitled 'A vindication of the present government of Ireland under . . . Richard, Earl of Tyrconnel (Dublin, 1688), 31.

9. William Petty, *The political anatomy of Ireland* (1691; Shannon, 1970), pp. 34–5, 124–5, 127. William Molyneux, *The case of Ireland being bound by acts of parliament in England, stated* (Dublin, 1698), 97–8.

10. Cited in J. G. Simms, *William Molyneux of Dublin*, ed. P. H. Kelly (Dublin, 1982), pp. 103–4.

11. The best account of these proceedings is J. I. McGuire, 'The Dublin Convention, the Protestant community and the emergence of an ecclesiastical settlement in 1660', in A. Cosgrove and J. I. McGuire (eds), *Parliament and Community*. Historical Studies XIV (Belfast, 1983), pp. 121–46.

12. Patrick Adair, *A true narrative of the rise and progress of the Presbyterian Church in Ireland, 1623–1670* (Belfast, 1866), p. 243.

13. R. H. Murray, 'The Church of the Restoration', in W. A. Phillips (ed.), *History of the Church of Ireland* (Oxford, 1933), p. 129; Boyle to Bramhall, 13 Nov. 1660; 14 Sept. 1661; *HMC Hastings Ms.* iv, 99, 109–10.

14. The English republican Edmund Ludlow remarked that Archbishop Bramhall conducted the consecration 'with as many superstitious and idolatrous ceremonyes as if he had received particular directions therein from the Pope himselfe': Edmund Ludlow, 'A voyce from the watchtower, pt. 5, 1660–1662', A. B. Worden ed. *Camden* 4th series, vol. 21 (1978), p. 284.

15. R. F. Foster, *Modern Ireland, 1600–1972* (Harmondsworth, 1988) 124–5; F. R. Bolton, *The Caroline tradition of the Church of Ireland, with particular reference to bishop Jeremy Taylor* (London, 1959), pp. xiii, 42, R. H. Murry, 'The Church of the Restoration', pp. 122, 136.

16. Adair, *True Narrative*, 251; Bolton, Caroline tradition, pp. 34–6; Murry, 'Church of the Restoration', p. 140.

17. Adair, *True Narrative*, 246.

18. Raymond Gillespie sees this period as a time of Presbyterian *consolidation*: 'The Presbyterian revolution in Ulster, 1660–1690', in W. J. Sheils and D. Wood (eds), *The Churches, Ireland and the Irish, Studies in Church History 25* (Oxford, 1989), pp. 159–70.

16. See, for example, the comments of Bishop Wilde, who complained that he could not properly enforce the law against dissenters because of 'the want of an experience justice of the peace about Derry [and] . . . the gentry here are thinly planted': Wilde to Bramhall, 4 Dec. 1661, *HMC Hastings Ms.* iv, pp. 122–3.

20. Adair, *True Narrative*, pp. 258–60.

21. J. M. Reid, *Kirk and Nation, The Story of the Reformed Church of Scotland* (London, 1960), p. 93; Marilyn J. Westerkamp, *The Triumph of the Laity, Scots–Irish Piety and the Great Awakening, 1625–1760* (Oxford, 1988), pp. 60–1, 68.

22. Adair, *True Narrative*, pp. xx–xxi, 276–81; *The horrid conspiracie of such impenitent traytors as intended a new rebellion in the kingdom of Ireland . . . published by authority* (London, 1663); R. L. Greaves, *Deliver us from Evil, The Radical Underground in Britain, 1660–1663* (New York, 1986), pp. 140–50.

23. J. C. Beckett, 'Irish–Scotish relations in the seventeenth century', in *Confrontations, Studies in Irish history* (London, 1972), pp. 34–43.

24. Oliver St John to Francis St John, 11 March 1689, Cambridgeshire R. O., Huntington, dd. M52/1; *A letter from a gentleman in Ireland*, 2: S. J. Connolly, *Law, Religion and Power, the Making of Protestant Ireland, 1660–1760* (Oxford, 1992), p. 118. Earlier, William Petty occasionally used 'British' in its inclusive sense: *Political Anatomy*, pp. 23, 27.

25. J. Smyth, 'Irish Protestants, ancient Britons'.

26. Connolly, *Law, Religion and Power*, pp. 311–12.

27. This point has been made about Catholics who prospered in spite of the Penal Laws: K. J. Harvey, 'The family experience: the Bellews of Mount Bellew', in T. P. Power and K. Whelan (eds), *Endurance and Emergence, Catholics in Ireland in the Eighteenth Century* (Dublin, 1990), pp. 192–3.

28. *Northern Star*, 22 September 1792; (Irish) *Parliamentary Register* (Dublin, 1792), p. 84.

29. Barnard. 'Crises of identity', pp. 54–5.

30. Long after the event, Ormond claimed that he had in fact anticipated divisions among the Catholics 'to the greater security of the government and protestants': Lady Burghclere, *The Life of James, First Duke of Ormonde* (2 vols, London, 1912), vol. II, p. 51.

31. Petty, *Political Anatomy*, pp. 99–100; Orrery, *An answer to the scandalous letter*, p. 10.

32. Hugh Reilly, *Ireland's case briefly stated* (1695), pp. 72, 77–9, 85, 122.

33. Connolly, *Law, Religion and Power*, pp. 12, 33–40.

34. William King, *The state of the Protestants under the late king James's government* (Dublin, 1691).

35. Thomas Bartlett, *The Fall and Rise of the Irish Nation, The Catholic Question, 1690–1830* (Dublin, 1992) pp. 13–16.

36. This contrast is drawn by P. H. Kelly, 'Ireland and the Glorious Revolution: from kingdom to colony', in Robert Beddard (ed.), *The Revolutions of 1688, the Andrew Browing Lectures, 1988* (Oxford, 1991), p. 163. On the Restoration in Ireland as a local initiative see McGuire, 'The Dublin Convention', passim; and Orrery, *An answer to the scandalous letter*, p. 26.

37. David Hayton argues that 1688–91 marked 'a critical moment in the expansion of English control over other parts of the British Isles; a step towards empire': 'The Williamite revolution in Ireland, 1688–91', J. I. Israel (ed.), *The Anglo-Dutch Moment. Essays on the Glorious Revolution and its World Impact* (Cambridge, 1991), p. 186.

Notes on the Contributors

Brendan Bradshaw is University Lecturer in History in the University of Cambridge and is also Fellow and Director of Studies at Queens' College. He has published widely on sixteenth-century Britain and Ireland and on the history of religious thought. His major work to date is *The Irish Constitutional Revolution of the Sixteenth Century* (Cambridge, 1979), and he has recently retired from the editorship of *The Journal of Ecclesiastical History*.

Ciaran Brady is Senior Lecturer in Modern History at Trinity College, Dublin, and the author of *The Chief Governors: The Rise and Fall of Reform Government in Tudor Ireland* (Cambridge, 1994). He has edited several collections of articles on Irish history. He is joint editor of *Irish Historical Studies*.

Mark Goldie is University Lecturer in History in the University of Cambridge and is also a Fellow and Director of Studies at Churchill College. He has published widely on late seventeenth- and eighteenth-century political and intellectual history, and he is co-editor of *The Cambridge History of Political Thought*, volume 3: *1450–1700*.

Derek Hirst is Professor of History at Washington University, St Louis, where he has been since 1974, having been trained at Cambridge and having been a Fellow of Trinity Hall. He has published extensively on seventeenth-century British history, most notably in *The Representative of the People?* (Cambridge, 1975), and *Authority and Conflict, 1603–1658*, in the Arnold History of England series (1986).

Hiram Morgan took his doctorate in Cambridge. He has held research positions at Queen's University, Belfast, at the University of St Andrews, and at the University of Ulster. He is currently Lecturer in History at University College, Cork. He has published *Tyrone's Rebellion: The Outbreak of the Nine Years War in Tudor Ireland* (1993) and several articles. He is the editor of *History Ireland*.

John Morrill is Reader in Early Modern History in the University of Cambridge and is Fellow and Vice Master of Selwyn College, and also a Vice President of the Royal Historical Society. He has written and edited many books and many articles, mainly on seventeenth-century British history. A representative selection of his more influential

320 NOTES ON THE CONTRIBUTORS

articles was published in 1994 under the title *The Nature of the English Revolution*. He became a Fellow of the British Academy in 1995.

J. G. A. Pocock is Professor Emeritus of History at Johns Hopkins University in Baltimore. He is the prolific author of many books and more than 200 published papers, including a series which inspired this book. He is one of those principally responsible for establishing the long-running series of conferences on early modern political thought at the Folger Institute in Washington, DC, which have explored English, Scottish and Irish, and British, colonial thought and their interconnections.

Peter Roberts is Lecturer in History at the University of Kent at Canterbury, Honorary Fellow of the University of Wales Centre for Advanced Welsh and Celtic Studies at Aberystwyth, and the editor of *The Transactions of the Honorable Society of Cymmrodian* and the author of a succession of influential articles on Anglo-Welsh history in the sixteenth and early seventeenth centuries and on Elizabethan politics.

Jim Smyth is Associate Professor of Irish and British History, University of Notre Dame, and the author of *The Men of No Property: Irish Radicals and Popular Politics in the Late Eighteenth Century* (Macmillan, 1992), and of several articles on late seventeenth- and eighteenth-century Irish and British history.

Jenny Wormald is Fellow and Tutor in History at St Hilda's College, Oxford. She has written extensively on fifteenth-, sixteenth- and seventeenth-century Scottish history and on the reigns of both King James VI of Scotland and King James I of England. Her books include *Court, Kirk and Community, Scotland 1470–1625* (1981), and *Mary Queen of Scots: A Study in Failure* (1987).

Index

flags, 154
Fleetwood, Charles, 216
Fletcher, Andrew, of Saltoun, 235, 237–45
Flight of the Earls, 106
Flodden, battle of (1513), 15, 69
forced loans, 145
Fordun, John (of), 7
Forth, Firth of, 236
fortifications, 95
France, 10–11, 12, 17, 22–4, 66–7, 70, 72–80, 93, 161
Franchises Act, 124
Francis II, King of France, 22–3
Fuller, Nicholas, 163
Fullerton, James, 87

Gaedhil, 7–9, 34
Gaeldom, 2–3, 7–9, 12–13, 56–8, 70, 76, 85–6, 90–1, 166–7, 311n
Gaelic language, 24
Gaelic lordships, 8
Gaell, 8–9
Galloway, 223
General Assembly of the Church of Scotland, 221–3, 234
Geoffrey of Monmouth, 4, 9, 67
Geraldine League (1539–40), 41, 72
Gerard, Sir William, 136
Giraldus Cambrensis, 67
Glamis Castle, 156–7
Glasgow, 306n
Glencairn's Rebellion (1654), 209
Glendower, *see* Glyndŵr
Glorious Revolution, *see* Revolution of 1688/9
Gloucestershire, 132
Glyndwir Rebellion, 119–20
Glyndwir, Owain, 119–20
Glyndŵr Rebellion, 49, 55
Godolphin, Sidney, 237
Goodman, Godfrey, Bishop of Gloucester, 157
Gookin, Vincent, 311n

Gott, Samuel, 203, 306n
Graham, James, 1st Marquis of Montrose, 185, 190, 229
Grandison, Viscount, *see* St John
Greenwich, Treaty of (1543), 22, 73
Grey, Arthur, Lord Grey de Wilton, 287n, 309n
Grey, Lord Leonard, 72, 75, 94–7, 287n
Grey, Thomas, Lord Grey of Groby, 309n
Gunpowder Plot, 168

Habsburg, House of, 11, 25
Hamilton, Sir George, 168
Hamilton, James, 87
Hamilton, James, 3rd Lord Belhaven, 245
Hamilton, James, Earl of Arran, 69, 78
Hamilton, John, Earl of Abercorn, 168
Hamilton, Thomas, Earl of Melrose, 158
Hanoverian succession, 236–8
Harley, Sir Robert (later Earl of Oxford), 145, 233, 243
Harrington, James, 182, 205
Harrison, Thomas, 306n
Hartlib circle, 211
Hartlib, Samuel, 308n, 310n
Hatton, Sir Christopher, 102
Hay, George, 1st Earl of Kinnoul, 30
Hay, John, 3rd Earl of Tweeddale, 225, 237–8, 242
Henrietta-Maria, Queen, 297n
Henry II, King, and Ireland, 58
Henry II, King of France, 22
Henry IV, King of France, 85
Henry VII, King, 51, 59, 90, 131–2, 137; and Scotland, 21–2, 161–2; and the Tudor Revolution in Government, 20–3, 32; and schism, 66; and the incorporation of Wales, 119–20; and the succession, 69; divorces and supreme

DATE DUE

Printed
in USA

HIGHSMITH #45230